THE MISSING PIECE OF
THE PICTURE OF HORROR

In this book you will meet the young women who died hideously. Some of them had much to live for. Most of them were already committed to a life of drugs, pimps and prostitution.

You will meet the men hunting their killer. Police officers who saw their careers destroyed and politicians defeated at the polls as clue after clue led to a dead end, suspect after suspect wriggled free, and new corpse after new corpse was uncovered.

But there is one person you will not meet. Not on these pages at least. The Green River Killer himself. Like London's Jack the Ripper and San Francisco's notorious Zodiac, the Green River Killer is an unsolved serial murder case.

THE SEARCH FOR THE
GREEN RIVER KILLER

THE SEARCH FOR THE
GREEN RIVER
KILLER

Carlton Smith and Tomas Guillen

AN ONYX BOOK

ONYX
Published by the Penguin Group
Penguin Books USA Inc., 375 Hudson Street,
New York, New York 10014, U.S.A.
Penguin Books Ltd, 27 Wrights Lane,
London W8 5TZ, England
Penguin Books Australia Ltd, Ringwood,
Victoria, Australia
Penguin Books Canada Ltd, 2801 John Street,
Markham, Ontario, Canada L3R 1B4
Penguin Books (N.Z.) Ltd, 182-190 Wairau Road,
Auckland 10, New Zealand

Penguin Books Ltd, Registered Offices:
Harmondsworth, Middlesex, England

First published by Onyx, an imprint of New American Library, a division
of Penguin Books USA Inc.

First Printing, March, 1991
10 9 8 7 6 5 4 3 2 1

 REGISTERED TRADEMARK—MARCA REGISTRADA

CONTENTS

BOOK TWO: ADAMSON, 1984–86

AUTHORS' NOTE
AND
ACKNOWLEDGEMENTS

Probably any attempt to describe events taking place over a seven-year period would be fraught with possibilities for inadvertent omission and misunderstanding. That is all the more true with the Green River murders because of the sheer complexity of the events and the great number of people who played roles as the events unfolded. As time passes, human memories alter the recollection of events, or people forget matters entirely. The fact that the police had not identified the killer at this writing was an additional obstacle; understandably, the police wished to keep much of the information about the crimes confidential to assist them with their investigation. We were likewise handicapped by the reluctance of two of the primary investigators, Detectives David Reichert and Fabienne Brooks, to share their recollections.

Nonetheless, we were able to reconstruct many of the events. We were assisted greatly in this regard by numerous members of the King County Police Department, including, principally, Sheriff James Montgomery and his command staff, who graciously consented to provide copies of numerous important documents. Other members of the department willingly shared their experiences and recollections in interviews, as did many victims' family members. Several political figures provided candid interviews, as did former King

County Sheriff Vernon Thomas. We owe special gratitude to John Douglas, special agent of the FBI, King County Senior Deputy Prosecutor Alfred Mathews, King County Police Major Robert Evans, King County Police Chief Frank Adamson, as well as Lieutenant Daniel Nolan and Major Richard Kraske, both now retired, for their assistance in numerous interviews over a number of years.

Most importantly, we owe an enormous debt to publisher Frank Blethen and the management of *The Seattle Times*. In addition to employing us nearly full time on coverage of the murders from 1984 through the end of 1988, *The Times* provided us with complete access to the texts of hundreds of news stories written as the murders were being investigated, thus providing us with a solid structure for this narrative. We are particularly grateful to former Special Projects Editor Tom Brown, and the staff of *The Times*'s library, who unstintingly gave of their time in the search for relevant articles and support information.

We would especially like to thank our editor, Michaela Hamilton of New American Library, for her belief in this project, and for her steadfast support throughout. Without her many hours of work with the manuscript and her suggestions for cuts and revisions, the project would never have been completed.

Most of all, we would like to thank our wives, Helga Kahr and Susan Guillen, for their support throughout this project, which often seemed interminable. Both read and critiqued these pages from their own unique perspectives, Susan as a former police officer and Helga as an attorney who formerly specialized in criminal defense. In addition, Susan and Helga both accepted more than their share of the many burdens of daily living that our preoccupation blinded us to; we appreciate their efforts and love them very much.

A word on style. We have tried to reconstruct many conversations as they occurred, basing these on the recollections of those involved. To the best of our knowledge, remarks that appear in quotation marks reflect what was actually said at the time, either as reflected in news coverage or in the words of the participants as they recalled them. In cases where the actual words could not be reconstructed but the essence of the conversation was available, we chose to leave out the quote marks but indicate through the phrasing that these were words substantially similar to what was actually said. Italicized phrases reflect participants' recollections of their internal dialogue.

> *—Carlton Smith*
> *and*
> *—Tomas Guillen*
> *Seattle, Washington, June 8, 1990*

PEOPLE

Abernathy, Debbie; victim, last seen September 1983

Adamson, Frank; captain, King County Police, Green River Task Force, 1984–86

Agisheff, Amina; victim, last seen July 1982

Antosh, Yvonne; victim, last seen May 1983

Authorlee, Martina; victim, last seen May 1983

Avent, Pamela; missing, last seen October 1983

Bello, Mary; victim, last seen October 1983

Bonner, Deborah; victim, last seen July 1982

Brockman, Colleen; victim, last seen December 1982

Brooks, Pierce; serial murder expert, Green River Task Force Consultant, 1985

Brooks, Fabienne; detective, King County Police, Green River Task Force

Bryant, Hilda; television reporter, KIRO

Bundy, Ted; serial murderer, 1971–75

Bush, Denise; victim, last seen October 1982

Buttram, April; missing, last seen August 1983

Chapman, Marcia; victim, last seen August 1982

Childers, Andrea; victim, last seen April 1983

Christensen, Carol; victim, last seen May 1983

Coffield, Wendy; victim, last seen July 1982

Douglas, John; Federal Bureau of Investigation Special Agent, Behavioral Sciences Unit

Estes, Debra; victim, last seen September 1982

Evans, Bob; captain, King County Police, Green River Task Force, 1988–89

Fatland, Rollin; deputy King County executive, 1985–present

Feeney, Maureen; victim, last seen September 1983

Foster, Melvyn; suspect 1982–84, cleared

Gabbert, Sandra; victim, last seen April 1983

Gies, Rick; detective, King County Police vice squad, 1979–84

Haglund, Bill; chief investigator, King County Medical Examiner's

Harrington, Penny; former Portland, Oregon, police chief, 1985

Hill, Tim; King County executive, 1985–present

Hinds, Cynthia; victim, last seen August 1982

Horton, Richard Terry; suspect 1985, cleared

Hunt, Cookie; spokeswoman, Women's Coalition to Stop the Green River Murders, 1984–present

Johnson, George; criminalist, Washington State Patrol Crime Lab, 1981–present

Kellams, R.D.; policeman, city of Kent, 1982–present

Keppel, Bob; special investigator, Washington Attorney General's Office, 1980–present

Kraske, Richard; major, King County Police, Criminal Investigations Division, 1982–84

Kubik-Patten, Barbara; housewife, psychic, and private detective

Kurran, Rose Marie; possible victim, last seen August 1987

Lee, Kase; missing, last seen August 1982

Liles, Tammy; victim, last seen June 1983

Lovvorn, Gisele; victim, last seen July 1982

Malvar, Marie; missing, last seen April 1983

Marrero, Rebecca; missing, last seen December 1982

Mathews, Gail; victim, last seen April 1983

McGinness, Keli; missing, last seen June 1983

McLean, Ernest W. "Bill"; suspect 1986, cleared

Meehan, Mary; victim, last seen September 1982

Milligan, Terri; victim, last seen August 1982

Mills, Opal; victim, last seen August 1982

Montgomery, James; sheriff, King County Police, 1988–present

Naon, Constance; victim, last seen June 1983

Nault, Michael; captain, King County Police

Nelson, Kim; victim, last seen November 1983

Nickle, Jim; acting sheriff, King County Police, 1983

Nolan, Dan; lieutenant, King County Police, Green River Task Force, 1984–88

Osborne, Patricia; missing, last seen October 1983

Pitsor, Kimi Kai; victim, last seen April 1983

Plager, Delise; victim, last seen October 1983

Pompey, Jim; captain, King County Police, Green River Task Force, 1986–87

Reay, Dr. Donald; King County Medical Examiner, 1979–present

Reichert, David; detective, King County Police, Green River Task Force

Revelle, Randy; King County executive, 1981–85

Rois, Carrie; victim, last seen March 1983

Rule, Ann; writer

Sherrill, Shirley; victim, last seen October 1982

Smith, Alma; victim, last seen March 1983

Smith, Cindy; victim, last seen March 1984

Stevens, William J. II; suspect 1989, cleared

Streed, Tom; detective, San Diego County Sheriff's Department

Striedinger, Ed; detective, City of Seattle Police Department

Summers, Shawnda; victim, last seen October 1983

Tellevik, George; chief, Washington State Patrol, 1984–present

Thomas, Vernon; sheriff, King County Police, 1983–87

Thompson, Tina; victim, last seen July 1983

Tindal, James Michael; taxi driver, 1982–present

Tripp, Earl; detective, King County Police

Ware, Kelly; victim, last seen July 1983

West, Mary; victim, last seen February 1984

Whitaker, Allen; special agent in charge, Federal Bureau of Investigation, Seattle

Williams, Delores; victim, last seen March 1983

Wims, Cheryl; victim, last seen May 1983

Winckoski, Bernard; sheriff, King County Police, 1981–82

Winston, Tracy; missing, last seen September 1983

Wood, Brian; television reporter, KIRO

Yates, Lisa; victim, last seen December 1983

NOTES ON AN INVESTIGATION

(April 1984)

Through subaqueous web of sleep
ringing telephone
shatters the design

my husband answers
and a voice
(disembodied as the news it brings)
tells of another bone find along the river

Frightful familiar words,
femur, pelvic, skeletal remains
usher in first light

Red breasted robin sounds his call note weep weep
As he scribbles the details of the find
on a scratch pad beside the phone

The "who" is strung together later
like dreadful pearls
and given teeth

Now his words fall heavy on fragile morning
"Dump site, body drop, sign of ligature?"
(Clenched fist at his side
only sign of troubled heart)

He dresses hurriedly: last longing look at warm bed
Before donning green coat
(That repels water and denies the weeping sky)

Commander ready for a place called Star Lake Road
Where he'll collect another piece
of a human being

He'll not have a good day

—Jo Adamson, 1984

PROLOGUE

July, 1982

At the beginning, there was only the man. He drove alone, keeping his thoughts to himself. It was as if he existed outside of the rest of the world, isolated inside his own skin, captivated by his own thoughts. He was a man with a face so common, so ordinary, that no one thought to look to see what was within. He passed by others quietly, as if he were not even there, and no one saw him at all. But he was a man with a secret, and the secret was death.

His favorite time was the afternoon. In his truck the man drove on the highway, looking, choosing, selecting. He made it a rule to drive until he found what he wanted, waiting for him by the side of the road. When it was right he would stop, and the game would begin.

He strove to look eager but shy, gentle perhaps, and undemanding. The fish would bite, how they loved to bite! He would open the door and invite them inside. Across the seat they would talk, tiny hands on the clasp purse that all of them carried, holding the secrets he craved. They thought they knew who he was, they had seen a hundred or more just like him, and knew just what to do. They wanted the money.

He drove into the deserted streets and found a good place, listening to them talk while he tested the wind. Then he would talk, softly at first—don't frighten them!—and watch while their eyes registered puzzlement. The words were summoned and soon they poured forth, the teachings. There! He could feel them backing away, they wanted to leave, he had disturbed them. Then they looked at the door and saw there was no escape, but by then it was too late.

Afterwards he would drive to the places he knew, his places, where the wind whispered through the trees. The silence felt good. He took what he wanted, not everything, but enough to remember. Sometimes he did other things, but tried to forget it when he did. At the end he would hide them, cover them up so they couldn't be found. Still later he would go back to see them, sitting there in the afternoon, in the silence, and remember. They were his secrets, and he would keep them forever.

BOOK ONE

KRASKE

1982–83

1

THE SLAUGHTERHOUSE

August 12, 1982

At a quarter after one on a cool, dark, drizzling Thursday, a man named Frank Linard climbed on top of a truck parked behind the PD&J Meat Company slaughterhouse near Kent, Washington, and fired up his first cigar of the day.

Over the noise of the truck's engine, Linard could hear the rattle of the chains inside the slaughterhouse as they carried off the steaming, fresh-killed meat, and the laughter and shouts of the men with their saws.

Linard liked smoking cigars; most of all he liked digging one out from under his gore-splattered rubber apron, lighting it up, then feeling the relaxation that came with the first draw of smoke. The cigar was a good escape.

After four months at the slaughterhouse, Linard had learned to ignore much of what went on around him: the cows in their chute, bawling and moaning as they were prodded forward to their fate; the quick death that came from the air-driven bolt to the brain, followed by the practiced slash of the neck that spilled all the blood. Then came the hooks and the chains that carted the carcasses away to the butchers with their high-pitched, whining saws.

It was part of Linard's job to clean up the mess that remained after the cows were cut into parts. Wearing galoshes and his rubber apron, Linard usually hosed the blood and small bits of flesh off the slaughterhouse floor and into the underground septic tank. Unless Linard emptied the septic tank into the truck each day, for transport to a nearby rendering plant, the bloody glop would back up in the tank and shut the slaughterhouse down.

As he smoked his cigar, Linard looked down into the river behind the building, the jurisdictional boundary between the Seattle suburb of Kent and the unincorporated area that contained the slaughterhouse. The river began high up on the flanks of Washington state's largest mountain, Mt. Rainier, and wound its way down through a series of valleys before emptying into Puget Sound just south of the city of Seattle. A century before it had been named the Green River, although, from what Linard could see, for most of the year it was gray or brown, not green.

In the summer, however, the river was clear and slow, placid, curving sinuously back and forth through the valleys as it piled up sandbars, occasional boulders, and waterlogged tree trunks. One hundred years earlier the river had served as a pioneer thoroughfare and rubbish disposal system, and as recently as twenty years before this day in 1982 the bloody water from the slaughterhouse had just been emptied into the river, where it carried downstream to the harbor a few miles to the north.

Right where the slow-moving current swept past the slaughterhouse, Linard saw a gravel hump poking up from the water. A few logs stuck out of the mud and weeds. A large mass of foam clung to one of the logs. As he gazed, the foam seemed strange to Linard: too much foam for too little current, he thought. Drawing on his cigar, Linard guessed it wasn't foam he was seeing, at all, but maybe a dead animal. Sometimes the carcasses of wildlife washed down the river from the mountains. Sometimes their pelts were worth money. Linard jumped down from the truck, telling himself he had some time before the tank filled to take a closer look.

Linard went to a small trail the fishermen had

beaten down through the blackberry bushes fringing the channel and worked his way down the bank. When he came out of the tall bushes, Linard saw that the foam was really a naked woman.

Linard saw she was hung up on a large log, bent over with her naked buttocks raised. He stepped into the shallow water for a closer look. The woman's arms dangled below her, swaying in the slow-moving current. Her hair floated on the water. She was very white, bleached from long immersion. A purplish heart tattoo marked one arm. Linard could see the woman's face staring down at the shallow riverbed under the water. Her eyes appeared to have no pupils, and Linard knew the woman was very dead.

Linard's brain at first refused to function. His first thought was to get away. He raced back up the bank to the slaughterhouse, where there was a telephone mounted on the wall. He called the operator and asked for the police. While he waited for them to come on the line, Linard told the slaughterhouse workers about the dead woman. The building emptied as the slaughterers and meatcutters stampeded to the embankment and gaped at the riverbed, all of them jabbering at once. The cattle bawled in their wooden chute, temporarily reprieved.

About an hour after Linard made his discovery, a plain sedan driven by a young man with jet-black hair, a mustache, and a network of scars across his neck drove up to the slaughterhouse and parked in front. King County Police Department major crimes detective David Reichert had arrived to begin an investigation of the death. Reichert's first task was to determine whether murder had been committed.

Reichert's most important task at this point was to make sure nothing that might explain the death was overlooked. He went down the bank to the river and looked at the dead woman, then came back and talked quietly to uniformed police, telling them to search the river banks for anything that might explain how the woman had come to be there.

Soon a nondescript gray van from the medical examiner's office arrived. Someone produced a folded blue plastic bag. Police and medical examiners went to the river and returned with the blue bag sagging heavily in their hands. They put the bag down on the concrete apron near the truck, behind the slaughter-house, out of the view of the television news crews now already setting up on the road, and gave the victim a quick inspection. Linard put down his hose and went over to watch.

It all seems so quiet, so ordinary to them, Linard thought, just like the body was an old piece of meat, not a dead woman. The medical examiner's patholo-gist unzipped the plastic bag and pulled it away. He watched as the pathologist rolled the body around, viewing it, looking for an indication of the cause of death. There was no blood, no obvious wound, just water-bloated white flesh. Linard now saw that the woman's body actually had numerous tattoos. The whites of her eyes bugged out, and he saw again that the pupils had disappeared. It was clear to the pathol-ogist that the woman had been dead for at least sev-eral weeks, maybe even longer. The skin of the fingers was already beginning to slough off from long immer-sion in the water. Fingerprints would be difficult, maybe even impossible. The putrefaction of the corpse and the number of small insect larvae present on the exposed skin surfaces indicated that the woman had died long before that day. The pathologist put the body back into the bag, and then the bulging sack was put onto the collapsible gurney for the trip to the gray van. The television cameras dutifully recorded the event. Overhead a television helicopter hovered, pre-paring for a live feed for the evening news.

Meanwhile, the uniformed police, assisted by police from the city of Kent, continued searching both banks of the river, looking for the woman's clothing or any-thing that might suggest how she had come to be there. One by one the uniformed cops returned to tell Reichert that the search of the riverbank had produced nothing: no clothes, no identification, not a shred of evidence to indicate how the woman had died. Reichert nodded. As things later turned out, believing there was no more evidence to be found was the first mistake, and probably the biggest.

2

REICHERT

August 12, 1982

Reichert drove back to the county detectives' squad room on the first floor of the King County Courthouse in Seattle. There Reichert told his sergeant the details of the discovery. The sergeant, in turn, went off to report to his superior, the lieutenant in charge of the investigation of major crimes. The lieutenant, in turn, reported to the major in charge of all criminal investigations, and later, the major would brief the King County sheriff himself, Bernard Winckoski. Police work had nothing if not a chain of command.

Reichert sat down behind his gray metal desk, surrounded by other desks with their detectives, the bookshelves, filing cabinets, coffee machines, and bulletin boards. This was the nerve center of life in "the dicks," as the cops in the county department informally called their detectives. Around Reichert the other detectives made telephone calls, typed reports, laughed, argued, drank coffee, and got ready to go home. The dead woman in the river occasioned little comment. It was just another routine tragedy in a job where *someone's* misfortune was a daily event.

Reichert had been in the county's twelve-cop major

crimes unit for less than two years. His fellow detectives weren't much more experienced than he was. Most of the top hands in homicide had left the department over the last few years. Now Reichert's six-cop homicide-robbery unit included Bob LaMoria, a veteran police officer with comparatively little homicide experience; Frank Atchley, who was waiting for a promotion to sergeant; Ben Colwell, another veteran detective light on homicide experience; Earl Tripp, a productive narcotics investigator getting his first crack at major crimes; and Larry Peterson, a quiet, steady detective who had a reputation for solid if unimaginative work.

Not far away in the bullpen was the county's two-person Sex Crimes unit, which handled sexual assaults. Here, too, the experience was short. The team included Fabienne Brooks, a woman who sometimes doubled as a police artist; and Spencer Nelson, who had just come in from the warrants section, located down the hall, where investigators searched for those wanted for arrest. Still in the warrants section was Detective Larry Gross, a streetwise veteran. Like Brooks, Gross was one of the few blacks in the department; he was also a man who was very good at finding people who did not want to be found.

Despite his relative lack of experience with murder, Detective Reichert was considered one of the brightest young stars of the county's department. Most saw him as certain to rise rapidly on the career ladder. Six feet tall, solidly built at 190 pounds, the thirty-one-year-old Reichert was a former small-college quarterback who still moved with an athlete's coiled grace. His hazel eyes and boyish grin made him seem younger than he was. Reichert's personable nature, his neat appearance, good looks, and demonstrated courage had marked him as one of the department's comers.

The scars on his neck were a visible reminder of both his initiative and his courage. Reichert got the scars when he climbed in the rear window of a house in which a woman was being held hostage by a man who had gone berserk. After getting the woman out through the same window, Reichert had gone through the darkened house looking for the hostage-taker to arrest him. The man saw Reichert's image reflected in a window. As Reichert came forward, the man attacked, leaping on Reichert and slashing his neck with a knife. An inch either way, Reichert was told later, he would have been dead. But as Reichert struggled with the man, other police broke down the front door and managed to pull the man off. In the King County Department, such bold, unilateral actions were a mark of distinction, and Reichert had the scars to prove it.

Reichert was also deeply religious, and not shy about expressing those views. His grandfather had been a minister, and at first Reichert had wanted to be one also. He had gone to a small college in Minnesota in pursuit of a divinity degree, but had to give up when his wife had gotten pregnant and money had run short. Maybe it was for the best. "I couldn't handle the Greek and Latin anyway," he later joked. Still, Reichert had continued to teach Sunday School every week at a church near his home in south King County. Becoming a cop was a good second choice, Reichert often thought. The job gave him a chance to get involved in people's lives, to really help. That meant a lot to Reichert, who wanted very much to make a real difference in people's lives.

It was one of Reichert's more engaging traits that he saw his cases in terms of athletic competition. Crime and detection still seemed something of a game to Reichert, a contest of both wits and endurance. In Reichert's book, quitting was only for losers. "This guy's not gonna beat me," Reichert would tell fellow detectives whenever he found himself stumped. For Reichert, solving crimes was *personal*, not merely something he was paid to do. More experienced detectives thought this attitude on Reichert's part was a bit silly or naive, or possibly even dangerous. Sometimes, they knew, taking crimes personally could lead to tunnel vision, and tunnel vision could lead to some bad, even fatal misjudgments.

Now, as he sat behind his desk, Reichert considered the dead woman who had been found in the river behind the slaughterhouse. If the woman had been murdered—as seemed likely, given the absence of any clothing—the killing would be the second in less than a month involving the river.

A month earlier, another woman had been found in the river, not a half mile from this latest discovery. Sixteen-year-old Wendy Coffield had been strangled with her own pants. Like this latest woman, Wendy Coffield had tattoos. Because the victim had been discovered inside the Kent city limits, that suburban police department was investigating the Coffield crime.

The question was: Were the two discoveries related? Reichert thought that might be a possibility, but not a certainty. While at the river, Reichert had talked with a Kent policeman assigned to investigate the Wendy Coffield case, and while R. D. Kellams of the Kent department felt the two cases were connected, Reichert wasn't so sure. The river, he knew, was a place for dumping things, and there was no reason to assume that just because a murderer had used the river in July, the same man would have returned in August.

But until he knew who the new dead woman was, Reichert could not rule out a possible connection. He had another possible connection as well.

Six months earlier, Reichert had investigated the death of a third young woman, someone who had been a friend of Wendy Coffield. Like Wendy Coffield, Leann Wilcox had been strangled. Although the body of Leann Wilcox was found miles away from the Green River, both girls had been involved in street prostitution. Now there was this third woman. Who was to say that all three deaths weren't connected? If the third woman also had a background in prostitution, it would be time to give serious consideration to the possibility that a single murderer was using the Green River as a place to dispose of victims.

But first, Reichert had to find out who the latest dead woman was, and how she had died. To do that, Reichert would have to go to a medical examiner's autopsy the following day.

3

DUB

August 13, 1982

Attending autopsies was perhaps one of the most dis-
agreeable aspects of being a homicide detective. Dead
bodies were taken from cold storage, rolled onto a
stainless steel operating table, and inspected, prodded,
photographed, and cut with a thoroughness that
shocked the uninitiated. Otherwise hardened police
officers were known to grow faint. Homicide detectives either got used to it or got out of the business.

The autopsy began around 9:00 A.M. Photos were
first taken of the dead woman's tattoos, which were
crudely done. One on the arm was mottled, but
appeared to be a heart around the the word "Dubi."
A technician manipulated the dead woman's hands to
obtain a blurred set of finger- and palmprints. After
x-rays, the cutting began.

A surgical inspection of the dead woman's lungs
showed the absence of water; therefore she had not
drowned. But while the length of time between her
death and the discovery of her body made it impossible to say with certainty what had caused her death,
it appeared that the woman had been suffocated, perhaps strangled, just like Wendy Coffield and Leann
Wilcox.

One by one, all of the internal organs were removed, weighed, and inspected; so was the brain.
Samples were taken of blood and bile for laboratory

testing. Teeth were x-rayed, and fingernails were carefully preserved. Hair samples were taken. A surgeon's knife performed the most thorough sort of gynecological examination possible. Forty-five minutes after the autopsy began, the eviscerated body was photographed again, sewn back up, and returned to the cold room.

After the autopsy, a medical investigator gave Reichert a set of the photos and prints taken from the corpse. Reichert took the prints and the pictures back to his office in the courthouse, and gave them to a technician in the department's criminal identification section. Within several hours the prints and tattoos were tentatively matched to a name: Deborah Lynn Bonner, 23, a convicted prostitute and occasional striptease dancer who also sometimes used the name Pam Peek.

As Pam Peek, Bonner had been arrested for prostitution as recently as July 18, 1982 by the county police undercover vice squad. But dental charts would be needed to confirm the identification. Reichert sifted through the records and found the address of Bonner's parents in Tacoma. He decided to visit them the following day, a Saturday, and find out the name of Debbie Bonner's most recent dentist. It would be up to Reichert to tell the Bonners it was quite possible their daughter was dead.

On Saturday, August 14, Reichert drove to the home of Walter and Shirley Bonner in Tacoma. Reichert introduced himself to the Bonners, knowing that he was bringing the possibility of news every parent dreads. Sometimes it's best to be direct: There's really no good way to say it.

The Bonners were devastated. They told Reichert that their daughter was nicknamed Dub. That explained the "Dubi" tattoo. The Bonners told Reichert that Dub had been missing for nearly three weeks—about the same length of time the dead woman had been in the river, according to the medical examiners. The Bonners said they knew their daughter was in trouble; only recently they had put up their house as a bond to bail Dub and her boyfriend, Carl Martin, out of jail. Boyfriend? Reichert's ears perked up.

But Martin was no real boyfriend, the Bonners told Reichert, bitterly. He was a drug-dealing pimp. The Bonners blamed Martin for Dub's problems. Dub had always been a little wild, the Bonners said, but her troubles had really begun after she had taken up with Martin. After Dub and Martin had been bailed out of the Tacoma jail, Dub had disappeared. Then Carl had called the Bonners a few weeks ago wanting to know whether *they* had seen her. That meant trouble, the Bonners were sure. Shirley Bonner went to the Tacoma Police Department to file a missing persons report on Dub, but the police wouldn't take the report.

Did the Bonners have any idea what had happened to Dub? Yes, they did. Walter Bonner produced a note Dub had written in July, and had given to a Tacoma bartender who knew Walter and Shirley. The note said that Carl Martin owed another man several thousand dollars, the Bonners thought for drugs, and that the second man had threatened to kill Dub if Carl didn't pay up.

The second man, said Dub's note, was Larry Darnell Mathews, who lived in Tacoma and who was known to Carl Martin.

Now the investigation seemed to be getting somewhere: a possible identification of the victim, and two good leads—one a pimp, the other a drug pusher. Maybe it would turn out that the latest murder wasn't connected to the killings of Wendy Coffield and Leann Wilcox at all, Reichert thought. Maybe this one could be cleaned up quickly.

The Bonners gave Reichert the name of a dentist who had x-rays of Debbie's teeth. The dentist would be contacted on Monday, Reichert told the Bonners; he advised them not to go to the medical examiner's office to make a visual identification of the body. The Bonners wouldn't want to remember their daughter as she was found, he said. Until a positive identification was made, there was still hope.

Thanking the tearful Bonners for their help, Reichert began searching for Carl Martin and Larry Mathews. He called in and told his sergeant that he had some good leads in the slaughterhouse murder. Probably the killing wasn't related to Wendy Coffield or Leann Wilcox. The sergeant was pleased to hear the news.

But that night the slaughterhouse man, Frank Linard, bolted from his bed in a cold sweat. It was 3:00 A.M., and he had just had a terrible dream: He had been walking alone, peacefully, along a beach made of fine black sand. As he walked, he looked down and saw something flashing up at him from the blackness. As he looked the flashing grew brighter, and suddenly Linard knew it was a human face. His heart pounding, Linard was drawn on inexorably, and just as he came to the flashing place, the face suddenly erupted from the sand and flew up toward his eyes. Linard tried to step back but was frozen. The face hung in front of him, winking while he screamed. Linard realized that it was the woman with no eyes.

4

MANNEQUINS

August 15, 1982

By Sunday the rain had stopped, and the sun was out. The Green River continued to run low. Robert Ainsworth loaded his inflatable rubber raft into the back of his pickup truck and headed for the river for an afternoon of relaxed drifting.

Usually Ainsworth liked to go rafting with his wife Maureen and son Jeff. The family had long enjoyed rafting down the Green as a hobby. But on this day Maureen wanted to visit her mother, and at the last minute Jeff decided to go to Tacoma. So Ainsworth went rafting by himself.

Ainsworth drove his truck down to the Green River and stopped at a bridge near the West Valley Highway, a road that bisected the valley south of Seattle. He put his raft in the water and began slowly floating downstream, keeping his eye on the bottom, which was clearer than usual because of the low water and the sunshine.

At forty-one, Ainsworth had worked for a dozen years as a meat inspector for a Seattle area meat wholesale company. He also had a bad ulcer. Going to the river and floating downstream, Ainsworth found, was as calming as it sometimes could be lucrative. With his large rubber raft and a special hook he had made for grasping old bottles, Ainsworth liked to make a day of floating down the river, all the way to the southern outskirts of the city of Seattle.

As he drifted, Ainsworth searched for the old relics on the riverbottom. The Green River, Ainsworth knew, had been used as a barge route to farms upstream in the valley in earlier years. Now pioneer throwaways could still be found 100 years later when the water ran shallow and the currents revealed new layers of sediment. Old whiskey bottles, bottles of patent medicine, Mason jars, plates, utensils, farm implements, crockery, just about every nonperishable article that people could throw away could be found on the riverbottom, by those who looked closely. And some of that old-time trash was worth money to modern-day collectors. Ainsworth himself had a valuable collection of old bottles, jars, and other scroungings from the riverbed.

Just past the place where Ainsworth put his raft in, the river made a broad turn to the south. A half mile later, it doubled back on itself to head north once more, forming a giant horseshoe. From Ainsworth's vantage point, the channel seemed like a deep green canyon, with steep banks covered with blackberry bushes, yellow-flowered wild tansy, and tall grass. Rocks and logs stuck out of the mud and sandbars piled up on the riverbottom. Occasionally Ainsworth drifted over deeper, darker holes where fish rested quietly before continuing upriver to spawn.

Once in a while Ainsworth saw something on the bottom that attracted his interest. Lowering himself over the side, Ainsworth waded to the spot for a closer look. If the object seemed worth something, Ainsworth tried to snag it with his hooked pole. That morning, Ainsworth found a four-foot fragment of a waterlogged singletree, the wooden tongue used by the pioneers to harness horses to farm wagons. Ainsworth pried the ancient wood up from the muck and dumped it in his raft, then resumed his journey, keeping to the shallower water at the sides of the channel.

Shortly before noon, having drifted around the top of the horseshoe and heading north once again, Ainsworth could see the looming bulk of the PD&J Meat Company slaughterhouse, silent because it was Sunday.

Just after the turn, Ainsworth saw a man standing by the water's edge. There was a narrow trail beaten down through the grass from the roadway above. On top of the bank, Ainsworth was aware of another man behind the wheel of an old pickup truck. Ainsworth stopped his raft and waded over to the bank. The man at the edge of the water seemed to be in his late forties, tall, well-muscled, and balding. Ainsworth assumed that the man had been fishing. "Catch anything?" Ainsworth asked. The man shook his head. "Found anything?" the man asked Ainsworth.

"Just this old singletree," Ainsworth replied, pointing to the waterlogged wood. The man nodded and said, "You know, there's an old motor right down there, a car motor, in the river under the water." The man pointed to the near side of the river. Ainsworth turned around to look. "Yeah," he said. "I can see it right now."

Then the man in the truck—he seemed younger, to Ainsworth—shouted something, and the balding man went back up the trail and got into the truck. The truck drove off.

Ainsworth climbed back into his raft and floated downstream for another minute or so as the sounds of the truck faded. He looked down into the water again and saw a black woman floating face up under the water. Ainsworth was struck by the woman's hair, which bobbed gently along with the current under the water. Her eyes stared back at him without blinking. She seemed very small, almost a child. Ainsworth's mind told him he was seeing a mannequin which had been thrown into the river. He got out his bottle pole and tried to hook the figure. One of the legs was stuck under a submerged rock. The raft turned underneath him as Ainsworth reached out. It bumped into something. Ainsworth looked over his shoulder and saw another mannequin almost under the raft. Ainsworth suddenly realized the figures weren't mannequins at all. The awareness struck him with an electric jolt that made his ulcer scream: These were *dead* people.

Shaking, Ainsworth pulled his raft over to the bank and got out of the water. The tall grass formed a canopy over his head. Picking his way through the shallows, Ainsworth worked his way back upstream to the place where the man had been standing by the trail. Ainsworth went up to the road. The truck had disappeared. He sat down, unsure of what to do next. He waited for someone to come by. After about half an hour, a man and two children came by on bicycles. Ainsworth hailed them and told them about the bodies. The children wanted to go down to the river and look, but wisely, the man stopped them. Ainsworth asked him to call the police. The man said he would do it, and then he and the children pedaled off. Ainsworth sat down once more to wait.

Another half hour passed. Ainsworth's ulcer was starting to gnaw at him. He began feeling very sick. Finally, a policeman drove up. Ainsworth led the cop down the bank to the two bodies. Ainsworth told him that at first he had thought the bodies were mannequins. The cop stepped into the water to feel one of the bodies. It seemed to Ainsworth that the cop thought they might be mannequins too. Then Ainsworth and the cop climbed back up to the roadway where the cop called in on his radio. They sat down to wait for reinforcements. Ainsworth felt like he was going to throw up.

On the same Sunday Reichert took his wife and children to church. That afternoon he received a call from the department's communications center. Reichert was instructed to go out to the Green River again.

"Some guy out there says he found some bodies," Reichert was told.

Reichert didn't believe it. He guessed the report was somebody's idea of a bad joke. "They've got to be dummies," Reichert said. When Reichert learned the location, it was close enough to the Thursday body to make Reichert think somebody was pulling his leg.

For the second time in four days, Reichert drove out to the river area. By the time he arrived, several green and white county police cars were parked along the road about two hundred yards south of the slaughterhouse. Reichert stopped his car. Several of the police were busy stringing up the yellow crime scene tape. A uniformed cop in charge gestured with his thumb. Reichert found the trail down through the heavy grass and picked his way to the river's edge. He made his way along the water's edge until he came to more police officers. They were standing on the bank looking into the river. One of the bodies was almost ashore, half in, half out of the water. The other one, Reichert was told, was still submerged.

"The guy weighted 'em down with rocks," one of the cops told him. Reichert could see that the body almost on the riverbank appeared to be that of a black woman. Reichert could tell she hadn't been dead very long. Reichert realized that the rocks used to keep the bodies under water meant the bodies might have been there on Thursday when the body he had tentatively identified as that of Dub Bonner had been found. The police could have found them Thursday if only they had looked farther upstream.

Reichert now tried to put himself inside the killer's head. For openers, how did the guy get the bodies down the steep bank? Where? Reichert had an uneasy feeling that these two new victims might turn out to be prostitutes. First Leann Wilcox, then Wendy Coffield, then Dub Bonner, and now these two. If these victims were prostitutes too, he'd have to reexamine his thinking about the lack of connection between Coffield and Bonner, and maybe even Wilcox. In any event, Reichert knew there would be an uproar. The discovery of four bodies in a small stretch of the same river in less than a month almost certainly meant that at least some of the murders, if not all of them, had to have been committed by the same person. Reichert now had doubts about Martin and Mathews. What was going on?

* * *

Downtown at the courthouse headquarters of the police, ranking officers were trying to contact the sheriff, Barney Winckoski. Winckoski, appointed only two years earlier after a thirty-year career in Detroit, was widely seen as a caretaker sheriff awaiting his second retirement. He was on a fishing trip to Neah Bay, an isolated spot at the far northwestern tip of the state. It would be hours before Winckoski would be able to cut short his vacation and drive back to Seattle.

In the meantime, all the immediate decisions would be in the hands of Major Richard Kraske, the man in charge of the King County Police Department's Criminal Investigations Division.

Years later, Kraske would still remember the moment he first learned about the bodies in the Green River. Kraske had just returned from his neighborhood supermarket with a few sacks of groceries, and as he stood talking to one of his neighbors, his pager went off. Kraske went inside and called the department's dispatcher, and learned that two new bodies had been discovered in the Green River—making three victims at nearly the same spot in less than a week, and four in less than a month. His apprehension rising, Kraske drove immediately to the river, where it turned out the report was all too true.

For Kraske, it was a nightmare out of the past. Eight years earlier, Kraske had been the lieutenant in charge when a murdering maniac they knew only as "Ted" had kidnapped and killed at least eight young women in the Seattle area. The murders had created a sensation in the Seattle area. Try as they might, Kraske and his detectives had never been able to solve the crimes. Eventually Ted Bundy made his way to Utah, then Colorado, and finally Florida, killing everywhere he went. Eventually Bundy's death toll had reached at least thirty-three, and Kraske was haunted by the sense of failure, coupled with the suspicion that if only they had been better, if only . . . if only *something,* they would have caught Bundy before he got away to kill again.

Most detectives work their entire careers and never

see even one serial murder case, Kraske thought. Now it looked like he was going to have two in less than a decade.

Before doing anything else, Kraske decided to call in the department's divers for a thorough search of the river. And before allowing either of the bodies to be moved, Kraske also called for the medical examiner. Kraske remembered how potentially critical evidence in the "Ted" murders was improperly handled at the time those bodies were discovered, and how later confusion over which bodies had actually been found where had complicated matters. He also remembered a handful of television reporters in the "Ted" murders who worked their way around the police lines to walk through the areas where the skeletons had been found, possibly tearing up some of the evidence before anyone else had a chance to search. Kraske decided that *this* time, at least, *nothing* would happen until everything was ready.

Kraske next decided to go to a telephone and call the Kent Police Department and ask them to send their detectives. Since the Kent department was handling the Wendy Coffield murder, Kraske thought it might be smart to have their detectives present while this new crime scene was being processed. Soon R. D. Kellams and a Kent detective who had been helping him on the Wendy Coffield case were at the scene. While he was at it, Kraske thought, he might as well call a meeting of homicide detectives from all over the region.

The best way of solving these murders, Kraske realized, was to get as much help as he could from the surrounding police departments. After all, whoever the killer was, it wasn't likely that he would commit all of his crimes only on Kraske's turf. The other departments would certainly be affected too. After making his calls from a nearby telephone to minimize the radio traffic, Kraske returned and stood on the roadway to consider his next move.

Meanwhile, Detective David Reichert was making

his way downstream through the head-high grass, looking for some indication of the killer's route to and from the scene. About twenty or thirty feet away from where the uniformed cops were still standing near the immersed victims, Reichert almost stepped on yet *another* body. "I've got another one!" he shouted.

Three bodies! Kraske felt staggered. In the core of his being, Kraske knew it was happening all over again, just like the Ted murders. Quickly Kraske told Reichert to freeze. Other officers were told to rope off the area where Reichert was standing. No one except Reichert, *no one,* ordered Kraske, was to enter the area where Reichert was until the medical examiner arrived.

Temporarily immobilized, Reichert looked down at the body he had almost stepped on. This one, it seemed, had never been in the water. She looked like she had been killed within the past few days. She looked incredibly young. Could the body have been dumped there even while he was up at the slaughter-house on Thursday?

The girl had a light coffee-colored complexion. Possibly she was a very light-skinned black. She lay face down in the grass, one arm bent at the elbow as if she were sleeping. A pair of blue pants was wound tightly around her neck and knotted on the right side—just like Wendy Coffield. The girl's brassiere had been pulled up to expose her breasts. Reichert could see numerous bruises and abrasions on her arms and legs. The girl's tongue lolled from her mouth, and Reichert could see the broken blood vessels beneath the skin that had come from death by strangulation.

Up on the roadway, police were waving the traffic on through. Drivers, bicyclists, and joggers streamed by, with no stops permitted. Ainsworth sat by the side of the road and chain-smoked cigarettes while the police asked him questions. He felt horrible. Ainsworth told the cops about the balding man and his friend in the truck. He wondered whether the man had pointed to the motor in the river to deflect him from the bank where the bodies were. Was the balding man the killer? Was it just a coincidence? Finally one of the cops drove Ainsworth back to his truck.

Ainsworth then drove back to the place where the police cars were parked to pick up his raft. He loaded the raft into the truck and waited for his wife to come by. She had said she would meet him downriver. Ainsworth thought she would probably be worried because he wasn't there.

By now the divers were in the water. A helicopter was being summoned to search the channel by air in case there were still more bodies. Several of them were smoking as well, dropping their butts at random. Ainsworth thought that was odd. Didn't the police care about contaminating the crime scene? The way they were going, it was soon going to be impossible to tell what had been present before their arrival.

About an hour later, Ainsworth saw his wife driving by. He saw Maureen try to stop her car, but the police kept waving her through. She stopped anyway. Ainsworth could see her behind the wheel. She *was* worried. He could see that she had seen his truck. Probably she was thinking that he had drowned or something. Then he saw that she had seen him. "He's mine, he's mine," Maureen kept saying to the cop, pointing at Ainsworth. Ainsworth got up and went over to her in the car. "It's all right, Maureen," he said. "I'm fine. You go on home and I'll meet you there later." Maureen nodded. She decided not to ask any questions. She drove home to wait for her husband, who looked very sick.

Meanwhile, farther downstream, Frank Linard had come back to the river. His aunt and uncle from Boston had wanted to go blackberry picking. Despite his dream, Linard decided to take them and his mother to the Green River near the slaughterhouse, where he knew the berries were plentiful. As the four picked the dark juicy fruit from the long thorny branches, Linard looked south on the road and saw many police cars. *Oh God*, Linard thought, *not another one*.

* * *

About 6:00 P.M. Chief Medical Examiner Donald Reay and two of his assistants arrived at the river. The pathologist walked down to the river to look at the first two bodies. The victims had remained in the water while the divers finished their work. Then the bodies were removed. The heavy rocks that had kept them submerged were taken as evidence.

As he examined the victims, Reay used a hand-held tape recorder to dictate his findings:

The first body recovered is unclothed and appears to have been in the water three or four days. The body is generally quite well preserved although there are patches of skin slip. In addition, mud is diffusely adherent to the body surface. The head hair is black and curly. The facial features are those of a black. In addition, skin pigmentation indicates black race. The age of the victim is mid to late twenties. No obvious injuries are present on the body. There is no jewelry on the body. The hands are quite well preserved. A bruise is noted over the middle aspect of the proximal left forearm. The hands show immersion changes with no unusual features otherwise identified. The hands are bagged under my supervision by Mr. Rowley.

The second body is estimated to have been in the water about a week and shows moderate decomposition with gas distention of all body tissues. Patches of black discoloration are present over the trunk and right leg and these correlate with the placement of rocks over the body as noted in the water. The head shows decomposition with the tongue protruding between the lips. Much of the skin has slipped and there is diffuse mud deposition over the surface of the body. The hands likewise show the glove separation of the outer skin. In addition, the hair is starting to separate. The hair is black and multiple pigtails are present somewhat distributed uniformly over the head including the right and left parietal regions, occipital region, and a patch of hair which separates and is presumed to have come from the occipital region. The garment which remains on the body is a short sleeved and at this time appears dark blue in color. The brassiere is still on the body but is such that the brassiere is lifted above the front of the body. The brassiere is of the type that fastens in the front. The front fastener is undone and as a consequence the cups of the brassiere end up over the back. The hands are bagged. The body demonstrates no specific injuries at this time. There is a heavy coating of mud as previously noted. There is also skin separation in the glove-like fashion of the feet. The body is then prepared for removal.

Reay and his assistants moved up the bank to where the body discovered by Reichert still lay, and where finally Reichert was rescued from the "freeze zone," as the police called it. Reay continued his dictated description:

The third body lies in tall grass along the riverbank. It is in north–south fashion. It is unclothed except for the upper portion of the body where a garment with a zipper is entwined. The exact character will be established as the body is examined. The brassiere is rolled particularly over the back, and anteriorly it is likewise up over the surface of the breasts. The body itself lies face down. Over the right buttock there is a patch of abrasion. The right hand lies open-faced with the arm slightly flexed while the upper left extremity lies in a flexed fashion above the head. The head hair has a reddish tint but appears to be artificial with the main color of the hair light brown. In addition, this has a kinky-type appearance. The body still shows some faint rigidity. Lividity is well developed over the anterior portion of the body. The body as it lies shows a prominent degree of anterior lividity which is fixed. In addition, fly larvae deposition is present over the vulva recesses.

Likewise over the face, some fly larvae is noted.

About the neck, a pair of blue slacks are wound with an over and under type knot on the right side of the neck. The knot is not examined any further and will be preserved at the time of the autopsy. The face shows extensive congestion and in the conjunctivae, petechiae are noted. The lips are somewhat contused and swollen but a closer examination after cleansing during autopsy will be performed. The brassiere is pulled up exposing the breasts. The upper extremities aside from scattered scratches demonstrates no jewelry or other changes. The thighs are covered by loose adherent dirt. In addition, loose vegetation from the immediate scene is adherent to the body itself. The lower extremities likewise show scattered scratches. Fly bites are likewise noted. The hands are bagged and the body is removed under my instruction.

I depart the scene at 7:50 hours.

The presence of rigidity in the last body, the one found by Reichert, meant there were still faint signs of rigor mortis, the stiffening of muscles owing to the solidification of intramuscular fluids. Usually, rigor mortis disappears about twenty-four hours after death, longer when the weather is cooler. That meant the last body had probably been put on the bank sometime between Thursday afternoon, when Reichert was at the slaughterhouse, and Saturday night. Because the latest bodies had not been discovered on the previous Thursday, there had been no surveillance of the river for three critical days.

After Reay's inspection, Kraske conferred with the medical examiner. Reichert listened in. After Reay left, Kraske and Reichert conferred. Kraske asked Reichert to brief him about Dub Bonner. Reichert told Kraske about the note mentioning Carl Martin and Larry Mathews, and the reported friction between the two over money and drugs. Seattle detectives he had talked with, Reichert said, suggested that the murders could be byproducts of some sort of possible "pimp war" that might involve the two men. Kraske said he doubted that. Reichert looked away. "We're in trouble," he said.

Kraske just looked at Reichert. He was thinking that you didn't have to be a detective to figure *that* out.

By 10:00 P.M., the scene at the river had been cleared by the police. Somehow, no reporters had stumbled onto the story, in part because Kraske had tried hard to keep the reporters in the dark as long as he could. There were more important things to take care of first, Kraske knew. Like getting the bodies out of the river. *That* had been a struggle, especially getting them up the steep bank. Finally they had put a rope on the gurney and hauled it up, with Dr. Reay pushing and puffing along with the rest of them.

Reay had said it was hard to tell just how long the new bodies had been in the river—possibly as long as a week for the one under the water, maybe three or four days for the one partly on the bank. The girl Reichert had stumbled upon had only been dead a day or so—and as the remaining rigor indicated, maybe even only a matter of hours.

Kraske drove back downtown. In his office he sat down to compose a message to the press about the latest grisly discovery. Then Kraske went to the department's communications center to record the announcement on the department's telephone answering machine. Press people routinely called the machine when they wanted to know if there was any news. Well, tonight they would get a surprise, Kraske thought.

After delivering the basic facts of the three newest bodies, Kraske said he would hold a press conference the following morning. He played the message back to see if it covered everything he wanted to say. Then he went home to think about what had come his way again. Later that night he found himself wondering whether this was a second chance after Ted, or just Fate's way of torturing him some more.

5

THE MAJOR

August 15/August 16, 1990

At forty-five, Major Richard Kraske had long out-
grown the military brushcut that had been his trademark in his early years as a cop, back when he looked
so young others in the department first thought he was
a high school kid who had gotten into the department
by mistake. Now Kraske's blonde hair was moderately
long, combed across the top of his head to his left,
each strand kept in place just as meticulously as
Kraske had once shined his Marine shoes. The rock-
solid young infantryman's body had softened a bit,
and Kraske's broad Slavic face betrayed just a trace
of the puffiness that comes to middle-aged men known
to enjoy a drink or two. But Kraske was still a believer
in The Book, as in doing things by.

In his more introspective moments, Kraske strove
to eschew all manner of self-delusion. He was aware
of what his critics in the department liked to say about
him: that he was slow, too cautious by half, too meticulous to a fault; that he was more comfortable with
paper than with people. When he looked deep within
himself he could see the origins and even the truth of
those remarks, and they did not bother him. He took
comfort in order and procedure, he knew; whether he
took too much caution was not for him to say, as long
as he did things by The Book, the way things were

supposed to be done, and as long as The Book brought results.

Some of Kraske's love of order and precision could clearly be traced to his traumatic childhood. He had been born in Billings, Montana, in 1937. When he was five years old, his father was killed in an accidental shooting; five years later, to the day, his mother was killed by carbon monoxide fumes while sitting in a closed car with the engine running and the heater on. Kraske and his two brothers and a sister were taken in by their grandparents, and it was in their strict Catholic household that Kraske first learned to do things by The Book.

While Kraske's grandparents had fed and housed the orphans, the primary role models for Kraske were his uncles. All of them had been U.S. Marines— strong, confident men who believed in discipline and duty. When he graduated from high school at seventeen in 1954, Kraske also joined the Corps. There in the ranks Kraske found that while God may have worn the most stars, The Book was His platoon sergeant. In the Marines, Kraske learned to give his shoes a mirror finish, keep his weapon spotless, cut his hair to regulation length, wear his uniform crisp, and hop to it when his superiors told him to—all habits from The Book that he would keep for the rest of his life.

When, in 1955, Kraske's platoon was ordered to dig trenches in the Nevada desert just sixteen hundred yards from an atomic bomb codenamed Teapot Dome, The Book called for the trench to be six feet deep, which was the exact depth of the trench that Kraske dug. Shortly before sunrise, the Marines in the trench were ordered to duck. For the rest of his life Kraske would remember the loudest explosion known to man, then the rush of dust, rocks and sagebrush whistling over his head while he kept down in the trench dug to order by The Book.

Kraske would also remember the next command, which was to stand up and see what Teapot Dome had wrought. There, through the billowing cloud mushrooming up less than a mile away, Kraske stared at the newly risen, heliotropic sun. It had a horrible, deadly beauty, a poison lushness that seemed to promise a new evolutionary order, the genesis of a new kind of human being—a deadly, unfeeling species of human, Man Without Conscience, Psychopath Man, delivered fully formed into the world while arrogantly claiming equivalence with God Himself.

Eight hours after the explosion, Kraske's platoon was ordered in to Ground Zero. The Book said Move Out, even though no one knew then—or at least admitted—that ionizing radiation left over from the test was likely to give a few good Marines a fatal dose of cancer. But then, as The Book also said, who wants to live forever?

Doing things by The Book remained Kraske's guide even after he left the Marines and became a cop in Seattle. The Book said young recruit patrolmen had to spend time as guards in the jail, and nowhere did The Book say the recruits had to like it. Kraske spent nine months as a guard. Later Kraske was sent to the department's identification section, where his meticulous paperwork and organizational skills won him praise. Then there was a tour as the department's official crime scene photographer, partly because Kraske was one of the few men in the department who knew how to use a camera and develop film. Other similar technical and organizational assignments followed, as Kraske earned a reputation for thoroughness and meticulousness in completing written work, rare traits in a department where many members were recruited first for their size, strength, and toughness, and only secondarily for their ability to think and write.

It was only after he became a lieutenant in charge of the department's detectives in 1973 that Kraske began to doubt the capacity of The Book to resolve all problems. The killings they had all called simply the Ted murders had shown the limitations of The Book, he thought. But then, he realized, that only meant The Book needed to be revised, not thrown away. Kraske might be cautious, but that didn't mean he couldn't learn new things.

Before Ted, Kraske had believed that homicide was one of the easiest crimes to solve. Almost invariably, he knew, the murderer was someone known to the victim. All that was required was a process of elimination: Find the person with the motive, the means, and the opportunity to kill, then bore in. Collect the physical evidence, confront the prime suspect, and record the confession, case closed. In the rare cases where none of the victim's acquaintances could be shown to be responsible, one had only to look wider for the motive, which was usually robbery; and then work the street snitches until someone delivered the guilty person's name to the police.

But Ted was different. He wasn't known to the victims. He seemed to have no other motives than simply to murder and to confound. The crimes were aberrations, wild oscillations in the pattern of things. From his trench in the detectives' squad room, Kraske came to realize that in this case, at least, The Book would have to be rewritten.

One critical factor was information management. Traditionally, homicide cases were assigned to individual detectives, who maintained the case file from beginning to end. The names of informants were kept confidential by each detective, as were most sources of information. Rarely were seemingly disparate cases connected, and they were not, at least initially, in the Ted case. But as the Ted murders piled up, and as the evidence began coming together, Kraske knew there had to be a way to improve communications between detectives. Most of all, there had to be a better way of recording and retrieving the bits of information being developed that improved on the old single case-file method.

Equally important in a serial murder investigation, Kraske had learned from Ted, was the way the news media was handled. Whether they were aware of it or not, reporters could make or break an investigation. If the news media yawned at the crimes, so would the politicians, and if the politicians yawned, so would the department's top brass. On the other hand, if the media gave out too much information, it might prove impossible to separate the wheat from the chaff as detectives processed leads. Serial cases usually brought out the worst in news agencies just as they did with ordinary people, Kraske knew; because the cases were sensational, so would be the news coverage. The newspeople had to be carefully kept in line, given enough information so they could be supportive, yet not so much that they ruined everything. It was tricky. And if the media ever became hostile to the investigation, the cops might as well give up, because an investigation without public support was one that would never last.

And there were some other lessons as well. One of the detectives working for Kraske on the Ted murders was a young investigator named Bob Keppel. Keppel was a bit of an anomaly in the department. Bright, educated, often caustic in his contempt for those who kept doing things by The Book even when The Book wasn't working, Keppel had a reputation for unconventional thinking.

When the bones of the dead were found on the hillside, it was Keppel who read about such things as decomposition of bodies, who crawled around on his hands and knees in the mud in search of the remains, who learned to follow the brush trails made by small animals in hopes of discovering skulls, teeth, and finger and toe bones that taken together would help identify the dead.

And later it was Keppel who had come up with the idea of creating lists of people who might have come in contact with the victims by searching class rosters, lists of people who owned cars similar to the Volkswagen "Ted" was said to have driven during several abductions and attempted abductions; Keppel even assembled lists of people named "Ted" or similar variations who matched the approximate age and description of the suspect. By comparing the lists for commonalities, Keppel came up with twenty-five possible suspects. He was still working his way down the list, one name away from Ted Bundy, when Bundy was first arrested in Utah.

Kraske had also learned about serial murderers from the Federal Bureau of Investigation, which had begun a program of psychological profiling of crimes, using evidence from the crimes themselves. Kraske knew that profiling was a new, largely untested tool, but anything that might give an investigator an edge had to be considered seriously. They hadn't had a profile for Bundy, so no one had known what to look for.

As the years passed after Bundy's first arrest, his subsequent escape in Colorado, and then his recapture in Florida, Kraske decided that despite his initial shock at the wanton nature of Ted's crimes, similar psychopathic killers were actually everywhere: John Wayne Gacy in Chicago, Son of Sam in New York, two weirdos who killed teenaged boys in Houston, several women killers in Florida, a child killer in Michigan, and later, a man in Southern California who kidnapped men, cut up their bodies, and left the pieces in garbage bags strewn around the metropolitan area. There were the Hillside Stranglers, one of whom had been caught in Bellingham, Washington, just ninety minutes north of Seattle. The more Kraske read, the more it seemed that the country was undergoing a chain reaction of motiveless murder.

But of all the lessons Ted had taught, Kraske thought, the most important was the need for police departments to put aside their jurisdictional jealousies. Serial killers like Ted usually traveled. By the time one murder was discovered, the killer was likely to be committing another one miles away. Often, no one knew that the crimes were connected unless and until someone was caught. The full extent of the horror was usually realized only during the interrogation.

Even worse, pettiness over jurisdictional matters kept police agencies from effectively communicating with one another, and prevented recognition of the patterns involved in a series of crimes. City police in

Seattle had steadfastly insisted at the beginning of the Ted murders that the victims' disappearances were isolated situations, unrelated to one another. Even Keppel had at first rejected the idea that all of the crimes were committed by the same person.

Police academics and management consultants had a phrase for reluctance to see connections, Kraske knew: "linkage blindness," the reluctance to believe that one killer could be responsible for so many widely separated crimes. Such a concept simply flew in the face of conventional police experience. The solution to linkage blindness, Kraske now knew, was cooperation and communication. As he considered his situation the night after the new bodies were found at the river, Kraske resolved to open his eyes to the possibilities. Five murders in less than a month, and all the bodies dumped in or near the Green River. Six murders, if one counted Leann Wilcox. A serial killer was at work—no one should doubt that, Kraske thought. The trick would be to get all the area police departments to work together, and that wasn't as easy as it might sound.

Take the murder of Wendy Coffield, Kraske thought. *That* was a matter for the city of Kent, not his department. But what about Leann Wilcox? Hadn't she been friends with Wendy Coffield? Kraske thought of Keppel's approach in the Ted murders. If they could somehow assemble a list of people who might have come into contact with Coffield and Wilcox, then compare it to a similar list for Dub Bonner, and other lists for the three latest victims, the revised Book said that the killer might be isolated, in the same way that doctors hunt for a deadly virus.

That was the way to go, Kraske thought. But first the Kent detectives must be willing to share *all* their information about Wendy Coffield with the county's detectives, and the county detectives had to do the same for Kent. Then both departments would have to work cooperatively on the cases until a connection could be proved or disproved.

Nor should the cooperation include only the county

and Kent, Kraske realized. The Seattle Police Department had three homicides similar in many details to the deaths of Wendy Coffield and Leann Wilcox; so far, Seattle detectives insisted that not only were none of their crimes connected with either Coffield or Wilcox, they *weren't even connected to one another*. Were there really *nine* separate stranglers marauding the streets of Seattle and King County, all in the same six-month period? Kraske thought that was hardly likely, after the Ted experience. Suddenly it seemed that young women were dying and police of three different police departments weren't solving any of the crimes—the same way it had happened with Ted.

The Ted murders, Kraske thought. Sometimes he hated the man for what he had done. When he thought about Bundy—and he tried not to—Kraske recalled the initial police confusion, the disjointed efforts by various departments to get a grip on what was going on, the agency turf wars, the meddlesome press screaming for action, the long hours, the frustration, and the days spent on that hillside polluted with evil, while detectives searched laboriously for the bones of the dead. But mostly he remembered the steady fear that had eaten its way into his guts, conjuring up a dark, panicky vision: that "Ted" would somehow, some way seek out and kill Kraske's *own* daughters.

There had been the arguments with his wife, some of them bitter, some of them about the hours, but most over the safety of the girls. Kraske's wife wasn't about to let their daughters' lives be dictated by some vague fear, however palpable. The girls had a right to grow up normally, and that didn't mean with a police bodyguard always in the vicinity and paranoia as a constant companion. Somewhere during the Ted investigation, Kraske's wife had taken their daughters and moved out, and a part of Kraske had never recovered.

It seemed crazy now, but at the time it had been his private nightmare. The girls had only been in high school, but who knew for sure that a deviate who had killed so many college coeds wouldn't go after the children of one of his pursuers? Simply for the sport of it? That, after all, seemed to be the killer's only apparent motivation.

Because no one had really known what "Ted" would do. This was a killer who had never been imagined in any police management textbook. Kraske and the rest of his department had been forced to learn as they went, and the first thing *he* had learned was that there was never enough time. The second was that all the experience detectives had in the world of ordinary murders meant nothing when it came to a serial killer. No one knew what serial killers would do. *No one.* And that was the most important chapter in The Book on serial killers.

6

ROCKS

August 16, 1982

The next morning Kraske was in his office shortly after seven. As the man in charge of all investigations, he had the power to pull investigators off pending cases and reassign them, at least temporarily, to the river murders. Unfortunately, in the understaffed county department, there just weren't many detectives to begin with. Help would be needed. Kraske wanted to convince Winckoski to let him use members of the department's plainclothes patrol unit, the so-called "proactive" squad. While not trained investigators, the proactives were the best and brightest of the department's patrol force. Kraske also decided to use the four detectives assigned to the department's intelligence unit, Detective Fae Brooks from the sex crimes detail, and Larry Gross, the detective who specialized in finding people who didn't want to be found, from the warrants section. Kraske hoped Gross might be able to help them find out who the latest dead women were.

The links between Leann Wilcox, Wendy Coffield, and Dub Bonner and prostitution seemed readily apparent. Wilcox and Bonner had been arrested for prostitution, and Coffield had been known to frequent places where prostitution was occurring. It seemed quite likely to Kraske that all three women had encountered their killers while working as prostitutes. For that reason, Kraske assigned two members of the department's plainclothes vice squad to covertly watch prostitutes, their pimps, and the customers. Usually the vice squad concentrated on making arrests in bars and massage parlors in addition to undercover patrol of areas where street hookers strolled. Simple surveillance of the traffic rather than first baiting, then arresting the hookers was only rarely done, but Kraske thought the situation called for something new.

A little after eight Kraske went to see Sheriff Winckoski. After his thirty-year career with the Detroit Police Department, followed by several years with the federal Law Enforcement Assistance Administration, Winckoski had joined the King County Police as a former sheriff's administrative aide, assigned primarily to tap into federal money. When the former sheriff resigned to take another job, Winckoski took over. Coming in at the top that way caused some top officers to see Winckoski as little more than a political hack; certainly his status as an outsider made many of the rank-and-file cops suspicious of his motives. Rumors were rampant that with a new county executive in his first year of office, Winckoski's days as sheriff were numbered. Kraske wondered whether Winckoski understood what was going on with the river murders, and whether he could count on the sheriff's support for the size of the investigation he knew would be necessary.

Kraske sensed that the river murders could prove crucial to his own career. The county police were headed by an appointed sheriff, Winckoski. But operational control belonged to two top subordinates, designated as chiefs. A third chief's job had just been proposed—to head investigations—and Kraske hoped to be considered for the post. Solving the river murders wouldn't do any harm to Kraske's chances for the job. Kraske explained about serial murders to Winckoski. Winckoski nodded. He would need a task force of detectives to assemble information on the victims' backgrounds, Kraske said. Winckoski said he understood. So far, so good, thought Kraske. He explained that meant the use of the intelligence unit, all of the department's major crimes detectives, and the dozen or so patrol officers assigned to the department's plainclothes details. Winckoski agreed. Then Kraske told Winckoski that he intended to ask the FBI to develop a psychological profile of the murderer. Good, said Winckoski. Next Kraske briefed the sheriff on a ticklish point: exactly what to say to the news media.

Already the newspapers and the television stations were up in arms about the murders. Kraske explained how he had withheld notification to the news media about the bodies, and why. Winckoski told Kraske he would have his support.

The morning newspapers bannered the story across the tops of their front pages. "Three more young women found slain," said *The Seattle Times*. Kraske's announcement Sunday night over the message telephone had caused the news organizations to scramble for facts. Based on rumors about the victims' ties to prostitution, reporters were already canvassing hookers in downtown Seattle for information.

The Times that Monday morning also reported that a meeting of police from Kent, Tacoma, and both the county and the city of Seattle had been scheduled to discuss information about "a pattern of violence against young female prostitutes in the Seattle area." Other unnamed sources provided more "details."

"One police officer," *The Times* reported, "asking not to be named, said investigators are probing reports that some of the recent killings of young prostitutes may stem from a 'pimp war,' a battle for territory among those who profit from the young women's activities." Pimp wars! That was the Seattle Police Department talking, Kraske was sure. It was ridiculous. Even assuming the dead were actually prostitutes—a reach without any confirmed identification—the idea of pimps killing their meal tickets was laughable. Beat them, yes, frequently. Shoot them full of dope, certainly. But kill them? Highly unlikely. Winckoski wanted to know about the "pimp war." "That's nothing but sheer speculation," Kraske told him

The papers also said that police had made a tentative identification of one of the victims, but were withholding the name to check dental records. That was true at least, Kraske told the sheriff.

Already Reichert had talked to the parents of Dub Bonner, who had been missing for three weeks, Kraske told Winckoski. She could be the girl found Thursday, he said. The parents had given Reichert the names of two men who were involved with Bonner and who might know something about her disappearance. Further investigation would have to be conducted to see whether the two men were involved at all. Whether either of the two men were also connected to the latest three victims also had to be resolved. Personally, Kraske told Winckoski, he didn't think the two men had anything to do with any of the murders, but further checking would have to be done. At the very least the two men might be able to tell detectives where Dub Bonner had gone after getting out of jail in late July.

The truth was, Kraske told Winckoski, the whole situation made him think of Ted Bundy. Winckoski looked worried as Kraske left.

Back in his office, Kraske called an acquaintance at

the Seattle office of the FBI. The agent was sympathetic and cooperative. She promised Kraske that the bureau would provide a psychological profile of the murderer based on information Kraske's detectives would supply.

At the medical examiner's office, the autopsies of the three newest victims began shortly after 8:00 A.M. Reichert was again in attendance. Finger- and palmprints were taken of all three victims. An assistant medical examiner drew the first body from the cold room, a concrete enclosure about four hundred feet square kept at a constant temperature in the low forties to retard decomposition. The dead women lay on their own gurneys, covered with white sheets.

The first to be taken into the autopsy room was the young woman found by Reichert. The body was rolled onto the stainless steel operating table and the overhead lights were turned on. The pathologist noted several bruises and lacerations on the face and lips. As with Wendy Coffield, the left forearm was badly bruised. The right arm was scraped as if it had been dragged over rocky ground. A tiny puncture was found on the outside of the right knee. More scrapes were found on the victim's lower back and buttocks.

A closer examination of the knee revealed microscopic traces of pigmented, shiny material—perhaps some sort of colored glass. The pathologist went over the whole body with the magnifying glass. He found minute particles of what appeared to be tiny glass beads all over the body. These were scraped off and preserved. Further inspection revealed traces of intact sperm in the victim's vagina. X-rays were taken of the victim's teeth in the hope that dental charts might later be obtained to confirm the victim's identity.

At 8:45 A.M., the pathologist started on the next body. Within a few minutes he discovered something shocking: a pyramid-shaped rock about three inches long and about three and one half inches wide at its base had been shoved into the victim's vagina. The rock had to be surgically removed; it too was placed into evidence. The pathologist noted the presence of injuries in the woman's neck cavity, and concluded that the woman had been asphyxiated in some manner, possibly by hand.

While Reichert was in the autopsy room, Kraske left his office on the first floor of the county courthouse and took an elevator to the fourth floor of the same building, where the offices of King County Executive Randy Revelle included a large conference room. As Kraske walked into the room he saw that the television cameras had already been set up. The room was filled to capacity. He could tell from the faces of some of the reporters that it was going to be one of those mornings. His decision to withhold notification to the news media of the discoveries in the Green River while the police were at the scene had the newspeople sharpening their knives. Kraske's thoughts flashed back to the fiasco on the mountainside when the reporters had outflanked him. "I can't help it if they don't listen to their [radio] scanners," he later told acquaintances. If the newspeople had missed the story, it was their own fault, Kraske thought.

But Kraske had too much experience as a professional to put those thoughts into words. Instead, as he sat down before the cameras, Kraske kept his face impassive—the picture of a calm, composed policeman just doing his job.

Kraske began by announcing that the police were assembling a twenty-five-officer task force to investigate the murders—"the biggest task force since the Ted murders," he said. After describing the discoveries briefly, Kraske said police had concluded that all five victims found in the river, including Coffield in July, had probably been killed by the same person. Kraske said the county police had requested the FBI's help in preparing a psychological profile of the murderer. Then the questions came pouring in.

How were the victims killed? Were there any obvious wounds or violence? "No," said Kraske, keeping silent about the pants tied around the last victim's neck. "It appears that all five were dumped at different times from the same location," he added.

Where was that? "We think from a gravel shoulder just off the road," he said. "This is a remote area," he said. "It's a natural place to dump things. It's a good location for that." When were the victims killed? "Sometime within the last few weeks," Kraske said evasively.

Were the bodies decomposed? "Yes," Kraske said, keeping the information about the last victim's apparent time of death to himself. Who found the bodies? "Two were found just before noon by a man floating down the river on a raft, looking for bottles. At first he thought he saw a mannequin, then saw it was a human being. Our officers discovered the third victim." Kraske kept quiet about the rocks used to weight the victims down under the water.

Can you tell us the name of the man who found the bodies? "No," said Kraske. "He was very upset by his discovery, and he doesn't want to be contacted by the press." Do you have any leads? Any idea of how long it's going to take to solve the crimes? Kraske gritted his teeth. Of all the questions, that was the dumbest. *It's like asking if I know when the world's going to end*, he thought. But Kraske maintained his placid demeanor.

"We are working on some things. We'll know more after the autopsies are completed." When do you expect to identify the victims? "We're working on it," he said. Kraske terminated the press conference and walked back to his office to get his investigators organized to handle the hundreds of tips the publicity was sure to bring in.

Just before noon the pathologist began the examination of the third victim. Bruises were noted on the neck and top of the left shoulder, more evidence of violent struggle and probable strangulation. Examination of the vagina showed another pyramid rock, this one two and one half inches long and a little less than two inches wide at the base. Two victims found in the water, each weighted down with rocks and each with rocks in their vaginas. Clearly those two murders were the work of the same killer. Reichert took the finger-print cards, the rocks, and the pigmented material, and the glass beads back to his office.

One of the fingerprint sets matched with depart-ment records: another arrested prostitute, Belinda Bradford. Then the same prints were matched to another name, Marcie Woods, and then, to Belinda Woodies, Marcia Bradford, Belinda Jean Chapman, and finally, to Marcia Faye Chapman. Who was the dead woman, really? Further checking would be needed to determine her true name. The prints of the other two victims produced no identities.

That afternoon Kraske presided over the meeting of police detectives from Kent, Tacoma, the city of Seattle, and his own department. Kraske had invited Bob Keppel, the Bundy expert, from the attorney gen-eral's office, as well. There are a *lot* of homicides involving young women, Kraske realized, as detectives from each agency briefed the others on their cases. And there were several young prostitutes who had been reported missing as well, particularly in the city of Seattle. But a difference of opinion arose over whether the murders were really a serial case or whether the murders of Wendy Coffield and Leann Wilcox were separate cases, and over Bonner, if that was who the slaughterhouse victim was. Most agreed, however, that at least the two young black women found in the river were probably killed by the same person or persons, and also probably the third victim, the one that Reichert had discovered.

The meeting also reviewed the meager leads detec-tives had for the various cases. Reichert talked about Leann Wilcox, Dub Bonner, Larry Mathews, and Carl Martin. A Seattle detective described his department's investigation of the murders of Joan Conner, Theresa Kline, and Virginia Kay Taylor, all known to have hitchhiked, but said he doubted that they were connected to the Green River crimes. Another detective filled everyone in on prostitutes who had been reported missing. Kellams from Kent talked about Coffield. The Tacoma police brought with them information on Mathews and Martin, as well as on several others involved in Tacoma's world of drugs and prostitution.

After listening for awhile to the wrangling over whether the murders were a serial case, Keppel snorted in disgust. If ever murders met the criteria for a serial homicide case, Keppel said, they certainly did in the river murders. Keppel reviewed the facts: The victims were similar in age and possibly background; it appeared likely that the victims were dumped from the same spot along the river; two of the victims had the same sort of rocks forced into their vaginas, almost certainly a psychological signature of the same sexual psychopath; two of the other victims, Wendy Coffield and the woman found by Reichert, were both strangled with their own pants, and in both cases the same kind of knot was used, again a signature.

"I can tell you one thing," said Keppel. "This probably isn't the first time this guy has killed, and not only that, he's not going to stop until he's caught or he dies." Furthermore, said Keppel, it was almost a certainty that the killer or killers would soon be getting victims from all over, not just King County.

Many of the detectives disagreed with Keppel. Some pointed out that the rocks used to weight down the two black victims in the water didn't seem present with the slaughterhouse victim, and certainly not for Coffield, who was found floating. But Keppel wasn't so sure about that; maybe the current of the river had dislodged the rocks on the first two victims. Some said the girl found on the riverbank could be connected to the two blacks found in the water, but then again, not necessarily.

Some detectives also pointed out that the riverbank victim might have been placed there as late as Saturday, which would have been well after the Thursday night television broadcast about the discovery of the body near the slaughterhouse. Wouldn't the killer of the two river victims have worried that the river area was under police surveillance? In that case, wouldn't he have gone elsewhere to dispose of his last victim?

The riverbank victim could be the work of a copycat killer, some detectives suggested, or of someone who was unaware of the publicity. Either way might suggest the last victim was killed by someone other than the person who killed the two river women, because serial killers were known to pay close attention to news media accounts of their crimes. Keppel responded by saying that because serial killers were often motivated by the challenge of getting away with the crime, going back to the river with the last body despite the danger might have been a real turn-on for the killer.

But Keppel said he thought it was more likely the last victim had been dropped in the grass on the riverbank at almost the same time Bonner's body had been discovered at the slaughterhouse. The tall grass had kept the last victim's body cooler, hence the traces of rigor mortis. Keppel guessed that the killer had intended to put the last victim in the water, but had been frightened off by all the commotion at the slaughterhouse.

The other detectives listened noncommittally to Keppel. Many did not like him. Keppel's reputation as a bright but often caustic critic of traditional police methods made them feel defensive. Worse, some saw Keppel as a tireless self-promoter—stubborn, opinionated, and sometimes difficult to work with. "Bob Keppel is the biggest egomaniac I've ever met," said one disgruntled colleague several years later. Because Keppel by 1982 had earned a national reputation as an expert in serial murders and outdoor crime scenes, some detectives believed Keppel was likely to see serial murders where none existed. "That's Keppel," they told one another later. "He sees serial murders everywhere."

Connected or not, the crimes had to be investigated. Kraske asked for suggestions. Keppel had one. "It's my guess," he said, "that this guy is a reader. He's read about the Atlanta case. He's read about how water can be used to clean trace evidence off the victims. It's just like in Atlanta: this guy may go back to the river, or some river, somewhere. If I were you, I'd stake the river out. That's how they caught Wayne Williams in Atlanta, with a stakeout on the river."

Kraske agreed. And in fact, he had already ordered undercover surveillance of the river area, too late perhaps, but maybe not. In the meantime, the detectives from the four departments would follow their own leads and funnel information to Reichert. The Seattle Department would look into pimps and pimp wars; Kent would continue working on Coffield; and Tacoma would mine Bonner's drug connections for word on Mathews, Martin, and other possible suspects.

That afternoon, the identity of the dead woman found by Frank Linard near the slaughterhouse was confirmed. Deborah Lynn Bonner, known as Dub to her family and friends, would never be frightened again. Later that night, police released her name to the news media, and the race for the first of the Green River families was on.

7

FAMILY TIES

August 17, 1982

Things started going bad for Carlton Marshall not long after Dub had disappeared. Dub was Marshall's "ho," as they said on the streets. When Dub had worked for Carl, those were the good times. The twenty-seven-year-old Marshall, using his street name of Carl or sometimes Robert Martin, liked to idle his hours away inside the cool dark of Tacoma's downtown taverns while Dub hit the streets, looking for business. Then, when the cops made things hot, Dub and Carl left the Teapot Motel in downtown Tacoma and moved into south King County to the north. There the two had taken a room at the Three Bears Motel at South 216th Street and Pacific Highway South. That was in the heart of the so-called Sea-Tac strip, a locus of street prostitution near the Seattle-Tacoma International Airport. The motel offered x-rated movies and managers who asked no questions, probably because they didn't speak any English.

Then on July 25, Dub had disappeared, leaving Carl with all her clothes—the tools of her trade, fixings he'd paid good money for—and the maroon '72 T-Bird they jointly owned. Dub left the motel to hit the strip about 8:00 P.M. and never came back. Carl told friends that Dub was "missing in action."

Carl wondered whether Mathews had anything to do with Dub's disappearance. He'd called Dub's mother a few days later, and she said she hadn't heard from her. Carl couldn't believe that Dub would leave him, not after everything they'd been through. Hadn't they been arrested together?

But after Dub had vanished, Carl decided it was time to take care of business. He'd gone up to Lynnwood, just north of Seattle, and had gotten involved with a man up there. Carl needed to make a score. The other dude put him on to some stolen credit cards. With a little money, he could make things right with Mathews and maybe Dub would come back to him.

Then on August 4 Carl and the other man were busted by the Lynnwood cops for the stolen credit cards and were taken to the Snohomish county jail. The T-Bird was impounded while the cops searched the car, and it took Carl six days to raise the money to get out.

Then it turned out Dub was dead, one of the women found in the Green River. Carl found that out from the cops. He'd been out of jail less than a week when here on Tuesday morning the cops had landed all over him. Right in front of his own mother. What did he know about Dub's dying? Had he wasted her? Who was this Mathews? I don't know, man, he kept saying. All I know is that, we were at the Three Bears Motel in Seattle, and she just disappeared. I haven't seen her since, Carl said. You know, we were real close, too. The cops asked him about Dub's note, the one about Mathews. Silly woman had said that Mathews was going to kill her if she didn't get money to pay off Carl's debt. Sure, he'd told her that, but it was just for *motivation*, dig? But it put Carl in all kinds of trouble that she'd written that stuff down. Carl said that he and Mathews had a business disagreement, nothing to get excited about. Carl didn't think the cops bought that, but what the hell. They seemed like they were more interested in Mathews than in him. Good, thought Carl. It served Mathews right for threatening him.

The day after Bonner's identity was released, editors at *The Times* decided to step up their coverage of the murders. Shortly after 9:00 A.M., reporter Carol Ostrom was assigned to interview the Bonner family. "Try for pix of the dead girl, too," an editor had written on a slip of paper containing the Bonners' address.

Ostrom was generally regarded as one of the newspaper's best interviewers. Her skills depended in large part on her ability to seem ingenuous as well as empathetic. The *Golly!* approach seemed to work well, especially when interviewing people touched by trauma and tragedy, even if Ostrom wasn't entirely sure exactly how it worked. It was almost as if those being interviewed wanted to help *Ostrom*. "I kind of go unconscious in these situations," Ostrom later said. "I really don't know what I do."

Ostrom and a photographer headed for the Bonner family home. Driving into the neighborhood, both were struck by the poverty that seemed so abundant.

At the house, Ostrom and the photographer picked their way cautiously through a tattered front yard populated by numerous dogs. The front door was open; a screen door had been placed laterally across the lower half of the doorway, apparently to keep the dogs out, and Ostrom had to step over it to enter the living room when the Bonners invited her in.

Shirley Bonner was still crying. Soon, so was Ostrom.

Shirley poured out the tale to Ostrom. How Dub had started hanging around with Carl Martin. How Martin had called when Dub vanished. How Shirley had gone to the Tacoma police, who refused to take the report. How Reichert had told them on Saturday that the police thought Dub was dead. How the police had called on Monday and said that Dub *was* dead.

Shirley Bonner told Ostrom that Dub had dropped out of high school, and had quit the only job she'd ever had, working in a Dairy Queen, when the manager accused her of stealing. Ostrom nodded. "She tried other jobs," said Shirley, "but they just wouldn't take her because she didn't have a high school education.

"She was doing real good until she met this Carl a little over four years ago," Shirley said. "And then, she went downhill.

"She really loved us, and that . . . but like, if we'd say anything—I think she was really in love with Carl. In plain words, he was a pimp. We tried to keep her out of trouble, but if we ever said anything bad about Carl, she'd blow her top. She was just so hooked into him." *Or hooked on something,* Ostrom thought.

Over the years, said Shirley, Dub would go on trips with Carl: California, Colorado, up to Seattle, and other places. She would be gone for months at a time, but would still call home once or twice a week. "She'd say, 'I love you,' and 'Tell Dad I love him,' and stuff like that."

Dub's last call came a few days after July 20, Shirley said. They remembered the date because it was that day Walt Bonner had his eye operated on. "I don't know if she was on something or not," said Shirley. "Her voice was fine, but it was just up a little higher. She said, 'Mom,'—and she's never said this before— 'I've been a prostitute for four years.' She's never said that over the phone before."

Then Walt and Shirley told Ostrom about the note naming Larry Mathews that Dub had written and given to the bartender, and that Reichert had taken with him. Ostrom asked the name of the bar and the bartender. The place was called The Lucky Spot, the Bonners told her.

Then, as Ostrom and the photographer were leaving, Shirley Bonner said, "For the last three or four weeks, I'd get such happy feelings. I could hear her coming, or see her pulling up and getting out of the car and coming up the sidewalk . . . and all this time, she was dead."

While Ostrom was talking to the Bonners, the county police positively identified the first of the black women in the river. Marcie Woodies, aka Bradford, was in truth Marcia Faye Chapman. Chapman was thirty-one and the mother of three small children. Known as Tiny to her friends and neighbors because of her diminutive stature, she had worked as a prostitute near the Seattle-Tacoma International Airport for several years, using the money she earned to pay the rent on a nearby apartment and to feed and clothe her children. Chapman's mother was taken down to the morgue, where she provided visual identification of her daughter's immersion-bloated body.

Reichert learned that Chapman had been arrested on June 28 on Pacific Highway South not far from her apartment and had appeared in court about a month later. Nine days after that, at about 8:30 P.M., she told her children she was going to the store. She never came back. The following day one of Marcia's children called Chapman's mother, who came over to take care of them until Chapman turned up. But the hours dragged on with no word. Finally, just before midnight on August 2, Chapman's mother called police to report her daughter missing.

After leaving the Bonner residence, Ostrom went to see a close friend of Dub's, another prostitute. The woman directed them to a bail bondsman who had done business with Carl and Dub. Supposedly, the bail bondsman had possession of a telephone book kept by Dub that listed some of her customers. But the bail bondsman was out, and his clerk refused to say anything at all about Dub, or whether the enterprise had Dub's phone book. Then Ostrom stopped at the house of Carl Martin's parents. Carl wasn't in. Ostrom said she would call back.

Next, Ostrom headed for The Lucky Spot, the tavern mentioned by the Bonners. The Spot was in a two-block area of downtown Tacoma hard up against pornographic bookstores, peepshows, pawnshops, a credit furniture store, and the Greyhound bus station. The district was directly in the shadow of the newly built glass box of Pacific Northwest Bell. Heavy-lidded, short-skirted prostitutes lounged against the buildings, eyeing the passing traffic, on the lookout for possible customers.

Inside the tavern, Ostrom discovered that the bartender was aptly named. Ron "Shorty" Best stood just over five feet tall. Best told Ostrom he was too busy to talk right then, but gave her a telephone number where she could reach him later.

Finally, Ostrom and the photographer drove back toward Seattle, stopping at the Three Bears Motel on Pacific Highway South just south of the Seattle-Tacoma International Airport, where Dub Bonner had last been seen. Ostrom tried to interview the manager, but the manager only spoke Korean—or so it seemed.

Ostrom was not the only journalist digging into the victims' backgrounds. *The Seattle Post-Intelligencer's* George Foster, the paper's regular police reporter, was keeping an ear tuned to what the county police were saying. Foster soon learned that police now believed that all five Green River victims had been killed by the same person, and that county detectives were focusing their investigation along the Sea-Tac Strip. A cop told Foster that all five victims had died the same way, and that none were victims of shooting or stabbing. The county's detectives were showing pictures of the victims to bar operators, fast-food waitresses, motel managers, and others on The Strip in search of leads.

Foster also drove down to Tacoma to see the Bonner family. So did reporters from KIRO, the CBS affiliate in Seattle; Walt and Shirley told them the same things they had already told Ostrom. The television people then dropped in on The Lucky Spot and put Shorty Best on camera.

Meanwhile, the police were being deluged with telephone calls by reporters from all over the country. The police press spokesman, Pat Ferguson, met several times with Kraske and Reichert in an effort to keep the story under control.

That afternoon, Kraske had a special bulletin distributed to area police agencies. The bulletin contained two full-face photographs of the two remaining unidentified victims. Short physical descriptions of each were provided.

"Attention missing persons, homicide units and vice units," said the bulletin. "Between 07-16-82 and 08-15-82 the bodies of two white females and three black females have been found in and/or near the Green River near the city of Kent, Washington. Three of the five have been identified and indications are all three have been involved in prostitution.

"Request any agency having info on the possible identity of the two above victims to please contact Det. Reichert, King County Police."

Foster obtained a copy of the bulletin and took it back to *The P-I*. There an artist began transforming the faces of the two victims with their dead staring eyes into reasonably lifelike drawings. The paper planned to use the drawings to illustrate a story it intended to publish Friday warning the city's fluid population of street people to watch out, that a murderer was on the loose.

At the same time all the reporters were driving to Tacoma, King County Executive Randy Revelle was taking the first step toward ending Winckoski's command of the King County Police.

In an afternoon press conference, Revelle announced that he had hired Vernon Thomas to run the county's jail. Thomas, a fifty-six-year-old deputy chief in the Seattle Police Department, had for almost a decade been one of the most controversial figures in Washington State's law enforcement circles. Eight years earlier, while in command of the city's vice squad, Thomas had led a highly publicized revolt against a newly appointed police chief, suggesting starkly in public testimony that the new chief would give then Seattle mayor Wes Uhlman veto power over where and when to make gambling raids. Revelle was on the City Council at the time, and chaired the council committee in charge of the police. Thomas had become Revelle's key exhibit in the councilman's effort to tie Uhlman to the scent of possible police corruption.

Uhlman and his chosen candidate for the chief's office denied the charges, and counterattacked by claiming that Thomas had been behind what they claimed was an illegally recorded tape of the prospective chief's commitment to Uhlman regarding the gambling raids. Revelle lost, Uhlman's man was installed as chief, and Thomas spent the next five years in police oblivion, first handling the traffic patrol, then commanding the graveyard patrol shift.

But now, eight years later, Thomas was back at the top of the Seattle city department after having been rescued by a new chief, and Revelle was in power as the county's top elected official, the county executive. In appointing Thomas, Revelle was coming through on his debt to the controversial police commander.

True, the jail post was only a side pocket, but Revelle made it clear that Thomas's work in the jail would only be temporary. Bigger things were ahead for his old ally. Within minutes of Revelle's announcement, the perception of Winckoski's lame duck status that had troubled Kraske hardened into utter conviction among the county police. Winckoski would be gone; that was just a matter of time.

How much this looming change of leadership would influence Winckoski's willingness to get the resources from Revelle to undertake the murder investigation would remain unclear, even years later. Long after he retired, Winckoski insisted that Kraske told him that he had what he needed to solve the crimes, and that it wasn't necessary to obtain new resources from County Executive Revelle. But Kraske believed that once the departing sheriff knew he was on his way out the door, he lost all interest in the investigation.

What was certain on that day in August, however, was that Winckoski was hardly in a position to make expensive demands for resources on a politician who had effectively fired him. And as matters turned out, Kraske was on his own.

That evening, a television helicopter overflew the Green River with a live report for the evening news. The airborne reporter announced for the world to know that the police had the Green River under surveillance. The police erupted. Maybe the killer wouldn't come back to the river again, but after the broadcast the chance seemed more remote than ever. Detectives cursed the news media for blowing their best chance to catch the killer almost before it could be put into play. The relationship between the detectives and the media was already severely strained, less than two days into the investigation. The distrust and suspicion between the police and their natural critics would henceforth mark the Green River murder case to its very end. At the time, the irresponsible broadcast seemed a bad omen to Kraske.

*   *   *

Later that night, Ostrom telephoned Shorty Best from *The Times*. This time, Best was more talkative about Dub.

"She come in here close to little more than a month ago," Best told Ostrom. "She was real worried and scared, and started crying. She told me that if anything ever happened to her, that this was the guy, and she told me his name. Said this man had been following her around."

Best said Dub told her that she needed to raise several thousand dollars to pay off Carl's debt.

Ostrom asked Best if he thought that Carl was responsible for Dub's murder. "No," said Best. "Pimps don't kill their women. If they kill them, then they ain't got the money. I think," he said, "it's one person following one pimp."

The next morning Kraske was already in the first political squabble of the investigation. In announcing at his press conference that the FBI had agreed to do a psychological profile, Kraske inadvertently stepped on the toes of the special agent in charge of the bureau's Seattle office, Allen Whitaker. Whitaker thought the announcement of the FBI's role in the case should have been made by *him*, not Kraske. Now the bureau was complaining that the county police were being uncooperative with its agents. Jeez! thought Kraske.

Maybe he should have talked directly to Whitaker, but things had been happening so fast. Now the bureaucracy was uptight, saying, "Why wasn't *I* notified?" Kraske thought there had been enough time for the FBI agent he talked with to notify Whitaker, but apparently that hadn't happened. "The only reason I made the announcement," Kraske said later, "was because I got a commitment from the person I talked to. If the agent can't talk to Whitaker, I can't help that."

Meanwhile, police in King County wanted a missing persons report on Dub Bonner from their counterparts in Tacoma. The Tacoma police were both embarrassed and a little defensive about their failure to take the report earlier, when Shirley Bonner had reported her daughter missing. A report was immediately filled out, and dated to the day Shirley Bonner had come in, July 30. Shirley Bonner had told the Tacoma detective about the note Dub had left with Shorty Best, the note about Larry Mathews, but the threat didn't seem to impress the Tacoma detective as an urgent problem. He couldn't remember the name of the motel Shirley Bonner had said Dub was staying at, but he did have the telephone number. The number matched that of the Three Bears, which confirmed Carl's story. The detective said Shirley Bonner told him that Dub was a prostitute, and that another friend had said that Dub was going to California. In the absence of any compelling reason to believe that anything criminal had happened to Dub, the detective decided not to file the report.

Now, in the report the King County police insisted on having, the Tacoma detective tried to explain why he hadn't filed the report on July 30. "Mrs. Bonner appeared to be more concerned about her daughter showing up for a pending trial due to the fact that Mrs. Bonner had put up her house to bail Deborah and Robert Martin out of jail.

"R/D (reporting detective) advised Mrs. Bonner that she should report Deborah missing with Seattle P.D., if that's where Debra had been living." The report didn't say why the Tacoma detective didn't bother to contact the Seattle police himself with Shirley Bonner's information.

The same morning Ostrom headed for Chapman's mother's apartment in an effort to learn more about the murdered mother of three. No one was home, so Ostrom then drove to Wendy Coffield's mother's apartment in Puyallup, located about fifteen miles east of Tacoma.

There Ostrom talked to Virginia Coffield, Wendy's mother. Ostrom showed Ginny Coffield a snapshot of Dub the Bonners had given her. "Never saw her, never heard of her," Ginny said. She had never heard of anyone named Larry Mathews, either. Nor could she remember the names of any of Wendy's friends.

Great, thought Ostrom. This is going nowhere. Ostrom asked Ginny to talk about Wendy. Wendy drank and sometimes worked as a prostitute, Ginny told her. "I just couldn't control her." The state had taken custody of Wendy, Ginny said, and placed her in a temporary foster home in Tacoma, but Wendy had run away.

"Wendy and I were a lot alike," said Ginny. She told Ostrom how *she* had been raised by foster parents, and how she had spent two years in the state's school for troubled girls. It was the best thing that had ever happened to her. Ginny said she told Wendy *she* should be locked up, too. But the state wouldn't take her, Ginny said sadly, because Wendy didn't have enough "points."

"Points?" asked Ostrom. Ginny Coffield explained that because bedspace at the school was so limited, the state reserved the beds for those kids with the worst criminal histories. Wendy just wasn't *bad* enough, Ginny said, and although she kept earning new points every time she was arrested, the state kept increasing the points required. By the spring, Wendy had arrests for burglary, forgery, auto theft, and petty theft, and was frequenting a truck stop on Pacific Highway South to earn money as a prostitute. Despite all this, said Ginny, Wendy was still short of "points."

After the Kent police had notified her of Wendy's murder, Ginny identified the body at the morgue. Later she had Wendy's remains cremated, and Ginny scattered the ashes "all over the place. I wanted to see my baby one last time. She's gone, she ain't going to suffer, ain't nobody going to hurt my baby no more. She was wild in a lot of ways but I didn't think it was a harmful kind of wild. The only one it hurt was herself."

Shortly after Ostrom left, a reporter for the *Tacoma News Tribune* showed up. Ginny told the story one more time, and then again later for the television cameras. "I'm all cried out," she said.

*   *   *

While Ostrom talked to Virginia Coffield, other
reporters burrowed into Chapman's background. Some
of Chapman's neighbors near the airport knew she
worked as a prostitute. They called her by her nickname, "Tiny," because, at five feet two inches and
just over 100 pounds, she was so small. The neighbors
said "Tiny" had occasionally left her children home
alone to work the streets, but usually called her
mother first. In mid-July, a man in the apartment
complex had broken into Tiny's apartment and raped
her after pistol-whipping her. Tiny had been taken to
the hospital with a cut lip and facial bruises. Police
arrested the man. He was later released on bail. "How
do you rape a prostitute?" the man asked Tiny's
neighbors afterward.

An editor at *The Times*, meanwhile, was concerned
that *The P-I* was getting details about the murders that
his own reporters were missing. He asked a veteran
reporter with inside police contacts to see what he
could come up with. A little before 6:00 P.M. the
reporter phoned in with some information.

"The two tattooed girls," said the reporter, "each
had the same kind of tattoo linking them with a Kent-
area motorcycle gang. These guys are heavy into guns
and drugs. The cops' intelligence people say they are
watching these guys real closely. There are about fifteen or twenty members. The tattoos are often put on
the club's groupies, the hangers-on. It's like, if you
wanta hang around, you gotta be willing to have the
tattoo.

"The second thing is, the cops say all of the victims
bear in some way the same signature. My source
wouldn't say what that is, whether it's a cut, a wound,
or some kind of message on the body. The signature
could be interpreted as the work of a whacko, but it's
common to all five victims." That wasn't true, of
course, notwithstanding the rocks.

"One more thing. The county did a number on the
FBI on the psychological profile. They announced it
before getting clearance from the FBI. The criteria for

doing a profile requires some sort of pattern, like the signature. Something repeated, anyway. But the information hasn't been made available to the FBI. The agent in Seattle went to the county and didn't come close to getting the kind of information he needed to make the determination as to whether there was a pattern. The agent left the courthouse and picked up the afternoon paper and saw a story saying the FBI was doing a profile.

"The FBI feels the county set them up. It's like the county was trying to spread the heat. A profile can be done fairly quickly, but it usually takes a couple of months. It's a complicated process, but it can be expedited."

Later that night, Tomas Guillen, another *Times* reporter, armed himself with copies of the police special bulletin and photos of the five dead women and went into Tacoma's red-light district. There Guillen learned that Marcia Chapman, Dub Bonner, and Wendy Coffield had all been known to loiter near The Lucky Spot, and that the three women knew one another. One pimp told the reporter that Wendy Coffield was thought to rob customers while hooking. And a prostitute said one of the unidentified women looked like a prostitute she knew as "Cookie." The woman said she thought Cookie and Chapman had been friends. To Guillen, it was beginning to look as if all five women may have been connected.

The following day, *The Times* reported that Wendy Coffield, Dub Bonner, and Marcia Chapman "may have known each other," and that "it may be that all five victims have worked in Tacoma."

"Prostitutes and other street people there said last night they recognize the two unidentified black women pictured on police fliers," Guillen reported in *The Times*. "One anonymous source said one of the girls may have gone by the nickname 'Cookie.'" The police immediately disputed the story.

The next night, *Times* reporter Duff Wilson also dropped in on the red-light district. He reported on the atmosphere. "Except for a heightened undertone of fear," Wilson reported, "it was business-as-usual.

"Two Tacoma vice squad officers in plainclothes were citing an eighteen-year-old woman for being in a tavern without identification. The night before, the same officers arrested the same woman for prostitution.

" 'It's a game,' the vice officer said, and as if to prove his point he nodded to an attractive brunette in white pants walking by, and said, 'Hi, Donna, how are you tonight? Be careful now.' Donna, who doesn't deny her line of work, smiled back and said, 'I've heard they found two more girls.'

" 'I don't think so,' the officer said. 'It's scary,' said Donna as she left."

The police believed that prostitution in Tacoma's district had actually increased in the past week, Wilson reported. One vice cop said he noticed new faces in the area since the discovery of the bodies in the river. The cop guessed that some of the women had left Seattle to get away from the murderer.

Wilson found that indeed, rumors about the murders had raced far ahead of the facts. "A bartender claimed that one of the unidentified victims' cousin 'was in here the other night, but she won't come forward to identify her because she knows more or less what happened and she was scared for herself.'

"There's a rumor that police plants are working among the new prostitutes. There was a rumor last night that the police thought the killer was coming back and were ready to swoop down on him. That caused the block to be cleared of prostitutes in fifteen minutes.

"One prostitute said she agreed to a sex act with a man yesterday, but after she got in his van to drive to her place, he drove toward the Green River instead. The man made it seem like he was the killer, the shaken prostitute told friends, so she let him rape her. 'If that maniac wasn't still loose, I'da used my straight-blade on him,' she said, referring to the razor she carried in her purse, 'but I did just like I was told.

That maniac's still loose and it could be anybody.' The man later freed her near downtown Tacoma, the woman said."

But the feeling Wilson most noticed was one of anger. "Bonner was a regular here," he reported. "She's the one who is most missed, and one man warned that the police aren't the only ones looking for the killer. 'If they don't get him, somebody else will,' the man said angrily. 'And they might chop him up, too.' "

8

CONNECTIONS

August 20, 1982

Two days later, just after 1:00 A.M., the police arrested Larry Mathews.

Mathews had just walked into Browne's Star Grill, not far from the Lucky Spot, when Larry Gross, the detective who specialized in finding people who didn't want to be found, put the arm on him. For several nights, Gross had been cruising the streets of downtown Tacoma with a pair of Tacoma cops looking for Mathews. As Gross approached him, Mathews quickly drew a knitting needle honed to a fine point and threatened Gross. But after a brief wrestling match, Mathews was down on the floor and in handcuffs. Mathews was taken to the county detectives' offices in Seattle. By morning, Mathews was talking freely, but police weren't learning very much they didn't already know. It appeared that Mathews knew nothing about any of the murders.

Shortly after nine that morning, Kraske held another press conference and announced the arrest, which had already leaked from the county police. Kraske refused to name the man who had been arrested. He said that the man reporters had already identified as Mathews was one of four or five potential suspects in the murders. "We can't call him a prime suspect," said Kraske. "We are only investigating the possibilities." The other four men, he said, were still being sought for questioning.

Was the man cooperating? "Sometimes after an arrest there is a reluctance to be cooperative," Kraske said, "but we hope that can be developed."

Kraske said the detectives were trying to learn more about the man's involvement in the prostitution business in Seattle and Tacoma. "We don't believe he was a customer of prostitutes," he said, "his involvement is something more than that." Was the man a pimp? Kraske wouldn't say. What about the pimp war?

"That's the lowest of our investigative priorities," Kraske said. "For a pimp to go out and kill a bunch of prostitutes that belong to another pimp is most unlikely," adding that it was equally unlikely that a pimp would kill his own prostitute. "You don't kill your source of money," said Kraske.

The media firestorm was actually increasing, Kraske knew. Already detectives were complaining that it was almost impossible to talk to potential witnesses who hadn't already been interviewed by some reporter from someplace. Worse, the reporters were generally untrained in conducting investigative interviews. Often they inadvertently contaminated the witnesses' recollections by telling them things the witnesses wouldn't have known. A case in point was *The Times*'s report a few days earlier about the supposed connections of the women. A reported fact soon had the effect of becoming an actual fact, at least in the minds of potential witnesses. Soon, witnesses were telling police that sure, all the women had known one another, and it was impossible to say who *really* knew that and who had only read or heard it.

Then, that morning *The Times* had written about the squabble with the FBI over the damned profile. "Tempers were described as 'frayed,' " the paper said.

"The FBI said yesterday that it had not been asked officially to draw up a profile—contrary to an announcement made by police earlier this week. In fact, the agency had received no information, said Allen Whitaker, special agent in charge of the Seattle FBI office. 'We don't know,' he decided, 'if they are collecting it.' "

Criminy! As if Kraske didn't have enough to worry about. Now the newspapers were using Whitaker to make the county police look bad. Kraske wondered whether the papers were still mad because he hadn't notified them of the three Green River victims on Sunday. Or maybe they were paying him back for the Ted failure.

Now all the reporters were watching him describe the arrest of a man who probably wasn't even a good suspect in the first place. The thing to do was get the focus back on track, to show what the police had been doing.

"So far," Kraske said, "we have talked to more than one hundred and fifty people in areas where the three identified victims have lived and worked. In addition, we have searched the entire river from the West Valley Highway to Tukwila. Everything we know now tends to point to one suspect at this time." The West Valley Highway was where the bottle collector, Ainsworth, had launched his raft the Sunday before. Tukwila, downstream, was the place where Ainsworth's wife was to have picked him up.

Would the killer strike again? "There has been conjecture the suspect may strike again." Kraske paused. "We do not discount that statement."

What about the FBI's statement yesterday that they hadn't gotten information needed for the profile? "I would like to discuss that with the FBI," Kraske said evenly. Then, more firmly, "As it was stated at the first of the week, we have requested the assistance of the FBI to develop a psychological profile of the suspect."

After the press conference, Kraske finally heard some good news. A county prosecuting attorney had sworn an affidavit in support of a search warrant to comb through Mathews's Tacoma house, and a judge had approved the warrant. Detectives were on their way. Maybe, just maybe, they would find something to prove that Mathews *was* involved, despite his denials.

Even better, the two drawings of the unidentified victims published that morning in *The P-I* had generated several telephone tips from people who said they knew the victims. Dental charts were being sought on some of the names in an effort to finally identify them. Publicity wasn't always bad, Kraske knew. It was just that it was so hard to control.

That afternoon, a team of King County and Tacoma city detectives searched Mathews's house from basement to rooftop. The basement was particularly interesting. The searchers found a pair of handcuffs and chains bolted to the ceiling. There appeared to be dried blood underneath the restraints. Samples were taken of this. After several hours, the police finally emerged from the house, carrying away two cardboard boxes. Reporters from *The Post-Intelligencer* were there, watching; *The Times* was not. The police had ways of making the media more tractable; one way was by "forgetting" to let offending reporters know that something was up. If that didn't deliver the message, Kraske thought, he might just consider telling the newsies publicly: *Back off*.

On Sunday, August 22, one week after the bodies were found, medical investigators identified the remaining two women. One was seventeen-year-old Cynthia Hinds, sometimes known as "Cookie." The other was sixteen-year-old Opal Mills. Mills had been the one found by Reichert on the riverbank. The following Monday, police refused to release their names, and the medical examiner's office said it wouldn't either.

"We don't want to give out this information at this point," said police spokesman Pat Ferguson, who had been assigned by Kraske to take up the offensive against the interfering reporters. "We feel that releasing it could hinder our investigation. We've already seen that with the first three. We want to get a little head start. Before, the stories appeared before we had a chance to talk to families and friends of the victims."

With this head start, Reichert learned from the Mills family in Kent that Opal had left with a friend known only as "Cookie" on August 11, the day before Bonner's body was discovered. "Cookie" and Opal had gotten summer jobs painting apartments, the family told him. Opal was to ask the painting contractors whether another job might be available for Opal's brother.

On Thursday, Opal had called collect from a pay telephone and left a message. There were no other jobs. The family didn't know where she had called from. Reichert made a note to ask the telephone company if there was a record of the collect call. That way he might be able to find out where Opal had been.

It appeared that Cynthia Hinds, who had a record for assault and seemed to be a familiar face to the county's vice squad, might be "Cookie." Detectives talked to Hinds's family, who provided the names of some of her friends. From the friends, it was learned that Cynthia had been seen the night of August 11 at a convenience store located at South 200th Street and Pacific Highway South—about twelve blocks from the place where Marcia Chapman had last been seen on August 1, and sixteen blocks from The Three Bears Motel, where Dub Bonner had vanished on July 25. It was starting to look more and more like the suspect was a prostitution customer, a "sick trick," as the women called them.

Later Reichert found out where Opal Mills had placed the collect telephone call. The call had been made August 12 from the pay telephone at Angle

Lake Park, located at South 193rd Street and Pacific Highway South. That put Mills's last known location between Cynthia Hinds and Marcia Chapman; it also put four of the five victims on the Sea-Tac strip at the times of their disappearances. It seemed that the murderer had to be cruising Pacific Highway South, looking for victims. There were hundreds of prostitutes out there near the airport, Reichert knew, and as far as he knew, all of them were now potentially at risk.

Reichert also noted the time of Opal's telephone call: 12:55 P.M., only thirty-five to forty-five minutes before Linard had discovered Dub Bonner's body in the river at the slaughterhouse. Hadn't Keppel speculated that the killer had dropped Mills's body in a panic because of the commotion caused by the discovery of Bonner's body?

Reichert visualized the man carrying the body down the steep grassy bank, hearing sirens or seeing the flashing red lights, and then dropping Mills's body unceremoniously in his haste to get away.

On the other hand, there was the medical examiner's evidence about the body's rigor mortis and lividity. That could mean the body had been dumped later on Thursday, perhaps at night after Reichert and the others had left, or Friday, or even, possibly, early Saturday. In that case, the police might have caught the man in the act, if *only* they had placed the river under surveillance after Bonner's body had been found. How could the murderer have known there would be no surveillance? Was he showing his contempt for the police by going back? Or was it just that he didn't care? Maybe he was just stupid. Certainly he was lucky. Reichert was starting to get mad at this guy.

On Monday, August 23, the police relented and provided the names of Opal Mills and Cynthia Hinds. As before, the newspeople swarmed over the families. Photographers and television cameramen took pictures as the victims' family members stared glumly at the cameras. Reporters described the victims' final days, including their brushes with the law.

By now, Ostrom of *The Times* was starting to get the picture: These girls were coming from low-income homes where alcohol and abuse were facts of life. All of the girls had been in juvenile trouble, often underage drinking, shoplifting, or similar petty crime. The parents of Opal Mills maintained that as far as they knew, Opal had never been involved in prostitution.

"I've read the things in the newspaper," said Robert Mills, a retired Boeing forklift operator, "and she just didn't fit in. My little kids have had everything . . ."

"Everything we could give them . . ." Kathy Mills amended.

Robert Mills said he had just had a minor stroke. He said he had suffered the stroke while protecting his daughter from a man who had chased her home from downtown Kent. "She ran in all screaming, her hair standing on end," Robert Mills said. "My little girl . . . he chased her within a half block of here."

Robert Mills was black. Kathy Mills was white. Both parents said they thought Opal might have had some problems at school because of her mixed race. "She was black and proud of it," said Kathy Mills. Minorities were uncommon in Kent, they said. They thought the schools were partly to blame for Opal's juvenile troubles. "I don't know how this happened," said Robert Mills. "I think she was just in the wrong place at the wrong time." Ostrom could see that Kathy Mills was angry at Robert. There is tension in this house about Opal, Ostrom thought.

"Just say," said Kathy, "that Opal had a lot of problems, and leave it at that."

Ostrom asked Opal's brother Garrett about the man who had chased his sister. Garrett described a man in a red Cadillac, and said he thought the man was in some way connected to the Ku Klux Klan. Ostrom wrote that down.

Then Kathy Mills told Ostrom that the family planned to play Opal's favorite song at her funeral: *Love Begins with One Hello.*

*   *   *

Cynthia Hinds's brother told other reporters that the family hadn't seen his sister for more than two weeks. The last time any family members saw her, he said, she left without telling anyone where she was going. He said the family later learned that Cynthia had returned home with a man in a red Cadillac. She picked up her clothes, said Cynthia's brother, and prepared to leave. A neighbor begged her not to leave with the man in the Cadillac. Four days later, her brother said, a family acquaintance saw Cynthia on Pacific Highway South near the airport, getting out of the red Cadillac and into a black jeep. "Everyone says the man in the Cadillac was the connection," Cynthia's brother said.

Reporters decided Cynthia's brother and Opal's brother were describing the same car. The red Cadillac could be a pimp. Teams of newspeople were assigned to go to the airport area on Pacific Highway South and look for red Cadillacs and black jeeps. There seemed to be scores of them.

On the same afternoon, police acknowledged what *The Times* had printed the previous week: that all five women found dead had been involved in prostitution, and that the murders seemed to be connected with Seattle-Tacoma International Airport and Pacific Highway South, the area popularly known as the Sea-Tac Strip.

9

THE STRIP

August, 1982

Ten miles south of Seattle's downtown, Pacific Highway South leaves the flat river valley on the city's southern edge to mount a long bumpy ridge. The ridge, about four hundred feet above sea level, runs for about fifteen miles to the south and Tacoma. The Pacific Highway, before the construction of the Interstate 5 freeway, was the state's main road tying Seattle to Tacoma, Olympia, Portland, and points farther south. The ridge and the highway, with their proximity to Seattle-Tacoma International Airport, were to be the main stage for the depredations of the unknown man who came to be called the Green River Killer. Partly, this was because of the area's topography and history.

Throughout the first part of the century, the ridge—known to locals as the Highline, for the roads connecting Tacoma to Seattle—remained rural. Dense forests of Douglas fir were cut down, then regrown. Scattered farms were hidden in the trees, accessed by dark, graveled roads. Orchards, subsistence farming, and livestock raising were the most common means of employment for most of the ridge's population. Small game hunting was common, as was trapping and fishing in and around the small streams, ponds, and hillocks that gave the ridge its features. Numerous two-lane blacktop roads ran east and west off the north–south highway, through tall firs, down narrow, winding, unpopulated canyons to the Kent Valley below, affording knowledgeable drivers quick access to both areas, much like secret passages between rooms of a house. The domain of the King County sheriff, throughout the 1920s and 1930s, the entire area was known as the lair of gamblers, bootleggers, cathouse operators and out-and-out thieves, who often used the dark, narrow side roads for their illicit commerce.

Much of the rural character of the ridge began to change in 1942, when the Port of Seattle accepted a grant from the Civil Aeronautics Administration to build a new airport on top of the ridge. The Seattle area's existing airfield in the valley below had originally been built by the Boeing Company, which later turned the field over to the King County government to operate. But Boeing Field—Boeing's Field to Seattle's oldtimers—was too low in elevation to handle the large volume of air traffic government visionaries imagined for the Seattle area for the rest of the century. Fog often lay along the Duwamish River, where the Green River met the Black River before emptying into the harbor, and the larger aircraft necessary for profitable commercial flight operations needed some new place to land, preferably above the weather. The ridge, with an average elevation of nearly 450 feet, was perfect.

In 1942, earthmoving equipment began tearing out hundreds of acres of trees and Scotch broom, and leveling the rolling hills for the new airport's runways. Evicted in the name of this progress were two rabbit farms, a riding school, a frog ranch, a mushroom farm, a dog kennel, and perhaps forty residents. By 1945, the airfield was done.

In 1948, construction began to widen Pacific Highway in the area of the airport. Soon, most of the remaining trees and farms along the highway's route made way for highway-oriented businesses. By the mid-1950s, both sides of the road were crowded with gas stations, motels, diners, used-car lots, honky-tonk saloons, truck garages, billboards, parking lots, junk stores, gem shops, real estate offices, and the like, all jammed elbow-to-elbow along the highway's edge in a mad scramble to skim some of the money off the increasing traffic generated by the larger highway roadway and the airport it served. The hurdy-gurdy of the highway, its twenty-four-hour-a-day character, the elongated pattern of the virtually unregulated development, and the area's rollicking past soon conspired to give the area atop the ridge the image of a frontier settlement, the natural habitat of hustlers, men on the make, and outright outlaws. "The Strip," with its connotation of Las Vegas-style action, was born. But the dark, narrow roads down to the valley below remained essentially unchanged.

As Seattle grew in the 1960s and 1970s, so did the air traffic to and from the new airport. At the end of the 1950s, air passengers arriving or departing at Seattle-Tacoma International Airport—"Sea-Tac" to the locals—had reached 1.6 million. By the end of the 1960s, the annual passenger traffic was up to 4.5 million, and by the end of the 1970s, to 9.8 million, or nearly 27,000 people each day. As the air traffic jumped, so did the highway traffic. By the early 1980s, there were nearly 80,000 vehicles driving The Strip every twenty-four hours.

With the growth of the airport and the expansion of the highway came large hotels. The first wave, represented by the Hyatt House, the Holiday Inn, and the Hilton Hotel, arrived in the late 1950s and early 1960s. The 1970s brought the Red Lion, and the late 1970s, the Marriott. Other hotels and scores of smaller motels took root as well. Virtually all of these facilities catered to the ever-expanding air traffic generated by the airport, most of it composed of single businessmen, temporarily away from home, many on their way to Alaska, the Far East, or on their way back from those destinations.

Men away from home often do things they would not do otherwise. Often they drink, sometimes to excess. Fueled by alcohol, sometimes they go looking for women. Sometimes women go looking for them.

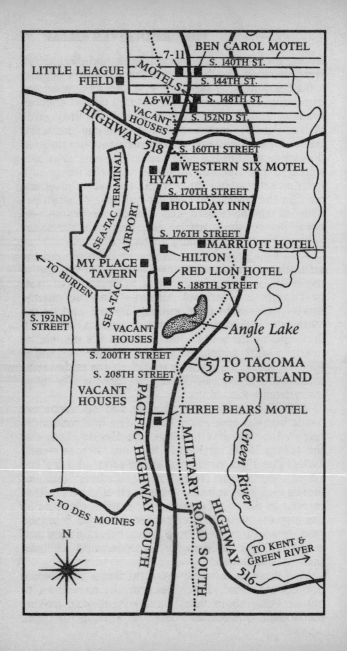

Such men are often vulnerable, as in the early 1970s, when many Alaska pipeline workers flew into Sea-Tac for R & R with billfolds bulging. Partly because of The Strip's sheer volume of traffic, with tens of thousands of people on the move around the clock, and because of The Strip's wide-open reputation, it was perhaps inevitable that prostitution would begin to flourish in the area.

By the late 1970s, street prostitutes began appearing on The Strip. In contrast to prostitutes who frequented the area's hotels and concentrated on out-of-towners, or women working in message parlors, the streetwalkers worked the highway traffic. Many were very young, often in their teens. Most were runaways with drug habits. Often they were accompanied by pimps, whom they called their "boyfriends." The pimps provided the drugs, handled most of the money, bought the women their working clothes, and ferried them from city to city on a sort of prostitution circuit that included Tacoma, Portland, Las Vegas, Hollywood, San Francisco, Vancouver, B.C., and sometimes Minneapolis and Denver. The circuit meant the women were constantly changing—three weeks or so in one place, then on to the next town.

In the beginning, the business plan was simple. A streetwalker simply staked out a likely location on the side of the road and began hitchhiking or waving at the traffic. A driver would stop. The woman would lean through the window of the vehicle and ask if the driver wanted to go to a party. If the driver said yes, the woman would ask how much he might be willing to spend. After a bargain was struck, the woman would get into the car, direct the driver to a private spot off the highway, collect the money, and then provide a sexual service, usually oral copulation. This was known as a "trick." Then the driver would take the woman back to the highway and leave her to find a new customer, or "john." The price of oral sex varied, but averaged about thirty dollars. The best business hours were between 3:00 and 9:00 P.M., at the peak of the vehicular motion on the highway. In a profitable day, a streetwalker might earn as much as $300. Most of the money, however, went to pay for drugs provided by the pimps.

To keep the women working even when they were tired, the pimps kept them high on cocaine, amphetamines, or heroin, and often a combination of the drugs. The drugs numbed the pain of standing and walking for so many hours on the highway, and clouded the mind to any reluctance or anxiety that accompanied getting into strangers' cars.

Not every streetwalker had a pimp, however. Some, like Marcia Chapman, were independent. Often pimps would attempt to capture such women with blandishments or threats, and sometimes the women would succumb. The rape and beating of Chapman only weeks before her disappearance may have been one such instance, but Chapman did not give in. "Why should I give the money to a man?" she asked one of her neighbors. "I need it for my kids, not for some man."

In trying to convince a woman to work for him, however, a pimp might offer a woman protection—from other pimps to be sure, but also from "johns" bent on robbing or raping them. In actual practice, however, this protection was very limited. Often when a woman ran into trouble during a "trick," the pimp was in a motel room cutting drugs or socializing with other pimps. It was unusual for a pimp to keep watch over his "ho"—patois for "whore," as the pimps called their women—unless the pimp was unsure of his "ho's" loyalty. The main thing the pimps were interested in was the "ho's" income, and if the "ho" didn't generate enough, or complained about the work, the pimp often terrorized her, sometimes beating her with wire coathangers, burning her with cigarettes, or inflicting small cuts with a knife. Most women were so frightened of their pimps they refused to testify against them or otherwise provide any information about the pimp's activities to anyone. If a woman reported that she had been beaten, raped, or robbed during a trick, the pimp usually shrugged it off as one of the breaks of doing business.

While the original clientele of the prostitution on The Strip was among traveling men, with the coming of the streetwalkers a market of local "johns" also developed. The locals were usually men who lived in south King County who worked in the area, down in the valley at Boeing, or in Tacoma. After getting off work, such men would drive to The Strip, cash their paychecks, and start drinking in the taverns along the roadside. Between 5:00 and 7:00 P.M., many would start home, see a prostitute waving by the side of the road, and pick her up.

By the early 1980s, the number of streetwalkers working The Strip had exploded. At the peak in 1982 and 1983, literally hundreds of women shouted, waved, gestured, and pantomimed their wares on the stretch of highway that ran from the beginning of The Strip at South 139th Street and extended south to about South 272nd Street, a distance of perhaps ten miles.

The street prostitution problem was compounded enormously by a federally funded Port of Seattle program to acquire and remove thousands of houses under the airport's flight paths north and south of the airport. Beginning in 1975, the Port bought the houses, boarded them up, and shut off all power, water, and lighting to the old neighborhoods, pending the eventual removal of the houses. The resulting clear zones of vacant residential lots, overgrown landscapes, and boarded-up houses, all under the shrieking blanket of incoming and outgoing airliners, was a perfect place for prostitutes to take their tricks. It was also a perfect place to commit murder, as it turned out.

At the beginning of 1982, the King County Police Department's vice squad was composed of seven plainclothes patrolmen and one sergeant. Two of the patrolmen were assigned primarily to undercover gambling investigations; the remainder were detailed to prostitution enforcement. Of those, two spent much of their time making arrests in the massage parlors. That left just three officers to patrol the entire ten miles of The Strip looking for prostitutes to arrest.

On some nights, a single undercover cop might arrest as many as six or seven prostitutes. Virtually all of them were taken downtown to the courthouse jail, booked, fingerprinted, and placed in a holding cell pending the arrangement of bail. Most were usually released the following day, and by the afternoon, would be back on the highway looking for new business. The cops changed their cars, their clothes, their appearance, anything to shuffle the deck. After two or three weeks of this revolving-door process, with perhaps three or four arrests, a woman might be facing several trial dates and the prospect of several hundred dollars of fines, or even a month in jail. At that point the woman and her "boyfriend" would pull up stakes and head to downtown Seattle to work, where there was a different vice squad and a different court system. Or they would go to Portland, or Tacoma, or Vancouver, B.C., where the woman would adopt a new identity. When a woman failed to appear for trial, a bench warrant would be issued for her arrest. But because prostitution was a misdemeanor, serving such warrants was usually confined to only Seattle and King County, and then only when police happened to apprehend the woman for a new offense. If the arrest papers hadn't been served within three years, the order was recalled and stamped "Unable to Locate," and the entire cycle began all over again.

In the meantime, a woman might be arrested scores of times in other jurisdictions under her own and different names. But because police agencies considered prostitution a local problem, there was no exchange of information on those arrested. And in any case, the costs of bringing a woman back to face a trial were simply not worth the revenue that might be gained from the fines.

Under such circumstances, the police as well as the women came ultimately to see their activities as a sort of game, a contest of wits and patience that seemed to have no real purpose other than to keep the two sides occupied and to provide the government treasury with a flow of dollars. But the failure to maintain adequate records on the prostitutes' identities, travels, and associations was later to cost police vital time when it was desperately necessary to know just who had been killed, and when.

Now, in the first weeks after the discovery of the river murders, the police found themselves outnumbered by the news reporters, who were likewise combing The Strip for answers, talking to relatives and friends, and in general, doing a fine job of bollixing up the information. By now it was becoming harder and harder for detectives to be sure that what they were being told hadn't originated with a reporter, or been seen on television, heard on the radio, or read in the newspaper.

Kraske by now believed that all the publicity was generating a swamp of confusion and contradictions, threatening to bog his detectives down in worthless and even erroneous facts. There was no way to keep track of the information, he realized. He pirated a microcomputer from somewhere within the department to use in the investigation, but the leads and tips were coming in so fast it was impossible to get them all into the small computer, or indeed, even to make sense of them. Instead, the twenty-five cops assigned to the case simply scribbled information down on paper while trying desperately to sort through the chaos for good leads. Somehow, it had all fallen to Reichert, as the lead investigator, to sort through the information and assign priorities. But Reichert was busy chasing down his own leads as well. Inexorably, the confusion grew worse and worse. This is beyond a nightmare, Kraske thought.

And the nuts had already come out to play. High-profile cases like the Green River murders, Kraske knew, always excited people. People wanted to help the police, and many of them believed they alone held the key to the mystery. It was hard to make people who called in with tips understand that thousands of other people had also called in.

The trick was to figure out who really knew something and who didn't, and the uncontrolled publicity was making that task extremely difficult. Kraske was reluctant to devote any of his scarce resources to investigating each and every yarn, but some had to be looked into, which was often a further waste of time.

And there were others who kept trying to insert themselves. One was a matronly forty-five-year-old woman who described herself as a combination psychic/private detective. Barbara Kubik-Patten was sure she had known Opal Mills. She thought she remembered picking up Mills while Opal was hitchhiking one day earlier in the summer. Mills was, she said later, a friend of her own daughter. Barbara told anyone who would listen that she had warned Mills against hitchhiking, but that Opal seemed unconcerned.

Then, when Opal turned up dead in the Green River, Kubik-Patten felt the peculiar jolt that comes with the discovery that someone one knows has been murdered. Barbara thought her psychic abilities might help her find the murderer.

On the day the three bodies were found in the river, Barbara later claimed, she told the police an interesting story.

After reading about the discovery of Bonner's body the previous Thursday, and recognizing the murder as the second one involving the river in less than a month, Kubik-Patten and a friend had driven down to the river on Saturday, August 14—the night before the three newest bodies had been discovered. There Kubik-Patten had seen a man acting furtively and, to her, suspiciously. The man was walking around on the riverbank. While they watched him, the man went back up the bank, got into a small white car, and drove off.

The following day, about the same time Ainsworth was putting his raft in the Green River, Kubik-Patten and her husband and children had gone down to the river to look around. Near the bridge where Ainsworth had cast off, Kubik-Patten said she found a bloody shirt and a piece of bone. She immediately drove to the Kent police station to report the discovery. There she and her husband and children learned that new bodies had been discovered. She said the police had taken her to the scene. There Barbara was put into the back of a police car and interrogated. She told the police about the man in the white car. She said she kept hearing the word "Opal" in her mind, and thought that the word related to the small white car she had seen, which might have been an "Opel." Told there were two bodies in the river, Barbara said later she had insisted there was a third victim. Reichert, she said, had argued with her, saying he did not believe in psychics. Later Reichert had discovered the body of Opal Mills.

But the police denied they had talked to Barbara that day, or that she had predicted a third body would be discovered. Indeed, Kraske said he had never heard of Barbara Kubik-Patten until she began appearing on The Strip, several weeks after the Sunday at the river.

In any event, when Kubik-Patten found out Opal Mills had been one of the three victims, she began thinking this was *proof* that she was psychic. Maybe, she thought, she had been called down to the river by Mills's spirit.

Her confidence in her psychic abilities thus bolstered, Kubik-Patten began haunting The Strip throughout the rest of August and into September, searching for a glimpse of the small white car and the face she had seen. Pulling on her detective hat, she also began talking to scores of prostitutes. Frequently, the woman told her that while they were nervous about being on the highway, they could take care of themselves. And the women told her that the murderer was probably a policeman, or at least someone pretending to be one. Several told her stories about a man who had flashed a badge at them and ordered them to get into his car. Fortunately, the women told Kubik-Patten, *they* were too smart to fall for that one. Barbara called the police faithfully every few days to report her findings, adding to the growing pile of paper. Detectives sighed and wrote down the new information even as Barbara pumped *them* for new information.

Soon Barbara was also talking to the reporters, many of whom were interviewing the same prostitutes, and trying to talk to the same detectives. Stories and rumors were exchanged, and as the weeks went by and reporters continually asked police about the stories Barbara told, it became increasingly difficult to separate truth from wild rumors. Kraske began to wish Barbara Kubik-Patten had found a better use for her time.

Meanwhile, because of the danger posed by the killer, the vice squad's "john" patrols were stopped. The john patrols—in which the customers rather than the prostitutes were targeted for arrest—were usually trotted out by the department whenever prostitution really got out of hand. Essentially, policewomen who dressed as they thought prostitutes might were placed as decoys in the prostitution areas. Men who unwittingly solicited the decoys were invited to a nearby motel room, where they were promptly arrested. Nearly forty men were bagged during three separate patrols in the first seven months of the year. But now, with the killer on the loose, the patrols were stopped.

No one wanted a policewoman to wind up dead the way the women in the river had. But the termination of the department's best available tactic to identify the killer may have cost the police another excellent chance to identify the man.

By late August, Kraske had had enough of the circuslike atmosphere surrounding his investigation. The first thing to do was to get the press to back off. Kraske had police spokesmen Pat Ferguson deliver the message. "I'm not bitching," Ferguson told the *Tacoma News-Tribune*. "We've had a lot of fine press cooperation on this case . . . but the problem has been the aggressiveness and the competition among the news media for the stories. Some papers have their hotshot investigative reporters on this case and they think they have to come up with something big every day.

"It's been the sheer number of reporters on every scene in connection with this story that has us overwhelmed," Ferguson continued. "They have been reaching witnesses and acquaintances of witnesses and the victims before we had a chance to get to them.

"With people like those who have been involved in a crime like this, it changes the way people talk to a police officer if they have been interviewed on television first or if the newspapers have been talking with them.

"We cringe each time we see a vehicle description or a nickname of a possible suspect appear in the newspaper or on the air before we have a chance to locate the vehicle or find the subject."

Within a few days of Ferguson's complaint, executives at most Seattle-area news media outlets had pulled off the teams of reporters assigned to the story. Instead, editors waited for Kraske and the police to give them the news. But as the weeks, then months unfolded, there was little news to report.

And much of that turned out to be wrong.

10

GISELE

August 1982

But while police had their hands full with all of the tips pouring in and with the reporters who kept interfering, and with the nuts who kept propelling them on wild goose chases, others were busy dying.

These were the young women of The Strip, most of whom were teenaged prostitutes just like Leann Wilcox, Wendy Coffield, Cynthia Hinds, and Opal Mills. On the run, often supporting drug habits, driven to prostitution by fear and a need for money, these girls were in continuing jeopardy from the murderer.

Worse, their lifestyles made their disappearance seem quite ordinary. Despite all the intensity of the initial hunt for the murderer, few thought at first that the killings might be continuing, despite Keppel's warning. Certainly, no one in their wildest imagination in August of 1982 believed that by the time the terror was over, at least forty-nine would die. The undiscovered key to the puzzle lay in the way police treated reports of missing people.

As in any other major city, scores of people in Seattle and King County were reported missing every month. Neither the Seattle Police Department, the King County Police Department, nor, for that matter, any other police agency, had enough detectives to look for them all. Priorities had to be established, and first call on the limited resources went to small children and to cases where foul play was strongly suspected.

Most adults who go missing often do so on purpose, police knew from experience. There was no law against not coming home again if one didn't feel like it. Police believed there was little sense in wasting effort to find people unless there were strong indications that a crime had been committed.

The problem of the missings was particularly complex when juveniles were involved. How to tell if a teenager was in trouble, or simply tired of living at home? There wasn't any sure way. Often, when detectives took a missing report involving a teenager seriously, the teenager when located simply refused to go home. Following a U.S. Supreme court decision granting children the same legal rights as adults, the Washington State Legislature had passed a law which in effect legalized the right of children to run away. Legally, police kept telling parents, their children were the same as adults, and they had a right to run away from home if they wished to do so.

To look for a missing teenager with a record of prostitution arrests was an even larger waste of time, many police officers felt. Because prostitutes generally were such a transient group, police had a tendency to dismiss reports of missing prostitutes as simply "moved, left no forward address." In cases where obvious pimps had turned in the reports, police cared even less. In their own minds, detectives thought that was just too bad for the pimp; maybe the missing girl had gone home for good. Detectives rebelled at seeing themselves as a property recovery service for drug-dealing, low-life scumbags wearing gold chains and driving hot wheels.

Police therefore tended to simply file reports of missing teenagers as "runaways" and take no further action, unless clear evidence indicated the matter should be treated differently. Most runaways, police knew, sooner or later returned home. Of those who did not, the odds were, sooner or later, that they would be arrested for some petty offense—like prostitution—and thus "found."

Even when parents wept for their teenagers, pleading for police to do something, police would only shake their heads sorrowfully and blame the situation on lawyers and the legislature. The reports went into the file, the name went into the computer, and that was the end of it. Then, every thirty days, the names of the missings were routinely and automatically purged from the computer system. Unless a parent was insistent, the disappearance of a troubled teenager was quickly forgotten.

By the early 1980s, experts estimated that about six hundred teenagers of both sexes were living on the streets of Seattle and King County. Some were as young as eleven years old. Many worked as prostitutes to pay for a repetitive diet of fast food, alcohol, and psychoactive drugs, crashing for the night in abandoned buildings or at the houses of strangers, some of whom were likely to rape and rob them. Some maintained a precarious existence as "single hoes," as prostitutes unaffiliated with pimps called themselves. But most soon fell into the hands of pimps, and afterward had only the most sporadic contact with their families, who repudiated them as bad seeds.

Thus, on the run from abusive or otherwise dysfunctional homes, alienated from familiar friends and places, confused about life, frightened of authority, driven into petty crime, bitter with an affected cynicism, muddled on booze and drugs, ignored by authorities and the public at large, preyed upon by exploiters, these juveniles were perfect victims. In August of 1982, few thought to connect this problem of missing teenagers with the murders, so ordinary and common were the reports of the missings. As events so tragically illustrated in the years to come, the failure to make this connection proved to be a major breakdown of the system.

Among those who reported a teenaged prostitute missing in the summer of 1982 was taxicab driver

James Michael Tindal. As with most others who had filed such reports, Tindal initially received scant police response. Tindal then began looking for seventeen-year-old Gisele Lovvorn himself. It was as if the character in "Taxi Driver" had come to life.

A bright and articulate son of a California aerospace engineer, Tindal nevertheless seemed to have a talent for self-destruction. He had been a police-sponsored Explorer Boy Scout in the Los Angeles area, and even years later retained a strong interest in police matters, working periodically as a security guard. He attended college, but never graduated. He moved to the Seattle area in the late 1970s, but had to leave town when he was arrested on charges of credit card fraud.

Back in Los Angeles, the problem continued. In 1980, while working as a security guard again, a car wreck while drag racing led to his being fired. Later he met Gisele, then a 14-year-old runaway from a middle-class family who lived in Northridge, California. Tindal was later to claim that he and Gisele had fallen in love in Los Angeles, and that while he had asked Gisele to marry him, she had refused. Nevertheless, the two decided to move to Seattle and live together in the spring of 1982. Tindal, hoping the fraud charges had been forgotten, was able to get a job as a taxi driver near the airport.

In his Los Angeles days Tindal kept his hair short and wore a tie, in a moderately successful attempt to keep at least one foot in the straight world. But after returning to Seattle with Lovvorn in the spring of 1982, Tindal changed his image by growing a ponytail and donning a leather vest and a working man's cap. In this way, Tindal essentially adopted the protective coloration of a biker-turned-cab driver, and merged into the colorful, sometimes seamy, and often chaotic nightlife of The Strip. Tindal gave himself a nickname, "Catnip," and decided, when police couldn't or wouldn't do anything when Lovvorn disappeared, that "Catnip" would have to rescue her himself, just like in the movie.

Lovvorn had left the apartment she and Tindal

shared with several others on Saturday afternoon, July 17, two days after Coffield's body had been found in the Green River. To get around, Lovvorn usually hitchhiked. That day she had been headed out to The Strip to turn "three or four tricks," Tindal later said. Afterward, she was to meet Tindal at his airport cabstand.

Instead, Lovvorn had simply vanished, leaving behind her backpack, clothes, money, and cigarettes. She had taken her small clutch purse, the one she used to carry her knife and her condoms—both tools of her trade. When Lovvorn failed to turn up at the airport that night, Tindal started calling hospitals and police departments. No one knew anything, nor, to Tindal, did they seem to care. He also called Gisele's parents in California, who seemed relieved that she was no longer with Tindal, but, Tindal thought, not particularly concerned. Gisele had always been independent, even headstrong.

The following day Tindal tried to file a missing persons report on Gisele, without success. He came back a day later and raised such a fuss a uniformed officer finally filled out the document, as much to placate Tindal as anything else. No one from the police came to see him. A few days later, Tindal called county detective Earl Tripp, the officer who had arrested him years earlier on the fraud charges, and told Tripp about Lovvorn's disappearance.

Gisele was just under five-feet-five, with blonde hair and blue eyes. She weighed less than one hundred twenty pounds. When Tripp asked for a picture of Gisele, Tindal gave him a snapshot of a smiling, animated Gisele that made her look like a junior high school student.

Gisele was a prostitute, Tindal admitted to Tripp. When they arrived in Seattle in the spring, Tindal had been arrested once more on the fraud charges he had hoped would be forgotten, the same charges that had brought him together with Tripp the first time. Tindal told Tripp that Gisele started walking the streets in May to earn money to bail Tindal out. He had begged her not to, Tindal told Tripp, but Gisele had ignored him. Tripp checked the records, and discovered that in late June, Gisele had been arrested by the county's vice squad for prostitution while using the name Gisele Lewis.

Tindal told Tripp that Gisele wanted to work the streets only long enough to build a base of regular customers. Then she intended to be a call girl instead of a streetwalker. She kept the names of all of her johns in a notebook at the apartment, Tindal said. But Tripp wasn't particularly interested in Gisele's john book. He thought it was far more likely that she and Tindal had had a fight, and that Gisele had walked out.

"Without her backpack?" Tindal pointed out. "That was her baby. She wouldn't go anywhere without that." But Tripp had seen countless cases where missing people had left behind prized possessions. Often, he knew, the sheer joy of getting away from someone made mere possessions unimportant. "She'll turn up," Tripp told Tindal. "Someday she'll call you from someplace and say she's coming back."

Bullshit, Tindal thought. if the cops wouldn't do anything, he would. He spent the next two weeks cruising The Strip, showing Lovvorn's picture to strangers, haunting cabstands and coffeeshops where cabbies, pimps, hookers, and cops hung out. Everyone just shook their heads. No, man. Never saw her before. Tindal offered a $500 reward to anyone who had information about Gisele. "Just ask for Catnip," he told people.

By late July, Tindal had twice heard rumors that Gisele had been kidnapped by two pimps nicknamed "Peaches" and "Pretty Tony." Once one of Gisele's johns had called asking for her. The john said he'd seen Gisele downtown that afternoon, sporting a black eye and looking dazed. She hadn't even recognized him, the john said. Then, another man told Tindal that he had seen Gisele in the coffee shop of a downtown hotel, sitting with a pimp. Gisele had dyed her hair black, Tindal was told.

"He described her to a tee," Tindal said. "She had a little scar, like a smallpox vaccination, on her forehead. It didn't show up on her picture. The guy described this scar. He described her teeth, which were bad. This guy saw her two weeks after she disappeared."

That clinched it. The dirty pimps were holding his Gisele prisoner, just like in "Taxi Driver"! But when he reported this to police, they said they had no record of any pimps using those names.

Then, in the first week of August Tindal picked up a pair of black prostitutes in his cab and took them to an address at the Puerto Villa Apartments, the same complex where Marcia Chapman had lived with her children. On the way, Tindal overheard the two women talking about "Pretty Tony," and heard them mention Peaches.

"I came unglued," Tindal said later. "I pulled over to the side of the road and said, 'What do you know about Peaches and Pretty Tony?'" The women told him Pretty Tony was the top enforcer for the man known as Peaches. Tindal showed his picture of Gisele picture to the women, who told him they hadn't seen her around for "a week or so." In Tindal's mind, this confirmed his conviction that Pretty Tony and Peaches had Gisele. This he also reported to police, who yawned.

But in mid-August, after the bodies were found in the Green River, police had decided to drop in on Tindal to see what he knew. Tripp came with Reichert and introduced the other detective. They showed him pictures of the dead girls and asked him if he knew them. "I might have seen them around," Tindal told the two detectives. Tindal tried to tell Reichert about "Peaches" and "Pretty Tony," but Reichert again said there were no pimps who used those names. Tindal asked police to publicize Gisele's disappearance, but Reichert declined. If they did that, Reichert said, they'd have to do the same for hundreds of people. It just wasn't practical. Reichert and Tripp then left. Tindal didn't know it then, but Reichert wanted to see whether Tindal might be a good suspect in the murders.

In the meantime, Tindal called Hilda Bryant, a television reporter for KIRO, the television station. Bryant had been covering the story of the Green River murders. Couldn't Bryant put Gisele's disappearance on television? Couldn't she do something about Peaches and Pretty Tony? But Bryant told Tindal the same thing the police had said. They couldn't very well broadcast Gisele's picture, Bryant said, or soon they'd have to do the same for hundreds of similarly missing teenagers.

Finally, in desperation, Tindal contacted a psychic he knew in Idaho. He gave the woman a vest Gisele had worn. A few minutes after giving her the vest the woman put the garment aside and said, "Well, she's dead. She's laying face down without any clothes on, in mud. There's a big tangle of bushes next to her. I think they're like briar bushes. Something's around her throat. And she is not in water."

"Can you give me a better location?" Tindal asked.

"She's not far from home," the woman told Tindal.

Tindal began driving the backroads of The Strip looking for tangled, brushy areas "not far from home." There were, Tindal soon learned, hundreds of such locations. The movie was going wrong. Soon the taxi driver quit looking altogether. Instead he found a new girlfriend.

11

SICK TRICKS

August 1982

By late August, the ranks of the "hoes" were thinning out along the highway. While many of the girls might have been foolish, only a few were stupid. The murders, with all the publicity, had made it obvious to everyone except the most drugged-out, desperate, or overconfident that it was too dangerous to stroll for tricks in the Sea-Tac area.

One woman, eighteen-year-old Shirley Sherrill, had actually been arrested by one of the county vice cops the night of the day Bonner's body had been found. After getting out of jail the following Saturday, Sherrill joined a group of women who were heading south to Portland, away from the murders. Others headed for California or Las Vegas. Some decided to stay put, but stroll only in downtown Seattle for awhile, since the killer seemed to like The Strip so much.

Those prostitutes who remained were interviewed by the news media, and almost universally rejected the idea of the murders being related to a "pimp war." Instead, some pointed fingers at the traditional enemy, the police. The killer, said these women, was a cop, driven mad by frustrated lust. But most believed that the murders were the work of a "sick trick." The cops would never solve the murders, the women said, because they didn't care about prostitutes anyway.

But if most women were cooling it for awhile, a few

others continued to believe the unknown killer would not get them. They saw themselves as plenty street-wise; they would be able to "vibe out" the killer if he approached them. And even if the killer tried to get them, they were prepared. They showed reporters the guns, knives, hatpins, knitting needles, razors, and canisters of mace in their armories. If the killer came after *them*, he would surely regret it, they said.

By the last week of August, having backed the press off from his investigation, Kraske and his team of detectives began working The Strip in earnest. It was beginning to look obvious that the killer was a john, but probably a john who knew all five of the victims. Something about *these* five victims had set the killer off. Kraske wanted his detectives to find out what it was.

Already they had discovered that Coffield and Mills had gone to the same junior high school and knew one another; that Chapman and Bonner had hooked in Tacoma at the same time and had sat together in the same barroom; that Hinds and Mills might have been together shortly before Hinds disappeared; and that Hinds may have been acquainted with Chapman. Coffield, Bonner and Chapman were known to use heroin or cocaine whenever they could get them. These links between the victims were too close for coincidence, Kraske thought; the killer *had* to be someone who knew them all, maybe someone who frequented both The Strip and The Lucky Spot. The thing to do was to find out everything about the five victims' johns from the remaining prostitutes.

Two undercover cops from the vice squad were detailed to cruise The Strip bars where the pimps hung out in an effort to pick up any rumors about "sick tricks"; later, someone else would try to see whether those men might have been known to the five women. The pair was also supposed to check out whether there really was anything to the stupid "pimp war" idea. The two cops had drinks at the Red Lion, the Hyatt Hotel, and the Marriott, but learned little. Everyone had a theory about the murders, but no one seemed to know anything worth getting excited about.

Other members of the vice squad were sent to The Strip's only topless bar, "My Place," a magnet for prostitutes and johns, to see if anyone had heard anything there about "sick tricks." Nothing came up.

Meanwhile, other detectives on Kraske's 25-member task force continued sifting The Strip for prostitutes, telling them they had no intention of arresting them for prostitution, but wouldn't they please tell them about their customers? Had anybody seen or experienced anything weird? Any threats? Narrow escapes? Kinky demands?

Little effort was made to link the reports involving missing teenage prostitutes like Lovvorn to the murders. After all, there were scores of them at any given time, and if Kraske spent all his effort running those people down, the investigation was sure to go way off track. His job was to find the murderer, not missing teenagers. Finally, because no new victims had been found in the Green River, or any other river for that matter, it seemed likely to Kraske that, for some reason, the murders had stopped.

Despite the intense effort by Kraske's detectives, the prostitutes continued to be suspicious of the police. Weren't the cops the enemy? Many of the women feared they would be arrested if they told the police about bad experiences they had had while prostituting. Wasn't it like a confession or something? Some of the pimps likewise discouraged cooperation. Once a "ho" began talking to the cops, who knew where it might lead?

The barriers against cooperation were insurmountable in many instances. Slowly, however, some stories came trickling in.

Several prostitutes told about a big slobby guy in overalls and a plaid jacket who said he was a cop; the word on the street was that the big guy was someone to watch out for. Kraske knew that description matched one of his own vice cops, in fact, one of the two men he had sent out looking for sick tricks. *He* couldn't be the killer, Kraske realized. Another claimed a uniformed cop had arrested her, taken her in handcuffs down to the Green River in his patrol car, and raped her in the back seat. Afterward, the cop had taken her to jail, the woman said, and had the gall to say the used condom was evidence of her prostitution! There were no records of any such case.

Another woman told of being picked up in Seattle's central area and also driven toward the river. The driver told her that if she didn't cooperate she would end up like "those other bitches they found," the woman said. She said she was able to escape from the man's car only when it broke down at a stop light. Who was the man? police had asked, "I never saw him before," the woman said. What did he look like? "Average," said the woman. That was the trouble with this case, Kraske thought: The potential victims were the best chance they had, and they were unreliable.

But not every story reached the police, at least immediately. Late on the night of August 22, even while Kraske's detectives were deciding they had no evidence to implicate Larry Darnell Mathews in the murders, a thirty-seven-year-old meatcutter picked up twenty-one-year-old Susan Widmark in the heart of the prostitution area at South 144th Street and Pacific Highway South. The man agreed to pay Widmark for oral sex. Widmark directed the man to drive to a nearby house, but instead the man drove north on Pacific Highway South at a high rate of speed. As he drove with one hand, the man produced a pistol and pointed it at Widmark.

"If you don't want to get hurt, you'll do what I tell you," the man told her. He pulled off the highway and drove down a dirt road. In a dark spot, he ordered Widmark to take off her clothes; then he raped the terrified Widmark while holding the pistol to her head.

Afterward, when Widmark started replacing her

clothes, the rapist put the barrel of his gun to her head and told her to stop.

"You don't have to bother with that. You won't be working anymore tonight, anyway," he said. "Haven't you heard about all those hookers they found in the river?"

What do you mean? Widmark asked, but the man only laughed. He started his pickup truck and headed for the darkened riverbank, still holding the pistol on Widmark. At a stoplight, the man's pistol wavered briefly, and the half-naked Widmark bolted from the truck. The man sped away, but not before Widmark was able to memorize part of his license plate and the make of the blue and white vehicle. Badly shaken, she hitchhiked back to Pacific Highway South and told her pimp about the experience. But the pimp didn't want to call the police.

Five days after the attack on Widmark, sixteen-year-old Kase Ann Lee went to an appointment she had with a volunteer probation counselor working for the Airport District Court in nearby Burien, where most of The Strip prostitution cases were heard. Kase had been arrested in downtown Seattle earlier in the spring, and then again in May and June on The Strip. A week after the bodies had been discovered in the river, Kase was arrested again, this time back in Seattle. After a couple of days in jail, she had been released on her promise to keep up with her court dates, including the August 27 appointment with the probation counselor, Pat Bucy.

When she was arrested, Kase had been using one of her twelve different street names, "Wanda Mercury." Her Mercury ID said she was twenty-five. Kase never told the counselor her real name. Kase also didn't tell the counselor about her husband, Anthony Craig Lee, and "Pretty Tony's" penchant for dealing drugs and making her work as a prostitute. Tony terrified her, Kase once told her mother, Marilyn Harrison, who lived in Spokane in eastern Washington State. But Kase had nevertheless married Tony, while

Tony was in jail the previous April. Marilyn Harrison thought the only reason Tony had married Kase was to prevent the authorities from using Kase as a witness against him. She was sure Tony didn't love her daughter. But then, as Marilyn admitted, she had no use for Tony anyway. Marilyn and Tony had never gotten along.

Bucy brought up the subject of the murders. With the killer still on the loose, wasn't "Wanda" frightened? Didn't she know that she could be killed? "Wanda" said she *was* scared. "I'm going to stay off The Strip," she said. "It's safer downtown." Bucy didn't say anything to "Wanda," but concluded that since the girl had admitted working as a prostitute for nine years, her immediate reform was unlikely. Bucy thought it might do "Wanda Mercury" some good to do some time in jail, and that's what she recommended on the report she would give the judge at "Wanda's" sentencing October 1. Maybe, thought Bucy, jail might even save her life.

The same day Bucy was talking to Kase, the Mills family buried their daughter Opal. "This is a very rotten society," the Rev. James Young told a hundred mourners in the funeral chapel. "Let what happened to Opal Charmaine Mills rest on the minds of other girls, because what happened to Opal could happen to them."

But about noon the next day, a Saturday, Kase Lee left the apartment she shared with Tony Lee on South 208th Street, about two blocks east of The Strip. When she didn't come home that afternoon, or that night, or the next night, Tony decided to report her disappearance to the police. Tony told the police Kase was going to buy hamburger to cook for dinner. Kase had been carrying a brown clutch purse, and was wearing red shorts, a white blouse, and blue sandals. Tony told police he was sure the Green River killer had gotten Kase. Why? Because she had never gone missing before, said Tony. Did Kase have any other names? Yes, said Tony: Wanda Mercury.

Then Tony called Marilyn Harrison and told her what he had just told the police.

The day after Kase disappeared, Terri Rene Milligan put in a full afternoon waving at cars from the intersection near South 144th Street and Pacific Highway South. Her ten-month-old baby was with her mother in Seattle, and her "boyfriend" Mark was in the motel waiting for Terri to bring in some money. About 6:00 P.M., Terry decided to take a break. She told Mark that she wanted to go to a nearby Wendy's for some food. Wearing a red-striped top, brown shoes, red panties, pinstriped blue jeans, and no bra, Terri set off for the fast-food outlet some five blocks away. That was the last Mark saw of her. The following day, he called Terri's mother to see if she had seen Terri, but she hadn't. The day after that, Mark called the King County police and reported Terri missing. Police patrol units were told to keep an eye out for both Kase Lee and Terri Milligan, but no investigator was immediately assigned to either case.

On Sunday, August 30, the day after Terri Milligan disappeared, a girl who called herself Betty Lorraine Jones hitchhiked south on Pacific Highway South. When she had been a small child, her mother and father had nicknamed her "Muffin." Now, as a fifteen-year-old loose on The Strip, she instead used the nickname "Star," except when the police arrested her for prostitution. Then she was "Betty Jones."

Once described by her parents as "twelve going on twenty-five," the girl who called herself Betty Jones had been arrested twice in the spring of 1982 for prostitution by the Seattle police, and twice more by the county's vice squad. The court dates were piling up. Betty Jones decided to change her appearance. In late August she dyed her hair black from its natural blonde, and moved in with a drug-dealing pimp who set up his headquarters in a Pacific Highway South motel.

By accident or perhaps by unconscious design, the

motel used by "Betty Jones" and her pimp was directly across the street from the office of a small trucking business owned by Tom and Carol Estes. The Esteses were the parents of a runaway girl they had long ago nicknamed "Muffin."

For months the Estes couple had been reporting to police that their daughter Debbie was a runaway. The police greeted these persistent reports by Debbie's parents with sympathetic indifference, saying, as usual, there was little they could do to locate runaways. Once, in July, Tom and Carol even filed a theft report charging their daughter with a petty theft in an effort to induce the police to actively go looking for her, to no avail.

Then, in August, after the discovery of the bodies in the Green River, the Esteses called the police again. The discoveries unnerved Carol Estes. She was sure Debbie had been working as a street prostitute. She feared that Debbie might be one of the unidentified victims. The police had asked for Debbie's dental charts. None of the dead girls was Debbie, the police told her later. Moreover, they said, there was no record of anyone named Debbie Estes—or even Muffin—ever having been involved with prostitution. Once again they explained to the Esteses that they just didn't have the time to go looking for runaways. Carol Estes thought the police were secretly disgusted with her for her failure to keep her child at home.

Nevertheless, "Betty Lorraine Jones" had been arrested at least four times for prostitution during the time Tom and Carol were looking for their daughter. The problem was, police had no way of knowing who "Jones" actually was, and really, didn't much care.

And while police knew *where* "Betty Jones" was, Tom and Carol Estes had no idea that the police knew *that*. Neither Tom nor Carol Estes ever had the slightest inkling their long-sought daughter was working as a "ho" just across the street from their office. Debbie Estes had so thoroughly become "Betty Jones" that she fooled everyone. In the end, it was a fatal masquerade.

Like Gisele Lovvorn, Debbie Estes had first run away from home when she was twelve. By thirteen Debbie had made friends with the slightly older daughter of a Puerto Rican family living in a subsidized housing project in South Seattle. By fourteen, Debbie and seventeen-year-old Becky Marrero were sharing an apartment in another housing project, also in south Seattle. By the time she was fifteen, both Debbie and Becky were walking strolls in the three major King County prostitution areas in downtown Seattle, North Seattle, and on The Strip. Becky had a two-year-old child. Her contacts had helped Debbie get the false "Betty Jones" identification. Both girls used each others' identities interchangeably; that way, they could later claim in court that the vice cops had arrested the wrong person. They thought this was quite clever.

On August 30, as "Betty Jones" walked south on The Strip to a nearby shopping mall, she had seventy-five dollars in her purse, and no intention of doing any business. This was to be a day off.

Just before 4:00 P.M. a man in a blue and white pickup truck pulled to a stop and offered her a ride. She accepted. After starting up again, the man turned to her and pointed an automatic pistol at her. "I won't use this," he said, "if you do what I say. Take off your blouse." When Debbie said she wouldn't, the man pulled the hammer back on his pistol. Debbie took off her blouse. The man turned the truck into a dirt road. He stopped the truck and ordered Debbie to take off her blue jeans. She did. "Give me a blow job," he said. Debbie told him no. The man hit her with his pistol. Debbie gave in. Afterward, the man tied her hands behind her back and stole her money. Then he walked her at gunpoint into some nearby woods, untied her hands, and left her, warning her to stay where she was until he left. A few minutes later Debbie heard the man drive off. She went to a nearby home for help. The residents there called the police. Sex crimes detective Spencer Nelson came to interview her. Debbie told Nelson her name was Betty

Lorraine Jones. Nelson took the report of the attack back to the Green River detectives, saying that it sounded like something they might be interested in.

What was "Jones's" relationship to the five dead girls? That wasn't immediately clear. But a check of similar unsolved cases netted at least four other nearly identical crimes. Six days later, when Susan Widmark was arrested on The Strip for "O&A—offering and agreeing to prostitute," detectives learned about that attack as well. Widmark also provided the partial license plate number she remembered. Was the man in the blue and white truck the killer? That possibility couldn't be discounted until the man was found and questioned. But now, at least, the police had a real lead.

12

DOUGLAS

September 1982

The week after "Betty Jones" had her frightening encounter with the man in the blue and white truck, the special agent in charge of the FBI in Seattle, Allen Whitaker, flew east to Washington, D.C. With him was a special package prepared for the bureau by King County Police: backgrounds on the Green River five, a description of the terrain where the bodies were found, autopsy reports, and a number of eight-by-ten color photographs of the victims and the crime scenes.

After arriving in Washington, Whitaker drove south on U.S. Highway 95 for about an hour, then turned right off the highway and headed for the FBI's training academy at Quantico, Virginia. There Whitaker wound his way through the academy's labyrinthian corridors until he found himself at the bureau's Behavioral Sciences Unit.

The Behavioral Sciences Unit was a comparatively recent innovation for the bureau. For years the bureau had offered training courses to local police officers around the country. Part of the training was grounded in behavioral sciences: how to handle suspects, mental cases, hostage negotiations, and the like. As the training program grew in sophistication, the bureau's trainers found themselves confronted with questions from police about real-life situations like the Manson case, Richard Speck's murder spree in Chicago, and other psychological puzzles. Often the cases were unsolved, and the agents were asked their opinion about what might have occurred, or how an investigation might proceed. By the time of the Atlanta child murders in 1981, through a process of trial and error, some of the principles of psychological analysis of violent crimes began to emerge.

Seeing the details of so many cases helped agents sharpen their perception of what a police detective might expect from a given set of crime circumstances. Later, the Bureau began offering police departments advice on the psychological backgrounds of known suspects in an effort to help police conduct effective interrogations. These "suspect evaluations" often proved invaluable to police officers in interviewing suspects, particularly in breaking through a suspect's resistance to admitting his crimes.

The next step was to hazard some prediction about the type of personality involved in a specific crime. Simply by looking at the evidence left by a killer at a crime scene, agents were able to suggest some personality traits—a "psychological profile"—that detectives might expect to encounter if and when any suspects were unearthed. Thus, first the psychological profile told investigators what sort of person had committed the crime; then, second, the evaluation of a known individual helped investigators interrogate him.

But both the suspect evaluations and the psychological profile were still only educated guesses on the part of the agents assigned to the Behavioral Sciences Unit. There was little hard data on convicted murderers to back up agents' gut instincts about such crimes.

In early 1982, two BSU agents and a psychiatric nurse from Boston obtained a National Institute of Justice grant to study convicted serial murderers. The study was the first ever undertaken into the murky inner workings of the minds of repeating killers. During the eighteen-month course of the study, thirty-six multiple murderers were extensively interviewed on their family backgrounds, personal habits, ordinary lives, frustrations, and their conduct immediately before, during, and after their crimes. The study was well under way when Whitaker made his way to the office of John Douglas, one of the study's architects, and asked him to drop everything else. Whitaker gave Douglas the packet of information from the King County Police, and told him Seattle had a big problem.

Douglas was thirty-seven, a six-year veteran of the Behavioral Sciences Unit. He held a master's degree in psychology from the University of Wisconsin and was working on a doctorate in education. He had spent six years in the Milwaukee field office of the FBI and was trained as a hostage negotiator. In the course of his duties, Douglas often found himself briefly alone with a wide variety of people arrested by the bureau.

"In those days," Douglas recalled later, "it was strictly conducting investigations on unsolved bank robbery cases, fugitive cases, that sort of thing. And of course you get involved in the interviews and interrogations with these people once you have a suspect and they're arrested . One of the things I always did, I always felt compelled to ask questions, even nonrelated to the crime, or indirectly related, as to the why's of his behavior. Why he did certain things the way he did. Why he went to certain places." The criminal mind held a fascination for Douglas.

After talking to Whitaker about the case, Douglas reviewed the material the Seattle agent-in-charge had brought with him. Then Douglas went up to the third-floor library of the training center, gazed out the window at the surrounding forest, and began visualizing what might have happened at the Green River.

Several things about the crimes were immediately obvious to Douglas. In the study with fellow BSU agent Robert Ressler and Boston nurse Ann W. Burgess, the agents had found that virtually all serial murderers' offenses were related to an internal fantasy process that had begun prior to the crimes, often years before. The fantasies were frequently led by a fusing of pornography and violent imagery that allowed the fantasizer to see himself in complete control of his victim.

As years went by, the fantasy would grow more elaborate, more detailed. At the same time, more and more, the fantasy required making the victim into an *object* rather than a person. Ultimately, the fantasy would burst out in overt behavior as the fantasizer tried to replicate his daydreams in real life. Usually, the first crimes did not completely match the fantasies; in real life, victims tend to act differently than in daydreams.

But if the killer was not immediately arrested, and instead became more experienced in murdering, future crimes tended to match the fantasies with increasing accuracy, almost ritualistically. Each crime, therefore, had subtle indicators as to how far the murderer had progressed in matching his crime to his fantasy, and how idiosyncratic the fantasy/ritual had by then become. Such indicators over time became unique, a sort of psychological signature of the murderer.

The keys to understanding the ritual, the fantasy, and therefore, the personality of the murderer, lay in the assessment of the perfection of the ritual involved. From their research, Douglas, Burgess, and Ressler had already concluded that there were two broad categories of serial killers: those in the early stages of their ritual, and those who were more advanced. To that end, the evidence available at crime scenes yielded further clues, revealing killers who had acted on impulse, and those who had methodically planned their crimes in advance.

Reconstructions of the scenes had also revealed two broad types of pre- and post-offense behavior: disorganized and organized. Some killers were both impulsive and disorganized, leaving clues inadvertently through their behavior at the crime scenes; these would be killers early in the fantasy process, and therefore probably younger and less experienced in killing. Wayne Williams was seen as an example of this type.

Other scenes showed aspects of impulsive killing but still organized pre- and post-offense behavior. These would be people farther along in the fantasy/ritual process, evidence of more experience in murder. Probably this killer would be somewhat older than the first type. Albert DeSalvo, The Boston Strangler, was an example.

Still others showed aspects of meticulous preplanning: bringing ropes or weapons, readying a kill site in advance, and the like, followed by clearly organized post-offense behavior, such as burying a victim, washing the body to remove evidence, or similar actions. These would likely be most experienced of all, and oldest. Ted Bundy, John Wayne Gacy, and Dean Coryll were models here.

The Green River killer Douglas saw at once, had elements of both impulsiveness and organization. The apparent randomness of victimization and the unpredictability of the availability of victims, as well as the use of the victims' clothing as a murder weapon, was an indication of the killer's impulsiveness.

Arguing for organization were the actions of the killer in weighting down the bodies of Chapman and Hinds under water with rocks. That meant the killer had spent time at the dumping site. The killer therefore felt comfortable at the site and capable of organized thinking after the murder. The fact that the victims had been killed at different times over a month and their bodies left in the same general location buttressed that conclusion.

Had the murderer been more the disorganized type, the disposal site would have indicated far more evidence of panic dumping, as well as inadvertent clues to his identity. Placing all but the last victim in the water also indicated planning. Why wasn't Mills, then, also in the water? Douglas didn't know, but he guessed that somehow the killer had been disturbed while carrying her toward the water.

The discovery of the bodies in a stream known for its fishing, coupled with the steep terrain, made Douglas think the killer was an outdoor-type person, perhaps someone with a background in recreational hunting and fishing. The fact that all five victims had links to prostitution tended to indicate that the killer would hold strong feelings about sex-for-pay and sexual fidelity. The casual dumping of the victims indicated that the killer felt no remorse over his crimes.

The killer, guessed Douglas, might be a man with strong religious feelings. Was placing the bodies in the river suggesting some sort of religious aspect to the ritual, perhaps a form of baptism? That was a possibility, Douglas thought. It was also possible that the killer's mother or some other significant female relative may have been a prostitute. And Douglas agreed with Keppel: The killer had almost certainly murdered before, and was likely to kill again.

Another critical question was whether the killer had *wanted* the bodies to be discovered. Some serial killers, Douglas knew, liked to display their victims as a sort of statement, while others preferred to conceal them. The psychology of displaying or "staging," as the experts referred to it, versus concealing was really a continuum. Like impulsiveness and planning, or organization and disorganization, most serial crimes had elements of both. But understanding the elements was essential to an understanding of the psychic forces at work in the killer's personality.

Douglas wasn't sure, but it seemed to him that the

killer's use of the rocks to weight the victims down was reflective of the desire to conceal.

On the other hand, the fact that several victims had their clothing in disarray was something of a psychological statement, an aspect of staging. It seemed to Douglas that the killer was someone who wanted to make a statement, to declare to the world that he had power over his victims. The contradiction provided an insight into the killer's own feelings of impotence or lack of control over his own life, Douglas thought.

The killer's relationships with women, Douglas guessed, were particularly humiliating to him. Accordingly, the killer in turn would humiliate his victims. That meant investigators should be looking for an inadequate personality, someone likely to be given to braggadocio and exaggeration, especially in his relationships with women; it was also likely that the person would be unemployed or chronically underemployed. Studies had shown that fantasy murderers spent increasing amounts of their waking hours embroidering their internal visions, and therefore had little time or energy for demanding employment.

At the end of the week, Douglas gave Whitaker a quick copy of a twelve-page profile of the probable personality of the Seattle killer, along with some advice for the King County authorities.

There was a good possibility, he said, that the killer was someone with a strong interest in police work, just as Wayne Williams had been in the Atlanta murders. The King County police should be alert to calls from men who wanted to help police solve the crimes. And they should be on watch for any "helpers" with a previous history of assaultive behavior. The Green River killer was an opportunistic killer. He wasn't the kind who started out the day with a firm decision to commit murder. Instead, it began to happen at the point of contact between the victim and the suspect. A trigger might lie in the conversation between the victim and the killer. At first, the victim would feel that she had the suspect under control. But then the suspect would somehow turn the tables on the victim, get control of her so that he could get her to the river, where he felt most comfortable with his organized, post-offense behavior. The killer, it seemed obvious, was very familiar with the river area. Whitaker thanked Douglas. He returned to Seattle, and the following week gave the Douglas assessment to the King County police for use when and if a good suspect was identified.

13

SUSPECTS

September 1982

Finding a good suspect was just what Reichert badly wanted. By the first week of September, he and Bob LaMoria had someone in mind, a person who, just as Douglas was to warn about, had repeatedly and insistently offered help to the police. The man was a chronically underemployed taxicab driver named Melvyn Wayne Foster, who had called the police several times in August to offer advice on how to catch the killer. Interestingly, Foster himself seemed to know prostitutes and street people suspiciously well.

Foster had worked off and on as a taxi driver in Seattle and down on The Strip for several years. He lived in the small community of Lacey, located just outside the state capital of Olympia, where he and his two small sons lived with his father, Daniel. Melvyn had twice served terms in state prison, once for auto theft, and he also had a stretch in a federal pen under his belt. But that had been when he was younger.

Now that he was settling into middle age, Foster liked to think of himself as a supporter of the police. Who knew? Maybe he could tell the cops a thing or two about their business. Foster saw himself as wise in the ways of the world.

He first called the police August 13, the day after Debbie Bonner's body had been found near the slaughterhouse. A police operator took the call, but Foster wouldn't give his name. "Haven't you people considered the possibility that a cab driver might be doing this?" he asked, and then hung up.

Foster called a second time the next week, after the three bodies were found. This time he was put through to the detectives. Earl Tripp took the call.

"You guys should be looking at the cab drivers," Foster told Tripp. "They're the ones who know all these hookers."

Did Foster have anyone specific in mind? Tripp asked. As a matter of fact, Foster said, he did. Foster gave Tripp the name of a cab driver, a man named Smith. Tripp wrote it down and hung up. The same name had been provided to the county police by a Seattle Police Department detective the day before. Almost ten days went by before Detective Larry Gross, coming back from a trip to Tacoma, spotted the cab mentioned by Foster and the SPD man. Gross jotted down the cab's license plate, and an investigation was started.

By September 1, Foster's suggested suspect, Smith, had become a focus of the investigation. Reichert found the North Seattle mobile home where Smith lived, but Smith himself couldn't be located. Detectives patrolling The Strip were advised to watch for Smith's cab. Smith's arrest record was checked. It appeared that he had no criminal history.

Two days later, late on a Friday afternoon, a worker at a center for runaways being operated by the YMCA brought three street kids to see the detectives. Detective Bob LaMoria met them. The three kids told him about a strange man named Mel Foster who had warned them to stay away from Smith. LaMoria asked

the trio what they knew about Smith, and also about
Foster. Foster, it appeared, liked to take care of street
kids. He often gave them advice and sometimes
money. And sometimes, he would have sex with them.
After the teenagers left, LaMoria found himself wondering whether Foster might be a viable suspect
instead of Smith. Sometimes, LaMoria knew, a killer
might attempt to intervene in an investigation by raising a red herring.

On September 9, LaMoria and Reichert called Foster back. They invited him into the major crimes
offices to discuss the case. They questioned Foster for
more than an hour about Smith. Foster identified a
driver's license photo of Smith as the man he was
talking about, and claimed Smith had been forcing
street kids to work for him as prostitutes. Reichert
and LaMoria then showed Foster photographs of the
dead women. Foster told them Bonner looked familiar
to him, but the others were strangers. Had Foster himself ever had sex with any street kids?

"Hell, no," he said. "Anyone who would have sex
with a fourteen- or fifteen-year-old is a pervert." Why
was he hanging around with so many teenagers, then?
He just wanted to help them, Foster said. He didn't
want them to become "losers" and spend the rest of
their lives on the street. Foster boasted that he had
spent nearly four thousand dollars of his own money
over the past year trying to help the kids. Foster
admitted that he had spent time in prison, but said
that he hadn't been in trouble since 1965.

After Foster left, the detectives decided to obtain
his complete criminal history. Both detectives thought
there was something strange about the Lacey man and
his motives for coming forward.

The next day Reichert and LaMoria contacted
Smith at his mobile home. The man agreed to accom-
pany them back to the office for an interview. Smith
inspected the photographs of the victims, and said he
knew none of them. After an hour, Smith agreed to
take a polygraph test. Twenty minutes later, the test
was completed. The man named by Foster had easily

passed. Reichert and LaMoria decided to look even harder at Foster himself.

The day after Smith was cleared, county police announced they were looking for two new possible victims of the killer. Secret bulletins put out by the department listed Kase Ann Lee and Terri Rene Milligan as missing. But police refused to name the missing women for the news media.

But wouldn't publicizing their names prompt them to come forward if they were still alive? a reporter asked. "We want to protect their families," said a homicide lieutenant, in a glancing and unstated reference to the missing women's activity in prostitution. Besides, said the lieutenant, "There is no assurance that they *are* the victims of the Green River Killer."

While Reichert and LaMoria sorted through the conflicting stories from Foster and about Foster, other detectives continued to scour the highway in search of the man with the blue and white truck. Three days after the police announced the new missings, two patrol officers stopped a man in a blue and white truck who was obviously cruising The Strip area. They asked for the man's license and identified him as Charles Clinton Clark, a meatcutter at a local Safeway market. Detective Gross checked the county's concealed weapons permit records and found that Clark owned two handguns. He obtained a copy of Clark's drivers' license photograph and constructed a montage of six pictures, including the one of Clark. Susan Widmark readily identified Clark as the man who had terrorized her. A second victim also picked Clark.

On September 15, Reichert, Brooks, and several other detectives served a search warrant at Clark's house. During the search, clothing and boots worn by Clark in the attacks were discovered. Simultaneously, Clark was arrested at the supermarket just as he arrived to go to work. Police handcuffed him and took him back to his house, where the search was still underway. Searching Clark's blue and white pickup truck produced a gun described by one of the victims. The truck was vacuumed for bits of hair, fibers and dirt.

Detective Spencer Nelson of the county's sex crimes squad read Clark his Miranda rights. After a half-hour, he turned the questioning over to Reichert. Reichert reminded Clark that he did not have to answer any questions without a lawyer present, then asked Clark if he would mind answering some questions about the Green River murders. Clark told Reichert he didn't mind talking about the Green River crimes at all, because he wasn't involved. He admitted having committed several kidnappings and rapes, but no murders. The detectives allowed Clark to say good-bye to his wife and two children, then took him to jail.

Could Clark be the killer? Certainly the man was committing crimes in the area where the Green River victims had last been seen. He also seemed to have a penchant for violence against prostitutes. And Widmark's story about the man had him making references to the murders and driving her toward the river. But there were some differences as well. For one thing, why would he let these victims go while killing the others? And wouldn't he shoot the victims, rather than strangle them? It also appeared that Clark might have alibis for at least some of the victims' disappearances: he could have been at work, cutting meat in a Kent supermarket. Reichert decided that Clark was not the answer. Just in case, though, he and LaMoria decided to ask the state crime lab to compare the hairs and fibers found in Clark's truck with those recovered from the victims. Meanwhile, Clark agreed to take a polygraph test on the murders. He passed.

At the same time detectives were booking Clark for the highway rapes, eighteen-year-old Mary Bridget Meehan decided to take an evening stroll. The brown-haired, green-eyed Mary was more than eight months pregnant. She was staying in a room at the Western Six Motel, located just across The Strip from the

Hyatt, with her boyfriend Ray. Mary had never been arrested for prostitution, but she had a history of running away from home. She was estranged from her parents, who lived in a middle-class section of Bellevue, a city across Lake Washington from Seattle.

Mary's boyfriend waited for her to return. When several hours passed, he went out to look for her. He couldn't find her.

Returning to the motel room, Ray called the county police for help. He was told that at least twenty-four hours had to pass before a missing persons report would be taken.

The next night, when Mary had still not returned, Ray called the police again, who this time took the information. The case went into the communications in-basket. The following week it was routed to a sergeant, who routinely assigned the case to Detective Earl Tripp.

The sex crimes detectives, meanwhile, worked to close the case against Clark. On Sunday, September 19, Clark was taken to a lineup in the jail. Several of the victims, including "Betty Jones," were unable to identify him. Clark had shaved his mustache on his attorney's advice, he told Detective Fae Brooks. After the lineup, detectives showed all the victims a montage of photographs that included one of Clark with his mustache, and this time they all picked Clark.

After the lineup, Detective Spencer Nelson drove "Betty" back to Pacific Highway South and asked her to show him the place where Clark had picked her up, and the place where the attack had occurred. Nelson looked the locations over and made notes for his report while she waited.

Little was said about "Betty's" recent arrests; "Betty" was doing the police a favor by agreeing to testify against Clark.

"In this case she was a victim," Nelson said later. "If you want their cooperation, you have to treat them with a certain amount of respect. You don't treat them like suspects."

After visiting the scene of the rape, Nelson dropped "Betty" off at the Stevenson Motel—the place just across the street from where the Estes couple had their office.

Presumably, "Betty" went out for an afternoon stroll later that Sunday. No one ever saw her again, and after a week, the motel manager assumed she had simply left without paying her bill. He didn't give it another thought. Later, when Detective Nelson went back to the motel to pick her up for another court appearance, he learned she was no longer there. Nelson obtained a warrant for "Betty's" arrest as a material witness in the case against Clark.

As the weeks dragged on and still "Jones" did not turn up, Nelson told Tripp and Reichert that they probably had another missing hooker to deal with. But, the three men reasoned, it was always possible—probably even likely—that "Betty" had just decided not to go to court after all.

14

MELVYN

September 1982

A day or so after Clark had been cleared, the profile written by Douglas was delivered to the county police by Whitaker.

It was vital, Douglas warned, that the profile remain one of the investigation's most closely guarded secrets; otherwise, tips from the public could be skewed as well-meaning people began tailoring their information to meet police expectations. Or worse, the killer could read about the profile and consciously attempt to alter his behavior. The profile would remain a closely guarded secret for years afterward, until it was obtained by the authors. By that time, Douglas's initial assessment of the crimes had been superseded by other events.

Douglas cautioned that the profile would be no substitute for investigation, that it would only be a tool useful for prioritizing leads and evaluating suspects. The assessment could only be general in its conclusions in the absence of more evidence, he warned, and it was entirely possible that the real killer might fit only some of his predictions. Certainly, no suspect should be eliminated only on the basis of the profile.

Douglas began the document with a description of some of the facts of the case, particularly focusing on the victims' backgrounds and the evidence available at the river scene. That the victims were all known to be prostitutes or street people, wrote Douglas, shed a considerable amount of light on what type of person the killer would likely be. Then Douglas went on to outline some of the characteristics the detectives might expect to discover in likely suspects:

Their ages and race [Douglas wrote of the victims] show a variance which indicates that the offender demonstrated no personal preference for race. It has been determined through studies at the Behavioral Sciences Unit that even the best of the so-called street people can be tricked or fooled, and a frequent tactic repeatedly observed is where the offender impersonates a law enforcement official. During his contact with the victim, her safety will be the prime entree he will use and he may even promise to take the victim home or to the police station. He may also admonish the victim for walking the streets in the evening hours and for soliciting sexual favors. The offender's biggest obstacle will be to gain control of the victims and while the victims will initially be willing to go with him for the solicited act of prostitution, at some point he will have to demonstrate power over the victim.

While in this particular case the victims are of different ages and races, including variances in modus operandi, the assumption is still made that all the deaths are related and all are committed by the same individual. This is based on the location where the victims were initially confronted, that being the Pacific Highway South "stroll" area near the Seattle-Tacoma International Airport, and the location of the disposal of the bodies. Also due to the probable cause of death being strangulation, asphyxial. All of the victims are categorized in this matter as high risk victims due to their involvement with drugs and prostitution, their lifestyles, which make them susceptible to be a victim of a violent crime. In other words, they are characterized as victims of opportunity, they are easy to approach on the street, and probably initiate the conversation with their prospective "john."

An analysis of crime scene reflects a primary focal point being the disposal site for the offender. In the case of the Green River victims, namely, Bonner, Chapman, Coffield, Hinds, and Mills, the offender dumped his victims in or near the Green River. Crime scene analysis further reflects the offender was comfortable with the crime scene, where some of his victims were anchored down with rocks. His efforts to secure victims to the bottom of the river by placing rocks on top of them demonstrates the fact that he spent a considerable period of time in or at this location. The other body [Mills] that was dumped on the side of the Green River [is] evidence that the offender had to quickly dispose of his victim. The method of disposing of the victims indicates the offender does not, or will not, demonstrate any remorse over the death of his victims and what the offender is telling police is that the deaths of these victims are warranted and justified and he is even providing in his own mind a service to mankind.

The crime scene further reflects that the offender at this particular point in the investigation is not seeking power or recognition or publicity as he is not displaying his victims after he kills them. He does not want his victims to be found and if they are eventually found, he has the mental faculties to understand that items of evidentiary value, because of the bodies being placed in the river, will not be found.

The offender is very familiar with the areas where the victims are disposed, does not seek publicity, and demonstrates no remorse.

From the Medical Examiner's reports and autopsy reports, it is learned that the victims die from some sort of asphyxia. In some of the cases, the offender leaves a ligature around the neck where in other cases, none is evident. The primary element that surfaced with each victim is that the subject is not planning to kill his victim each night [as] he sets out to the area where the victims solicit sexual favors. He does not bring a rape or murder kit with him, nor does he plan to put his victims through some sort of ritual sexual act or body positioning.

We learn that the offender commits postmortem acts on two of the victims, that being placing pyramid rocks in the vaginal canal, and by doing this act, the offender reveals further elements of his personality.

The offender is profiled basically as a psychopathic personality in that the offender is mobile, drives a vehicle quite a bit. The vehicle, according to the profile, will be conservative in make and model. Offenders of this type favor vans and four-door conservative automobiles. These vehicles will be a minimum of three years old, and will probably not be well-maintained.

The offender, in all probability, has a prior criminal or psychological history, comes from a family background which includes marital discord between his mother and his father, and in all probability was raised by a single parent. His mother attempted to fill the role of both parents by inflicting severe physical as well as mental pain on the victim [offender]. She consistently nagged her son, particularly when he rebelled against all authority figures. The subject had difficulty in school which caused him to probably drop out during his junior or senior year and he has average or slightly above average intelligence. The offender has dated and in all likelihood, if he has been married, he is separated or divorced at this time. He does not [have], nor has he ever [had] an aversion toward women. He has felt that he has been "burned" or "lied to and fooled by women one too many times." In his way of thinking, women are no good and cannot be trusted and he feels women will prostitute themselves for whatever reason and when he seeks women openly prostituting themselves, this makes his blood boil.

He is drawn to the vicinity where there is open prostitution because of recent failure with other significant women in his life, and in all probability, he has been dumped by a woman for another man.

He seeks prostitutes because he is not the type of individual who can hustle women in a bar. He does not have any fancy line of speech as he is basically shy and has very strong personal feelings of inadequacy. Having sex with those victims may be the initial aim of the subject but when the conversation turns to "play for pay" this causes flashbacks in his mind to uncomfortable times he has had in the past with women. These memories, as stated previously, are not pleasant. The straightforwardness of prostitutes is very threatening to him. They demonstrate too much power and control over him, because of his personal feelings toward women and the action of prostitutes, that will make it mentally comfortable to him to kill them.

The offender will be in relatively good shape and not be extremely thin or fat. He is somewhat of an outdoorsman, and would be expected to have an occupation that required more strength than skill, a "laborer, maintenance [man], etc." He does not have an aversion to getting wet or soiled. His employment or hobbies will get him this way all the time.

He will not be very meticulous, neat, and/or excessive compulsive in his everyday lifestyle. He is a beer drinker, and probably [a] smoker. Since these homicides, he, in all probability, has been doing more drinking than he has in the past.

When it comes to determining the race of the subject, the probability factor is decreased inasmuch as some of the victims are white, some are black, some are mulatto. Generally, crimes of this type are intraracial, black-on-black, white-on-white. Using the hypothesis that the first victim was white and is related to the other four victims, this would lead to the fact that the offender, in all probability, is white.

The age of the offender can be determined by the amount of control and confidence he exhibits in initially confronting his victims, as well as mobility. These factors place him in an age category between his mid-twenties to early thirties. If the age grouping is correct, a previous criminal and psychological history can be found. Criminally, cases of assault and rape would be his typical criminal background. If institutionalized in [a] mental hospital, diagnosis of paranoid schizophrenic or manic depressive psychosis is almost typically found. It is felt, however, that the offender is not insane as evidenced by his ability to conceal his victim, leaving little or any tangible evidence, and [to] drive a vehicle. Someone [who] is insane does not rationally think of concealing his crimes nor is he capable of driving a vehicle safely.

It should be noted that any suspects developed cannot be eliminated by age alone. There is no burn-out with these types of offenders and they can kill easily at 40 years of age just as at 20 years. These homicides reflect rage and anger on the part of the subject and he will not stop killing until he is caught or moves.

Under post-offense behavior, it is noted that the offender does not stay idle. He is a nocturnal individual and is a cruiser in his automobile. He feels comfortable during the evening hours, and when there is stress at work or at home he cruises to the area where prostitutes are available. He, in all probability, has returned on several occasions to the disposal dump sites, both prior and subsequent to the victims being found and he has in all probability had additional encounters with prostitutes since these homicides. His primary topical area of conversation with the prostitutes would be the homicides.

He has followed the newspaper accounts of these homicides, has clipped them out for posterity, and for further fantasy and further embellishment.

If items belonging to the victims are missing, he will take them as souvenirs and will in all probability give them to [his] girlfriend, wife, or his mother.

He has had difficulty sleeping and has been experiencing periods of anxiety. He fears being detected particularly if newspaper accounts report that investigators are conducting a thorough and exhaustive investigation.

The similarities between the personality described by Douglas and some aspects of Foster's behavior seemed immediately obvious to the detectives, particularly the references to nocturnal behavior, compulsive driving, and drinking and smoking. The prediction that the killer would pretend a concern for the victims' safety rang a bell. Like the prototype in the profile, Foster had slightly above average intelligence and was menially employed or, as the FBI studies suggested the killer might be, periodically unemployed. Like the prototypical killer, Foster had a history of instability in intimate relationships, with his five marriages. Foster frequented the areas where the prostitutes worked and even sought them out, just as Douglas's profile suggested the killer might. Foster grew up not far from the river, as Douglas suggested the killer probably had; and Foster had a previous criminal record and had threatened assault on numerous occasions. Foster drove an older, conservative four-door sedan that was not well maintained. Foster continued having contact with prostitutes and street girls even after the killings, warning them to be careful and talking to them about the murders. He had followed news media accounts of the murders with rapt attention. And most of all, as Douglas had suggested the killer might, Foster had gone out of his way to inject himself into the investigation.

True, there were some differences between Foster and the Douglas prototype. Foster's mother had died years earlier; he lived with his father, not his mother. There was no indication that Foster was much of a hunter or fisherman, or that he was any sort of outdoorsman. While he was not an excessively neat person, there was little indication that he routinely got himself wet or soiled, or that he felt comfortable doing so.

The problem with the profile was that in many respects it was so general as to apply to a sizeable chunk of the male population of King County, Kraske realized after he read it. In the Pacific Northwest hunting, fishing, and outdoor work was the rule rather than the exception; *that* characteristic was so common as to be almost meaningless. Thousands, if not tens of thousands, of men in the area had histories of violence toward women; after all, didn't the police spend half their time breaking up family fights? Police in both the city and the county annually made up to two thousand arrests for street prostitution. That probably meant there were at least three to four times that number of men who were drawn to the prostitution areas, if not more. At least half of them drove older cars, had unstable intimate relationships, worked outdoors, and smoked and drank. Probably more than half were raised only by their mothers. God, this was a hundred times worse than Ted, Kraske thought.

Still, by this time, his detectives had begun to feel that Foster was a good bet. One of them decided to call Douglas to get his opinion. But Douglas was out of town. Douglas's boss, Roger Depue, urged the police to wait several days before interviewing the cab driver. Douglas would be back by then, he said.

"What's the rush?" Depue asked. Depue knew that interviewing suspects in serial cases was a fine art. The subject had to be coaxed into cooperating. The best thing to do would be to allow Douglas to compose a suspect evaluation on Foster. The worst thing would be to have an inappropriately timed confrontation. That could shut down any possibility of inducing the suspect to admit the crimes, as serial killers often did. But Reichert had already invited Foster to come into the office for further "consultations," and the detectives didn't want to wait. They had a feeling about Foster, and the feeling told them that he was their man.

15

CONFRONTATION

September 20, 1982

Melvyn Wayne Foster was happy but a little nervous: After badgering the cops for more than a month, it now appeared that someone was finally taking him seriously.

The cops had called on a Friday evening and asked if he wouldn't mind driving up to Seattle the following Monday, September 20. Reichert said the police needed a bit more information. If it wasn't too much trouble, could Foster come in again? And by the way, would Foster agree to take a lie detector test? It was just routine, the police assured him. No problem, said Foster. It was a decision that was to change his life.

Fond of wearing leather jackets and boots that seemed to make him grow or shrink as the occasion required, just about everything Foster said about himself made Foster look good. Foster was tough, but fair; Foster was idealistic and smart; Foster protected the weak while fearing no man. Much of his conversation was laced with violent imagery, with Foster delivering the violence—all directed, of course, toward the bad guys, who richly deserved it.

In Foster's world, Foster was The Hero, the Shane of the Streets, always ready to defend the weak and exact certain retribution on behalf of the oppressed. Especially when the oppressed was Foster. He would "bust someone's skull," or "kick their butt," or "knock them on their ass." He would "clean their clock," or worse. Foster liked to tell people he was six feet tall and that he weighed 190 pounds, "all of it solid muscle," of course, but that was a bit of poetic license useful in building the image of Foster. In truth Foster was slightly shorter and at times as much as 30 pounds lighter. His physical condition had long ago slid into the memory hole.

Foster wore his thinning hair slicked back, the remnant of a bygone era of ducktails and dungarees, when James Dean had set the pace and Jerry Lee Lewis called the tune. He drank, sometimes excessively, and smoked a pack of Salems every day. He could use drug slang with anyone, although he professed never to use drugs himself.

But at forty-four, Foster's personality seemed to be in a state of flux. What was he now, the tough guy, schooled in the hard knocks, yet generous to a fault, who walks off with the girl in the last reel? Or was he your kindly uncle, bifocals slipping down the nose, a wry grin with some friendly advice? Foster had cultivated both masks, but which one to wear? At one moment he might rave violently at some outrageous injustice, threatening the worse kind of righteous retribution; in the next instant, he seemed to shrink inside his very frame, metamorphosing into someone's vision of a genial relative, pipe in hand, ready to assist wherever needed.

Perhaps nowhere was Foster more confused than in his relationships with women. Foster had been married five times. One of his previous wives had died; all the others had left him. All of them had been teenagers when they began living with Foster. Foster seemed incapable of developing an intimate relationship with a woman his own age. Consequently Foster found himself attracted to young girls. Sometimes Foster was the worldly-wise lover; other times he was daddy.

Driving a cab on The Strip had brought Foster into contact with scores of young women. Most of them had run away from home after fights with their fathers. Mel could be the Daddy these girls had both avoided and wanted at the same time. If the girls wanted to sleep with him, who was he to stop them?

In other words, as he prepared to meet with Reichert, Foster was everything the straitlaced, religious Reichert despised. At the same time, Foster saw Reichert as wet-behind-the-ears, pompous, and stuffy. Thus, the seeds were planted for a personality conflict that was to bedevil the Green River investigation for years to come.

Foster drove into Seattle and parked his car in the county's gray concrete parking garage next to the courthouse. Public parking was limited to two hours. I'll be back in plenty of time, Foster thought.

Reichert and Bob LaMoria were waiting for him. They invited Foster back into the major crimes unit and seated him in an interview room and closed the door. Both detectives were glad to see him, Foster thought.

Reichert and LaMoria have never commented publicly about this critical encounter with Foster. Foster has, however, and quite volubly. Much of what may have happened remains secret; the version recounted here is taken from Foster's recollections, and from certain facts gleaned from two police documents, and one entirely unauthorized tape recording of some of the events.

The way Foster told the story later, the interchange began pleasantly enough.

According to Foster, Reichert and LaMoria again pulled out a stack of photographs of young women, most of them booking pictures from the jail. Did Foster know this girl? How about that one? As the interview progressed, Foster said, he identified numerous women, and told the detectives the girls' street names, where they liked to hang out, stories about their pimps, and other anecdotes. "I knew more about the street than their entire vice squad," he later boasted. Periodically, either Reichert or LaMoria would get up and leave the interview room, and return a few minutes later.

Foster said he told police that he had warned the women about the killer, and that he had urged several girls to contact the police for their own safety. The detectives nodded. Coffee was brought, followed by soft drinks. The morning became the afternoon. As time wore on, Foster said, he started getting "halfway mad . . . I come in expecting to be interviewed and it turns out that's not what they had in mind."

This time, Foster identified pictures of Coffield, Chapman, and Hinds, and seemed to recognize Mills. The detectives bore in: How did he meet Coffield? Who had introduced him to Bonner? To Mills? Had he ever given a ride to Chapman? He had? When? What about Hinds? Her too? Where had he last seen her? Suddenly the detectives started seeming skeptical.

Just how had Foster come to know so many of these women, anyway? Didn't Foster realize that he knew *all five* of the murdered women?

"When you drive cab at night, you meet 'em," Foster said lamely. Foster could tell from the detectives' expressions that they doubted this. Foster plunged on. "On a wet nasty night they want to crawl in a cab, ride out and dry up and warm up. They will flag you down to take their business . . . sometimes they'll take their customer with them to wherever so they can do some business." The detectives were staring at him. Foster began to get the picture.

What was Foster up to in July and August? He had two street girls staying with him at his father's house in Lacey, Foster indignantly told the police.

"On a celibatic basis, of course," Foster added. He had offered to let the girls stay at his house because they were afraid of the murderer.

Oho! said the detectives. Who *were* these girls? And where was his father while this was going on? Foster said his father had been visiting relatives in Colorado. As for the girls, the cops could check with them and see if he wasn't telling the truth. Foster gave the detectives the girls' names, and where they might be contacted.

"It sounds like you guys think *I* might have had something to do with it," Foster said. He became indignant. "I'm going to tell you up in front, you're nuts." Besides, said Foster, his car wasn't working during much of the time. And he had injured his knee a few months before. He told the police it would have been physically impossible for him to carry the bodies down to the river. The detectives shook their heads. They told Foster it seemed to them that he knew too many of the victims too well.

The detectives asked him if he would take the polygraph test. They told him if he took the test and passed, they could clear him and he could go on his way.

"Anytime you're ready," Foster shot back, and so Foster was taken to another room where a civilian expert employed by the county was waiting with the machine. The expert, Norm Matzke, strapped Foster in. Bands stretched across the abdomen and chest monitored Foster's heartbeat, blood pressure, and breathing. A third wire was connected to Foster's skin to measure perspiration. Someone telling a lie, so the theory went, would exhibit various physiological signs. When matched with a thorough interrogation, the machine was believed to be accurate more than 90 percent of the time.

Just relax, Foster was told. We're going to ask you a number of questions to establish a pattern. On some you'll be asked to lie, so we can measure that. We may go through these questions several times. If you don't understand a question, just say so. Go ahead, said Foster.

The detectives took Foster through the questions. Did Foster know Bonner? Chapman? Mills? Hinds? Coffield? Yes, said Foster. Was he telling the detectives the truth? Yes. Did he know who had killed the women found in the river? No. Did *he* kill the women in the river? No. Did he know what was done to Chapman? No. To Hinds? No. Was his name Melvyn Wayne Foster? Yes.

And then it was over. Matzke was packing up his machine. The whole thing took less than thirty minutes. Foster, who knew a little about polygraphs, was perplexed. A thorough polygraph was supposed to take a lot longer, Foster thought. The way it was supposed to work, the longer the polygraph went on, the more the guilty sweated. Long, repeated polygraphs were supposed to be good for the innocent. But Reichert and LaMoria took Foster back to the interview room while Matzke analyzed his charts.

Now the detectives peppered Foster with new questions. Why had he come forward? Where was he exactly when the murders took place? Why did he sleep with young girls? They showed Foster photographs taken at the river. The bloated bodies stared up at Foster sightlessly. "You've got the wrong guy," Foster insisted. The detectives left Foster alone in the room while they went back to consult with Matzke. Foster realized he had been locked in.

According to police records, Matzke pointed to the charts and said he thought Foster had lied on four important questions. The tests showed that Foster was attempting to deceive when asked whether he was telling the detectives the truth; when asked if he knew who had killed the women; on whether he had killed the women; and on whether he knew what had been done to Chapman and Hinds, an unstated reference to the rocks. Four other county detectives with experience in giving polygraph tests reviewed Matzke's examination and analysis and agreed with his conclusions.

The detectives went back to Foster and told him that he had failed the polygraph. Foster still insisted that he was innocent.

We can clear this up right now, Foster said he was told. Why don't you let us search your house? That way, we can get this problem resolved. "I got nothing to hide from you guys," Foster said. "You can look through anything you want."

Reichert and LaMoria took Foster out of the major crimes unit and picked up another detective from the vice squad, who glowered at Foster but said little. The four men used LaMoria's car to drive down to Foster's house. All the way down, the two detectives kept taking Foster through his story on how he had met the women, where he had taken them, what they had said to each other. Foster kept adding new details and retracting parts of what he'd already said. He was getting confused, but didn't want to admit *that* weakness.

By now it was almost 7:00 P.M. Foster's father Daniel and Foster's two sons were at the house when the men arrived. They were met there by deputies from the Thurston County Sheriff's Department, who asked him to sign a paper consenting to the search. No one paid much attention to one of Melvyn's small sons, who was on the living room floor playing with a tape recorder. A football game was on television.

Daniel Foster was thunderstruck. He defended his son.

"What in the heck is this all about?" asked Daniel Foster. "I would like to know that."

"Well, he's been accused of something and this is

one of the easiest ways to clear him of it," said LaMoria. "And he's agreed that, he believes that's the thing to do and he signed one too."

"Hopefully, it will only take a few minutes," said one of the Thurston County deputies.

"Search the car, too," said Melvyn Foster. "You won't find all that much in it."

"Does he ever drive your car?" LaMoria asked Daniel Foster.

"No. Nobody drives my car but me."

"We probably should look through it while we're here," said Reichert.

LaMoria agreed. "We probably should look through it while we're here. That way we can say we did . . . so nobody can say it was in the car and you didn't look there."

"When did all this supposedly happen?" asked Daniel Foster.

"It's been over a period of the last two months," said LaMoria.

"I was gone all last month," Daniel Foster said.

Daniel Foster signed the consent to search.

"Who's winning the game?" Reichert asked.

"The Giants, I think," said Daniel Foster.

"O.K.," said one of the detectives. "Where do you sleep? Where do you keep your clothes?"

Foster showed them. "Right here," he said.

"I know he went no place in that car in June or July or August," said Daniel Foster.

"What happened?" one of Melvyn's sons asked Daniel Foster. "What happened?"

"I don't know," said Daniel Foster.

"Mel, why don't you sit out here?" one of the detectives suggested, to make sure Foster didn't interfere in the search.

"Sure," said Melvyn.

"What happened?" Melvyn's son asked him. "Some questions were raised and we're going to get it cleared up," Mel told him.

The son holding the tape recorder produced a long

raspberry and giggled. "That was a policeman. He farted."

The kids followed the police outside. One of the detectives began poking through a shed. One of the sons offered commentary to the police as the search went on. "He mostly keeps jars in there," said the son. "He makes jam. And in the other cabinet he has like . . . jelly . . ." The detectives moved the jars around.

They went next to the small barn. "Is that the barn?" one of the detectives asked. "Yeah," said one of the kids. "There's nothing in it yet. We don't have any animals."

The detectives and the two kids went back to the house. One of the kids offered help to the detectives. "There's a closet you forgot to check."

"Where?" said one of the detectives.

"Inside the house."

" 'Aha!' " said one of the kids, mimicking the detectives' reaction to this information. Then one of the kids began whispering into the tape recorder: "These are police searching our house *right now!* I'm not faking this."

The son turned the tape over, and, like any good radio journalist, announced, "Second half of the police searching the place. My dad's talking to one of the policemen."

"This is where they're looking through our drawers," said the son into the recorder while the drawers were being opened and closed.

"There's nothing in that chest," said one of the kids. "Dad, they're leaving. Daddy, they want you."

Daniel Foster was mad at the condition of the house. "They left one hell of a mess," he said to Mel. Mel and the kids started picking things up.

LaMoria approached Daniel Foster and held up some articles. "We're going to take some pieces of paper and a bra," he said.

"That bra belonged to [one of Foster's former wives]," said Daniel Foster. The detectives said they wanted to take Mel back to Seattle with them. They left. The son with the tape recorder marked the end of the search. "This is the end of the story," he said. But it wasn't.

Back in Seattle that night the two detectives zeroed in on Foster once more, in Foster's version of the events. By now it was nearing 10:00 P.M., and Foster was arguing with the detectives. Finally he blew up when the detectives accused him of committing the murders.

"If that's where you're going," Foster said, "this interview is over." He stood up to leave. Foster later remembered that Reichert smiled. Not quite, Foster said he was told. We've got a warrant for your arrest. Reichert showed him. The warrant said Foster was wanted for failure to pay $427 in parking tickets. " 'In fact,' " Foster said he was told, " 'you've been under arrest since this morning.' " Foster got mad all over again.

"Well, I guess you blew it on the Miranda business, didn't you?" Foster told the police. "How come I haven't been given an opportunity at a reasonable hour to arrange bail?"

" 'We didn't think it was necessary until now,' " Foster said he was told.

He wasn't going to let the cops get away with this, Foster said. "Well, you blew it," Foster said he said, "and I'm not going to let it slide. We're all done talking."

The two detectives then handcuffed Foster and took him across the street to the city's Public Safety Building, where he was booked into the city jail on the parking tickets warrant.

The following morning Foster was brought back to the major crimes unit for more questioning. This time the detectives worked again on his alibis for the dates when the murders occurred, in Foster's versions of the events.

About 2:00 P.M., Foster said, the detectives asked him whether he would be willing to voluntarily pro-

vide samples of his blood and hair. Foster told the
detectives to give him the consent form. "Let's get it
on," he said he told them. A technician came and
clipped hairs from Foster's head, arms, legs and pubic
area. Blood was drawn. All of the samples were sealed
in an evidence envelope. Reichert was called out of
the room once more. Then LaMoria left, leaving Foster alone. The door was locked again.

After a short wait, the door opened and Detective
Fae Brooks from the sex crimes detail entered. She
sat down and peered at Foster closely, he claimed
later. "Fae Brooks came in and she sat down and she
looked down her nose," Foster said. "Through them,
what looked like, coke-bottle glasses. [Brooks wore
glasses.] They're not really that thick but the way she
was sitting at the moment they looked like coke bottles. She looked down her nose and stuff and she
started on me . . ." Foster later gave a blow-by-blow
description of his version of the conversation:

" 'Why'd you get those girls?' " Foster said Brooks
asked him.

" 'What girls? I'm not a pimp.' "

" 'No, what I mean is, why did you *kill* those
girls?' "

" 'Hey, just between me and you? . . . I . . . didn't
. . . do . . . it!'

"And she said: 'Well, you're a sick, sorry son-of-a-
bitch and I'm going to see your nuts hang.' I said,
'Hey, look, nigger . . . [Brooks is black.] . . . I said,
'Hey look, nigger, you take your shoe-shine ass out
of here before I stick a shoe in it. And do it now.'
And I started to get up and boy, she was out that
door *that* quick.

"Reichert come back in . . . Reichert come hot-
footing it back in, and he said 'She's really upset. You
blew your stack.' I said, 'You send that fucking nigger
back in here again and I'll pull her teeth. That's a
nigger cunt, not a black officer.'

"That's what I told him," Foster said afterward. "I
called Reichert out here. Those were the exact words
I used."

Foster claimed that Brooks had baited him. "She blew it," he said. "She raised my boiling point and normally I didn't get into ethnics. I don't like that stuff. That's for the redneck idiots down south.

"She got me so mad I got into ethnics. And I just don't do that. That's not American."

Foster said Reichert asked him what had happened. "He said: 'What started that?' I told him exactly what happened. I told him, 'You send her in here again, I won't repeat to you what I've said once. I will make an exception, for the first time, I will put my hands on a female in anger.'

"And he said, 'Well, I don't think she'd want to come back in now, anyway. She's out there, kind of shook.' Then he said, 'Why'd you call her a nigger for?' I said, 'David, just between you and me, I don't do that. That's not American. It's not the way I was raised. But she got me so mad that's the only thing I could think of to call her, because it's a shiftless, worthless person with no values. And it doesn't matter what color. You got white niggers, you got black ones.' "

Later, Reichert and LaMoria returned to their own interviewing. They made Foster answer still more questions. Finally, about 9:00 P.M., another cop opened the door and told Reichert that Daniel Foster was outside the courthouse demanding the release of his son. Bail had been posted earlier in the day, but the release order had not been processed.

"How long ago was the bond posted?" Foster said he asked. About six hours ago, Foster claimed he was told. Foster got mad once more.

"You've been blocking my release for six hours by not telling me that bond has been posted? I'm walking out of here right now, unless you're prepared to shoot me in the back. Open this goddamn door, I'm gone." Foster said he got up and left. No one tried to stop him, he said.

Foster went over to the bail bondsman's office and signed some papers with his father. Daniel Foster started back to Lacey. Foster walked back to where he had parked his car two days earlier in the county's garage. There was a new parking ticket on it. It looked to Foster like the car had been vacuumed clean inside. The dashboard and doors were covered with sticky fingerprint powder. He got behind the wheel and turned the ignition key. The starter wouldn't turn. He walked back to the bail bond office and waited for Daniel Foster to get home.

"For crying out loud," said Daniel Foster when Mel told him he needed him to come back and pick him up. "All right. Boy, this is going to be a long night."

An hour later, Daniel Foster came back to Seattle, picked up his son, and drove them both home. Neither man noticed the cops who were trailing them. Beginning on the night of September 21, Melvyn Wayne Foster would be under twenty-four-hour surveillance for the foreseeable future.

In the meantime, detectives would work to run down all of Foster's alibis. Perhaps some old-fashioned detective work would be able to tie Foster closer to the murders.

16

CATNIP

September 1982

On the Saturday evening of September 26, five days after the start of surveillance on Melvyn Foster, an employee of the Red Lion Hotel on his day off decided to give his dirtbike a workout in a sandy, brush-covered area near the condemned houses south of the airport.

As the rider maneuvered his bike around near a small hillock some distance north of what used to be South 202nd Street and 18th Avenue South, he got a whiff of something rotten. He stopped and throttled down, sniffing. Yes. Something dead.

The man shut his motorcycle off and followed his nose to a clump of blackberry bushes. Parting the foliage, he looked down on what had once been Gisele Lovvorn.

"Catnip" Tindal's psychic had been almost right. Lovvorn had been discovered less than three miles away from "home." She was nude, lying on her back with her legs spread apart; a pair of men's socks, black, had been tied together and knotted tightly around her neck. Her clothes, boots, and the clutch purse with the condoms and the knife were nowhere to be found.

Because Lovvorn's body had been found on Port of Seattle property, the Port Police had legal jurisdiction.

The Port sent its officers to the scene to secure the area, but decided to call in the King County Police to handle the investigation. Homicide wasn't really the Port's line.

The following morning, an assistant medical examiner arrived at the scene shortly before 10:00 A.M. The detectives and Kraske greeted him in a light rain. The police had already cleared away most of the brush. The pathologist and one of his assistants put plastic bags around the hands. The body was badly decomposed, but not yet skeletonized. The pathologist and his assistant slipped the remains into the regulation blue body bag. Shovels of the dirt from underneath the body were poured through small screens into buckets in an effort to isolate any trace evidence. None was found. An hour later, the medical examiners left, taking the last of Gisele Lovvorn with them.

What was it Douglas had said? It was possible that the killer might return to the dump site? Kraske asked the medical examiner's office to keep the discovery quiet for the time being. Medical investigators agreed.

But was this a victim of the same killer who had put the five bodies in the Green River? That's the way it seemed to Kraske: After all, there was the use of the socks to strangle. "Does not bring a murder or rape kit with him," Douglas had said. One thing was clear: These were not the dead girl's own socks.

Back at the office, Detective Earl Tripp was pretty sure he knew who the dead girl was. He remembered the cab driver Tindal telling him that his girlfriend Gisele Lovvorn had a tattoo of a bird on her breast. This dead girl had a tattoo on her breast too. And there were the rings. Gisele wore a prized gold ring that formed a snake's head. So did this girl. Tripp told his sergeant, who told Kraske. There were some discrepancies, though. Lovvorn was a blonde, but the dead girl appeared to have black hair.

An autopsy was scheduled for Sunday, September 27. That morning Kraske told the Medical Examiner's office that the girl might be Lovvorn. Kraske asked the Medical Examiner's office to get in touch with Lovvorn's parents in California, to see who Gisele's dentist had been. Because of the decomposition, it would probably be best to get a positive identification from dental charts.

That left the problem of Tindal. While Kraske's best guess was that this latest victim was connected to the earlier murders, one first had to be completely sure that Tindal wasn't the one who had killed her, if indeed the victim was Lovvorn. For that matter, it was possible that Tindal had killed *all* the victims, wasn't it?

That was pretty much Reichert's thinking too. On Sunday, he, Earl Tripp, and Bob LaMoria went hunting for Tindal.

A patrol cop found Catnip working on his car at the gas station where his roommate worked. The cop told Tindal to call the county police department's airport-area precinct office. Tindal called and was told that a body had been found. He demanded more details.

"Is it a blonde?" Tindal asked. "Is it female? Does she have a tattoo on her right breast?" Sorry, Tindal was told, the police couldn't tell him anything. Would he please come in to be interviewed?

Tindal drove to the precinct office. The detectives were waiting for him.

"Look, for God's sake," said Tindal, "if it's Gisele, let me go view the body, I'll tell you in a second."

No, we can't let you do that, Tindal was told.

"Then can you take a photograph of the right breast?"

No, we can't do that either, the detectives said.

"How long before you identify the body?"

It could be up to three weeks, the detectives told Tindal.

Then the detectives took Tindal over his story again. How Gisele had left. How they were supposed to meet at the cabstand, but Gisele hadn't shown up. All about Peaches and Pretty Tony. Tindal spent four hours at the precinct, and at the end still didn't know whether Gisele was dead or alive.

The next day, Monday, a medical investigator called Gisele Lovvorn's Los Angeles-area parents and obtained the name of her dentist. The dentist said he would send her dental charts north for comparison to the teeth found in the dead girl's mouth. It might take up to a week before final confirmation, the investigator told Gisele's parents.

Meanwhile, county police released the news of the discovery, but kept the tentative identity back. A police press spokesman told reporters the county's detectives had concluded that the latest victim had been killed by the same person who had murdered Wendy Coffield, Dub Bonner, Marcia Chapman, Cynthia Hinds, and Opal Mills. Why?

"The circumstances surrounding the apparent cause of death," the spokesman said, along with the victim's apparent age, her unclothed condition, and the fact that she had been killed in the same time period the others had been killed.

That put the official Green River death toll at six.

On Tuesday, the detectives asked Tindal to come downtown to take a polygraph test. Tindal agreed. The test lasted for several hours. The detectives asked Tindal many of the same sort of questions they had asked Foster, but this time focused on Gisele Lovvorn.

The detectives finally released Tindal. No one told him whether he had passed the polygraph or not, but Tindal figured that he did. If not, he would have been in jail. Maybe now, he thought, the cops will start looking for Peaches and Pretty Tony. Tindal called Hilda Bryant, the television reporter, and told her what the police believed. Within hours, Lovvorn's name was on the evening news. Now Bryant was all over Tindal, seeking information, including *his* picture. Soon other reporters were calling Tindal, and hearing all about Peaches and Pretty Tony.

While Tindal was talking to the press, the police

announced that two more young girls were missing and possibly victims of the killer. Unlike the last time, this time the names were released. "Ann Lee Kase," a police spokesman said, getting Kase Lee's name completely confused, and Terri Rene Milligan had been last seen in late August. The spokesman refused to release either girl's address, or confirm that both had been involved in prostitution, "out of deference to the families."

But the very next day, the police reversed themselves about Lee and Milligan. Detectives, said the spokesman, had been told that Milligan had been seen recently in eastern Washington, while Lee had been spotted in Alaska. Reporters were confused.

So was Kraske. He didn't know what to think. The problem was that nobody involved in the prostitution business was really reliable, he thought. That was the big difference between the Green River case and the Bundy business. At least in the Bundy case, with college girls the victims, missing people were *really* missing. With hookers, no one knew anything for sure.

Kraske gave news interviews the next day. True, he said, there hadn't yet been an outstanding lead in the case, and detectives weren't anywhere close to making an arrest.

"But the investigation is not at a dead end," he insisted. Work was still going on. Patience and persistence would be the key.

"This is not a one-hour TV show," Kraske said. "It takes time. But we *are* making progress." The investigation was hampered by the fact that the victims were involved in prostitution, he said. "They get into so many cars, and it's not necessarily the car of the killer." But the prostitutes were frightened and information was starting to come in.

"Usually our people are out there trying to arrest them," Kraske explained to the reporters. "The prostitutes have their own communication system and that's where a lot of our information is coming from.

"We have been getting more help—quite a bit more—from the prostitutes than the pimps. Some of the women are very credible, are very concerned, and some of them are terminal space cases.

"The prostitutes talk to each other and warn each other. They tell each other, 'That guy is kinky, that one is weird. I saw a gun in the door pocket of that guy's car. Stay away from that guy.' They know and recognize the weirdos."

Kraske said his detectives had sent bulletins around to other police departments asking about similar homicides involving prostitutes. "We didn't get anything back on that at all," he said. "So we feel it's probably someone who lives in this state." What about the pimp war theory? *That* was out, he said. Drugs and debts, as with Larry Mathews, had also been discounted as a connecting factor.

The best guess, said Kraske, was that the killer was a customer of the prostitutes.

But a john, Kraske did not add, who didn't *seem* to be kinky or weird in the least. That was the problem: Except for this one thing, the killer was probably perfectly normal.

17

GOING PUBLIC

October 1982

By October 1, Foster, aware that the police had him under surveillance, had had enough of it. He decided to go public. He thought of a way to do it that would be as entertaining as hell.

One of his neighbors had told Daniel Foster that

the King County Police were using a nearby driveway to spy on his son. Foster checked; sure enough, every time he drove away, someone was on his tail. I'll show the bastards, he thought.

Foster drove to Seattle, his shadow following. He went off the Fairview off-ramp and drove around for awhile, then stopped at a Denny's Restaurant. He went inside and telephoned Hilda Bryant. Several days earlier he had told Bryant that the police considered him a prime suspect in the Green River murders. Bryant was interested, but no story was broadcast. Now Foster called Bryant again. The police still thought he was the murderer, Foster said; in fact, the police were following him *right now*! And he could prove it. How? Be out in front of the station with a camera, Foster suggested.

"Give me five minutes," said Bryant, and hung up.

A few minutes later, Foster drove up and parked in front of the KIRO broadcasting offices. Bryant and a cameraman were waiting. I'm Mel Foster, he said, and these are the King County police officers who are following me. The camera panned over to the shadow detail that had pulled up not far away. Another car was further back. With her microphone, Bryant went up to the nearest man.

"Hi, I'm Hilda Bryant with KIRO News. What are you doing?"

"Nothing," said the detective. "Just driving around, that's all."

"Are you following this man?" Bryant pushed the microphone in the detective's face.

"No, no, of course not," the detective said.

"Who are you?" Bryant persisted. "Are you a King County police officer?"

"No, no."

"Are you sure you're not following this man?"

"Like I said, just driving around, that's all," said the detective. But just then his two-way radio started squawking.

Flushing, the detective opened his glove compartment and removed the embarrassing instrument. The detective was tersely ordered to move off by a hundred yards or so. He left. Foster laughed and laughed.

Three nights later both Foster and the police were featured on the nightly news. What an embarrassment, Kraske thought. He couldn't decide who he was maddest at—Foster, Hilda Bryant, or his detective, who had fallen right into it.

The next day the newspapers had the story as well. "Cabbie says he's suspect in murders," headlined *The Times*. "Man reports he's suspect in 6 deaths," said *The P-I*. The police confirmed that they had questioned Foster, but denied that he was the only suspect.

Foster was in his element. "I feel like the basic rights of a citizen have been trampled on," he said. He was going public, he said, to force the police to "lay an egg or get off the nest."

But the surveillance would continue.

Three days after Foster entered the public eye, on October 8, twenty-three-year-old Denise Darcel Bush took a phone call from her friend Jody Blair, who was spending some time in the King County Jail. Bush and Blair were both prostitutes. Denise was an epileptic who took antiseizure medicine on a regular basis. She had a large scar along the right side of her neck and a hole in her skull about the size of a nickel. But the health problems hadn't prevented her from working the streets. She had been arrested in July, and then Jody had been nabbed in early September.

Now Denise was out of jail, but Jody was in. Both girls were fans of the soap opera *All My Children*. Jody made a practice of calling Denise every day from the jail to get updated on the soap's characters.

About noon, Jody called, and Denise filled her in on the latest turns of the plot. Afterward, Denise and her pimp flipped a coin to see which one would leave their room at the Moonrise Motel at South 144th Street and Pacific Highway South to buy a pack of cigarettes at a nearby convenience store. Denise lost. She pulled on her jeans and a hooded sweatshirt, and left the room, her hair uncombed. She was never seen again.

Some time over the next few days, eighteen-year-old Shawnda Leaa Summers was watching for likely tricks near the intersection of South 146th Street and Pacific Highway South. Summers already had one arrest for prostitution as a juvenile; she had never appeared in court. Shawnda's mother and brothers were living in San Diego. She had begged her stepfather Steve Summers to be allowed to live with him in Seattle, where Shawnda had a boyfriend. Against his better judgment, Steve Summers had allowed the girl to live with him. When she was arrested for prostitution, Summers made her spend the night in jail. Later, Shawnda had left with the boyfriend, and had never returned.

By early October, Summers was an experienced hooker. She had left her boyfriend and was keeping company with another man; the old boyfriend was angry at Shawnda for deserting him. Steve Summers was mad at the old boyfriend for making Shawnda work the streets.

Then, on the night of October 9, Shawnda disappeared. It would be several weeks before any of her family members tried to report her missing, and even then they were unable to say with any certainty where she had been seen last. The Seattle Police Department refused to take any report. "She'll be back," the police told Steve Summers. "She's just gone off with her boyfriend."

But Shawnda's "boyfriend" hadn't seen her either, and in fact, Shawnda was very dead.

18

CLOSING IN

November 1982

While the surveillance of Foster continued around the clock, other detectives were busy prodding his story for holes. It appeared by early November that there *were* some serious deficiencies in Foster's explanations.

For one thing, detectives had tracked down the two young girls who stayed with Foster during the month of August. They told police that Foster had warned them about the murderer, and that he had invited both of them, at different times, to stay with him in Lacey.

Most significant of all was the statement by one of the girls that Foster had called her to discuss the murders, and that he had mentioned the names of several women who had been killed, and that one of the victims he named had been a girl named Opal.

When had Foster made those telephone calls? The detectives pressed hard for this information. The girl thought it might have been late in August. Are you sure? the detectives asked. Was it earlier than that, maybe? The point that excited Reichert and the others was the prospect that Foster had known *before anyone else* that Opal Mills had been murdered. That would be strong evidence that either Foster himself was the killer, or else knew who was.

Arrangements were made to secretly subpoena Foster's telephone records. State law permitted a prosecutor or police to obtain such private records, including credit card accounts and other bank records, merely by making a secret request to a judge designated as the county's "inquiry judge."

The star-chamber inquiry proceeding had been used in place of the usual grand jury process for some twenty years, after dozens of indictments of police and public officials had been thrown out because of improper testimony before the grand jury. The grand jury law was still on the books in Washington State, but it was never used.

Instead a policeman or prosecutor, meeting in chambers with an "inquiry judge"—so designated by the county's presiding judge—had only to make an oral or written argument in favor of the issuance of so-called "inquiry subpoenas." Often the entire process was only conducted on paper, the better to insure its secrecy. The target of the process was neither represented in any way, nor advised of the conference's outcome. The only time a record of the proceedings was presented to defendants was when they were formally charged with a crime.

Thus armed with Foster's telephone records, the detectives were able to determine that Foster had made telephone calls to the girl on three separate dates—August 13, the day after Dub Bonner's body was found near the slaughterhouse; August 15, the day the three bodies were found but before anyone but the police knew about it; and on August 24, the day after Opal Mills's identity was released to the public.

The detectives showed the girl a calendar, and after some consideration, the girl decided that she had initially been in error, and that the discussion with Foster had taken place in mid-August, after all—*before* Opal Mills's name had been disclosed to the public. That was definitely incriminating information, everyone agreed.

The detectives next decided to give the girl a polygraph test. Norm Matzke, the polygrapher, was brought in once again. After putting the girl through the test, Matzke concluded that she was telling the truth about the date and content of the conversation with Foster. The ties of circumstance were drawing ever tighter around Melvyn.

With Foster now aware of the surveillance, little effort was invested by police in concealment. Officers in unmarked cars often parked on the side of the road near Foster's home. Others followed him wherever he drove. Twice, Foster went to a nearby hospital, once to undergo knee surgery, and a second time two weeks later for a postoperative checkup. Both times detectives went into the hospital and hung around the waiting room for Foster to emerge.

And Foster claimed to others that his mail was being tampered with. Once, he said, he had hidden behind a bush near his mailbox. When the postman delivered the mail, Foster had quickly plucked it from the box, then hid again. Soon two plainclothes detectives pulled up at the box, opened it, and reached inside, he said. When they saw Foster staring at them, they jumped back in their car and roared off.

At night the detectives parked across the street from Foster's house and played their headlights through the front window, he claimed. Foster's children began receiving taunts from other students at school, and the younger son began having trouble sleeping. One night Foster came out of his house and began yelling at Detective Pat Ferguson, who had drawn the surveillance duty. Detective Larry Gross watched from some distance away from the saddle of his motorcycle. Ferguson drove off. The irate Foster got in his own car and gave chase. Gross fired up his bike and chased after Foster. And Kraske, pulling surveillance duty as well, started his car and chased after all three, down Foster's street to the freeway, then onto the freeway, heading north. Ferguson pulled off. So did Foster, then Gross, then Kraske. Pulling alongside Ferguson, Foster yelled epithets at him, then drove home, never noticing Gross or Kraske behind him.

In early November Foster sent a letter to King County Executive Revelle complaining about the surveillance, and calculating its cost at nearly $100,000. In the letter, Foster reiterated his alibis, and complained that Reichert was bent on depriving him of his civil rights. Legal action was next if the cops didn't back off, Foster threatened.

But on November 19, Kraske signed an affidavit in support of a formal search of the Foster house. Kraske's affidavit was approved by a deputy prosecuting attorney and then signed by a judge. Three days after that, five dozen policemen fell on Foster's house in Lacey and tore it apart.

19

THE SEARCH

November 22, 1982

Foster first learned of the search about 10:00 A.M. when Kraske personally knocked on his front door, accompanied by a busload of Explorer Boy Scouts and two search dogs.

"I'm Dick Kraske of the King County Police," Kraske said, introducing himself to Foster for the first time. "We'd like to search your house—", and here Foster seemed on the verge of agreeing "—but just in case you don't want to give us permission, we *do* have a warrant." Kraske handed the paper to Foster, then walked past him into the house. Foster asked Kraske if he could make a telephone call. Kraske told him to go ahead. Foster called Hilda Bryant at KIRO.

Meanwhile, the police closed Foster's street to traffic on both ends. Teams of detectives and Explorer Scouts fanned out across the two-and-one-half–acre property, tearing up the flooring in Foster's barn, collecting mud samples from around the yard, and yanking the sheets off Foster's bed. Foster was placed into a county car by Detective Bob LaMoria, and driven to Seattle. New samples of hair and blood were taken there; LaMoria explained to Foster that the first samples hadn't been good enough.

Meanwhile, another team of detectives went to the elementary school attended by Foster's sons, and attempted to gain custody of the children. The principal of the school, however, refused to release the boys without formal authorization. Frustrated, the police backed off. But when the school decided to let the boys go home early to relieve them from the taunts of their playmates, the police were waiting. They picked the boys up outside the school and quizzed them about their father. Finally a Thurston County deputy took them away and delivered them to the home of one of Foster's neighbors.

By noon, the news media had arrived in force. Television helicopters hovered overhead, carrying live feeds back to Seattle and videotaping the events for the evening news. Scores of news media trucks jammed the narrow street. Police strung up some of the yellow crime scene tape to keep everyone back. Foster's rural neighbors were agog.

In Seattle, Foster answered more questions, these about the operability of his car during the summer months, and the surgery on his knee. LaMoria brought up Foster's relationships with street kids again. This time, however, Foster refused to say anything more without an attorney present. So LaMoria put Foster into the car and took him back to Lacey.

By the time they got back, the search was over. The house was a mess—drawers dumped, swatches of carpet snipped, the bedding torn apart, closets turned upside down. The news media was still waiting, though, for Foster. Someone told him there had been a rumor that he and the Thurston County Sheriff's Department SWAT team had been in a firefight. Foster, surveying the wreckage, said it looked like there had been a battle, all right. He gave extensive interviews, blasting the King County Police and again threatening lawsuits.

Following the search, the round-the-clock surveillance on Foster was ended, to be replaced by intermittent surveillance. Now the case would go to the crime lab. If a match could be made between the hairs, fibers, soil, and other materials taken from Foster with similar materials found on the victims, Foster would get his day in court.

In the meantime, Kraske would redeploy his task force back to their regular duties. Other crimes were taking place. The Green River case and Foster would be left in the hands of just two detectives, Reichert and Fae Brooks. They would keep looking for more and better links between Foster and the victims.

In early December, two weeks after the search of the Foster home, Rebecca Marrero, eighteen, received a telephone call at her mother's apartment in a housing project in the southwestern portion of the city of Seattle. The caller wanted Marrero to go someplace. Marrero argued for awhile, then slammed down the phone. She took a bath, then got ready to go out. She asked her mother, also named Rebecca, to take care of her year-old baby. Where are you going? her mother asked. When will you be back? "Just take care of the kid," Becky said, and left. Marrero had no idea what had happened to her friend "Star," also known as "Betty Jones," but she did know that she had to go to work.

The following night Becky obtained a room at the Western Six Motel, the same place where Mary Meehan had last been seen three months earlier. Becky didn't know Mary. But that night, Becky went out on The Strip, and disappeared forever.

20

ADRIFT

December 1982/March 1983

On Pearl Harbor Day, it became official: Winckoski was out. As expected, his replacement was Vern Thomas, the former Seattle Police Department commander who had been running the dilapidated and overcrowded jail. But County Executive Randy Revelle held off making the announcement of Thomas's appointment for the time being. He wanted to gauge the reaction of the King County Police to the idea of having the controversial Thomas come in at the top.

For Winckoski, leaving was a relief. For most of the past year, he had felt estranged from Revelle. Earlier in the year, a budget crunch had threatened to cut as many as twenty jobs from his already severely underfinanced department. It wasn't that Revelle was hard to get along with, Winckoski told friends; it was just clear that Revelle wanted his own appointee in charge of the police. Revelle had asked him to stay on the job until the new man could come in. Winckoski, sixty-one, had agreed, but he knew that any initiatives to improve the police would come from his replacement, whenever he arrived.

Thomas would be under no such handicap. Revelle's plan called for Thomas to finish up his work reorganizing the jail while he was being confirmed as the new sheriff by the nine-member elected county council. Revelle expected that to take place in February, when Winckoski would officially depart.

Randy Revelle was just beginning to feel comfortable as the top elected official in the state's largest county. An intense man with a shock of dark hair atop his head, slightly overweight, with a infectious grin, and sometimes, a ferocious temper, Revelle possessed a magic name in King County politics. His father, Thomas Revelle, was a former U.S. attorney in Seattle, and had later been named a judge. The older Revelle was widely respected throughout the state for the sharpness of his legal mind, but mostly for his intense commitment to public integrity. Both father and son were liberals in the tradition of Roosevelt and Kennedy. For Randy Revelle, government was an instrument, a powerful tool that was only being used properly if it was improving people's lives.

After serving several terms on the Seattle City Council in the 1970s, Revelle in 1981 used his widespread name familiarity to run for the county's top elected position, that of King County executive. One of his predecessors in the job, former County Executive John Spellman, had been elected governor while serving in the post; therefore, some saw the job as a possible springboard to higher, statewide office.

But it had taken Revelle nearly one year into his first term to consolidate his grip over the county's bureaucracy, including the police department. That meant moving his predecessor's appointees out and his own people in. Vern Thomas was one of Revelle's people. Thomas had been there for Revelle during the battles over the city police in the 1970s, and Revelle wasn't the sort of politician to forget loyalty like that, not after Thomas had been so severely punished by his commanders for his outspokenness while siding with Revelle. Now it was time for Thomas to have his reward: command of the King County Police Department.

Thomas's earlier battles with his commanders in the city department had earned him a mixed reputation. Some saw the wiry, gray-haired, tough-talking Thomas as a hothead, quick to bristle over criticism, obstinate to the point of combativeness. Others, including Revelle, preferred to see him as the very embodiment of police integrity: After all, hadn't Thomas sacrificed five years of his career by having the courage to attack the city power structure?

Still others called Thomas a "bluenose" for his insistence on aggressively policing gambling, prostitution, and other vices that many liberals saw as "victimless crimes." But among the police he had commanded in his thirty-two years with the Seattle department, Thomas was seen as a man who was both fair while being a strict disciplinarian. After being returned to the city department's hierarchy, he was named to head the department's internal investigations unit. Thomas quickly caused a half dozen officers to be fired and scores of others to be disciplined for illegal or inappropriate behavior.

Thomas's years as a detective in homicide, robbery, narcotics, vice, and intelligence had marked his management style. He tended to methodically, inexorably gather information before drawing conclusions. Not for him were the quick intuitive leaps that so often brought on tunnel vision and wasted energy.

In his conversations with Revelle, Thomas was given three priorities: to clean out any remaining corrupt officers left over from the department's bad old days of the fifties and sixties; to reorganize the department's command structure to improve efficiency; and to take a hard look at the Green River investigation. Revelle told his aides that he had a "nagging feeling" that something had gone wrong with the investigation of the murders. Why hadn't anyone been caught? Had the killer simply left? Or was it really Melvyn Foster?

No one could say for sure, and that troubled Revelle. His government would be a government that worked for people—even prostitutes. The last time he looked, Revelle told his aides, prostitution was not a death-penalty offense.

For Kraske, the departure of Winckoski and the imminent arrival of Thomas meant his personal ambitions would now go on hold. True, Revelle and the council had approved the restructuring of the department as the management team had recommended in July, but Winckoski's leaving meant that now it would be Thomas who would choose the new chief. In fact, Thomas, when he took over, would have the right to choose all the chiefs. That meant the current chiefs and all the majors, like Kraske, would go back into the pot for Thomas to choose from.

Kraske was nearly convinced that Melvyn Foster was indeed the Green River killer. The most important evidence in support of that contention, Kraske believed, was the apparent absence of similar river murders after Foster had been identified.

Foster was the only person who knew all five of the victims. And for good measure, the search of Foster's car had turned up—glory of glories!—small beaded material that appeared to be identical to the substance found on Opal Mills's body. Some experts thought the beads were bits of reflective material found on road signs, or in reflective paint. But no one knew for sure, and arrangements were made to send the stuff back to the FBI's laboratory in Washington, D.C. All these things took so long. But even if no match was made, the force of circumstances surrounding Foster was making him look better and better. That was one reason Kraske had ordered Foster kept under intermittent surveillance. Now, if the FBI agreed that the samples of beaded material were the same, the Green River murders might well be solved.

No, The Book as rewritten by Ted said that Foster had to be the killer. Kraske felt that his investigation had worked, that it had done its job in identifying the culprit. Now all they had to do was get the evidence to charge him.

In the meantime, the largest problem faced by Reichert and Fae Brooks was the sheer mass of information that had been collected in the late summer and fall. Normally a homicide case could be contained in one three-ring binder. Rarely, if the case was exceptionally complex, as many as three binders might be used. The Green River case was already pushing fifteen binders. The information was all spread out. It was impossible for one person to be familiar with everything.

Having spent so much time shadowing Foster, too little effort had been invested in correlating the information already collected. Worse, much of the information was superficial, partly because too few of the detectives drafted by Kraske for "the biggest task force since Ted" knew what to ask. Crucial follow-up interviews had never been done. And, in December, the microcomputer that Kraske had pirated from the vice people suffered an unprotected power surge, and all the data that had been so laboriously loaded in was zapped from the machine's memory. All the department had left were the hard copies of the material.

Irritating as all those things were, Kraske was not perturbed. The main thing was to find the evidence in the pileup that could convict Foster.

In late January, after a polygraph test, lab tests, and because of a firm alibi, the last of the other priority suspects besides Melvyn Foster was cleared. That left the Lacey man as the detectives' last and best suspect. Kraske confirmed this publicly. "He's the only one we've got," he admitted.

Kraske's remarks made Foster furious. "They better have an airtight, watertight case before they jump," he warned. "I have counted 112 violations of my civil rights, and I am going to pursue this all the way."

The police were still watching him, Foster contended. Kraske wouldn't say if that were true or not. "We are in contact with him," Kraske said. "But we haven't talked to him."

But in February, the FBI reported back on the tiny glass beads. The FBI lab man had taken both bed samples to one of the laboratory's clean rooms for analysis. Then, for some reason, the expert had gone out to the parking lot. When he returned, he examined his footwear. The special clean room slippers the man had worn to the parking lot were literally covered with tiny glass beads, and the beads were identical to those found on Mills and in Foster's car. The material was so common that one could even find it in the FBI's parking lot. It was worthless as evidence.

Now, for the first time, Kraske began to have some doubts. The Book after Ted said it had to be Mel. *But what if The Book were wrong?*

21

DOUBTS

March 1983

By early March Kraske's doubts had grown even larger. Several things continued to bother Kraske. First, there was the old, worrisome specter of Lovvorn: She alone of the victims had *not* been dumped in or near the Green River. Why would the killer put Wendy Coffield in the river, Gisele on dry land, and then go back to the river? One explanation was that perhaps Lovvorn had not been killed until after the river victims had been found, despite her July 17 reported disappearance date. Maybe that meant there were other victims near the airport, too. God knew the land surrounding the airport was isolated enough and overgrown enough to hide scores of bodies. Or maybe, thought Kraske, there were two different killers, and they had erroneously assumed there was only one. Whatever the explanation, Lovvorn's differences with the river victims caused Kraske to look more skeptically at Foster.

Second, the crime lab reported again that Foster's

blood and hair did *not* match the blood and hair found with some of the victims.

In fact, nothing found at Foster's father's house—like carpet fibers or other similar microscopic evidence—in any way tied Foster to any of the crimes. And the intermittent surveillance on Foster hadn't caught the man doing anything. Kraske himself had continued participating in the surveillance, both to be sure it was airtight and also to keep up his detectives' morale. Kraske wondered if Foster might have slipped the net, somehow. Maybe he went out the back way and stole a car from time to time. Hadn't Foster done time for auto theft? But that was nothing more than speculation, Kraske knew.

Most maddening of all were the continuing reports about missing prostitutes—now Reichert and Fae Brooks had a near dozen of those, and more continued to come in. A lot of time was being spent tracking people down. Most of the time the prostitutes weren't missing at all, just working in another city. Still, there seemed to be at least five who couldn't be located. Maybe there were others as well. Some of them were last seen while Foster was under surveillance.

How could that be, Kraske asked himself, if Foster were the killer? Maybe the missing dates were off, Kraske thought. More likely, the women had just gone someplace else and hadn't told anybody yet. Perhaps they would turn up, like Lee and Milligan.

Meanwhile, Reichert and Brooks remained convinced that Foster was the killer, and they had been sifting through the lives of the latest missing women, looking for a connection to the Lacey man. Nothing had turned up. Now it appeared that the missing reports were increasing, not decreasing, and that didn't seem right. Reichert told his sergeant that the workload was increasing too quickly to be adequately handled by just two detectives. They couldn't afford to overlook any leads, Reichert argued. Any one of them might be the break that could bring the case to an end.

The sergeant shipped Reichert's complaint up the

chain, to the lieutenant, then the captain, then to Kraske. Kraske sighed. Now was not the time to ask for new positions, not with a new sheriff coming on board. He would have to borrow more manpower. Kraske dipped into his dwindling supply of goodwill inside the police bureaucracy and begged three new detectives to help Reichert and Brooks out. Pat Ferguson, Larry Gross, and Ben Colwell were transferred to the case. Kraske found another detective, Elizabeth Drouin, to assist the five with keeping track of the growing pile of information. As lead investigator, Reichert was to give the new detectives their assignments. He was the one who understood the case the best anyway.

Soon Ferguson, Colwell, and Gross were running down missing prostitutes. Reichert and Brooks had the idea that some of the missing women had disappeared because Foster had either frightened or killed them. He and Brooks continued to sift their existing information for new leads to the former cab driver.

But by March Kraske had decided it was time for another opinion. He called Bob Keppel, the Bundy man, in the attorney general's office. Would Keppel be willing to come in and look over what had been done so far? Give a critique of the investigation? Wasn't that what Keppel was always saying, that serial murder cases demanded "peer review?" Keppel agreed to look the case over.

On March 7, Keppel went to the King County police headquarters in the county courthouse and found his way to the mezzanine level of the building. There Reichert and Brooks and the four other detectives were closeted in a small office next door to the vice unit. A sign over the door read "Green River crew—members only." The walls were covered with the pictures of the six victims and maps of The Strip and the river area. Filing cabinets were jammed against the walls. Telephoned tips that had been filled out on slips of paper were stacked on the desks. Papers were everywhere in the overcrowded office. To Keppel, it looked like chaos.

Across the hall, the vice unit continued business as usual. Because it seemed that the murders were over, the "john" patrols had resumed in January. The Green River detectives were generally too busy to attend to looking over the would-be customers. But there were other problems as well. By now a low-level feud simmered between the two units, partly because Reichert, Brooks, and the others remained so secretive. The homicide detectives demanded information from the vice squad, but weren't willing to give anything back. The vice people decided Reichert and his crew were snobs. So much for cooperation and communication.

Keppel began looking through the files. The more he looked, the more discouraged he got. No one had yet bothered to organize the information in any coherent way. Facts about suspects were strewn through the victim files, and facts about victims were strewn through the suspect files. Facts that were in some files were missing in others. No one had yet created a master list of recovered evidence. There was no ready way to evaluate the investigation and to set strategy.

Keppel explained to Reichert that the material had to be reorganized. Reports should be photocopied, related paragraphs snipped out with scissors, and pasted into new files, which would then be rephotocopied and placed in new binders. To do the job right, Keppel said, the detectives needed to get control over their information. When that was done, Keppel said, he would be back.

22

THOMAS

April 1983

On April 18, Vernon Thomas was sworn in as King
County sheriff. As if to symbolize the new job, Seattle
Police Chief Patrick Fitzsimons presented Thomas
with a cowboy hat.

But Thomas was no cowpoke. While running the
jail over the past nine months he had plenty of time
to look over the county police department. He also
had some ideas on how it could be run better.

One of the first moves Thomas made was to replace
the lieutenant in charge of investigating major crimes
in Kraske's Criminal Investigations Division with a
captain. The captain Thomas picked was Michael
Nault, one of the department's whiz kids.

The shift came as news to Kraske. Thomas hadn't
consulted with him about the move. What did *that*
mean? Kraske also noticed that Thomas was in no
hurry to fill the empty chief's slot, even though it had
been approved by the county executive and the
council.

The next thing Kraske noticed was that Nault never
seemed to be available to him for consultation, and
when he was, Kraske got the feeling that Nault barely
listened to what he had to say.

Kraske hadn't been in the police department for
more than twenty years without being able to see the
signs. He was becoming a pariah in the department

just as the new administration was coming in. That meant he was being set up to take the fall, to shoulder the blame for the failure to catch the killer. Other commanders looked away from him when he passed them in the hallway. Nobody wanted to get near him, or be seen as being friendly with him.

A few nights after Thomas took over, Kraske was sure. Hilda Bryant on television was delivering a report on the murders. At the end, after using her standard question—when will the murders be solved?—she looked straight into the camera and gave the answer herself this time: "With Major Kraske in charge, who knows how long it will take?"

That was definitely a bad sign, Kraske thought. Definitely.

23

THE ASSESSMENT

April 1983/May 1983

More than a month later, on April 25, Keppel returned to the detectives' office and began to read the newly reorganized files. Several problems with the investigation were immediately obvious. The more he read, the more appalled he became. This investigation wasn't just stuck, he thought, it was mired to its wheelwells.

After reading, making notes, and thinking for three weeks, Keppel delivered a thirty-three page report on his findings to Kraske, Nault, and Thomas on May 18. With every page stamped "CONFIDENTIAL," Keppel's report was as devastating as it was prophetic. It remained secret until 1989, when it was released with deletions.

Keppel picked apart the investigators' work on each case, victim by victim. Were follow-up reports taken on this witness statement, or that one? When did so-and-so live with Bonner? Had she ever met any of the suspects? Why hadn't investigators interviewed Chapman's children? Had anyone checked Chapman's bank accounts to see when she last withdrew money? Had she paid the rent? Had Hinds ever been driven down to the river by [deleted]? What about [deleted's] statements about killing people? Why had [deleted] said this? How had [deleted] said he killed people? How many times? When? What were the circumstances of the conversation? What was he talking about? Did Mills have any of her favorite clothes missing? What did she wear most of the time? When Opal called home on the same day Bonner's body was found, who was she with? Did she give any hint as to where she was going? How was Lovvorn dressed when she left? Did she leave on foot, or was she picked up? Had she written about her tricks and all her contacts with people? Where were Lovvorn's belongings now? Had Lovvorn's remains been examined for trace evidence and compared with Mills's? If not, why not? Keppel's questions ballooned as the investigation done so far was torn apart.

The Keppel report fell on the department's top command like a collapsed building. Kraske had known the investigation needed reorganization, even more manpower, but this? If Thomas needed any encouragement to give Nault a free hand to run the investigation, this should certainly do it. Keppel's report made it look like Kraske was running a floating crap game, not an investigation.

Still, if Keppel's plan were implemented the way Keppel recommended, it might take every single cop in the entire department, Kraske realized. And the cost! What did Keppel think the county should do, start printing its own money? What about all the other things the county police had to do, like burglaries and drugs and family fights, all the usual stuff? Would all that go on the back burner while Keppel's manhunt unfolded? How would that go over with the voters?

Kraske could see it now: "Officer, I called you people two hours ago, and I'm still waiting for someone to show up. What's the deal? Don't I pay taxes? It's all those cops you have working on those hooker murders, isn't it? Big deal. When am *I* going to get some service?"

Most painful of all were Keppel's attacks on the quality of the investigation done so far. All those questions, those unfollowed leads. Maybe Keppel was just rubbing salt in old wounds, trying to make himself look good. Kraske knew there were problems, but making the sort of turnaround Keppel had in mind was going to take some time, never mind a political commitment of the county's top politicians.

Kraske asked Reichert to provide a written response to Keppel's gloomy assessment.

Reichert reviewed Keppel's report. He was both angry and embarrassed. He had helped reorganize the material the way Keppel wanted it, and *this* was the result? Besides, Keppel had consistently overlooked work that *had* been done. Some of Keppel's statements about the lack of follow-up were just plain wrong. Reichert's frustration boiled over.

What did they expect from him, anyhow? He was just one man, and every day new information had to be checked out. It was all he could do to keep up, and every time he asked the department's muckety-mucks for more help, he was told the budget couldn't support it. Now to have Keppel's report criticize them for the things that hadn't been done was almost too much. Reichert hurled his pencil across the room.

24

OUT OF CONTROL

April 1983/July 1983

On the night of April 17, seventeen-year-old Sandra Kay Gabbert went to the Seven-Eleven store near South 144th Street, the same place Denise Bush had gone to on the day of her disappearance back in early October of 1982. Sandy—sometimes she liked to call herself Sand-e—was known to her family as Smurf. She was a cute, personable girl who had become involved with a pimp and drug dealer. Her mother, Nancy McIntyre, knew that Sandy worked as a prostitute.

"I said, 'Sand-e, you could get yourself killed doing this,' " McIntyre said later in an interview with *The San Francisco Chronicle*. "She said, 'Oh mom, I'm not going to get killed.' " It was no use trying to talk Sandy off the streets. It was the money, Sandy told her mother. "She could turn one trick, take half and hour and make as much as she made when she worked for two weeks. Now you try to show someone the logic of getting a legitimate job," Nancy McIntyre told *Chronicle* reporter Susan Sward.

Shortly before she disappeared, Sandy and her mother had gone to a Mexican restaurant together, McIntyre told Sward. After dinner they returned to McIntyre's house.

"I put my arms around her," Nancy said. "I said, 'I love you, baby, please be careful.' She said, 'I love you too. I am careful.' I watched her walk down the front steps, and I knew I wasn't going to see her for a long, long time."

On April 17, just the day before Vern Thomas was to be sworn in as sheriff, Sandy picked up a trick near the Seven-Eleven around 8:00 PM. and vanished.

And on the same night, perhaps an hour later, seventeen-year-old Kimi Kai Pitsor was walking in downtown Seattle with her pimp when she caught the eye of a pockmarked man driving a green pickup truck with a camper on the back and a primer spot on the passenger door. Pitsor motioned to the man to drive around the corner at Fourth Avenue and Blanchard Street, and then went after him. The last her pimp saw of Kimi Kai, she was climbing into the truck of the pockmarked man in a nearby parking lot, and then the man was driving away.

Meanwhile, Reichert and Fae Brooks plodded on. The task sometimes seemed overwhelming. The main thing was the new disappearances. The cases had first been assigned to Earl Tripp, but now Larry Gross, Ben Colwell, and Pat Ferguson were working to find the missing. Most of the women were quickly located after a lot of tedious checking. But some remained missing. The detectives kept thinking those still missing were somehow connected to Melvyn Foster. But how? Foster had gone on television again; this time he had taken a polygraph examination arranged by KIRO's Hilda Bryant. He passed.

And relations between the Green River contingent and the vice squad were still headed downhill. Conversations were distant and cool. No plans were laid to coordinate activities between the two units. The people who knew the prostitution scene best were being kept on the sidelines.

Meanwhile, Thomas had begun his own review of the case. "I'm an old homicide man," Thomas said, and he wanted to see if Revelle's nagging fears had any basis.

*   *   *

Two weeks after the disappearances of Sandy and Kimi Kai, but before either had been reported missing to police, eighteen-year-old Marie Malvar and her boyfriend, Bobby Woods, were working Pacific Highway South near the Three Bears Motel at South 216th Street. About 10:00 P.M. on April 30, a man in a dark-colored pickup truck with a primer spot on the door swung into a nearby parking lot and gestured for Marie to get in. Marie opened the door and got in. The truck pulled back onto the highway and started heading north. Bobby followed in his own car. As he pulled alongside, Bobby said later, it looked to him as if Marie and the man in the truck were arguing about something.

Some distance up the highway, the man in the truck pulled into another motel parking lot. Bobby turned off the highway and made a U-turn on South 208th Street. He let the car idle as he watched the man and Marie in the truck across the highway. Suddenly, the man put the truck in gear and pulled back out onto the highway and started heading south. Bobby pulled out after him. The man started going faster. Soon the two vehicles were speeding south, back toward South 216th Street, with Bobby trailing. At the left-turn pocket the man in the truck slowed down and caught the arrow light. Bobby jammed on his breaks for the red. The truck with Marie went up the hill of South 216th Street and disappeared. Bobby never saw Marie again.

On May 3, Bobby reported Marie missing to the Des Moines, Washington, Police Department, but didn't tell the officer who took the report what he and Marie had been up to when she had disappeared. A detective there was assigned to investigate. The suburban detective, Bob Fox, believed that Bobby Woods had something to do with Marie's disappearance, and in a way, of course, he was right.

Several days after Marie had vanished, Bobby was visited by Marie's father, Joe, and Joe's son, James, Marie's older brother. Joe had been born in the Philippines. A war veteran, he had come to Seattle to work at Boeing. The years in Seattle had been good to Joe, and he and his wife had prospered. The family owned both a restaurant and a small grocery store in Renton. But now Joe was mad at Bobby Woods.

Get in the truck, Joe told Bobby. Bobby did. Together the three men drove to the area near South 216th Street where Bobby had lost sight of the dark truck. They drove around for hours in the neighborhoods off South 216th Street. Sometime in the afternoon, they turned into a small cul-de-sac a short distance south of South 216th Street. In the driveway of one of the houses Bobby saw a dark-colored truck with a primer spot. That's it, he said. That's the truck.

Joe pulled over the side of the street and parked. Together the three men watched the house for awhile. Two men appeared to be inside. Finally Joe told James to go to a house on the street, borrow a telephone, and call the police.

Because the cul-de-sac was just over the Kent city limit into the city of Des Moines, the call was routed to the Des Moines department. Soon Bob Fox drove up with another cop. The two officers went up to the house and knocked on the door. They did not go in, and after some discussion at the front door, both lawmen left. Fox came up to Joe Malvar, still sitting in his truck. There's no woman in that house, Fox told him. Joe nodded. To him, it figured. Bobby Woods was a liar, anyway, Joe thought. He hated Bobby Woods.

Just after the first week of May, a family hunting for mushrooms in a wooded area off Southeast 244th Street near Maple Valley, a rural area many miles east of The Strip, discovered the body of a fully dressed human figure lying about thirty feet off a dirt road. There was a brown paper grocery sack pulled down over the head. At first the family thought that the figure was a store mannequin. But when the man in the family carefully extended a stick to the sack and pushed it back, everyone saw that the body was that of a dead woman. A fish had been placed across the woman's throat, and another over the left breast. Some freshly ground raw meat lay on top of the left hand. Both hands were crossed over the abdomen. A large green wine bottle lay between the woman's legs, with the neck under the right hand. The family called the police.

The differences between this corpse and the Green River victims found the previous year seemed obvious to the police who responded. For one thing, this victim was fully dressed, right down to the shoes and socks. And the food items: While weird, they seemed to be full-blown examples of the staging Douglas and Keppel were always talking about. The presence of staging in the Green River cases was far more debatable. Finally, investigators searching the woman's clothing found a Washington State driver's license in the right breast pocket of the victim's nylon parka. Since when had the Green River killer bothered to leave his victim's name and address behind?

A closer look at the neck showed that the woman had been strangled by a narrow cord of some sort, possibly a piece of clothesline or narrow rope.

The following day at the autopsy, the examiners noticed that the woman's bra had been put on inside out. That, along with the fact that the woman's shoes had been untied, led credence to a theory that the woman had been redressed after death by her killer. The final stages of rigidity from rigor mortis were still present, an indication that the murder had taken place sometime within a day or so prior to the discovery. But faint "washer woman" wrinkles in the hands and the soles of the feet seemed to suggest that the body might have been immersed for a short time. Faint doubts began to creep in. If the victim had been in water, could this case be connected to the Green River cases after all?

At least figuring out who the woman had been wouldn't be difficult. The driver's license identified her as Carol Ann Christensen. She had lived at an address three blocks off The Strip. The grocery sack was from a food store located next to the Seven-Eleven at South 144th Street, in the heart of the Green River killing ground.

As the weather warmed, the number of women working The Strip increased dramatically. By late May 1983, small knots of women gathered at intersections up and down the highway to gesture at the drivers of passing cars and trucks. The vice squad tried to do what it could, but it was like trying to bail a rowboat with a thimble. There were just not enough cops and way too many prostitutes.

All the previous year's publicity about the murders had died away to a whisper. Many women believed that the killer had either left the area or had been identified as Foster. Patrol cops, kept in ignorance of the true facts by the secrecy of the investigation, inadvertently added to that impression by telling women that it looked as if the killer had moved on.

But he had not, and this was to be, in retrospect, the county department's darkest hour. Between the discovery of Carol Christensen's body and the end of the month, at least three more women would die, and it would be more than a year before anyone but their killer knew it.

The next to vanish was Martina Authorlee, an eighteen-year-old who was working the intersection around the Red Lion. Sometime in the afternoon or evening of May 22, 1983, Authorlee picked up her last trick.

The following day, Cheryl Wims, also eighteen and living in Seattle's Rainier Valley, went out to work the streets and never returned. And then on the last day of May, another eighteen-year-old, Yvonne Shelly Antosh, a heavyset, auburn-haired woman, left the motel room she shared with a friend and her pimp near South 142nd Street and was never seen again. None of the three women was reported missing to the police.

One other event *was* reported to police, but because of the confusion of jurisdictions and lack of cooperation between the multitude of police agencies responsible for The Strip, nothing was done. As things later turned out, the failure to act may have cost the police another excellent chance to identify and catch the Green River killer.

About midnight on May 27, on the "B" concourse of the Sea-Tac Airport, a custodian was running his vacuum cleaner over the short-weaved, sturdy carpet of Gate B4. As he pushed aside some of the plastic chairs arrayed around the waiting area, the custodian found a driver's license in the name of Marie Malvar. He picked up the license and put it on his cleaning cart. At his break about an hour later, the custodian took the license to the lost-and-found office operated by the Port of Seattle Police. An officer there took the license and typed the name into the department's computer terminal, which was linked to the state's criminal information computer system. The computer coughed up the information that Marie Malvar was a missing person, whose case was under investigation by the Des Moines Police Department, where the case was being investigated by Detective Bob Fox.

The following morning, another Port officer called the Des Moines Police, and notified them of the recovery of the license. The Des Moines department noted the information in their files. But no one ever bothered to drive up to the airport and collect the driver's license. It remained in the Port of Seattle property room until October of 1983. Then it was routinely destroyed—along with any fingerprints it might have contained. The prospect that the license may have been dropped at the airport by the killer was never considered, at least that year. It would not be until 1985 that someone finally looked into the possibility that the killer may have been at the gate the night the custodian found the license. But by then, all of the flight records had been destroyed.

On the afternoon of June 8, a twenty-year-old woman named Constance Elizabeth Naon, who worked at a sausage factory in Seattle, got off work in the early afternoon and drove to the Red Lion Hotel. She parked her car in the parking lot, went inside the hotel, possibly to the bar on the top floor, and made a phone call. Connie told her boyfriend that she would arrive at the house they shared just off The Strip in about twenty minutes. She never showed up. Five days later, after checking with Connie's friends, family, and at the sausage factory without results, Connie's boyfriend called the police to report her missing.

The day after Naon vanished, sixteen-year-old Tammy Liles picked up a trick near the Pike Place Market in downtown Seattle. She also disappeared. No one reported her missing.

And still later in June, Keli Kay McGinness, eighteen, left her room at the Three Bears Motel to work the intersection near The Strip and South 216th Street. When McGinness didn't come back that night or the next day, her pimp called the police. The case was assigned to Detective Bob Fox of the Des Moines department.

Meanwhile, Reichert was still smarting over some of the things Keppel had written in his review. One of the loose ends was Mike Tindal, Gisele Lovvorn's cab-driving boyfriend. Keppel had suggested that detectives obtain Lovvorn's reported "trick book" for the names of her customers. No one had ever bothered to do that, so Reichert, Brooks, and several other officers went to see Tindal on a Sunday morning in June.

Tindal later said he was made aware of the police presence when he was awakened just after 6:00 A.M. by someone knocking on the front door of his apartment on South 208th Street—the same complex that Connie Naon's mother lived in, and where Kase Lee had last been seen by her husband Anthony Lee some ten months before.

"I'm wearing my robe and that's all I'm wearing," Tindal later said. "I answer the door, my door is kicked in the minute I unlock it. I'm knocked into my closet. Reichert walks in with a uniformed police officer who looks like Godzilla.

"So they come in there, Heidi [Tindal's new girlfriend] is still in bed, she sits up, Fae [Brooks] walks back there, starts talking to her, Reichert gives me this story that if I don't cooperate and let them search my apartment I'm going to jail, period. For suspicion of murder.

"I said, 'I've got nothing to hide, go ahead. If your searching the apartment keeps me from going to jail, fine.' He says, either you give us permission to search right now or you're going to jail and we're getting a warrant. I'm standing there in my robe six o'clock on a Sunday morning. What else am I going to do?" Tindal said the police then locked him in the back of a county police patrol car.

Five hours later, according to Tindal, the police brought him back inside.

"My house had been torn apart, from the carpet to the pillows to the furniture, taken apart. Every single book I owned had been gone through, the whole bit. They had a big pile of stuff they were taking. They did not have a warrant. I used to be with the Los Angeles County Sheriff's Department Law Enforcement Explorer program years ago. I had a bunch of memorandums, paperwork, all kinds of memorabilia and stuff from that when I was there. They took all that. They took my scrapbook with all my photographs of Gisele, our love letters, they took her journals, they took the poetry she wrote and I had and everything. They took concert ticket stubs, everything that was in this scrapbook. Even including some of the articles about some of the killings going on with the Green River case.

"They took all my *Playboys*, they took all my *Penthouses*, they took some of the photographs I had of some other girlfriends I'd had before I'd met Gisele. Some of them were nude. This one cop's sitting there looking at this picture of this girl. He says, 'What's this chick's name? I know this chick.' I say, 'Buddy, if you lived in Los Angeles maybe four or five years ago, maybe you know her.' He says, 'This is a fifteen-year-old girl, what are you doing with her nude photograph? Her name is Angela, she's fifteen years old.' I say 'Her name is Angela Cartwright,' thinking of this chick who played Penny on *Lost in Space*. The cop says, 'Yeah, I know her.' Right, dummy. Making a fool of himself. They took all this stuff.''

The police began asking Tindal more questions about Gisele. Soon the conversation turned to Heidi.

"They're talking about pressing charges against me if not for murder, at least for immoral practices and stuff with Heidi and all this stuff. She's like sixteen. Reichert sits there and talks to me. He gives me this church lecture about what a bad dude I am, and about how I'm corrupting her morals and on and on and on. Why do I do the things I do, and I'm sitting there apologizing up and down and the whole bit. I'm thinking I'm going to jail. I'm going to be dragged to jail in my robe. This is very intimidating.''

But in the end, Reichert and Brooks let Tindal go. Heidi was placed in a foster home. Tindal later heard that Reichert began taking her to church. And June turned into July.

176   Carlton Smith & Tomas Guillen

25

HELL'S HIGHWAY

July 1983/September 1983

Nowhere was the need for coordination and communication spotlighted by Keppel's blistering report so acute as on The Strip. By the end of June 1983, prostitution on the highway had once again reached enormous proportions. Yet the uniformed officers assigned to routine patrol in this potential abduction zone remained woefully ignorant of what to be watchful *for*. Many cops, in fact, had come to believe that the murders were over. When asked for information by the prostitutes, some cops still told the women that the killer had left the area. Others talked about "that taxi driver" as if he had already been convicted, thus ending the danger.

The county's vice squad, meanwhile, was still trying to hold back the tide. Cooperation between the vice detectives and the murder investigators was now at an all-time low. Often the vice officers sat drinking coffee in the enclosed A & W stand near South 146th Street and the highway, watching the women they were supposed to arrest wave down passing motorists, get in the cars and pickup trucks, and drive off. Yet few of the officers bothered to write down the license plates of the vehicles. Certainly none of the information was relayed to the detectives working on the murders.

And when vice did make arrests, the women were rarely interviewed about the murders. What were they supposed to ask, anyway? Reichert and his crew were shut up in their secret headquarters, sharing nothing. The vice people felt ignored, discounted. If Reichert and his people were so hot, let *them* go out and find the hookers, the vice cops told one another.

It wasn't as if the vice squad had little else to do, anyway. Literally hundreds of women were out working on The Strip. At some intersections on the highway, women actually came over to idling cars and sat on the hoods while the drivers waited for the lights to change. At other intersections, the women gathered on each of the four corners, shouting at drivers and pursing their lips suggestively. In motel parking lots, pimps and drug dealers lounged against parked cars, openly trading drugs and cash. Two motels near South 146th Street blatantly advertised hourly rates and x-rated, closed-circuit movies, and did a brisk business.

But the cops, the prostitutes, and their johns and pimps weren't the only people cruising the highway in the summer of 1983. By that point, Tom and Carol Estes had learned of their daughter's friendship with Rebecca Marrero. Contacting Rebecca's mother, the Esteses learned that Becky was missing too. That seemed very significant to the Esteses. Still, county police kept insisting they had no indication that Debbie Estes had ever been involved in prostitution, despite the link to Marrero. As before, they merely took a runaway report on Debbie and filed it. As for Becky, she had disappeared inside the city limits, so that was a city problem. The county police kept implying to Mrs. Marrero that they had enough to do without doing the city's work too.

Frustrated, the Esteses and Mrs. Marrero decided to take matters into their own hands. Every chance they got, Tom and Carol drove over to the housing project where Mrs. Marrero lived and picked her up. Then the three parents would drive downtown, or to The Strip, looking for their daughters. They saw hundreds of young girls, but no Debbie and no Becky. Carol cried frequently, alternating between inconsolable grief at the disappearance of Debbie and the guilt she felt for her inability to handle her child, and rage at the indifference of the police. Tom felt helpless. Mrs. Marrero kept hoping that Becky had been captured and was being held in a basement somewhere by some pervert, and that somehow, Becky would miraculously escape. The alternative was too grim.

Meanwhile, Joe Malvar hadn't yet gotten over his anger at Bobby Woods. At night he would drink and think about killing him. But that wouldn't bring his daughter back, he knew. So, unknown to the Esteses and Mrs. Marrero, he and his wife were also driving The Strip in search of Marie. Every time they spotted a short, dark-haired woman, their hopes soared. But always it turned out to be someone else.

Finally, unbeknownst to the Esteses, Mrs. Marrero, and Joe Malvar, Jodi Summers, Shawnda's mother, was also searching. She came up from San Diego to look for her daughter. But Shawnda had also vanished. No one seemed to know anything about her, or even care.

By early July, Thomas was under tremendous pressure from the owners of legitimate businesses along The Strip, and from the nearby residents, to do something about the flagrant prostitution. Community leaders pressed the commander of the area precinct, who simply pitched the problem back downtown. Little could be done to stop the activity, said Major Ray Jenne, unless he were given more resources to stop the activity. Soon the complaints were being directed toward the politicians, and the county councilman who represented the area began howling for action. Revelle himself forwarded numerous complaints about the prostitutes to Thomas.

Surrounded on all sides, the sheriff asked for a report, along with some proposed alternatives, from the vice squad's Don Christianson. One idea: Rent a billboard along The Strip and publicize the names of the men arrested for soliciting prostitutes. That idea had worked in Portland, Oregon, Christianson advised.

*   *   *

As the afternoons lengthened and the weather warmed up, Gina Serrett liked to put her baby in a stroller and walk from her house just east of The Strip on South 150th Street to her parents' house about three miles away on the other side of the airport. Gina had grown up and gone to school in the airport area. But the area had changed so much that Gina was often disgusted with what she saw on her walks. As she walked she carried a stout length of wood for protection. Gina called the club her pervert stick.

Pushing her baby stroller through the prostitution zone nearby, Gina often had to pick her way around used condoms, drug needles, beer bottles, and other trash left behind by all the nightly goings-on. The old corner grocery store now had an entire backroom given over to hardcore pornography. And the prostitutes were so brazen Gina had seen a prostitute giving a man oral sex right in broad daylight in a Pacific Highway bus shelter; sometimes they even solicited Gina! "Wanna have a good time?" they asked. It gave Gina the creeps. Men cruising The Strip honked and waved at her, even with the baby in the stroller. On her walks to her parents' house, Gina usually walked down South 146th Street, a hub of the prostitution activity. Gina knew South 146th Street by its local name: "Raper's Road," for its lonely stretches. Kids who had grown up in the area liked to scare each other with stories about rapists who lurked there after dark. After South 146th rose over the slight bump of the ridge, it then ran downhill toward a timbered flat area cut by a small muddy stream called Des Moines Creek. A Little League baseball field had been laid out on the flat area.

With all the houses now removed, Raper's Road was scarier than ever. At the corner of 16th Avenue South and South 146th Street, Gina always turned right and headed north to get to a dirt track that bisected the timbered part of the flat area. It was a telephone company easement, and a telephone company shack was back in the woods. Gina would push the stroller through the woods and come out on Des

Moines Way South, then head back to South 146th Street and her parents' house. The whole neighborhood was like an old friend to Gina, even with the changes. Occasionally as she walked down the dirt track near the telephone shack, Gina would see a beat-up, older, two-toned tan and green van parked near the trees, but had never seen its driver. Once she had looked into the van and had seen an infant's car seat, but that was all.

Late in July or early in August, Gina put the baby in the stroller, walked down "Raper's Road," and turned into the dirt track. As she approached the shack, she smelled a horrible odor in the trees to her left.

"We came around the corner," Gina said later, "and right at the intersection there was just this godawful smell. Just something I've never, ever smelled before, which made me sick to my—I mean I had to hold my breath." Gina pushed the stroller away from the smell as fast as she could. When she got to her parents' house she told her father about the stink. Usually Gina's father, Francis, gave her and the baby a ride home. This time Gina asked her father to stop and see if he could smell what she had smelled earlier. Francis stopped the car and sniffed. He turned to look at Gina. He was pale. "Gina," he said, "when you get home you call the sheriff. This isn't a good smell."

Two hours later a King County policeman came to Gina's house. Gina told him about the smell. Gina offered to take the officer to the place. They went to the dirt track, and the officer smelled it too. He called it in. "This is not an everyday smell," the officer told Gina, and took her home. The patrol officer called other police and asked them to meet him in the area of the smell. Then he left.

Three hours later, the police dispatcher called Gina. The source of the odor had been found, the dispatcher said. Someone had dumped a pile of rotting fish in the woods. But Gina's father had been a fisherman in Alaska, and had once seen the dead bodies of two fishermen who had washed up on a beach after drowning. "They're wrong," he told Gina. But neither he nor Gina wanted to look any closer. After three weeks, the smell went away, and Gina's family liked to tease her about the time she had called the police about the rotting fish.

Still later that summer, however, kids playing at the Little League field noticed a terrible odor emanating from the center field area. Some kids told their parents they didn't like going out to play in the outfield because of the smell. And even the adults noticed the odor when they went out to raise the flag just before the games began. This time, no one bothered to call the police.

Shortly after the Fourth of July, Thomas called Lieutenant Daniel Nolan into his office. A lifelong resident of Seattle, the trimly built Nolan was an excitable, spontaneously enthusiastic cop who inspired intense loyalty from his men. Thomas wanted Nolan to take the prostitution problem on as a special project with one objective: Get the women out. Nolan said he would as long as Thomas backed him up when the heat came on. Thomas agreed.

Beginning in the middle of the month and extending into the middle of August, Nolan's special patrol squad "lit up The Strip," as he put it later, following pimp's cars, rousting prostitutes to ask for their identification, citing women for failing to walk facing the traffic, pulling drug dealers over and writing tickets for defective equipment (often created by a casual billyclub tap to the taillight), stationing patrol units with red lights flashing in the motel parking lots, anything to get the women and their support structures on the move.

Arrests for prostitution in June had totaled only twenty-three, all of them women. By the end of July, just as Nolan's Raiders were getting cranked up, the month's total of vice arrests increased to thirty-five. August brought thirty-six more, and September, a whopping sixty-two. By the end of September, as

Nolan's force went back to their regular duties, The Strip had been virtually cleared of prostitution.

But that didn't mean the activity had stopped. Driving the women off The Strip may have been good politics, but it did nothing meaningful about the problem. Instead, the women simply moved into downtown Seattle, to the city's heavily minority Rainier Valley. Perhaps worse, from the point of view of the murder investigation, putting the women on the move made it even more difficult to track down crucial witnesses.

At the same time, the stampede into new strolling territory destroyed the women's feeble existing safety network, which was primarily based on exchange of information between prostitutes. New locations meant new johns, new working associates, new, untested places to "date," and new dangers. Additionally, efforts by investigators to use the potential victims as reliable sources to investigate the crimes was greatly disrupted by the crackdown, which added considerably to the prostitutes' already deep distrust of the police.

Thus, because of political pressure brought to bear on Thomas and Revelle, the prostitutes became the city's problem. Inevitably, the killer followed the women into the city, although it would be years before anyone knew that.

The county did try to warn the city, however. On July 15, the one-year anniversary of the discovery of Wendy Coffield's body in the Green River, Kraske held a press conference to summarize the progress on the investigation. The bad news, said Kraske, was that the number of victims involved in the murders may have been twice as many as previously feared. And the killer was probably still at work, he said.

It now appeared, he said, that as many as seven other women were permanently missing, and possibly dead. Kraske listed them: Kase Ann Lee, Terri Rene Milligan, Mary Bridget Meehan, and Denise Darcel Bush, all missing since the summer and fall of 1982; and Marie Malvar, Constance Naon, and Keli K.

McGinness, missing since the spring and early summer of 1983. Malvar and McGinness had been reported missing to the suburban Des Moines Police Department, and the detective involved in those cases, Bob Fox, had decided to turn those two cases over to the county. All but Denise Bush and Mary Meehan appeared to have had experience in street prostitution, Kraske said, then unaware that Bush had been arrested for prostitution on the same day the previous summer that Bonner had last been seen.

Hadn't police said last fall that Milligan and Lee had been found? "Our information was wrong," said Kraske. "They are still missing." Now there were these new names as well. Kraske didn't explain why police hadn't announced the disappearance of the last five far sooner; he didn't want to explain, again, how difficult it was to know when people like this were really and truly missing. But fortunately, none of the reporters pressed him on the question.

In addition to the known dead and the missings, said Kraske, police were still trying to decide whether the May murder of Carol Christensen and the June murder of an unidentified woman in Federal Way were connected. If they were, Kraske said, the Green River killer could be responsible for up to fifteen murders. The murders were in danger of transcending tragedy and turning into a mere statistic.

"We've put thousands of man-hours into this," said Kraske. "It's frustrating. We have no solid leads on any single suspect. We've looked at more than two hundred people, and we know of at least one hundred more who might be responsible. The manner in which the victims were killed, the locations in which the bodies were found, and the backgrounds of the women have led us to believe all of the killings are related."

His detectives now had little doubt, he said, that the murders were the work of a single person, perhaps someone whose name had come up early in the investigation but had been overlooked. There was a need to cross-check information on a continuing basis, Kraske said, and that was taking time.

"One of the main problems we've had has been the difficulty in finding acquaintances and street people who might have known what the women were doing just before they were killed. We've also had problems relying on the credibility of the people we have been able to find."

What about the crime lab? Kraske was asked. Any help there? "We've put about seven hundred and twenty different items of evidence into the crime lab for analysis," Kraske said, avoiding the politically sore subject of the lab's slow progress in examining the materials, and including every single item that the crime lab had found among the seventy or so articles submitted by the police. "That includes body hair, soil samples, all kinds of things. They are still being examined." Any links so far? "I'd rather not say."

What about the pimp war theory? Kraske shook his head. "That's never had any credibility as far as a theory goes," he said. "Besides, it's usually the pimp that gets killed and not those who are making the money."

What was Kraske's advice to the women who were still working on The Strip? "We've said it before, and we'll say it again: Don't get into cars with people you don't know. All signs point to a psychopathic personality who is preying on single women. All the prostitution out on the highway has given the killer a virtually unlimited supply of potential victims. These girls are just walking to their fate."

Hilda Bryant wanted to ask a question. *Here it comes*, thought Kraske. "Can you give us any indication of when the case might be solved?" Bryant wanted to know.

"As I've said before, Hilda, these cases can't be solved overnight. This isn't much different from any other serial homicide case I've read about. And if you check, you'll see that most serial homicide cases take from three to five years to solve. And while we're frustrated that a single suspect hasn't been identified and charged, we're aware that it's going to take some time. Maybe even years."

*   *   *

Late in the afternoon of August 11, almost a year to the day after Dub Bonner's body was found near the slaughterhouse on the Green River, a man picking apples discovered a human skeleton under a pile of leaves and brush in a field north of the airport, near 18th Avenue South and South 146th Street—Gina Serrett's "Raper's Road." The bones were broken and fragmented. A small gold chain was found nearby. Police were initially confused about the jurisdiction. Was the field in King County or Port of Seattle territory? The property lines in the area were confusing. A surveyor had to be called in to make the determination: the county.

The following day, county investigators combed through the loose debris in search of more bone fragments, loose teeth, fingers, toes, and the like. Hours later, investigators had assembled enough of the skeleton to enable the medical examiner's office to make a stab at identifying the body. From the angle of the pelvic girdle, the skeleton appeared to be that of a woman. Too little was left of the skull to guess at the victim's race.

Kraske briefed the news media on the discovery. "We have seven still missing in the Green River case," he said, "five of them related to prostitution. As far as we're concerned, there is a strong possibility that one of them could be connected here."

But comparison of the recovered teeth the next day failed to match any of the dental charts of the missing persons already linked to the case. The case would go down as an unidentified, fifteen-to twenty-year-old woman for the time being.

Meanwhile, Melvyn Foster was still mad. Late in August he fired off a letter to Revelle, complaining once more about Reichert and the county police.

"I had hoped further contact with your office would not be necessary," Foster wrote Revelle, "but I find I have no alternative to this epistle."

Leave it to Foster to use the word epistle for letter.

Searching through the dictionary to find different words for common subjects was a Foster specialty.

Foster went on to complain that Reichert and other county police had stolen his mail, tapped his telephone, and harassed his sick sister. Foster warned that if anyone from the county ever contacted his sister again, or if his sister ever suffered from any ill effects from further police contact, he would sue.

Then Foster claimed that Reichert had personally participated in illegal wiretaps on his father's home telephone. He could prove it, Foster wrote, because Reichert had mentioned a trip being planned by Foster's father while interviewing Foster's sister.

"The only possible way he could have known of that trip being planned by my dad would be through a telephone wiretap of the telephone line to this residence," Foster wrote. "The only time I ever mentioned it was by telephone to Barbara Kubik-Patten, whose devout Catholicism rules out betrayal of conversation contents of that general nature."

For some time, Foster had been meeting with the Kent psychic/private detective to compare notes on the case. Now, suddenly, the relationship between Melvyn and Barbara had assumed the sanctity of the priest's confessional! That's how Foster avoided the conclusion that Barbara had been relating their conversations to the police.

Foster complained again about the polygraph test the police had given him.

"At six different points the King County polygraph taken on me on September 20, 1982, was invalid," Foster complained. "It contained multiple issues, as opposed to one; it was devoid of control questions in a 'search question' phase written by Detective Reichert, as opposed to containing control questions written by Examiner Matzke. I had passed the basic half of the exam and should have been cleared, but was not." Foster had obviously been talking to experts on lie detector tests.

"Any fair and unbiased polygraph examiner," wrote Foster, would have long since invalidated the King

County test. Then Foster launched into a long description of the lie detector test he had taken and passed for KIRO in late May, and concluded that Kraske and Reichert were out to get him, despite the absence of any links of either his blood or hair to any of the crime scenes:

"If I were black I would have been cleared of suspicion," Foster complained. "But I am white and Indian, and Detective Reichert and Major Kraske refuse to clear me.

"This tells me that even had I passed the entire King County polygraph instead of just the basic (culpability) half I did pass, Detective Reichert and Major Kraske would not have cleared me. Detective Reichert had made up his mind before that polygraph was even arranged that he would not be swayed in his theory about me no matter what evidence and tests established.

"We have a serious personality conflict between us that precludes his being objective on the case. With reference to myself, he and Major Kraske continue to exercise a presumption of guilt with the burden of proof of innocence on me, in total contravention of American justice . . .

"The King County Police have, upon me, committed slander, defamation of character, malicious harassment, invasion of privacy through repeated wiretaps, mail theft, unlawful removal from home, coercion into cooperation on hair samples and self-incrimination on taking care of runaways. I have seen my rights violated 132 separate times . . .

"Detective Reichert has made it a practice to drive to Olympia frequently to drive back and forth in front of my residence and harass my dad, my two sons and myself, block the driveway till my dad or I comes outside, then pull away, only to return in a few minutes. He has done this most recently four times in the past three weeks. It only ceases when either my dad or myself run him back to the Lacey on-ramp to I-5 northbound. Detective Reichert's actions have, aside from being devoid of legitimate purpose, inflicted an on-going stress situation that has finally gone too far."

A week before, wrote Foster, his father had suffered a minor stroke. Melvyn held Reichert personally responsible.

"If Detective Reichert is not stopped in his tracks, and my dad has a second stroke, incapacitating my dad, I cannot promise anything better than what my brother-in-law will do about my sister having a second heart attack. I'm sorry, I simply cannot. I cannot even promise to not visit Detective Reichert's house.

"Last night Reichert was down here again, harassing me, for over two hours, in his usual manner, and left only when, with him blocking my driveway, on the property line, I came outside with a baseball bat and told him to move and find something else to do or I'd crack his block."

Revelle immediately passed Foster's letter on to Thomas. A week later Thomas wrote back to Revelle.

The Criminal Investigations Division and the Green River Task Force have conducted an in-depth review of all information contained in Mr. Foster's correspondence. The allegations are untrue with regard to harassment and improper conduct on the part of Major Kraske and Detectives Brooks and Reichert. While we could refute each and every element of Mr. Foster's correspondence, I do not feel it would be productive to do so. This latest letter is but one of many received over the past year from Mr. Foster, falsely alleging improper conduct by members of this Department and personal harassment. Let me repeat again these allegation are without foundation and I would strongly recommend that no reply be provided to Mr. Foster since it would give him another forum to appeal to the media and thus complicate our investigation.

Revelle accepted Thomas's advice. No reply was sent to Foster. But the police took note of Foster's implied threat to find Reichert's house. Beginning with the first day of school in early September, a carload of King County police officers would follow Reichert's children as they rode the bus to school for the immediate future—or at least until Foster was disposed of, one way or another.

Meanwhile, Reichert began pressing for a search of the wooded areas around the airport. The pileup of missing persons reports involving prostitutes convinced Reichert that something was seriously wrong.

Two weeks after Foster's letter, a man searching for a lost chicken near 54th Avenue South and Star Lake Road—about eight miles south of the center of prostitution on The Strip, but only a mile away from where the bodies had been found in the Green River the previous summer—stumbled over another skeleton.

The Star Lake Road area was about a half mile east of the southern extension of Pacific Highway South; it was neatly bisected by Military Road South. Despite its proximity to the heavily traveled highway and the busy I-5 corridor, the area shared many of the characteristics of rural King County. Large expanses of open fields were separated by tall stands of fir trees. North of the isolated, two-lane Star Lake Road was a deserted, steep-sided canyon choked with brush and trees; on the south side, a small creek turned into a bog that flowed sluggishly eastward toward the Green River.

Expensive custom houses, mixed with older stucco ramblers, dotted the area. But farther away from the habitation, farther down the lonely road, trash, wrecked cars, abandoned toilet fixtures, broken lath and plaster, beer cans, faded newspapers, soggy old magazines, and ordinary household garbage were piled up after years of illegal dumping.

The latest skeleton, another female, was found face down in the woods along the north side of the road. Police called in a team of Police Explorers, Boy Scouts sponsored by the department, to pick through the nearby brush in an expanded search, but little was found that appeared to have any bearing on the murder. The bones and surrounding soil were collected and taken down to the medical examiner's office for closer inspection. Once again the recovered teeth did not match any of the known missing persons. A police spokesman refused to say whether the newest skeleton was related to the Green River crimes. It was too soon to know, he said.

26

BONES

October 1983/November 1983

On October 15, another partial skeleton was found, this one far to the east of the Green River, the airport, or Star Lake Road. The latest site was over the side of a steep embankment, near a creek at 140th Avenue Southeast and Auburn-Black Diamond Road—about twenty miles from The Strip, even farther by road. Another female, it appeared that Keppel's prediction that the killer would travel further and further away to find new dumping grounds was coming true.

By the middle of the month, Kraske, Nault, and others were engaged in intense discussions about the murders with Thomas. Keppel's earlier report, coupled with the discoveries of the newest skeletons, seemed to clearly require some action by the police. But on the other hand, there were the costs to figure. Even if a massive investigation such as that proposed by Keppel were somehow put in place, how long could the county afford to do it? And what if it failed? Wouldn't it be better to hope the murderer had left? Or, better yet, conclude that the murderer was Melvyn Foster, and that all these new skeletons were Foster's victims *before* he had been exposed?

As far as the police knew, nearly all of the victims so far—the five in the river, Gisele Lovvorn south of the airport, and the unidentified skeleton north of the airport—were all killed before Foster had been placed under surveillance, which meant that Foster *could* have committed those crimes. But what about the other two skeletons, the one at Star Lake and the latest one, the one found near Auburn-Black Diamond Road? Maybe they weren't related to the Green River murders, went the thinking. Maybe other people were responsible for those deaths.

Maybe, in fact, the county was just having a run of murders of prostitutes. There had been so many women out on The Strip, it only stood to reason that the number killed would increase.

On October 26, the skeleton found by the apple picker north of the airport near Gina Serrett's old "Raper's Road" was identified. Shawnda Leea Summers, who had gone missing in October of 1982 amidst police indifference, had finally been found. Police confirmed Summers's background as a prostitute, but said it was too soon to list her as a possible victim of the Green River murderer.

The following day the medical examiner's office identified the newest skeleton as well, the one found far to the east on Auburn-Black Diamond Road. The skeleton was that of Yvonne Antosh, the Canadian girl who had last been seen on The Strip at the end of May at the Ben-Carol Motel. This time, the police did have a missing persons report—one filed by Antosh's motel roommate, a childhood friend, in August.

The same evening the Antosh remains were identified, a nineteen-year-old girl and her boyfriend were looking for apples in some vacant lots south of the airport. The girl saw a small snake on a rock and ran over to catch it. Instead she tripped over a loose rock and fell, kicking up the dirt and leaves. Standing up, she noticed a leg bone and a pelvis, apparently disturbed by her fall. She looked closer and saw what appeared to be the top half of a human skull embedded in the dirt at her feet.

Because the lot belonged to the Port of Seattle, that agency was called in, and the lot was sealed off for a thorough search that would begin in better light the following day.

Shortly after 8:00 A.M., the Port police brought in a team of Explorer Boy Scouts to help with the search. Most police agencies sponsored a troop of scouts, most of them teenagers who acted as a sort of auxiliary for the police, directing traffic and handling crowd control at large events. Now the Scouts spread out across the lot, looking for anything that might resemble clothing or jewelry, while the medical examiner's experts carefully exhumed the newest remains. This one, investigators realized, had been buried. Moreover, whoever had buried this victim had carefully bordered the grave with piled rocks, outlining the grave site. As the experts picked through the dirt for the bones, one of them discovered a triangular shaped rock near the skeleton's mid-section. Had it been inserted, as in the cases of Marcia Chapman and Cynthia Hinds? Or was it just a coincidence?

About fifty yards away from the skeleton, a Scout stumbled on a second set of bones. *This* skeleton had been casually thrown into the heavy underbrush, and covered with tin cans and other debris. The foliage had overgrown it months before. The discovery meant that the bodies of three people had been dumped on Port of Seattle property in a little more than a year, all in the deserted clear zones either north or south of the runways. And there was the skeleton of Summers, who was so close to Port property a surveyor had to be called in to determine the legal jurisdiction.

While the second skeleton was being inspected by the medical examiner's pathologist and investigators, the Port of Seattle police chief knew he faced some important decisions. Homicide cases were a rarity in the Port's jurisdiction. The county had taken over the Lovvorn case, and had linked it to the Green River murders. The Summers case had also been connected. The odds were very high that these two newest skeletons were likewise connected. The county would have to be involved in the investigation, the Port chief decided.

But the larger problem was the vast expanse of empty ground surrounding the airport. All of those condemned houses, all of those overgrown lots, those deserted streets. Who knew how many other skeletons might be out there? The port had over two thousand acres of potential dumping grounds to search. And if the killer were burying some of the bodies, who was to say there weren't others similarly concealed?

The following Monday, the Port Police announced that a massive search of all airport property would be conducted. They said the search was expected to take weeks. The Explorer Scouts would help. Search dogs would be called in.

Meanwhile, Nault confirmed that the county department would investigate the latest airport skeletons in cooperation with the Port of Seattle, but reserved judgment on whether the latest two skeletons might be connected to the Green River cases.

Nault was still bothered by the difference between the water dumping, found in the Green River cases; the dry land discoveries of Lovvorn, Summers, and Antosh; and the three skeletons that still remained unidentified. To him it seemed like there was more than one killer at work—perhaps a copycat.

"The prospect of more than one suspect is being considered," Nault told the newspaper. "It wouldn't be logical to say there is one suspect." That was Nault's way of saying that Melvyn Foster could not logically be the killer of all the women.

But while police were planning the big search, others were equally busy.

One of these was Kim Nelson, a twenty-year-old

prostitute who had been raised in Michigan. She and her new friend, Paige Miley, decided to go out a little early looking for tricks. They left the Ben-Carol Motel at South 142nd Street and the highway just before 11:00 A.M., and sat down on a nearby bus bench to wait for some likely customers.

Paige, four months pregnant, got one almost immediately. She left Nelson on the bench, ironically only two blocks from the place where an old friend of Nelson's from her Michigan days, Denise Bush, had disappeared a little more than a year before.

Nelson had only known Miley for a short time. She had met her in San Francisco, where Nelson's pimp had met an old friend who turned out to be Miley's pimp. Miley, eighteen, and her pimp were already veterans of the prostitution scene in Las Vegas and San Francisco. During the summer, the four had moved north to the Seattle area. Nelson and Miley had already been arrested several times. Miley had used her own name, but Nelson had identification showing that her name was Tina Tomson, twenty-six years old.

One night in September, while Nelson worked The Strip near the Western Six Motel, she picked up a trick driving an old tan Ford. As the man stopped the car in a darkened parking lot, he pulled a piece of black iron rod about three feet long from under the seat and told her he was going to kill her, "just like I killed the rest of them. You bitches are all alike, nigger lovers." As the man whacked Nelson on the arms and legs, she reached for the door handles to get out. There weren't any. Nelson managed to roll down the window instead and pulled herself through while the man continued to hit her. She fell onto the pavement, then scrambled to her feet as the man started the car and sped off. Nelson tried to read the license plate but it was covered with mud.

Early in October Nelson had been arrested by the city police and jailed under the name Tina Tomson. This time she drew a twenty-day sentence. She decided that her experience with the man with the steel rod might be worth something, maybe an earlier release.

She sent a message to the detectives that she had information about the Green River killer. Detective Larry Gross went to see her. After hearing her story, Gross asked her to describe the man. Nelson said the man looked like Melvyn Foster.

Of course, by then Foster's photograph had appeared in the newspapers and on television so frequently that all the prostitutes had come to believe that Foster *was* the killer. Gross told Nelson that if she ever saw the man in the tan car again to try to get the license plate. Nelson agreed. She told Gross that the killer had already killed her friend Bush, and she wanted to get even. "I'm going to catch that prick," she told Gross. The promise failed to move Gross, and Nelson remained in jail until October 30.

Now, on November 1, 1983, Nelson was back on The Strip. Her heroin habit was demanding. The bus bench was a good spot to wait for a trick. Several cars and pickup trucks drove by before one stopped to pick her up. Nelson got in, and the man drove off. Fifteen minutes later, Miley returned to find Nelson gone. She never saw her again.

Several nights later, a man in a pickup truck saw Miley at a nearby convenience store. The man, an automotive painter at a nearby truck manufacturing plant, asked Miley where her "tall, blonde friend" was. Miley said she didn't know. But the incident stuck in her memory. How had this man noticed that she was with Nelson, when the two had been together on the bus bench for so short a period of time? The man made her feel uneasy. Two days later, the pimps cleaned out the motel room and disappeared, taking Miley with them. No one told the police about Miley's encounter until several years later. By that time the truck painter would be transformed into a major suspect in the investigation.

On November 3, Nault decided it was time for more assistance from the FBI. While the bureau had been helping Reichert with the case almost since the beginning, now there was new information. Nault still felt uncomfortable about the differences between the river victims and the bodies found on dry land, and the apparent exculpability of Melvyn Foster. Douglas's first profile had been based on the river bodies. Would it change because of the dry land people? Or was it possible that the new victims were the crimes of some entirely *different* person?

Throughout the fall, *that* had been the central question, with investigators and police officials split into different camps. Reichert, for example, continued to insist that Foster remained the best suspect for the river victims. But it just didn't seem possible that Foster could have killed all these other people as well.

Still, here were the bones. To Reichert, that meant a possibility there were two separate killers. The police had begun investigating one serial murder case, and in the course of that had stumbled on another one entirely. It was like one of those Russian dolls: Here was one murder series, and just as detectives were beginning to understand it, presto—another murder case was hidden inside the first.

Reichert discussed the case over and over again with Nault, and with the Port police. He discussed it with two psychologists brought into the case by the department on a consulting basis. He discussed it with Keppel. And finally, Reichert talked it over with the FBI's Douglas. Douglas and Keppel were the experts, and they believed that only one murderer was responsible for all the victims. The killer was simply finding new places to dump his victims, said Keppel, after all the publicity about the river, just as he had predicted last May.

The murders had to be connected, Keppel believed. What were the odds that two different killers would coincidentally dump their victims so close together? Probably astronomical. The same pattern could be seen operating at the river. And there were the similarities—like the rocks, for example, found with the river victims and with one of the latest discoveries, or the use of the socks with Lovvorn, reminiscent of the pants in Opal Mills and Wendy Coffield the previous summer.

But there were differences as well. Where the river killer had seemed to want to conceal his victims, the dry land killer seemed to take far greater pains to conceal them, like burying this latest one. And where did the still-unidentified Star Lake skeleton and Yvonne Antosh fit in? What about Carol Christensen, with the wine bottle and fish? For that matter, what about Leann Wilcox, Joan Conner, Virginia Kay Taylor, and Theresa Klein, all of those old Seattle Police Department cases that seemed so similar but had not been included on the list? Klein, it had turned out, was Wilcox's cousin. What did *that* mean, if anything? Nault assembled a list of all the victims and the missing people, including one found on a sandbar of a river in Pierce County to the south, and telegrammed it to FBI headquarters, and asked for a team of experts to come to Seattle.

Several days later, the FBI agreed to send Douglas and two other agents to Seattle to look over the situation. Douglas's schedule was crowded, Nault was told, but he would arrange to come to Seattle on November 28.

Meanwhile, the medical examiner's office had hired several forensic dentists to look over the remains unearthed south of the airport. Six days after the discovery, the partially buried skeleton was identified as the remains of Connie Naon. The bones were discovered just four blocks away from the Red Lion Hotel, where Naon had last been seen. The second skeleton, the one found by the Scout, matched none of the dental records so far accumulated by the medical examiner's office. The experts determined that it had definitely been a female, young, and probably white. But that was as far as anyone could go.

Ten days after Nault's November 3 telegram to the FBI, the Port's search produced more results. In another vacant lot just to the south of where the latest skeletons had been found, a trained search dog began acting strangely. The dog wasn't pointing at anything specific, but when its handler tried to induce the animal to leave the area, the dog whined and growled. The handler called in the supervising police, who began to carefully dig while a soft rain fell. Overhead, hidden in the dripping clouds, the booming shriek of landing aircraft created a palpable vibration. Less than a foot beneath the surface, the diggers found yet another decomposing skeleton.

27

THE MONSTER

November 14, 1983

The latest skeleton broke apart when it was removed from its shallow resting place. As with Naon, Antosh, Lovvorn, Summers, and the still-identified remains found at Star Lake, the grave was covered with cut branches. The medical examiner's office carefully placed the bones and the rotting flesh that still remained into.separate packages. A port officer with a video camera recorded the entire exhumation. The pathologist at the scene first removed the skull and jaw, and sent them immediately to the medical examiner's office so identification efforts could begin. Several fibers were recovered from a patch of skin that remained on the skull.

The following day, the pathologists conducted the autopsy, observed by a port detective and a technician from the state crime lab. A paper sack contained hair found with the body, and a third bag contained material removed from around the feet. A fourth package contained the remainder of the torso, arms, and legs, placed on a sheet when removed from the grave.

"The torso is caked with wet dirt," the pathologist dictated. "Some of this has fallen away from the left side revealing the left arm to be lying along the left side of the body. Also noted at this time there is a fairly large amount of black hair around the pubic region. Fibers are recovered by the crime lab at this point. The soil is removed from the body and sieved."

The pathologist probed further into the torso as the others watched. "For the most part, the internal organs are reduced to a homogenous, foul-smelling mass," he indicated. "Examination of this reveals recognizable fragments of heart, probably right ventricle, a somewhat more solid mass which probably represents liver, right kidney, diaphragm, and portions of the lower gastrointestinal tract." The pathologist stopped talking for a moment and looked closer. "My God," he said, and pointed to something inside the torso.

"In addition," he continued after a moment, "in the right lower quadrant of the abdomen there are multiple fetal bone fragments. This appears to constitute a complete fetal skeleton."

The victim had been pregnant—very pregnant. Whoever had killed this woman was so devoid of human compassion and decency that he had taken the life of a woman about to give birth. No one present said anything, at least for the record. But the thought kept returning as the autopsy proceeded: What kind of a monster were they dealing with?

At the end, the pathologists removed the remains from the sheet. The remaining mud and debris was sifted carefully for any other evidence. Nine different items were recovered, including three small bones, two halves of a yellow pencil, two halves of a clear plastic tube, and two small pieces of plastic, one about a half inch square with "15" printed on one side. What the hell was this? No one could say.

Later that day, a forensic dentist examining the teeth

left in the skull and jaw made a positive identification: The pregnant woman had been Mary Bridget Meehan, the eighteen-year-old woman who had gone out for a stroll September 15, 1982, and had never returned.

28

"FEAR IS TORMENT"

November 15, 1983

The following day, Nault held another news conference. Three more young women were missing, he told the reporters, bringing the total of missings to seven, and the total of known dead to eleven and possibly twelve, if one counted the still-unidentified skeleton that had been found near Star Lake.

The killer was still active, said Nault. It was clear that the police were dealing with a serial murderer, but beyond that, detectives had little to help them focus their investigation. "It's a person obviously bent on killing prostitutes in King County," Nault said, stating the obvious.

The new missings, Nault continued, were Sandra K. Gabbert, seventeen, who had last been seen in April; Tina Tomson, twenty-six, thought missing since October 31; and a third woman, twenty-two, missing since August.

His detectives, said Nault, were in constant contact with the Federal Bureau of Investigation. "I would not say we're close to making an arrest," he said, in answer to KIRO's Hilda Bryant.

Later the same day police announced that the third

woman heard that she was missing, and called the police to let them know she was all right. She was taken off the list.

The following day, Seattle police gave their county counterparts a list of six other missing women. Two of the six names involved women with records for prostitution: Mary Sue Bello, twenty-five, last seen October 11 in Seattle as she was headed out to The Strip, and Debbie May Abernathy, twenty-six, last seen in downtown Seattle.

Four other women on the city's list had no known links to prostitution, police said. They included Amina Agisheff, a thirty-six-year-old mother of two who had disappeared in downtown Seattle July 7, 1982; Maureen Feeney, nineteen, who had been hitchhiking to a job interview in Seattle; Cheryl Lee Wims, eighteen, reported missing the previous May; and another eighteen-year-old woman who later told police she was alive and well.

The county police thanked the city police for their assistance, but declined for the time being to put any of the six on the Green River list.

Meanwhile, the search of the Port property near the airport continued.

The Monday before Thanksgiving, an organized protest against prostitution was held on The Strip. About two dozen area residents picketed one of the two motels favored by prostitutes and their pimps, carrying signs that read "Fear Is Torment," "Money Is Not Everything," and "Who Is Next?" The news media gave full coverage to the protest.

"These girls have been dying," said Allen Cooter, a cemetary worker who helped organize the protest, "and our elected officials have not responded to these girls dying. This prostitution is caused by the businesses and pimps which allow them to flourish. We just want them out."

"The prostitutes have been treading this turf for five years, ever since the city started cracking down and moving them out," added Jeannette Baldwin, a local school board member. "We feel these motels cater to prostitution and help make our neighborhood a center for the kind of crimes and other behavior that surround prostitution. We've had a lot of discussion about prostitutes and the manner in which they are so flagrant about their lifestyle. We want to keep our clean community."

Another woman said her sixteen-year-old daughter attended high school in the area and had often been harassed by pimps and prostitutes. "When it's not even safe for your daughter, it's time to do something," the woman said.

Cooter talked about the killer. "Whoever is killing these women is a wacko, a crazy. That's our biggest fear—that sooner or later he's going to start coming after those of us who live around here."

The day after the demonstration, the county police changed their minds and decided to include Mary Bello and Debbie Abernathy on the Green River missing list after all. Both women, police said, had been arrested for prostitution, and had been known to frequent Pacific Highway South.

Meanwhile, Nault called Reichert and asked him to check into a report from the mother of a schoolboy, who had reported that in July he had smelled a foul odor coming from the vacant lot next to the Seattle Christian School. The school was located near South 194th Street and 28th Avenue South—two short blocks away from the same vicinity where the three latest skeletons had been found. Reichert and Ferguson arranged to meet the boy at the school, and asked him to show them where the bad smell had come from. The boy showed them. Reichert and Ferguson searched for signs of another grave but found nothing. But by this point, police had decided to check out all the bad smell stories. With so many dead and so many missing, no one could afford to be complacent anymore.

29

THE SELLING

October 1983/December 1983

Throughout the fall, as the new skeletons kept being discovered and as the debate over what to do about them raged within his department, Sheriff Vern Thomas was trying to make up his mind. What was he going to do about all these *murders?*

Thomas had reviewed Bob Keppel's May report several times. It would be nice to do it the way Keppel had suggested, but where was he going to find the resources? He couldn't gut his department to work on just one case. As an interim measure while he tried to figure out what to do, the sheriff had ordered Lieutenant Nolan's emphasis patrol to move the prostitutes and their pimps off The Strip, at least partially in the hope that it might disrupt the killer's pattern, if indeed the killer was still active.

But jumping on the case the way Keppel had recommended couldn't be done overnight. Important political obstacles had to be overcome. The Green River case wasn't like Bundy, where the victims had been young, clean-cut, fresh-looking college coeds. Thomas had to face facts. These Green River victims were throwaway kids; they didn't have a constituency of university parents lobbying for *them.*

Despite all his years with the Seattle Police Department, Thomas knew he was still an unknown quantity with the county bureaucracy and its political structure.

He couldn't simply tell the county's political leadership, "Here's what we've got to do, now give me the money to do it." There had to be some preparation first. He needed to be able to say how much it was going to cost, where the personnel would come from, how it would be organized, who was going to be in charge, and, most of all, why it was important to do it. He needed to get Revelle's backing, and he needed to help the county executive by lobbying for the plan with the county council, which had to find the money to pay for it, then help the council members defend it to the public, meaning the voters.

Throughout September and October, and into November, Thomas had repeated meetings with his command staff, searching for ways to get a grip on the case, which was turning into a major public relations problem for the department. To bring things into more concrete terms, he asked Nault to develop a plan for an expanded investigation. Nault took Keppel's ideas and scaled them back somewhat. He wanted a team of detectives to investigate the background of the victims, another team to process the suspects, and most important, an undercover arm to put The Strip under surveillance.

For the latter, Nault asked Thomas to authorize the use of up to a dozen plainclothes cops. That meant stripping those resources from two of the department's three precincts. Use of these plainclothes officers— the department's so-called "proactive" squads—almost certainly meant that petty crime would go up in those precincts. The bet was that the intensified effort would bag the killer before crime rates in the precincts got out of hand.

Thomas carefully reviewed Nault's proposal and accepted most of it. But where Nault asked for a dozen plainclothes officers, Thomas instead wanted to use *two* dozen—virtually the entire proactive force of the department. Thomas wanted to catch the killer in the worst way. "I had plans for the department when I came in," he said later, "and just as I took over, here was this enormous problem. I couldn't do any of

the things I wanted until that situation was resolved."
To get "that situation" taken care of quickly, Thomas
intended to play his political cards with County Executive Revelle.

In October, Thomas circulated a proposal to Revelle, proposing that a vast new effort to find the killer
be undertaken. Revelle questioned Thomas closely.
Could the job be done? What would happen if routine
crime in the precincts escalated to intolerable levels?
What if it took far longer than Thomas thought it
would? But Thomas was adamant; it *has* to be done,
Randy, Thomas told his old ally. And truthfully, Revelle was inclined to agree. What was government for
if it wasn't to protect people? Thomas and Revelle
made a bargain: Revelle would back Thomas with the
county council, and if problems developed in the precincts, Revelle would go to the council and ask them
to approve the hiring of more police officers, whatever
the cost. But Thomas had to promise Revelle: If it
ever appeared to the sheriff that the killer could not
be caught, Thomas had to be prepared to reassign the
resources to more productive tasks. Second, Thomas
had to help Revelle sell the program to the members
of the county council, who held the power of the budget. Revelle didn't want to be out there on his own
when the skeptics started taking potshots. Thomas
agreed.

Over the last few weeks of October and into mid-November, Thomas met repeatedly with the county's
politicians, pressing his case: The Green River murders, he said again and again, were a major problem,
something that needed to be addressed before things
got even worse. There was a possibility of more victims, he said, because the killer was probably still at
work.

Some members of the county council were sympathetic; others were more skeptical. Weren't there only
a half-dozen murders or so? some asked. Was there
any reason to panic here? Besides, what was the likelihood that the police *could* solve the crimes? Wasn't it
true that if a murder wasn't solved within the first

seventy-two hours, the odds against its solution went way up? Wasn't this nothing more than a quixotic attempt to do the undoable? Thomas argued his points in his intense, rapid-fire way, saying that to do nothing would be irresponsibile, that the case *could* be solved if sufficient effort were made, that no one could say for sure that the killer wouldn't begin branching out to, say, *school children*. Thomas brought up Bundy and pointed out that had the county police devoted the resources he was talking about to those murders, Bundy might well have been caught before going on to commit new murders in Utah, Colorado, and Florida.

He had confidence in his officers, Thomas said. *They* believed the case could be solved, and that it wouldn't even take very long if only enough man-power were devoted to the problem. And besides, said Thomas, think of the benefits to the community's rep-utation *after* the killer was caught. King County, unlike so many other places, would have first resolved to do something about a seemingly intractable prob-lem, and then would have done it. People all over the country would know that King County was a place where things *got done*.

After the glow of Thomas's salesmanship wore off, some politicians later felt they had been oversold by Thomas, that the sheriff, in his eagerness to convince them to support his program, promised an outcome that couldn't realistically be expected. And, truthfully, when disappointments in the investigation subsequently occurred, some of those politicians were quick to leap off the bandwagon Thomas had set in motion, saying they had expressed doubts about the wisdom of the attempt all along.

But at the time Thomas was given an assist by the murderer himself, or at least, by the discoveries of the three latest victims found on the vacant Port property. Grudgingly, the skeptics admitted that perhaps Thomas was right, that something *ought* to be done. By the end of November, just as Douglas and the FBI were about to arrive, Thomas had approval for the massive new investigation he wanted.

30

ONE BLACK SHOE

December 1983

On November 29, John Douglas and two associates from the FBI's Behavioral Sciences Laboratory arrived in Seattle. Douglas was very tired. He had been traveling the country constantly for the better part of a year.

Douglas had spent a considerable amount of time in Atlanta for the trial of Wayne Williams. That had been troublesome, mostly because the FBI felt it had only matched Williams, through forensic evidence such as fibers, to twelve of the city's twenty-six child murders. Atlanta authorities had nevertheless insisted that Williams was responsible for *all* the crimes, but Douglas privately believed that political officials in the southern city wanted to clear the books on all the crimes, regardless of the evidence.

After Atlanta, Douglas developed a psychological assessment of the man suspected of shooting civil rights leader Vernon Jordan. When Douglas came into the case, authorities already had the name of Joseph Paul Franklin, who had been a suspect in the shooting of two interracial couples who were jogging or walking together. No one knew where Franklin was. Douglas's assessment predicted that Franklin would go to Mobile, Alabama. That's where Franklin went. He was ultimately acquitted of shooting Jordan, however.

After Jordan, Douglas went to England to work on

the Yorkshire Ripper case, which involved a truck driver who had killed more than a dozen prostitutes; then to Germany; then back to Connecticut for a look at a case involving someone with a penchant for burning synagogues. After Connecticut, Douglas went to California to assist authorities there in searching for the Trailside Killer, a man murdering hikers in the San Francisco Bay area. Then Douglas went to Alaska for an assessment of a baker charged with killing sixteen topless dancers and prostitutes.

The pressure was intense. Douglas knew that all these investigations were depending on him, and that if he were wrong, it might create a disaster as detectives fruitlessly chased imaginary leads.

As the trip to Seattle neared, Douglas began to experience strange forebodings. At one conference in New York, before an auditorium filled with NYPD officials, Douglas was struck with a strange fear.

"I just had a premonition that something was going to happen to me," he said later. "I was going to be getting sick. There's about 350 police officers in this auditorium, and as I'm talking to that group I'm also thinking about where I'm going to be going next. And my next stop is going to be Seattle. And I'm thinking: 'My God, I'm bouncing all over the country.' I'm giving them instruction but my brain is thinking about Seattle. I start getting, like, an anxiety attack, a free-floating anxiety . . . No one in the audience noticed anything because this lasted about a minute. I'm saying to myself: 'Hey, regroup. Regroup yourself,' and then I was able to regroup. I just felt I was getting run down. I was just . . . so much pressure. Not only the Green River case, but cases all over the country. And I didn't have the support system in those days. I didn't have the ten people [now working with him]. And I was doing between 100 and 150 cases a year myself. When you do 150 cases this year, next year people still call you up on those cases, and it just builds, it snowballs."

Returning from New York, Douglas went to the FBI's personnel office at Quantico on the morning of

November 28 and took out an insurance policy to protect his income in case he got sick, and another $200,000 in life insurance, in case he died. The insurance would go into effect on December 1.

Then Douglas left work early to pack for the trip to Seattle. He stopped by the school where his wife, Pam, was a teacher, and told her about the extra insurance. "Why are you telling me about your life insurance?" Pam asked. Douglas couldn't say for sure. "It was weird," Pam Douglas said later. But she recognized her husband was wearing himself very thin. He kept getting headaches and felt like he was coming down with the flu. "Don't go to Seattle," she said.

"I have to," Douglas said.

The next day Douglas caught a plane for the coast.

That night Douglas checked into the Hyatt Regency hotel in downtown Seattle and went to his room to unpack. He was scheduled to give a presentation to the county police the following day. Unpacking, Douglas noticed that he had only one black shoe. Where was the lost shoe? Suddenly it seemed vitally important to Douglas to find his other shoe. He was going to talk to the police in the morning, and here he had only *one black shoe!* Douglas tore out of the hotel in a rush, pounding the downtown pavements frantically in search of a shoe store that was still open. Just before 9:00 P.M. he found one, bought a pair of black shoes, and, exhausted, returned to his hotel.

The following morning Douglas met with Nault, Nickle, Kraske, Thomas, Dr. Reay, and Reichert and the other detectives, including a team from the Port of Seattle. Also present were a pair of Seattle psychologists who had been helping the investigators. Nault and the others briefed Douglas on the new discoveries. Photographs were passed around, and the evidence possibilities were discussed. Would Douglas provide a new profile? It wasn't necessary, Douglas said, his head still pounding. The psychology of the killer wouldn't change very much. What was different was the increasing sophistication of the killer.

Were all of these crimes the work of the same man? Douglas shrugged. Probably, he said. But there just wasn't enough evidence from the skeletal remains to make that determination with certainty. Douglas could sense his audience sagging a bit. *That was the problem with these profiles*, he thought. It was as if the profiles had some sort of magic invested in them, when it didn't really matter too much whether there was one killer or a dozen. The fact remained that one or more persons similar to the profile was killing women, and what would apply to one would likely apply to all.

The problem was to get the police to take some concerted action to destabilize the killer, or killers, Douglas told his audience. Whatever actions were taken would apply to anyone preying upon the same group of victims, in this case prostitutes and street people. Then the police could answer the question of whether there was more than one killer. The profile was good only for categorizing all suspects into degrees of likelihood, nothing more.

Rather than sitting back and waiting for another victim, Douglas said, police should begin more "proactive" efforts to actually catch the killer, or somehow draw him into the net. He suggested that the police convene a community meeting to discuss the murders. The killer might actually attend the meeting, Douglas suggested. A sign-up sheet should be passed around, and someone else should note all the license plates of those who attend. And now that there were picketers against prostitution, police should keep an eye on them as well.

The police should use the news media more, Douglas suggested further. Have one of the investigators profiled by a newspaper or television station, and use the opportunity to promote the investigator as a "super cop" or as a relentless pursuer, in hopes that the killer might contact the police directly. The police might consider putting out some information about the crimes, suggesting broadly that there were witnesses to an abduction, and asking the public to contact police if *they* had seen anything as well. Sometimes, Douglas said, that ploy induced a killer to call the police with a cover story.

Douglas also discussed interview techniques that might be used if a likely suspect turned up. Interviewers might give a suspect the opportunity to talk about the crimes in the third person, or sympathetically suggest that the suspect might be suffering from the effects of a multiple personality disorder: 'I know there is a good Bill and a bad Bill,' the investigator might say. 'I know the good Bill wouldn't do this, but I think the bad Bill did. What do you think?' Or, priority suspects being interviewed might be placed in a room equipped with psychological stressors: candid photographs of the victims or of the suspect taken while under surveillance, or articles associated with the crimes, such as ligatures, weapons, rocks, and other similar triggers.

The suspect will want to be impressed by the interviewer's intelligence, Douglas advised. It was therefore very important that the interviewer *not* be younger than the suspect. A father-type investigator might induce the suspect to cooperate more.

More discussion of the killer's likely psychology followed. Douglas said he believed the killer felt locked into some sort of contest with the police, and would continue trying to challenge the detectives by committing new crimes. Douglas conjectured that the killer was continuing to have interactions with prostitutes, and that he may have preached to them without killing them. It was important for the police to be able to reach out to the prostitutes and encourage their cooperation. Douglas said he still believed the killer's rage was being triggered by prostitutes who rejected his preaching or who laughed at him. "He's a very angry person," said Douglas. "He enjoys the power he has over his victim, and all the publicity that he's getting."

Afterward, Douglas helped the detectives draw up a list of criteria for handling suspects generated by telephone tips. Most important among them were questions about the suspect's religious feelings, his interest in the murders, his attitude toward the police, and whether he had ever been to any of the places where victims were found.

After the meeting, the profilers were given directions on how to get to the victim dumping sites. The agents spent the rest of the day looking at the scenes.

That night, Douglas felt terrible. He went back to his hotel room and fell into bed. He slept all night. In the morning he felt worse than ever. A fever was raging, and the headaches were agony. Douglas told his two colleagues from Quantico that he wouldn't be able to see the police that day.

"I have to get over this," he said. "I probably won't even go tomorrow." The other two agents said they'd cover the meeting for Douglas instead. Douglas locked his door and went back to bed. That evening he woke up and tried to get out of bed. He could barely stand. The fever was killing him. He realized he needed help. He started for the telephone, but collapsed to the floor, unconscious.

The next morning, December 1, Douglas's two fellow agents went directly to the county courthouse to resume the discussions with the King County police. John was still sick, they said, and needed to stay in bed that day. The discussions lasted all day. No one checked on Douglas.

The main thing the police had to do, the agents told the detectives, was keep the psychological pressure on the killer. The change in the dumping grounds from the river to dry land was almost certainly due to the publicity, the agents said; after viewing the sites, the agents still thought that police were dealing with one killer, not several. The agents predicted that the missing victims would probably be found clustered together in a third area, not too far from the locations that had already been discovered.

The Meehan discovery was probably the detectives' best bet for increasing stress on the killer, the agents suggested. After all, Meehan had been buried deeper than any other victim, showing that the killer had obviously spent some time at the place. The agents suggested that the killer may have regretted killing Meehan because of her pregnancy, and that sympathy for the unborn child had perhaps prompted the decision to bury her. In turn, that showed that the killer could be made to react emotionally to intense public discussion of Meehan's murder, and that perhaps the killer might visit Meehan's grave, or send flowers to Meehan's parents, or engage in some similar act to bring attention to himself.

The agents said it appeared that the killer was likely to see himself as on a mission: saving women from the life of prostitution and the streets. Any suspect interviewed, the agents suggested, should be given ample opportunity to expound on his feelings about both prostitution and his mission. The police should give the suspect every reason to believe that the forces of law and order completely understood why he had done what he had done.

The following day, as the agents were getting ready to leave, they realized that neither one of them had seen Douglas since the morning of the day before. They telephoned his room. There was no answer. The two men went to the room and knocked on the door. There was no response. They went back downstairs and got a key from the manager, returned to Douglas's room, and unlocked the door. Douglas had closed the latch. Through the opening in the doorway the two agents saw Douglas on the floor, mumbling. It looked as if Douglas were trying to crawl across the floor toward the telephone.

The agents broke down the door and rushed over to the comatose Douglas. Quickly they called for an ambulance. Medical technicians rushed to the hotel and found that Douglas's body temperature was over 105 degrees, and that his heart rate was over 220 beats every minute. Douglas was paralyzed on his left side, and his brain was experiencing seizures. The ambulance raced Douglas to the hospital, where a doctor ordered him packed in ice. The right side of Douglas's brain had ruptured because of the fever. Immense quantities of central nervous system depressants were administered to stop the seizures. The doctor told the agents that Douglas was probably going to die.

The two agents then called the bureau in Washington, which in turn notified Pam Douglas and Douglas's father, who immediately flew to Seattle. One of the agents greeted Pam when she got off the aircraft. "It doesn't look good," the agent said.

Pam and Douglas's father went directly to the hospital. Douglas lay in the intensive care ward with his limbs strapped down and all manner of hoses, respirators, and intravenous lines connected to his body. The doctor explained to Pam that portions of Douglas's brain had been damaged by the raging fever, and that if he lived he would probably be blind, or worse.

Douglas would never be able to work again, the doctor guessed. A decision was made to give Douglas a CAT scan to see how much brain damage there was.

Lying in the hospital bed, paralyzed on one side, still in the coma, one part of Douglas's brain heard everything that was going on, even if he didn't understand it exactly.

"I could hear them talking," Douglas said afterward. "And there was this bright light, and I could see, but I didn't know what was going on. I thought I was being tortured . . . there was pain at times, with some of the things they were doing to me. I wanted them to know that when I heard my name . . . that had a calming effect on me." Images from his years of working around grisly homicides rampaged uncontrollably through his brain and blended with the efforts of the doctors to give him the CAT scan.

"My God," thought Douglas, "now I'm being murdered myself. People are trying to murder *me!*" He knew he was going through some kind of test, but at the same time, the test seemed like a diabolical attempt to kill him.

For five more days Douglas remained in the coma. Pam was a Roman Catholic, although Douglas was not. FBI agents called in a Seattle priest to pray for Douglas, but when the priest found out that Douglas wasn't a Catholic, he refused. The agents found another priest. The agents, Pam, Douglas's father, and the new priest formed a prayer circle around the end of Douglas' bed, joining hands and holding Douglas's hands as well. At almost the same time, Douglas emerged from the coma. He looked around the room, completely disoriented, partially paralyzed, and unable to think clearly.

"John, you're in the hospital," he was told. "You're very sick. You were in a coma." Douglas saw his father. *What the heck is he doing here?* Douglas wondered. Douglas tried to talk but couldn't. His voice sounded like Marlon Brando in *The Godfather*.

After another week, Douglas began to feel a little better, although the paralysis continued. The doctors told him he had been struck by viral encephalitis. The nurses told him they had never seen a worse case. Preparations had already been made to bury him at Arlington. Instead, Douglas would live; he just wouldn't be able to do any work for the next six months. The income insurance had come in handy.

31

EXIT

December 1983

In early December, as the FBI's Douglas lay hovering between life and death in the hospital, Thomas made a number of personnel shifts in order to accommodate the new investigation. One of those affected was Kraske.

Inside his green-painted office, Kraske knew that his fading hopes of becoming a chief in the department had just ended. The assignment orders issued by Thomas were explicit by what they did not say: that Thomas had lost confidence in Kraske's ability to direct the investigation. From now on, Thomas himself would have control over the Green River investigation. It would be out of Kraske's hands. Well, that was fair, thought Kraske. Thomas was the one taking the political risks, so he should be the one who reaped the benefits of success or the ignominy of failure.

Already, the chiefs were howling about Thomas's plan to catch the killer. The sheriff was stripping them of resources, pouring all the flexibility of the department into the fight against the killer. Everyone would just have to make do with less, Thomas told them. That affected the Criminal Investigations Division, too. Thomas's program would strip Kraske of most of his best detectives. Ordinary crime would have to take a backseat to the killer for a while.

Kraske thought back over everything he had done since the day at the river so long ago. He had tried to apply the lessons of Ted as best he could. He had believed for months that they had identified the murderer as Melvyn Foster. He still thought Foster might have committed at least some of the crimes, and was gratified that no one, not even Thomas, was discounting Foster's viability as a prime suspect. But while Kraske had been winding down his investigation over the winter, someone—was it really Foster, despite the surveillance?—had murdered and murdered, over and over again, while they had all been largely oblivious of the fact.

Kraske knew he should have pressured Winckoski for more help. But then, he thought, Winckoski should have known that it was needed. When Kraske thought back to the fall after the murders had been discovered, it seemed to him that the former sheriff was mostly interested in his retirement; anyway, Kraske wasn't the sort of cop who felt comfortable admitting that he couldn't do what was needed with what the department had given him. That was the way things were when he came on the department, where deputies were stuck in patrol cars and given an enormous swatch of territory to cover. No one asked for backup; they either did the job by themselves, like the Texas Rangers, or they got out of the business.

And Kraske knew that despite his hopes and ambitions, he had never had any real chance to become a chief, let alone sheriff. *I've never been one of those people who've been in the inside clique,* he thought. *I've always been out on the periphery. A lot of times, that was because of choice, because of what I saw after being on the department for a while. There were some stories I heard . . . well, I didn't want to be part of the clique, I saw what was going on back there. I didn't want any part of it, and that reputation followed me along.*

They look at you out of the corner of their eye, Kraske thought, *like when I made major. I'm sure I didn't have any fan club that really wanted me* that *bad. Well,* he thought, *I did the best I could. Maybe now someone else can do better.*

Kraske asked himself how he felt. After a minute, he knew. He felt relief.

Thomas has the ear of the boss, Randy Revelle, and Revelle's the head of the whole goddamn county, thought Kraske. *This is the way it ought to go. It should have gone that way in the first place.*

In his office a short distance away, Thomas was rejecting the screams of outrage from all of his top commanders. While Thomas had labored mightily over the previous six months to instill a sense in the department that it was a single organization, dedicated to a common purpose, all the instincts of his top commanders for bureaucratic self-preservation still ran strong beneath the surface. That was the way it had always been, as Kraske had discovered. Now that Thomas had told his command staff they were losing their staffing, he was being flooded with bitter protests. The protests were sure to go down the chain to the very bottom of the department.

Among the rank-and-file officers, the proactive units were considered to be the choicest assignment a cop could receive. Proactives operated something like a tactical squad, or a metro squad. Unit members were allowed to stay out of uniform and drive unmarked cars, and take those cars home with them. Each precinct had its own proactive team, assigned to work undercover in areas of high crime. Proactive patrol meant catching crooks, making collars. Exciting, challenging, a little dangerous, proactive patrol work was cop life at its most glamorous. Cops might spend years in the dull brown patrol uniform, cruising the highways, writing tickets, and breaking up family fights before finally getting a chance at proactive patrol, and this would create another problem, Thomas knew.

Just because the proactive *positions* would be thrown into the hunt for the killer, it didn't mean the people assigned to those jobs would go, too. The commander of the investigation would get the positions, not the people; the investigation commander would have first pick of the department's personnel. That meant some or even many of the existing proactives would be sent back to the uniform and the patrol car. More outrage and mutterings around the water cooler, Thomas supposed.

And who should he pick to run the new, augmented investigation? Thomas had been running *that* question through his mind for weeks, ever since a meeting with Kraske, Nault, and the chiefs in October. Kraske had proposed that Keppel be chosen to head the bigger investigation. It was clear to Thomas that Kraske didn't want Nault to get the job, and that events of the past six months had driven a wedge between the two men. Thomas conceded that Keppel knew about serial murders, but Keppel wasn't a member of the department anymore. Nor had Keppel ever administered anything, and administrative skill was going to be a primary consideration for what Thomas had in mind.

Besides, how could Thomas in good conscience turn the department's most important case—and that's what Thomas was saying the Green River murders had become—to an outsider? His subordinates would crucify him for showing such lack of faith in them.

Well, how about Nault? The mercurial Nault was intelligent and a quick study, Thomas knew, but he also tended to be acerbic with others. Thomas knew that some of the detectives working on the crimes had quarreled bitterly with Nault. Nault wasn't much for listening; once he had told a detective that he wasn't interested in his opinion. Nault had little patience for those who could not or would not keep up with him. Already, as Thomas had seen, Nault and Kraske had clashed more than once.

The new commander, moreover, would work directly for Thomas himself. If *he* was going to put his own political credibility on the line, Thomas thought, he wanted someone he could trust completely. Who could that be? Thomas considered all of his available commanders and the answer was instantly clear. There was only one operational commander that Thomas had worked with directly, the man in charge of the department's internal affairs unit—the policeman who policed the police.

For much of the previous year, Captain Frank Adamson had administered a highly sensitive internal department investigation of two officers, one a captain, the other a sergeant, who had been just a little too close to an unsavory man named Joseph Wiley Brown. For years, Brown had owned and operated a number of sex businesses in the Seattle and King County area—the waterbed stores, the nude counseling shops, nude modeling, all the usual places that the county and city cops had simultaneously been trying to shut down. The two officers were warned to stay away from Brown. Nevertheless, both had been caught up in a sting Brown had pulled with the FBI in an effort to broker a deal for a lighter sentence. Brown cajoled one of the officers to meet him in a motel room, where agents secretly taped the conversation;

the other officer had failed to report information about Brown and one of Brown's friends that could have prevented a kidnapping for extortion purposes.

Adamson had conducted the investigation slowly, methodically, quietly. It wasn't over yet, but Adamson was sure he could build a case that would stand up when the time came to fire the two officers. Thomas had promised Revelle he would get rid of the last of the bad old cops, and he intended to do just that, fair and square.

Fair and square. Much the same could be said about Adamson.

BOOK TWO

ADAMSON

1984–86

32

THE MOTIVATOR

December 1983

At forty-three, Frank Adamson was a stocky man with longish, thinning black hair that framed his pale face. Those who knew him well trusted him completely. Subtlety in Adamson was not inborn, but had been learned, laboriously, over the years. Left to his own instincts, Adamson's favored approach was straight ahead. Football was his favorite sport.

But what Adamson lacked in deviousness and creativity was more than compensated for by his abilities as an organizer, and most importantly, as a motivator. After nearly eighteen months of futility, the detectives assigned to the Green River case were in desperate need of an infusion of a sense of the possible. They had to be encouraged, to be assured that someone was behind them, that help was on the way, and that the case *could* be solved. Adamson could play that role admirably.

Most of all, Adamson had patience and persistence, and those were the main qualities Thomas was looking for in a commander for the investigation. For despite his sales job to the politicians, Thomas knew that in reality, it might take a long time to solve the case if even it *could* be solved.

Kraske, for one, saw Adamson as exactly the right sort of personality to put in charge. "He's not the kind who gets excited," Kraske observed. "He's very intelligent. He'll sit back and . . . whatever he's feeling underneath, you'll never know. Because he's easy-going and lets it come out slowly. He's very patient, very, very patient. I know at times I was very impatient, and I think Nault too was very impatient. But Frank is able to articulate well, and to get along with people."

"He'll be great," detectives told Kraske when Kraske told them that Adamson would be in charge. Kraske knew it was true. He'll get in there and pump them up, Kraske thought. Give them the old halftime talk. When everybody gets down, and when it looks like there isn't much possibility of solving the case, he'll get in there and pump them up. He won't let them let down. Every day it will be like first-and-ten, call the play in the huddle, clap your hands together, and hit the pile.

But that's just what this case needs, thought Kraske. Frank is a good team builder, and the most important job will be juggling all the egos—the detectives, the proactives, the department bureaucrats, the outside agencies like the FBI. Someone was going to have to keep everyone stroked, calm, and focused on the task at hand.

Adamson had no doubt of what was expected of him. "I'm a facilitator," he said, when Thomas announced his appointment, "and I'm a motivator."

Adamson had never intended to be a cop, and occasionally he still found himself surprised at the road his life had taken. Born in Spokane just before World War II, Adamson idolized his father, a hardworking man who had managed a furniture store while still in his teens, and had later put all of his younger siblings through college while supporting his own family despite the Depression. Childhood friends remember Adamson as having a hot temper, but by the time he was nineteen he had learned to present a calm facade no matter what was going on.

A friend recalled the day Adamson's father died. Frank, said the friend, "didn't seem to give a damn. I'd never seen anybody so . . . calm." Inside, of course, Adamson's feelings were churning, and he later told his wife Jo that on "the day his dad died, his whole world came apart." It was just that Adamson, because of his early temper, had learned to conceal his emotions so well.

The death of Adamson's father profoundly affected Adamson; when he died, Adamson's father had been working in a trucking company warehouse, a job he hated. Adamson resolved never, ever to work in a job he hated, never to become so stressed about his work that he ran the risk of killing himself. So Adamson learned to develop a certain equanimity about life, a distancing mechanism that allowed him to avoid seeing the ups and downs of his work as crucial to his own existence, unlike Kraske or Nault. For Adamson, there were other interests.

One of the most important factors of Adamson's steadiness was his wife and son, Brian, then fourteen. Jo Adamson was a year older than her husband. While outwardly a little more excitable than her husband, Jo also had an internal core that equipped her to deal with the storm that was to come. Both she and Adamson were voracious readers. The walls of their house in Seattle were lined with books; later, when they moved to a new house, one wall of the three-car garage was loaded with books the Adamsons could not bear to throw out or give away. For Christmas in 1983, Jo gave Adamson a book about Ted Bundy. Jo Adamson thought herself a feminist, and was an accomplished playwright, writing for Seattle's vigorous little-theatre scene. She also wrote poetry.

On the day Adamson was named to head the investigation, he came home and discussed the new job with Jo. Both resolved to not allow the problems ahead to interrupt their ordinary lives. Jo would continue writing plays and attending rehearsals at night. They wouldn't change their routines if they could help it. Their telephone number was listed in the book. They decided not to change the number, and it was nearly a year before they changed their minds. But by that time, a lot of other things had changed as well.

33

THE TASK FORCE

January 1984

By the middle of January, nearly all the assignments to the new investigation were completed. Thomas called a press conference to announce the stepped-up investigation, and said the new team would be called the Green River Task Force. The entire force would include two lietuenants, four sergeants, a dozen detectives, and twenty-two plainclothes street cops for surveillance of The Strip. Two detectives from the Port of Seattle were included in the group, as were two others from the city of Seattle. Thomas also traded one of his investigators to the state for the services of Bob Keppel, who would serve as a full-time consultant to the investigation.

Even before Thomas's announcement, Adamson had visited the five detectives in their hidey-hole on the courthouse's mezzanine level. Adamson walked into the room and saw a paper jungle. It was evident that the detectives were "completely at sea," as Adamson put it later. The investigators were drowning in their own efforts. The amount of information collected under the regimes of Kraske and Nault was so vast no one any longer had any idea of what it contained. Adamson was haunted by the fear that the answer was in the pile someplace, but that it would be overlooked. Something, he knew, had to be done to get the information under control.

Part of the problem was that the detectives continued to use their traditional method for case file management; even after Keppel's review, all of the murders remained keyed to the first case, that of Dub Bonner. Adamson knew that as the investigation unfolded, the amount of information was going to explode. He wanted to devise a system that would allow any investigator, not just Reichert, to quickly see links that would not otherwise be apparent.

Another major problem in the investigation so far, Adamson decided, was the physical separation of the detectives from The Strip, the place where the crimes had begun. Because they were headquartered in downtown Seattle, the detectives were forced to spend time on the road driving to and from the highway and the places where the witnesses could be located. Additionally, the detectives' work suffered from too much isolation. As Keppel had suggested months before, detectives needed to recognize and be ready to act on any clues provided by routine traffic stops in the vicinity of The Strip. Simultaneously, the uniformed patrol officers needed to know what the detectives wanted them to watch *for*. The best solution, Adamson decided, would be to put the investigation as close to The Strip as possible so that communications with the patrol officers and the potential victim population would be enhanced.

After considering several alternatives, Thomas and Adamson decided the best place would be at the nearest county police precinct, located about a mile west of the airport. That way, the investigators would be in constant contact with the patrol officers, and travel time to The Strip would be cut significantly. Putting forty new people into the precinct offices would be a tight fit, but it could be done. A large room in the precinct building used for community meetings and staff briefings was taken over and wired for telephones. Then all the files of the investigation and all the evidence that had so far been discovered were moved to the room, along with all the desks, bulletin boards, typewriters, filing cabinets, radios, and similar equipment used in the investigation.

A bonus of the arrangement was that the top floor of the precinct offices was given over to the Airport District court, where many of the victims and potential victims had been tried for prostitution. That meant that all the court records of the victims, possible victims, and many of the potential suspects were readily available.

Now, what to do with all the new people? The outlines of the assignments had been provided months earlier by Keppel, who had suggested a method of investigation and a rule of thumb for staffing: one detective team assigned to victims, with another team of detectives assigned to suspects. The idea was that the victims' team would work to assemble as much information as possible about the final days and hours of each victim, including the missings, while the other team worked to eliminate suspects. Hopefully, the information developed by each team would enable them to meet somewhere in the middle, much like two tunnelers digging their way to a connection.

That in turn meant the suspect team had to work a little differently than in most criminal investigations. Usually, police investigators worked to incriminate the most logical suspect. In the Green River case, that simply wouldn't work. There were literally hundreds of people police could target, and perhaps even take to court. But in this case, getting close wouldn't be enough.

The only way to make sure the real killer was identified was to go in reverse: Try to prove that Suspect A simply could not have done the crimes. To that end, obtaining the best possible information on where and when the known victims were last seen would be crucial. That way, if Suspect A had a clear and provable alibi at the time of a disappearance, he could be eliminated, and the next name subjected to the same test. In other words, it would be critical for the victim detectives to develop a matrix of time and place for use by the suspect detectives for elimination purposes.

Adamson therefore decided to assign seven detectives and one sergeant to a follow-up team to work on the victims, and another sergeant with seven other detectives to a second follow-up team to work on the suspects. Three other detectives would be assigned to a crime analysis section. They would have the job of giving investigation priorities to tips, evaluating information developed in a search for trends and investigative approaches, and making all the necessary charts, graphs, and maps.

That left the twenty-two street cops, most of them former proactive patrol officers or veterans of the warrants section, like Larry Gross. They would be the Task Force's proactive squad, available for surveillance, for developing contacts with the prostitutes, and for working occasional suspects. They would go onto The Strip in plainclothes and unmarked cars, armed with the knowledge needed to see the clue that might solve the crimes. The proactive people would work with the department's intelligence section to plan their surveillance strategies.

In this way, Adamson resolved to let the terrain of the killing ground work for the investigation. That meant removing the routine vice patrol from the highway, which in effect created a clear zone for prostitution. The proactives would put the women under covert surveillance, and follow the men who picked them up, getting the drivers' license plates, and often stopping the drivers and subjecting them to interrogation.

Meanwhile, Adamson decided to use the vice unit primarily for running decoy patrols. Policewomen posing as prostitutes would be placed on the sidewalks of the highway while under surveillance from the proactives. When drivers stopped to strike a bargain with the undercover policewoman, the policewoman would be instructed to invite the men to a nearby motel room, where a routine arrest for prostitution would take place, along with the same identification check and interrogation. Those drivers who declined to go to the room would be followed by the proactives, and occasionally stopped and interrogated. In this way, the proactives would be used to help the victim and suspect teams find new leads and further refine their existing information. The best bet, thought Adamson, was that the killer would be someone who would try to get a prostitute or decoy into his car. In Adamson's mind, if a man looking for a prostitute refused to go into a motel room, that automatically made him a priority suspect. Detectives firmly believed that if that strategy had been employed in 1982 and 1983, the killer would have been caught.

That, at least, was the theory.

But plans, Adamson quickly realized, had a way of breaking down under all too human resentments. Almost from the start, Adamson ran into muted opposition from the other top commanders in the department, who soon came to view Adamson as Thomas's favorite son. While the other commanders had to scrape by and do more with less, it seemed to them that Adamson had a blank check. Need undercover cars? Lease 'em, and by the way, put some cellular telephones in while you're at it. Radios? Take 'em from the other precincts. Travel money? You want it, you got it. Overtime? Take it. "You guys think you're the Manhattan Project, don't you," one of the chiefs bitterly told one of Adamson's lieutenants when he asked for some travel money.

From the chiefs' point of view, Adamson got the pick of the department. All the cops with the most experience and the most initiative were detailed to the new task force. That meant the other commanders had to make do with the remainder.

That in turn set up a new problem: The cops who were left behind resented not having been picked. Within a month the mutterings could be heard throughout the department: The Green River cops thought they were hot shit, somehow better than the rest of the force. The Green River Task Force? Oh yeah, you mean the Green River Golf and Country Club, don't you? While the unchosen slaved away on the drudgery cases, the Anointed Ones got all the glamour, not to mention all the equipment and the bennies. The resentment in turn led to suspicions of favoritism: Those selected were best at kissing ass, or those not selected just didn't have friends in the right places.

The worst resentments were in the airport precinct itself. Just like the vice squad before them, uniformed patrol officers came to view their Green River colleagues as secretive and clannish. The whole precinct seemed to be run for their benefit. Ordinary cops had to wait in line for the copy machines. Locker space was jammed. And the Green River people got all the best parking spaces. The feeling of separation was worsened when one of Adamson's lieutenants, to build morale, ordered special green nylon windbreakers clearly labeled Green River Task Force for all the task force members. The new jackets did the job, signifying distinction, but contributed further to the alienation. And while every patrolman driving The Strip fantasized about the night *he*, rather than one of the Chosen Few would catch the killer, communications between the two groups first stuttered, then withered to a halt.

Despite these mutterings and resentments, Adamson and nearly everyone else assigned to the task force firmly believed that the job was a short-term proposition. The killer, most thought, would surely be caught within three to six months. So confident were Adamson and his top subordinates that the killer would be quickly identified that some officers initially declined to join the task force, fearing to disrupt their career paths. Why give up a job one had worked years to get to throw it all over for a sideshow? "We were confident that the whole thing would be over in a few months," one of the original task force members recalled afterward. "None of us believed it would take any longer than that. We all thought we'd have the guy in jail and that we'd all be back doing what we were supposed to be doing before anyone realized we were gone. Shit, were we *wrong*."

34

DATA CONTROL

January 1984/February 1984

Almost as soon as the detectives, the files, the telephones, and the street cops moved into the Burien precinct, Adamson encountered another problem: the need to get a better handle on the information that was finding its way into the news media.

The newspeople, naturally, wanted to know everything Adamson's investigators were up to. But Adamson moved to shut communication down almost immediately, refusing even to identify the members of the task force. Telephone calls to the task force were routinely bounced back to the switchboard once detectives realized they were talking to the news media. Only a persistent reporter could get through to Adamson, who made himself and Detective Fae Brooks the only people authorized to comment. Complaints about the restrictions piled up, particularly from the radio and television news media, who often needed to reach a task force source quickly and at odd hours, only to be rebuffed by indifferent police communications supervisors. The complaints went to Thomas, who passed them onto Adamson along with some advice: Treat the press nice, but don't worry about them. Thomas told Adamson that if the press people complained to Revelle, he would back him up.

Adamson sympathized with the news media's demands, but it remained vital to keep tight control over the information being developed by the investigators, lest it get out and contaminate what the detectives were doing. To improve his control over the information, Adamson had Brooks maintain records on what was printed and broadcast. Knowing what had been printed or broadcast was critical in evaluating witnesses and suspects.

But inside the task force, Adamson decided, the only way to make sure the critical key was not overlooked was to have the detectives keep one another fully informed. Every morning, briefings within each task force subunit were held, and once each week, a task forcewide meeting was conducted at the only place with enough room, the banquet room of a coffee shop on The Strip. At the daily briefings, detectives were required to discuss their activities with the others, who would offer continuing critiques. The meetings were stimulating in that new ideas and theories about the crimes could be floated and discussed. Flaws in the separate investigations could be examined, and new leads considered. That way, Adamson hoped, the investigation would be able to avoid the "tunnel vision" cited by Keppel the previous May. The briefings also were useful in developing priorities for the proactives, who generally came to work in the afternoon for night duty on The Strip.

As the meetings progressed, a pattern emerged. Occasionally, a detective assigned to a victim case might comment that he had learned of a witness who might be helpful in further clarifying a victim's last known location. Often, such a witness was a prostitute. Could the proactives keep an eye out for so-and-so? If they contacted the witness, could they ask them such-and-such? Along the same lines, proactives were routinely sent down to the jail to interview women who had been arrested for prostitution. Slowly, in this way, members of the task force constructed a new and far deeper understanding of the prostitution subculture: who was friends with whom, where people had lived, what drugs they used, who their pushers and pimps were, where people had come from, where they would go next.

And the proactives slowly became proficient at developing information from the prostitutes. As the women saw that the proactives were not bent on arresting them, but were in fact helping to protect them, tips about strange tricks began to come in. All these went into the suspect pile to be worked, and if possible, eliminated.

As January turned into February, Adamson came to yet another realization: The number of potential suspects and victims staggered the imagination. Already the suspect pile had tripled, and promised to run into the thousands very quickly. He had never fully appreciated the amount of violence directed against women in contemporary society, Adamson realized.

Tips about possible suspects were sorted into three different categories—"A" suspects, those thought capable of committing the crimes based on their proximity to The Strip and prior histories of violence toward women; "B" suspects, those capable of committing the crimes but not linked to The Strip in any definitive way; and "C" suspects, comprised of everyone else. Suspects were constantly being shifted from group to group as new information was developed, or as they were eliminated. Periodically, someone would have to review the cases to see whether they were properly classified. Occasionally, there would be errors in classification, or improper elimination.

And the possible victims: The department's existing missing persons records were entirely inadequate, and the city of Seattle's were hardly much better. Adamson realized that he would have to assign detectives to sort through the records of prostitution arrests to see how many women were unaccounted for. Two detectives began digging into court records to find out who hadn't shown up for trial.

The answer was shocking: Of the nearly two thousand arrests for prostitution in both the city and the county, representing as many as one thousand different women, nearly half had failed to show up for trial

Former King County Sheriff Vern Thomas. He formed the Green River Task Force.

Wendy Coffield, the first found victim of the Green River case, is pulled out of the Green River. (CREDIT: Duane Hamamura, *Valley Daily News*)

Self-proclaimed psychic Barbara Kubik-Patten, who found one of the victims; F.B.I. Profiler John Douglas.

Major Richard Kraske (left) & King County Detective Dave Reichert led the initial hunt for the Green River Killer.

First Green River Task Force Commander Captain Frank Adamson.
(Left) (CREDIT: Matt McVay © *Seattle Times*) Current King County
Sheriff James Montgomery.

Captain James Pompey (left), named Green River Task Force
Commander in November 1986; Captain Bob Evans, Green River
Task Force Commander from 1988-1989.

Green River Task Force Detective Bruce Peterson carefully excavates the remains of a victim. (CREDIT: Matt McVay © *Seattle Times*)

Bill Haglund (white overalls), Chief King County Medical Examiner's Office Investigator, leads a team of investigators to a shallow grave. (CREDIT: Mike Levy © *Seattle Times*)

These composites depict men seen with Green River victims before their disappearance. Police would like to interview them.

Former taxi driver Melvyn Foster became a Green River suspect after coming forward with tips on possible suspects in the summer of 1982. (CREDIT: Dave Ekren © *Seattle Times*)

William Jay Stevens II. A two-hour docu-drama led police to this lover of police paraphernalia who studied serial killer Ted Bundy.

These two cartoons, which appeared in the *Seattle Times,* show the community's frustration at the inability of the Green River Task Force to apprehend the killer. (CREDIT: Brian Basset © *Seattle Times*)

Kathy Mills, mother of victim Opal Mills. (CREDIT: Dick Baldwin)

An estimated 400 women marched in downtown Seattle on March 16, 1984 to voice their concerns over the yet unsolved Green River murders. (CREDIT: Greg Gilbert © *Seattle Times*)

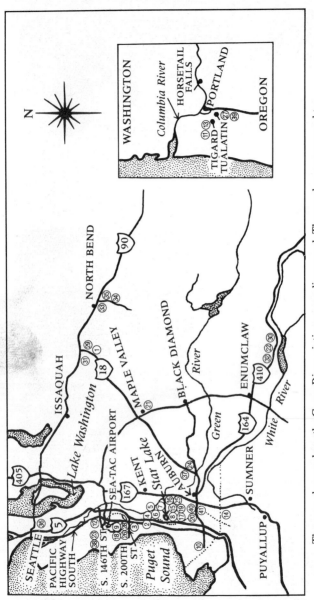

The map shows where the Green River victims were discovered. The numbers correspond to the photos on the following pages; underneath the photo appears the victim's date of disappearance.

(Map by Tomas Guillen & Carlton Smith with Pat Tobin)

1 Amina Agisheff
7-7-82

2 Wendy Coffield
7-8-82

3 Gisele Lovvorn
7-17-82

4 Debra Bonner
7-25-82

5 Marcia Chapman
8-1-82

6 Cynthia Hinds
8-11-82

7 Opal Mills
8-12-82

8 Terry Milligan
8-29-82

9 Mary Meehan
9-15-82

10 Debra Estes
9-20-82

11 Denise Bush
10-8-82

12 Shawnda
Summers
10-9-82

13 Shirley Sherrill
Fall 1982

14 Colleen
Brockman
12-24-82

15 Alma Smith
3-3-83

16 Delores
Williams
3-8-83

17 Gail Mathews
4-10-83

18 Andrea Childers
4-14-83

19 Sandra Gabbert
4-17-83

20 Kimi-Kai Pitsor
4-17-83

21 Carol
Christensen
5-3-83

22 Martina
Authorlee
5-22-83

23 Cheryl Wims
5-23-83

24 Yvonne Antosh
5-31-83

25 Carrie Rois
Summer 1983

26 Constance Naon
6-8-83

27 Tammy Liles
6-9-83

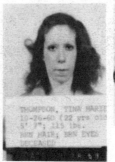

28 Kelly Ware
7-19-83

29 Tina Thompson
7-25-83

30 Debbie
Abernathy
9-5-83

31 Maureen Feeney
9-28-83

32 Mary Bello
10-11-83

33 Delise Plager
10-30-83

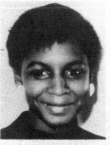

34 Kim Nelson
11-1-83

35 Lisa Yates
12-23-83

36 Mary West
2-6-84

37 Cindy Smith, 3-21-84: Smith is the last known victim of the Green River Killer.

BELOW: Four of the found victims remain unidentified. Various means were used to reconstruct their faces from their skulls.

38 White, 5′4″ to 5′7″, 12-18 years old. By Robert George.

39 White, 5′4″ to 5′7″, 17-19 years old. By Harvey Pratt.

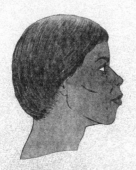

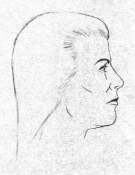

40 Black, 5′ to 5′4″, 20-25 years old. By Robert George.

41 White, 5′4″ to 5′8″, 14-19 years old. By Robert George.

Kase Lee
8-28-82

Rebecca Marrero
12-3-82

Marie Malvar
4-30-83

Keli McGinness
6-28-83

April Buttram
8-18-83

Tracy Winston
9-12-83

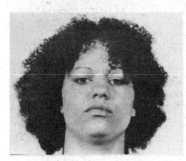

Patricia Osborn
10-20-83

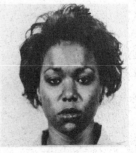

Pammy Avent
10-26-83

The above women are on the official list of Green River victims. They are missing and presumed dead. The dates refer to the day they disappeared.

at one time or another. All that information had to be pared down to the list of those who were still on the run. Then that list had to be further pared down to those who were truly missing, and not just avoiding arrest. It would be laborious, tedious work, complicated by all the false names used, the extreme transience of the potential victims, the lack of solid family connections in many of the cases. But it was the only way to get a handle on what they were dealing with. Once it could be established that someone was definitely missing, efforts could be made to obtain dental records, which promised to be the only sure way of identifying any newly discovered victims. Adamson had a bad feeling there would be more of those to come, and he was right.

35

ON THE STREETS

January 1984/March 1984

As the task force went into high gear, the proactives at first found it hard to keep up with the prostitutes. The whole nature of the business made it clandestine, and the women were skilled at avoiding the watchful eyes of the police. Larry Gross and others involved in the street patrols had to learn how to watch the women carefully, then follow them after they drove off with their customers. Soon the street team learned where the women would be most likely to direct their tricks, and the police carefully recorded the license plates of the vehicles, and often stopped the drivers and asked them for identification. Most of the men thus contacted were sheepish, if defensive; occasionally some were hostile.

One of the favorite locations was at the end of South 192nd Street where it dead-ended against a golf course. The fact that three victims' skeletons had already been unearthed less than two blocks away didn't seem to bother the potential new victims, who kept assuring the police they could take care of themselves. They could somehow sense when a trick was strange, the women said. The cops knew that just wasn't true. Probably, those who had already been killed had believed the same things.

Meanwhile, the digging by the victim detectives appeared to pay off with the first possible eyewitness account of an abduction.

Detectives had searched for Kimi Kai Pitsor's pimp, and after some weeks were successful in locating the twenty-one-year-old man. Once the youth realized the police did not intend to prosecute him, he tried hard to be cooperative. He was pretty sure about the last time he had seen Kimi Kai, the pimp told the detectives. They had been in downtown Seattle at night. A man had driven by in a pickup truck and had waved at Kimi. Kimi had waved back, and had motioned for the man to drive around the corner to a nearby parking lot. Then Kimi disappeared around the corner, heading for the truck and a trick.

When was this? the detectives had asked. The pimp wasn't too sure, but thought it had happened some time in April of 1983. By process of elimination and by using the known dates the pimp could remember, the detectives managed to pin the date down to April 17, 1983—the same night that Sandy Gabbert had disappeared on The Strip.

What kind of a truck was it? Again the pimp was unsure, but he thought it had been green, an older model, sort of like the GMC pickups driven by the Seattle City Parks Department. It had a silver metal camper shell on the back with a fold-down gate, the pimp remembered. Oh, and the door had a large spot on it—like there had been some sort of round sign on the door, but rubbed out.

What about the driver? Big, said the pimp. White. Dark hair, kind of curly. Pockmarked face. How old? Twenties or thirties. By himself? Alone, agreed the pimp. A police artist assisted the pimp in preparing a composite drawing of the man's face. The result looked suspiciously similar to Reichert—that is, if Reichert had had curly hair and a pockmarked face.

The detectives considered the information, then asked the pimp if he would be willing to undergo hypnosis. Sometimes, they said, a person under hypnosis could remember more details. The pimp was willing, and while in a state of relaxation recalled a few other details: the man had a tattoo on his arm, and the truck had large side mirrors and some sort of bar across the back end of the camper shell. But he could not recall any license plate.

Still, it was a start. The detectives prepared a confidential bulletin to be distributed to area police departments, and included the composite drawing and a photograph of a similar truck with a camper. Any officers who saw the man or the truck were asked to call the Green River Task Force immediately. But police stopped short of calling the man in the drawing a suspect. Until detectives had a chance to talk to him, he would only be a potential witness. After all, it was possible that the man might have left Kimi Kai elsewhere downtown before she took her last ride.

But the stepped-up investigative pace brought other problems as well as benefits. One was an upsurge in new tips about the murders, which seemed to wax and wane with the amount of publicity the case received.

On one hand, Adamson and the detectives welcomed the new tips. Every time the telephone rang, it brought new hope. But as the tips began to pile up, inevitably the detectives began to get bogged down. Worst of all, as usual, were the nuts and the false confessors.

Already, a notorious serial murderer in the Southwest had begun to claim that he and another man had committed many of the Green River murders. Henry Lucas had burst on the scene as a fully formed bogeyman, profiled in national magazines and publicly linked to the horrific murder of a small boy in Florida. Lucas had already claimed that he and his traveling companion, Ottis Toole, had killed as many as 165 people all across the United States. As the notoriety spread, homicide detectives from all over the country made a beeline for Lucas's jail cell. Bribing their way into Lucas's willing presence with offers of cigarettes and candy, these detectives asked Lucas who he and Toole had murdered in *their* states. Lucas cheerfully confessed to every murder the police asked of him. By the time the balloon burst a year later, Lucas would ultimately claim to have committed up to three hundred murders. Still later, Lucas would say he had lied: He had only committed one murder, he said: his own mother.

But after reading about Lucas, reporters from all over the country began peppering Adamson about the man's claims. What about these guys, Lucas and Toole? Couldn't they have committed at least *some* of the Green River murders, as they were claiming? Adamson laughed. Not very likely, said Adamson. For one thing, it seemed that the Green River murders had been committed over an extensive period of time, at least a year and perhaps longer. Lucas and Toole, by their own admission, had moved around the country quite frequently. Neither man had been in the Washington State area more than a few days, if even that. Besides, said Adamson, Lucas and Toole had already confessed to murders on the east coast that took place on the same day as some of the Green River murders. And it wasn't very likely that the vagabonds Lucas and Toole would be flying around the country to kill complete strangers when they could barely afford bus fare.

Meanwhile, Adamson hadn't given up on another well-publicized suspect. Melvyn Foster continued to be a "person of interest," as Adamson liked to characterize suspects. Foster was still subjected to sporadic surveillance, and occasionally, members of the street team were convinced they saw Melvyn cruising The Strip. Melvyn denied it, and claimed there was someone who looked just like him out on the highway.

He didn't have the resources necessary to watch Mel every minute, Adamson decided. The FBI offered its help. A high-tech surveillance camera was surreptitiously mounted on a telephone pole near Foster's house. That way, the police had a record every time Melvyn drove away from home. The camera was to stay up for the better part of a year. Foster never knew about it.

The camera wasn't the only asset the police had against Foster, however. They also got considerable assistance, wanted and unwanted, from an old friend— Barbara Kubik-Patten, the psychic/private detective.

Ever since Foster had entered the public eye in October of 1982, Barbara had an interest in the Lacey man. Some days she was sure Melvyn was the killer; other days, she saw Melvyn as the innocent man, wrongly fingered by the bumbling cops. Precariously, Barbara kept her balance between the two opposing sides for more than a year. Soon she was on a first-name basis with Foster, poring with him over the lists of victims and swapping rumors and leads, all over a weekly breakfast of steak and eggs at a coffee shop near her home. No sooner would Mel drive off than Barbara would call the police to let them know the latest. After the first few conversations, Reichert had lost interest. Another detective, Jim Doyon, had picked up the burden. Doyon refused to ridicule Barbara, and when the other detectives razzed him about his psychic, he simply shrugged it off. If nothing else, Barbara was helping the task force keep posted on Melvyn's moods and his comings and goings.

The publicity also generated other leads, albeit mostly of the wacky variety. Both newspapers and all of the electronic media began receiving numerous calls and letters about the murders.

Many evidenced the same theme: The writer or caller had seen something suspicious, and had called the task force, which had *ignored* them! A man who preferred to call himself "Agent X-2" telephoned from Tacoma and said that he was only an amateur detective, but that the answer to the crimes was obvious: Clearly, said X-2, the killer was bent on robbing the prostitutes, stealing their jewelry. The cops should stake out the pawn shops to get their man, X-2 suggested.

A woman from Pendleton, Oregon, wrote saying she was sure she had seen the face in the Pitsor composite at the Pendleton Roundup the previous September, and sent crude sketches to back up her claim. A very strange person sent in an anonymous letter comprising a series of cryptic sentence fragments that seemed to suggest the murderer was the leader of a famous symphony orchestra. A former Washington, D.C., lawyer, who had been disbarred for his involvement with a call-girl ring peripherally involved in the Watergate scandal, tried to pin the blame on a mildly retarded man who shared the basement of the house he was living in; police decided to investigate the former lawyer instead. And a retired reporter from the San Francisco Bay area thought that the murders might be the work of the Zodiac, resurfaced after a decade.

And so it went.

To all of these Adamson would only give his stock response: "Interesting," he would say. "Very interesting."

36

MORE BONES

February 1984/March 1984

On Valentine's Day, a man searching for moss stumbled over the skeletal remains of a human being near a state park not far off Interstate 90, about forty miles east of Seattle.

Within a short time, officers assigned to the task force were present at the scene. A search of the area was made as the medical examiner's office came to collect the remains, but no other bones were discovered. The skeleton, the experts said, had been that of a young woman.

The location of these remains were far away from the killer's normal dumping ground, Adamson thought. True, the skeleton was that of a female, but I-90 was the state's major east–west highway. It would be a mistake to assume too soon that this was another victim of the killer. After all, other people murdered too. Resolution of the question would have to await the identification of the skeleton, Adamson concluded. The medical examiner's office was working to obtain a library of dental charts of missing people. Maybe they could match the teeth found with this skull with those records. If the victim could be identified, and if she had been known to frequent The Strip, that might change things. For now, Adamson had decided not to include the skeleton on the list.

Adamson had already decided to try another one of Douglas's suggested techniques to draw the killer out. A community meeting was scheduled, and plans were made to collect the names and license plates of the crowd expected to show up.

Whether it was simple lack of interest, or lack of publicity, only four people attended. They were out-numbered five to one by the dozen police officials and ten reporters who did come. County Executive Revelle, who also attended, was clearly embarrassed, especially after he told everyone on arrival that he had come at the request of the people concerned about the murders. What people and what concern?

While police officers unobtrusively wrote down the license plates of all the reporters, the community meeting was transformed into a press conference of sorts.

"I don't measure the importance of this by who did and who didn't show up," said Revelle. The problem, he said, was that the region was suffering from the depredations of a serial murderer, and it was impor-tant to do something to stop the murders, whether people came to the meeting or not.

Did Revelle think that because the victims were prostitutes, the public didn't really care what hap-pened to them? Revelle had been a politician too long for fall for that one. "It doesn't matter whether they were prostitutes or what they were," he said. "They're still human beings, they have a right to the same police protection as any one else in our community. And as long as I'm county executive, they're going to get it."

Adamson was asked if he thought the killer would kill again. "Yes," he said. "We know that he was operating at least through November of last year, and I don't see any reason to believe he's stopped."

Three days later, a dog found the lower jawbone of a young adult about a half mile away from where Kimi Kai Pitsor's skull had been discovered near the ceme-tary in December. Examination of the jawbone showed that it did not fit with Pitsor's skull. Nor did the teeth in the jawbone match with the dental charts of any of the missings. A search was made of the area, but again, no other remains were discovered.

37

SKULLS

February 1984

The jawbone made a total of four complete or partial skeletal remains that could not be identified by the medical examiner's office. Naming the dead was crucial to solving the puzzle, and to that end, the people in the King County Medical Examiner's Office were vital. One of those people was a slightly built, bespectacled man who found death and burial fascinating; the unidentified bones, thought Chief Investigator Bill Haglund of the medical examiner's office, presented a puzzle within a larger puzzle: Who were the dead people, and how had they been killed? Were the unknown skeletons related to the Green River murders? And if so, was there anything about the bones that might help police identify the killer? Only by learning the identity of the dead could detectives hope to fill in the matrix of where and when the victim was last seen, so critical to suspect elimination.

A short, slightly built man, the forty-two-year-old Haglund began his career as a mortician's assistant for several years. Later he became an assistant in a pathology laboratory in a hospital in Long Beach, California. Dead bodies had long since become a familiar part of his daily life. Haglund had a fascination with the way cultures disposed of their dead. Already a graduate in biology, Haglund was working on a doctorate in anthropology at the University of Washington. Haglund's studies in anthropology, particularly in the techniques of analyzing human skeletons for what the bones suggested about the age, race, and sex of the dead, and the circumstances of the death, provided him with crucial skills in the challenge of identifying the remains of the Green River victims.

With assistance from one of his instructors at the University of Washington, Dr. Daris Swindler, who was one of the nation's leading experts on anthropological assessment of skeletons, Haglund soon adopted what amounted to archaeological procedures in the recovery of the remains.

Finding each bone was important, but most critical were the teeth. Dirt around the skeletons had to be dug up and sifted through progressively smaller wire sieves; the dirt was then examined for loose teeth, hairs, fibers, and other bits and pieces that might contribute to the growing amount of trace evidence the case was generating. Examination of the dirt for growth of insects, vegetation, and fungi helped narrow down the probable death date, which could be helpful in matching the skeletal remains to any reported missing persons.

The Green River case presented several challenges not often found at anthropological digs, however. Apart from the two skeletons that had so far been found buried, all of the others were simply dropped in out-of-the-way locations by the killer, and then often covered with cut branches for concealment. Natural forces then became the killer's ally.

Decomposition of bodies begins almost immediately upon death. Within days small animals appear to scavenge the remains, which break down rapidly under the effects of assaults by insects, sunlight, rain, and other elements. Over a period of a few months, a skeleton will inevitably become disarticulated as the small animals break away portions to carry them off. As a result, various bones may be distributed over a wide-ranging area. Years before, Keppel had seen the same phenomenon with the Bundy victims. A thorough examination of the trails left by small animals was essential to achieve a significant recovery of the remains. That meant investigators had to view the location where skeletons were found with an eye to where the small animals lived and nested so that various parts of the skeleton might be located.

The critical element, of course, was the skull. Over time, small animals often dragged the skull away, almost always downhill from the victim. As the flesh dried, the teeth loosened. Recovery of the teeth was vital to matching the remains to any dental charts. Following the trails made by small animals such as skunks, mice, squirrels, and other creatures could lead to the discovery of the teeth.

Once as many bones and teeth as could be found were recovered, the remains were brought back to the medical examiner's office. Haglund soon learned to interpret a dental chart with expert precision. But to back him up, the medical examiner's office retained two forensic dentists, Drs. Bruce Rothwell and Thomas Morton from the University of Washington. Simply by examining the teeth, the two dentists were able to guess the approximate age and sometimes even the cultural background of the victim.

Another crucial clue could be found by close examination of the skull. Males, for example, had larger ridges of bone over the eyes than females. Other differences in the size and shape of eye sockets might indicate race. Examination of the sutures on the top of the skull could indicate the approximate age. Finally, measurements of the length of the large leg bones indicated the approximate height and sometimes weight of the victim.

Haglund spent hours studying the four sets of remains, as he would a score of similar finds before the case was ended. Slowly, bone by bone, tooth by tooth, Haglund assembled accurate estimates as to the age, sex, race, height, and occasionally weight of each of the victims. As the estimates grew in their precision, they would be increasingly valuable to the detectives, who worked to narrow the field of possible victims.

Meanwhile, Haglund and the detectives continued to assemble their library of dental charts. By early March, the dental x-rays of thirty different individuals had been compiled. Each month, the library grew slowly larger as parents all over the country, worried about the killings and the prolonged lack of contact with their teenage children, called in, and arrangements were made to obtain the new records for comparison with the skeletons.

In this way, slowly but surely over the years, the bone faces of the dead began to assume flesh once again, and the hope was that they might say something about the man who had killed them.

While Haglund, Swindler, and the two dentists worked to narrow the field of possibilities posed by the unidentified skeletons, detectives studying previously ignored missing persons reports added four new names to the missing list: Shirley Sherrill, nineteen, who had been reported missing by her mother in December of 1983, a year after she had last been heard from; Tracy Winston, also nineteen, who had last been seen near the jail in downtown Seattle in September of 1983; Patricia Osborne, nineteen, last seen in late October of 1983 in the Aurora Avenue North prostitution stroll zone; and Carrie Rois, just fifteen, who, like Coffield nearly eighteen months earlier, had run away from a state-supported foster home in late March of 1983. Dental charts were obtained on each. Haglund and the dentists compared the records to the teeth found with the four skeletons, but the teeth did not match. That meant the four missings might be *other* victims of the killer.

The new missings brought that list to a dozen names: Kase Lee, Terri Milligan, Denise Bush, and now Shirley Sherrill, all from 1982; followed into limbo by Carrie Rois, Sandy Gabbert, Marie Malvar, Keli McGinness, Debbi Abernathy, Mary Bello, Tracy Winston, and Patricia Osborne, all from the year just past.

All these vanished women, thought Adamson, and in addition, the twelve known victims—Wendy Coffield, Dub Bonner, Marcia Chapman, Cynthia Hinds, Opal Mills, Mary Meehan, Gisele Lovvorn, Shawnda Summers, all from just six months in 1982; and Yvonne Antosh, Connie Naon, and Kimi Kai Pitsor from 1983.

All those, and the four unidentified dead. Adamson would leave for work early in the morning and come home late at night. Sometimes he would flop down in a chair, turn on the television, and just stare at it. He found himself snapping at Jo or his son Brian over small things. There was something about these crimes, he thought, that you couldn't escape from. A sense of guilt. Maybe it was a collective sense of guilt, recognition that somehow society had failed. But with each additional victim, the feeling was taking its toll on Frank Adamson.

It was crazy, Adamson thought. With each new identification, each new missing person, his hopes soared. Here, he thought each time, was surely an important piece of the puzzle. But at the same time, each new victim made him recognize how bad it *really* was. After twenty years as a cop, it was hard to be shocked, but here he was, stunned at the size of what they were uncovering.

The same day he announced Rois's addition to the missing list, Adamson made another decision. He would add Carol Christensen to the Green River victim list, even though her case was so different from the others.

The fact that Christensen had clearly been redressed after her murder, the availability of her identification, and the presence of such obvious staging props as the fish, the sausage, and the wine bottle, made her murder radically different than the others. Besides, the paper sack found over her head, said the experts, probably meant that Christensen's killer knew her very well. And there was no evidence at all that Christensen had ever committed prostitution, although she had been known to hitchhike.

But, Adamson thought, he had a lot of murders. Who could say that someone who had murdered Christensen wasn't also responsible for the other crimes, or at least some of them? Most telling of all was the fact that Christensen had last been seen on The Strip.

Christensen's addition made the known victim toll thirteen, while the known missings now totaled an even dozen. Add in the four unknown skeletons, and all of a sudden, in less than a year, the Green River murders had grown from just six to as many as twenty-nine.

Worse yet, as far as Adamson could tell, the killer was still out there.

38

THE TRIANGLE

March 1984

Sorting through the possible missings, the nuts, and the false confessors, and identifying the unknown dead weren't all that Adamson had to deal with. Beginning in early March, women's groups began attacking the police for not doing enough to stop the killings.

In San Francisco, a spokeswoman for a group calling itself the U.S. Prostitutes' Collective said her group felt that the murders had been taken too lightly by the police and the news media. Rachel West said her organization was thinking about going to Seattle to conduct a protest march.

And a second group of radical feminists calling itself the Women's Coalition to Stop the Green River Murders formed in Seattle. The coalition had already been involved in efforts to turn back an ill-considered proposal in the state legislature to establish a one hundred-dollar bounty for turning in a prostitute. And just as the task force was getting started, representatives of the coalition met with Kraske, not realizing that Kraske had been removed from the loop. What did he intend to do to stop more women from being murdered? The sympathetic Kraske could only offer what he felt was honest advice: Carry a whistle.

"The investigation by the police has been too slow," said Rachel West. "Money is being wasted. I don't think they're taking women's lives seriously."

Adamson calmly denied that the police were not taking the lives of women seriously. But then a new event added momentum to the charges.

On March 13, 1984, five days after West's criticism, a U.S. Army convoy of trucks and jeeps, traveling to maneuvers at a firing range east of the Cascades, stopped briefly at the same isolated turnoff of Interstate 90 where the February skeleton had been found. One of the soldiers in the convoy walked into the trees to relieve himself. About twenty-five yards off the pavement he discovered a fragmented human skeleton. Some flesh remained on the skeleton, as did much of its hair. The soldier reported the discovery to his superiors, who in turn called the police. The new skeleton was less than three hundred yards from the last one. Police hadn't searched far enough the last time.

Two days after the newest discovery, the Women's Coalition to Stop the Green River Murders announced that it would hold a "Take Back the Night" protest march in Seattle.

"Friday night," said Melissa Adams of the coalition,

"women will mobilize to take back the night and to claim our rights to live after sunset.

"We are calling on all women to end the farce of the Green River murder investigation. It is the responsibility of all of us to take action, and we must do it now—because women are dying."

Adams said the coalition had tried to arrange for local prostitutes to participate in the march, but no one wanted to publicly identify themselves as a prostitute. Instead, the coalition would pay to bring two prostitutes up from San Francisco to participate in the protest.

The focus on prostitution was all wrong anyway, she said, and the news media were doing the victims a terrible injustice to report on their prostitution activities.

"The issue is the killing of women," Adams said. "But we are showing unity with prostitutes who are victims of this killer—and victims of a sexist society. Violence against women is an all-American sport." Men would be welcome to watch the parade, she said, but they wouldn't be allowed to participate.

Two nights later nearly four hundred women marched through downtown Seattle carrying candles in protest of the murders. And at a march-ending rally in front of the county courthouse, speakers accused the police of minimizing the true number of Green River victims, and attacked the police for delaying for more than a year before putting enough resources on the investigation.

"The police didn't allocate significant resources until a few months ago," said a woman who would only identify herself as Winnie. "As a result, they've got evidence stacked to the ceiling that they haven't had time to process." The late start in the hunt was a disaster, Winnie said, and every day that went by further reduced the chances of finding the killer.

"Major Kraske tells us to carry a whistle," jeered another speaker at the rally, Cookie Hunt. "Take away his gun and let *him* carry a whistle," a woman in the crowd yelled back.

Hunt scored the police for not working hard enough on the crimes. "If fifty-two white, middle-class, college girls were missing or dead there would be an entirely different response," she said, citing the number of dead and missing women that *The Seattle Times*, from police reports, had previously reckoned might ultimately be involved. The problem was the news media, Hunt said, which insisted on telling the public about the girls' prostitution. The constant harping on the prostitution issue, Hunt said, only created a climate that fed the craziness of the killer; worse, it detracted from community support for the investigation.

At least two people cared far less about their daughter being identified as a prostitute, however, than simply finding her. As 1983 had edged into early 1984, Tom and Carol Estes continued to try to interest the police in looking for their daughter Debra. Even after the expanded Green River Task Force was created, detectives remained adamant: There was no evidence that Debra had ever been involved in prostitution, and since the investigators had their hands full with trying to locate missing prostitutes, there just wasn't enough time to look for the Estes's teenaged runaway.

Frustrated, the Esteses finally went directly to the Seattle city vice squad, and convinced a detective there to allow them to look through police photographs of known prostitutes. There in early March, the Esteses saw a booking photograph of Betty Lorraine Jones and immediately identified her as their daughter. Borrowing a copy of the photo, the Esteses returned to the task force, and then saw pinned to the wall an identical photograph of "Betty Lorraine Jones" as a possible Green River missing person.

The Green River detectives were horribly embarrassed by their previous reluctance to accept the Estes's story. They hastened to assure the couple that detectives had been searching for "Betty Jones" for more than a year, ever since she had disappeared from the Stevenson Motel. Where? asked Tom Estes. The

Stevenson, on Pacific Highway South in Federal Way,
replied the detectives, and showed the parents the
missing persons report that had been turned in by
Detective Spencer Nelson of the sex crimes detail in
late 1982. That was when the Esteses learned for the
first time that the daughter they had been seeking for
so long had last been staying just across the street
from their own office when she disappeared.

On March 21, 1984, a man who was preparing the
Little League field north of the airport for play
noticed that his dog had a bone in its mouth. The man
recognized the bone for what it was—a human leg
bone—and immediately called the police. A Port
policeman followed the dog back into the brush and
found a nearly complete human skeleton, minus a leg
bone. The Port police then called the task force.

The following day the entire field was searched,
including a stand of trees bisected by a dirt track leading to an old abandoned telephone shack just beyond
the center field fence and the flagpole. Within an
hour, a searcher handling a bloodhound had found a
second skeleton—this one very near the spot where
Gina Serrett and the Little Leaguers had smelled the
bad smell so many months before. Both new skeletons
were those of young females, Haglund decided soon
after he arrived.

A day later, Haglund identified the second skeleton
as the remains of Cheryl Lee Wims, one of the four
missing Seattle women county police had originally
decided not to include among the Green River missings. *That* decision, thought Adamson, would have to
be reevaluated.

In the morning briefings, an idea began to take
shape, then crystallize: The killer had followed a distinctive pattern in deciding where to dump his victims'
bodies. Looking at the maps and charts, it was apparent that the killer had used several dump sites *contem-
poraneously*, and that the locations were all connected
by secondary state highways in the region. The key
connector seemed to be Highway 18, a cutoff that

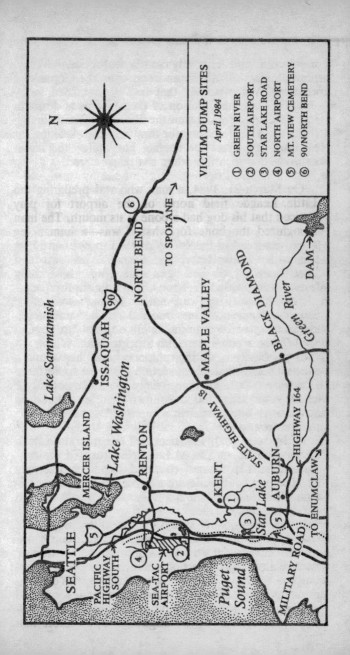

VICTIM DUMP SITES
April 1984

① GREEN RIVER
② SOUTH AIRPORT
③ STAR LAKE ROAD
④ NORTH AIRPORT
⑤ MT. VIEW CEMETERY
⑥ 90/NORTH BEND

connected Pacific Highway South near Federal Way with Interstate 90, the main road over the Cascades to eastern Washington.

Plotted on a map, the discovered victims and their dates of disappearance showed that the killer seemed to cluster his victims in several general locations: There was the river, of course, but while the killer was using that location, he had already started a new one with Gisele Lovvorn, south of the airport. And while police were watching the river, the killer had used that south airport location again with Mary Meehan; then, when Gisele Lovvorn was found, the killer had gone north of the airport with Shawnda Summers. He had returned in the spring of 1983 to both airport areas with Connie Naon and Cheryl Wims. Meanwhile, a new cluster had been started near I-90 with the two unidentified skeletons, and still another one near Mt. View Cemetery, where Pitsor's skull had been found the previous December. The cemetery, Adamson noted, was immediately adjacent to Highway 18, which connected The Strip to I-90.

Further analysis of the places where the victims were last seen filled in the picture even more. So far, there were two major areas where the killer obtained victims: The Strip and downtown Seattle. What he had to work with, Adamson realized, was a triangle of sorts: from downtown Seattle, out I-90 to Highway 18; Highway 18 southwest back to The Strip; and from The Strip north, back to downtown Seattle. The killer, Adamson was sure, traveled those connectors habitually. That probably meant the killer lived somewhere within the triangle.

To Adamson, the clusters of victims proved another thing: There probably was only one killer, after all. What were the odds that two different people, unknown to each other, would use the same sort of clustering system with the same sort of victims, connected by the same roads? The idea that there were two such killers operating independently seemed preposterous.

Finally, the dump sites—Adamson hated the word because it seemed so insensitive, but it had become such an integral part of the discussions about the murders that it was almost impossible now to use another term—had all the earmarks of the same person. Many of the victims had been concealed, if not buried, then covered with cut branches. The locations themselves were always isolated stretches of roadway that provided the killer with a clear view in both directions before getting rid of the victim. And nearly all the locations showed evidence of illegal dumping of household garbage and yard waste. What did that mean? Obviously, the killer was someone quite familiar with such locations. That meant he probably was a long-time resident of the south King County area, and had experience in using the illegal dumping areas before. And wasn't that consistent with the FBI profile? That the killer was trying to send the world a message? That, by leaving his victims with the garbage, wasn't he saying in effect that those he had murdered were just trash?

Publicly, Adamson kept up a positive attitude. No, he said, he was not discouraged. He still believed that the police would solve the case. It was just a matter of time. Was Adamson surprised at the number of new victims? No, he said. It was entirely apparent that the case was far bigger than anyone had ever dreamed. With a dozen missings or more still to be located, Adamson told reporters, he would not be surprised at all to learn of new victim discoveries. And to himself, Adamson said, they will probably be found in new clusters somewhere close to the deadly triangle.

Then, at noon on the last day of March, a man walking in the woods near State Highway 410, a scenic highway that ran from Highway 18 up the shoulder of Mt. Rainier, found the lower jawbone of a human being. The location was nearly thirty-five miles southeast of downtown Seattle in a straight line, much farther by the road, which passed through the small town of Enumclaw. The jawbone was just off an isolated stretch of the highway that provided a clear view in both directions.

Just two hours later, another man far away from the
first discovery, looking for wild mushrooms in another
stand of woods off Star Lake Road, stumbled across
a full human skull. Two new clusters had just been
discovered.

39

STAR LAKE

April 1, 1984

On April Fool's Day, the day after the mushroom
hunter made his discovery, the green-jacketed task
force members were out in force along Star Lake
Road shortly after daybreak. After the discoveries
near the airport, out on I-90, and at the Little League
field, the police had learned well how to organize
searches for more bones. The biggest problem was
covering enough ground.

Patrol units had blocked off the narrow road on
both ends. A uniformed patrol officer waved news
media vehicles through, but kept the general public
out. Another uniformed cop directed traffic past a
bend in the road bordered by a gravel turnout. The
usual gray medical examiner's van was already parked
there, along with another truck being used as a command post by the police. The media people were told
to park farther up the road. They walked back to
the command post and shared the little amount of
information while waiting for Adamson to appear. A
light rain dripped continuously from heavy gray skies.

The search began shortly after eight. Yellow crime-scene tape was tied around the trees just off the road to keep the curious out of the woods until the dense cover had been thoroughly searched. The Police Explorer Scouts were rounded up, and woods marked off into a huge grid with white string. Then the Scouts went into each sector of the grid, one after the other, for an intensive search of every square foot of the heavily overgrown, sloping terrain. The entire area, the size of a football field, was choked with brush, trees, blackberry bushes, and ferns. Fallen logs, tree stumps, and dead branches littered the forest floor. With the rain, the footing was treacherously slippery, and made worse by steep, hidden gullies that crisscrossed the area. Painstakingly, the two dozen Scouts, boys as well as girls, maneuvered their way through the string-marked plots, looking under bushes and logs, inside dense thickets of brush, anywhere someone might place a dead human body. Within two hours two additional skeletons were found south of the road, and the area immediately surrounding all three remains were marked off for more intensive inspection. Tired, wet, cold, and depressed from their grim work, the Scouts reassembled on the blacktop for a breather while the experts began processing the death sites.

One skeleton—the one discovered by the mushroom hunter—lay about fifty yards into the woods due east of the gravel turnout. A second one lay slightly further into the woods about a hundred feet to the north. The third lay over the side of a steep hill, south of the turnout, wedged against a fallen log, and like the others, covered with cut brush. With this last victim, carefully laid head-to-toe against the skeleton as if guarding it, the searchers also discovered the bones of a large dog.

Just before noon, a professional tracker from the U.S. Border Patrol was brought in to look over the area. Adamson didn't want to miss anything that might give his detectives an edge, and the tracker made a discovery that was as electrifying as it was tantalizing. Peering losely at the dirt around the victim found with the dog, the tracker discerned the faintest outlines of shoe prints.

"There was a great deal of foot sign immediately uphill from the body," the tracker reported, "[made] clear by moving the brush from the uphill side to the body. One track was found approximately eighteen inches from the head of the body. All of the tracks were of the same time period as the deposit of the body. The age and development of the vegetable matter appeared to be about a year old.

"The shoe impression is quite indistinct," the tracker continued. "However, it leaves some characteristics: a composition sole shoe; without a distinct heel; straight line from heel to toe; not a casual shoe; shallow sole; only a faint side indentation at instep; gentle curve at ball; well-shaped, not irregular; about size 10, could be as large as an 11.

"The tracks were obviously made when the person could see quite well, probably during daylight. The person could see the trail to carry the body to the location, find the brush and cover the body. Sign gives no indication as to predetermination of depositing the body by the log, however, there is sign of only one person, no wasted motion, cool, calm, organized thinking, not hurried or panicked. He didn't just throw the body into the brush, but attempted to cover it with leaves, ferns, loose debris."

A shallow, composition sole. No distinct heel. Straight line from heel to toe. Not a casual shoe. Size ten or eleven. Who would wear such a shoe? Someone, possibly, who did a lot of walking. A security guard, perhaps. Or maybe a policeman.

Whatever, this was the faintest trace of the killer, an actual indication of the murderer's physical presence. Suddenly the man they were seeking became more palpable. It was as if seeing the footprints made the killer real. Assuming the tracker's analysis were accurate, the prints had to have been left by the man who had put the body against the log. If the tracks had been left by someone else, why hadn't they reported the body? Besides, the shoe prints were covered by the same brush that had been piled on top of the victim—just like the other victims nearby.

And what of the dog skeleton? What did *that* mean? Had the murderer killed the dog at the same time as the victim? Or had he come back later with the dog? Why? Was this another message of some sort? Whose dog *was* this, anyway? For every new fact, Adamson and his investigators gained more new questions.

The skeletons and the tracks were not the only things present at these newest dump sites. Indeed, it appeared as though this particular stretch of the usually isolated Star Lake Road was one of the most popular uncontrolled garbage dumps in the county. Just about everywhere one looked, trash and debris could be found. How much was pertinent to the murders— if any? Did a beer can not far from a skeleton mean that the killer had consumed *that* beer? If so, would his fingerprints be on the can? Was this nearby piece of rag meaningful? What about these threads caught on that bush? Left by the killer—or not?

As each of his detectives reported back to him with descriptions of the items found around the skeletons, Adamson realized that his investigation's inventory of possible physical evidence was about to explode. Well, there wasn't much that could be done about it; the only safe course was to take everything into evidence, and *inspect it all*. But even Adamson had no real idea of how many items that might mean.

By this time, the police had learned a great deal about the careful isolation of possible evidence, particularly the types of evidence that required a microscope to be appreciated. This "trace evidence" often involved hairs and fibers, which had to be carefully removed from the bones of the dead, the dirt around the bones, and even from the nearby bushes and cut branches. Even more important, the evidence collection had to be carefully documented for legal reasons, in case the case ever went to court. A standard operating proce-

dure for the recovery of the remains had become
nearly inviolable.

First, one person was placed in charge of the recovery effort, often Reichert himself, as lead investigator.
The search supervisor had total control over the area
being searched and processed for evidence. The supervisor began by setting a large perimeter around the
search area with the crime scene tape. A second
perimeter was established around the widest possible
area where each of the remains may have been distributed, if the skeleton had been scavenged. A third or
inner perimeter was set up around the decomposition
site itself.

Once the search perimeters were established, investigators inspected the entire area all over again, this
time looking for the most obvious routes to and from
each decomposition site, in an effort to replicate the
paths taken by the killer himself as he carried,
dragged, or possibly escorted his victim to the place
where the body was found. Then each of the possible
paths was inspected closely for any evidence that the
killer may have dropped on the way in or out. Sometimes hairs and fibers might be caught on brush, and
the height at which the fibers were found might indicate whether the murderer carried or dragged the victim to the location.

Once the possible crime routes were established, the
search supervisor then designated an official route to
and from the decomposition area. The official route
often had to be hacked out of the remaining brush so
as not to interfere with the possible crime routes. Each
of the routes was then marked with ribbons or ropes
to keep foot traffic to and from the area under control. Police also used two-by-twelve planks or plywood
sheets to mark the official route. Occasionally, ladders
had to be used to provide non-crime route access to
the skeletal locations.

Immediate inspection of the probable decomposition site allowed the experts to determine the stage of
decomposition, which gave some clue to when the
body had been left; the position of the body when

dropped, which helped indicate whether the victim had been dead or alive at the time; the clothing, if any, and how it might have been arrayed on the body at the time of death, and whether there were any obvious wounds or trauma. Tape recorders were used by pathologists and others to note all the findings, and a video camera was also employed while the inspection took place.

After the inspection, the pathologist, Haglund, and other police investigators inventoried the bones discovered at the decomposition site, and decided which bones were missing. Based on the weight and size of the missing bones, a wider search within the second perimeter would be undertaken, again on hands and knees, for the missing skeletal fragments. Each time a new bone was located, a metal rod with a small flag would be driven into the ground. After some experience, the searchers came to be quite proficient at following the trail of flags, which usually led to the recovery of related bones that had been scattered some distance away.

As the investigators conducted their hands-and-knees tour of the second perimeter area, they kept a wary eye for any items of evidentiary value. Every time something unnatural was discovered—such a cigarette butt, or a beer can, or an article of clothing—the search was stopped until the relevance of the item was evaluated. If the item were meaningful—or if the search supervisor even *guessed* that it might be—it was photographed and sometimes videotaped. The items were then carefully packaged to prevent contamination. Each item of evidence received its own evidence number. After collection, a stake was driven into the ground where the item had been discovered. The hands-and-knees inspection then resumed.

Once the second perimeter had been thoroughly searched, the investigators returned to the actual decomposition site, and began work on the exhumation. The decomposition site was the best bet for trace evidence, such as hairs and fibers, or for clothing or personal items. Hair masses often yielded fibers. The chemical changes as the body underwent decomposition usually rendered the surrounding soil acidic, which limited vegetation growth and often turned overhanging branches or vegetation yellow, which was another indicator of the victim's presence. In cases where the body had been scavenged into smaller pieces, analysis of the yellowed vegetation frequently led to evidence of intense insect activity, and a close look at the insect activity often provided the outlines of how a body had originally been dropped.

The brush around the original body location was cut down and collected. Each branch or twig was inspected for hairs, fibers, bits of flesh, or fabric. Then the decomposition area was divided into small grids, and any vegetation or debris on top of the remains removed and similarly inspected. Each item of trace evidence discovered was meticulously charted for its exact location. Close inspection of the debris was necessary to see what clues it might hold to the passage of time. Small hand tools, magnifying glasses, tongue depressors, tweezers, and the like were used to pick up the small hairs and fibers.

Once the brush was cut and the obvious trace items collected, the pathologist and the detectives carefully inserted a thin sheet of metal under the remains. The hands, feet, and skull were often placed in separate bags. The remaining portions of the skeleton, along with any dirt still clinging to them, were then removed, wrapped in a paper sheet, and placed within one of the plastic body bags. After the remains were removed by the medical examiner for transport back to the morgue, a metal detector was passed over the rest of the area in case any metallic objects, such as jewelry, had been overlooked. Then the dirt still remaining in and around the site was carefully passed through progressively smaller screens in an effort to isolate still more trace evidence, overlooked bones, or anything else of evidentiary value, such as hairpins, fingernails, toenails, or even flecks of nail polish. Each screened segment of dirt was marked by its corresponding grid section number. The sifting process was maddeningly slow, with the diggers running far ahead of the sifters. As a result of all these steps, the processing of a single decomposition site usually took hours.

All of these activities were taking place in the rain on this April Fool's Sunday while the Police Explorers gratefully consumed cups of hot coffee and the news media waited for Adamson to appear. Finally Adamson materialized out of the trees, the rain streaming in rivulets off his pale face and thinning hair. He stood on the roadway while the reporters gathered around him. Pressing his hands together as if in an attitude of prayer, Adamson explained in basic terms what had been found, and how the search was proceeding. He kept silent about the dog, and about the shoeprint, however.

Would Adamson include the new victims on the Green River list?

"I'd have to say yes," he said. "These deaths are very, very similar to what we have seen before. And the fact that we had another victim found just a few months ago [Pitsor's skull at the Mountain View Cemetery] about six miles south of here in a place that is nearly identical to this one makes me believe that these crimes are related."

If these latest three were included, what would the killer's total now be? "Twenty, if you count the one found last night near Enumclaw," Adamson said without hesitation. Then were the police now counting the Enumclaw jawbone, too?

"We aren't sure yet, but probably, yes," said Adamson. And the skeleton found in September of 1983 at Star Lake, the one that was still unidentified? "I'd have to say yes. It's clear that whoever killed these women is very familiar with the roads of south King County. The m.o. in these crimes seems to be the same. So do the victims. At this point it would be wrong to assume that these crimes are not related." He still hadn't decided on the two skeletons found out near I-90, Adamson said.

Did Adamson expect that even more bodies were

yet to be found? "I hope not, but I have to be realistic. We have a dozen missing persons. We have a county with twenty-two hundred square miles, most of it just like this, isolated, overgrown with brush. I'd be very surprised if there weren't more victims."

The following morning, the Police Explorers returned to search the woods on the north side of the road, and found a fourth skeleton. The rain had stopped, the sun was out, and the narrow road was jammed with news media vehicles. At least a hundred reporters, television cameramen, and sound technicians, including one crew from West Germany, clogged the road, milling around while police did their best to ignore them. Overhead several helicopters hovered on station, poised to relay signals from the people on the ground to repeating stations for use in live feeds to New York, Atlanta, Tokyo, and London. The detectives began carting away pickup-truckloads of bagged evidence, including one long twisted shape that seemed to be a portion of a log, wrapped entirely in brown paper.

Adamson stood out on the road as he had the day before and answered all the same questions once again. No, he said, he couldn't say the police were any closer to catching the murderer, but he hoped they were. Yes, he said, he was sure the police would catch him eventually. No, he would not say what the police had found at the scenes.

Hours later, after the media circus had disbanded, while investigators continued to sift the dirt around the last skeleton, Adamson paused to think about what had happened. "What's so awesome about this," he said, "is the number that he's killed. It's just hard to believe.

"I'm sure we're going to catch him. We're like a fisherman, throwing our net out again and again. I don't know what he is. But from my perspective, he's a criminal, he's a killer, and we've got to catch him."

After leaving the site, Adamson drove back to his office in Burien, where he was confronted with a stack of telephone messages, mostly from more of the news media. Adamson wanted to be fair to the news media, but after the events of the past two days, he wasn't sure he cared to talk to anyone anymore. The woods on both sides of Star Lake Road had stories to tell, Adamson thought. The ambience of the whole place was funereal, oppressive. He was letting himself get discouraged, he realized, and that wouldn't work. The minute that he got down, so would everyone else. That would be fatal, he thought.

That night, when he got home, Adamson resolved to shut the murders from his mind any way he could. He needed to let it go for awhile, he knew. He picked up a book of poems by Dylan Thomas. He'd always enjoyed the poet's use of language. But as Adamson leafed through the book his eyes stopped on a page headed: "Death of a Child By Fire in London." Thomas was writing about children dying in the London Blitz, but he might as well have been talking about the Green River murders, Adamson thought. People might not be affected at first that others' children were dying. But as the toll mounted, he thought, the dimensions of the horror and the tragedy would begin to eat into the public's very soul.

While Adamson was reading, Haglund and the forensic dentists identified the first of the four latest skeletons. Terri Rene Milligan, who had only wanted a hamburger from Wendy's in late August of 1982, had finally been found; and while the missing list dropped to eleven, the number of known victims climbed to twenty-two.

40

AFTERMATH

April 1984

The Star Lake sites provided Adamson and his investigators with a huge haul of possible evidence. That was good. But it also created new problems for Adamson and the investigation. The biggest problem was time.

It would take time to organize the material, just to see what they had collected. More time would be required to categorize it in terms of its possible relevance to the investigation. And most time consuming of all, at least some of it would have to go into the state's overburdened crime lab for comparison to similar items. And in the crime lab, the new evidence would in turn generate still more evidence items as forensic scientists attempted to determine what the stuff *was*.

The state-run crime laboratory had been a major bottleneck right from the beginning of the case. Traditionally, the lab had been run not as an investigative agency, but instead as a forensic unit used to provide the proof *after* a suspect was identified.

In other words, the lab was perfectly capable of proving someone's guilt or innocence, but generally unsuited to helping detectives without suspects to know what to look for. When Kraske had given the lab the blood and hair from Foster, the lab had known exactly what to do. But there just wasn't enough time or personnel in the laboratory to have the criminalist peering through microscopes all day, week after week, month after month, in an effort to analyze possible clues to the murders in the absence of specific suspects.

The Connie Naon case was an example. On the surface of things, Naon did not fit the profile of the typical Green River victim. She appeared to have a somewhat stable relationship with her boyfriend. Unlike many of the other victims, she had her own transportation, a dark blue 1967 Camaro. And while she had a drunk driving arrest and a shoplifting conviction, she had no record of prostitution.

But after her disappearance, a friend of Naon's called the police and told them that she had been with Naon on other occasions when Connie drove to the Red Lion, parked, and then solicited passing motorists. The friend told police that Connie did this sporadically, mostly to earn money to buy drugs. The friend told the police to look in the Red Lion parking lot for Naon's car.

The police found the car, and conducted a thorough search of it. Among other things, the search produced a minute quantity of very small particles of a pink, glasslike substance on Connie's purse and on the passenger seat of her car. Five months later, when Naon's skeleton was found south of the airport, the same pink glasslike particles were found on her scalp and in the soil under her head.

Then, in February, when the first skeleton was found out near I-90, small pink glasslike particles were found on *that* victim's hair, and on a pair of woman's panties found at the scene. A month later at the Little League field, small pink glasslike particles were found on several articles of clothing found near one of the skeletons there, along with a strand of fiberglass.

What was this pink, glasslike material? No one knew, and the lab couldn't say for sure *what* it was. If only its origin could be identified, the police might be able to narrow their suspect parameters considerably. But for now, the lab could only go back to work on the items found at the newest and so far largest cluster. Maybe, everyone thought, they would find more of the pink glass.

In the briefings, Adamson heard his detectives build a picture of the Star Lake sites, which gave some clues to the man they were seeking. The road was one of the old side road connectors from the Highline ridge to the Kent Valley below. Unless a driver spent a lot of hours driving around sightseeing, it wasn't likely that he would find the road by accident. That probably meant the killer was familiar with the road from the days before newer connectors from the ridge to the valley had been built. Again, that fit with the theory that the killer had grown up in the south King County area.

Secondly, the west end of Star Lake Road formed a T-intersection with Military Road South. That older highway paralleled Pacific Highway South, and was dark, lightly traveled, and just two lanes, one in each direction. That meant someone who had abducted a victim from The Strip could drive east to Military Road, then directly south to Star Lake Road without much chance anyone would be able to see the victim in the vehicle. Then the killer could drive east on Star Lake Road, past the lake itself and all the houses, to the isolated eastern end of the road and the woods.

The two curves in the road meant the killer could park on the shoulder and have an unobstructed view in each direction. The isolation made the sound of approaching tires audible for a considerable distance. When the coast was clear, the killer could simply remove the victim from the vehicle, and in less than a minute, be deep inside the woods. Then, after dropping the victim, the killer could walk back to the edge of the road, wait for any passing cars to go by, then get back into his vehicle and drive further down the road to the valley floor below. The outlet of Star Lake Road, Adamson realized, was less than a mile from the place on the Green River where the five bodies had been found less than two years earlier.

*   *   *

Two days later, in the first week of April 1984, the skeleton found with the dog was identified as that of Sandy Gabbert. The missing persons report taken from Sandy's pimp showed that Sandy had last been seen about 8:00 P.M. at the Seven-Eleven store on The Strip on April 17, 1983. What was it the tracker said? "The tracks were obviously (by foot placement) made when the person could see quite well (daylight). The person could see the trail to carry the body to the location, find the brush and cover the body."

Sunset on April 17, 1983 was at *seven* o'clock. That meant Gabbert had disappeared in darkness. Was the tracker wrong? Having picked his way so carefully down the hillside where the skeleton was recovered, Adamson didn't see how it was possible for one man to carry a human body down that hill in the dark. Maybe the killer had carried the body up to the edge of the hill, and simply thrown it over. But there was considerable brush along the hillside that would likely have trapped the body before it reached the log. Besides, someone had stood next to the body and had spent considerable time concealing it with the cut branches. And there was the dog.

No, it seemed quite likely that the tracker was right, and that Gabbert's body had been deposited along the log, with the dog, during daylight hours. That meant the killer had kept Gabbert, either dead or alive, for a number of hours after he had first contacted her. If the killer were killing his victims in his vehicle—as seemed likely—that could mean that Gabbert's body had been hidden in the killer's vehicle at least overnight.

After learning of her daughter Sandy's confirmed death, Nancy McIntyre became very angry. She decided to catch the killer herself. She told Larry Gross of the street unit that she intended to find the man by dressing herself as a decoy prostitute and offering herself as bait. What can you do? Gross told his partner. We can't stop her unless she starts interfering with the investigation. But what if something goes wrong? The two detectives asked McIntyre where she intended to go. Nancy told them, and on several nights, the two cops waited quietly in the shadows while Nancy McIntyre tried to attract the attention of the killer on Aurora Avenue North. But finally Gross and his partner decided they had to get on with other business, and Nancy reluctantly gave up the hunt.

In mid-April, another skeleton was found, this one just before 4:00 P.M., off a logging road near I-90 and Highway 18, by a Weyerhaeuser Company worker operating road-building equipment. The task force immediately went to the scene; so did Haglund, who quickly determined that the victim was likely to have been a young woman. Because daylight was fading fast, the police put a guard on the scene and made plans to return the following day to process the site.

The following day, in her suburban sprawler in the Kent area, Barbara Kubik-Patten listened to the television reports of the latest discovery with utter fascination. For almost two years, she had followed the case intently while meeting frequently with Melvyn. For months she had attempted to talk to Reichert about the case, but Reichert had rebuffed her every effort. Barbara didn't think much of Reichert, and Melvyn Foster's anger at the detective only made things worse. But still Barbara persisted in attempting to make contact with the police, relaying information about Foster and others involved in the case to indifferent detectives. In January, when the new Green River Task Force had been formed, Adamson resolved to regularize this potential channel of information. In a conversation with Kubik-Patten, Adamson suggested that she confine her contact to a single detective, Jim Doyon. Unlike Reichert, Doyon refused to dismiss Barbara's claimed psychic abilities outright. That wasn't to say that Doyon necessarily believed in them, but Doyon was an experienced investigator, and he knew honey often worked better than vinegar.

In addition to keeping up the contacts with Foster

and Doyon, Barbara also maintained frequent contact with Hilda Bryant, the television reporter. Somehow Barbara had assembled a collection of all the photographs of the dead and missing women. She kept them arrayed on her coffee table as she conversed with Bryant, Foster, and Doyon over the telephone. For some reason her attention was drawn to the picture of Kimi Kai Pitsor.

While she listened to the news bulletins, Barbara got her vacuum cleaner out and started cleaning her living room floor. As she worked the appliance across the carpet, the photograph of Pitsor and the fact that the task force was processing another body site ran through her mind. Suddenly the living room disappeared and Barbara found herself in a wooded area that reminded her of the place near I-90 where the two skeletons in February and March had been found. She saw herself discovering a new body.

"It was like watching television," Barbara said later. "I recognized the intersection as Highway 18 and I-90. So I decided to take the kids out to North Bend for ice cream and a look at the woods also." Kubik-Patten rounded up her two children, packed them into her car, and rushed off to the intersection she had seen in her "vision."

Barbara drove out Highway 18 and came to the intersection of I-90. She stopped, confused. Where was the place she had seen in her mind? Just then she noticed a state patrol car parked under the I-90 freeway overpass.

"I went up to the car and I said to him I saw this psychic vision of this body being in the woods but I don't know where the spot is. I described this place to him." The state patrolman shrugged, and told her that if she found a body, the task force was working not far away.

Barbara drove back the way she came until she found a service road leading into the woods. "The vision said go into the woods, and go back twenty feet." Barbara parked her car and with the kids walked into the woods, past an old mattress and other trash.

"There was a lot of brush and stuff. We walked to the other side of the bushes and didn't see anything. Then the vision, it was like a voice, said go back twenty feet farther. I saw what I thought was an animal head and I went over to check it. It had been there quite awhile. There was no meat on it, just bones. It was a long animal's head of some sort. I thought, 'This isn't what the vision said,' and I turned around and my daughter was looking at the head and I saw this clump of plastic (tarp) and this numb voice said to go and pick up the tarp."

Barbara walked over to the plastic with her daughter right behind her. As she peeled back the plastic some of it stuck to what appeared to be decomposing bones. As she looked closer, Barbara saw dental fillings and long hair.

Barbara dropped the plastic and stepped back, gasping. She nearly stepped on her daughter. "What is it, Mama?" her daughter asked. "Go over there with your brother and stay there," Barbara told her. Barbara looked again under the plastic and saw that she had indeed discovered a human skeleton. She could tell it was a female because of the long hair that remained attached to the skull.

"We better get out of here," Barbara told the children. Suddenly Barbara had a fear that the killer might be watching them. "We ran right to my car and I was so nervous I couldn't get into my car." Fumbling with the keys, she finally got in and drove off to find the task force.

Some distance away Barbara found the outer perimeter of the task force's search area. She drove up to the command post. A cop assigned to controlling the outer perimeter refused to let her go any further. Barbara told him that she had found a body. The cop didn't believe her. Barbara told him she wanted to talk to Doyon. The cop got mad and threatened to have her arrested for obstruction of the investigation.

This wasn't working out at all the way it was supposed to!

Barbara drove back down the road, fuming. At the bottom of the hill she encountered a gathering of news reporters. "I told them I had found a girl's body in the woods, and that the task force guy had told me to get the hell out of there and didn't want anything to do with it," Barbara told the reporters.

Barbara asked them if they wanted to go with her to where the body was. Sure, said the reporters, let's go.

Just then a car came tearing down the road behind her. Jim Doyon got out of the car and motioned to talk to her. Barbara was still mad. She couldn't believe that the police had refused to believe her. Doyon listened to her story, then asked her if she would lead him back to the body. Barbara agreed. Everyone got into their respective cars and drove off. They came to the place where Barbara had first parked, and the police told the news media people to stay put. Then Doyon and the other two officers followed Barbara back into the woods. The kids stayed in Barbara's car.

Doyon peeled back the plastic. He got down on his knees and peered closely at the remains. Barbara stood about three feet away. Doyon said he was certain the skeleton was that of a Green River victim. Doyon went back to the police car and radioed to Adamson that Barbara had been right.

41

AMINA

April 1984/May 1984

The following day, April 23, the medical examiner's office identified the remains the police had been working on when they were interrupted by Barbara. The skeleton found by the Weyerhaeuser worker was that of Amina Agisheff.

The identity was a shock to Adamson. Agisheff had been on the Seattle Police Department's missing list since July 7, 1982. The county police had originally declined to list her as a possible Green River victim. And why not? She was thirty-six years old, and the mother of two children. She had no record of prostitution, not even any hints of it.

And yet, here was her skeleton, found altogether too close to three other remains. It seemed inescapable to Adamson that Amina Agisheff's killer was the same person who had killed the other three. The cluster theory seemed to be in working order.

But Agisheff? There was no way the woman fit the profile of the other victims. Older, for one thing. Had a stable relationship with a man. Had two children. Was close to her own parents. Had no connection to The Strip. Worked as a waitress in downtown Seattle. Was the discovery of her body in the midst of this cluster simply a coincidence? Or was it somehow a significant break?

A look at Agisheff's missing persons file showed that she had gotten off work on the evening of July

7, 1982, and had dropped in to visit her mother, who lived in an apartment near First Avenue and Virginia Street on the edge of Seattle's historic Pike Place Public Market. After drinking two beers with her mother, Amina had left about 11:30 P.M. to walk to a bus stop at First Avenue and Pike Street, two blocks away. First and Pike was the crossroads of the Seattle tenderloin and a frequent soliciting location for prostitutes working inside the city limits.

What had happened? Had the killer kidnapped Amina? Or *had Amina known the killer*? Had someone Amina knew personally picked her up near First and Pike, perhaps offered her a ride home? Was that person the same man who had later killed all the others after picking *them* up at random? An intensive background investigation of Amina's life had to be undertaken as a top priority.

One obvious possibility was that the killer they were seeking had been a customer at the restaurant where Amina had worked, and that Amina had made his acquaintance there. The date of her disappearance— if the Green River killer had gotten Amina, she would have been the first victim, even before Coffield— added weight to this idea. Sometimes a serial murderer's first victim was someone known casually to the killer.

But if the killer had gotten Amina, why had he put her body in the woods, and not in the river as he had with the other early victims? The dates of disappearance showed that Amina's disappearance was followed by Wendy Coffield, who was in the river; then Gisele Lovvorn, back on dry land south of the airport; then Dub Bonner, Marcia Chapman, Cynthia Hinds, and Opal Mills, all in or near the river. Why hadn't one or more of those four victims been placed on dry land? Particularly Mills, whose dumping would have been extremely risky to the killer? Was it possible that they were dealing with two independent serial murderers *at once*? A dry land killer, who started with Agisheff or perhaps even earlier, and a river killer, who had started and stopped in July and August of 1982? Did that mean, as Douglas and Keppel had so frequently suggested in late 1982 and throughout most of 1983, that the original investigators on the case had come very close to identifying the river killer? Was that why *those* crimes had stopped?

Was it possible they had mixed up the crimes of two different people entirely? What would that do to the matrix of disappearance times and places they were using to eliminate suspects? Already the detectives were of differing opinions on the question. The whole debate was central to the matter of Melvyn Foster. If there were two different killers, Foster's solid alibis for the dates when some of the dry land victims— Shawnda Summers, most obviously, because Foster had been under surveillance when *she* disappeared— would lose their importance. Any investigator looking at Foster had to keep in mind the fact that he seemed to be the only person who had contact with all five of the river victims.

The most troubling aspect about the two-different-killer theory was what it suggested about the police understanding of the crimes all along. It was as if they had set out to solve one problem, only to discover another, far larger problem buried deep underneath the first. How far did these crimes go back, anyway?

To answer that question, Adamson had the task force's three-member crime analysis unit begin researching unsolved female homicides throughout western Washington, going back a decade. Maybe they could uncover similar cases, and find the tracks of the killer back at the very beginning.

In late May of 1984, two children digging a play fort on Jovita Road, just over the King County line in Pierce County, discovered another skeleton. The Pierce County Sheriff's Department immediately called on the Green River Task Force to help process the site. Chief Medical Investigator Haglund quickly identified the new bones as those of a young female. This one, Haglund saw immediately, was so young she still had braces on her teeth.

42

HOAXED

July 1984/August 1984

By the middle of July, Adamson's detectives had made substantial progress on the missing persons problem. Using the Airport court's records of warrants issued for arrested prostitutes who failed to show up for trial, along with the arrest reports themselves, jail records, and any other records they could locate, two detectives, Rich Battle and Cherie Luxa, assembled a working missing list of nearly thirty names. Not all of the names had been placed on the official missing list, because not all the leads to their possible whereabouts had been investigated. But the detectives helped track down dental charts for most of the thirty, and several others besides. The dental charts were given to the medical examiner's office to join the growing "library." The sifting of all the lists resulted in three new names for the missing quotient.

Among the new missings, said police, were Becky Marrero, last seen in early December of 1982. Also missing, they said, were April Dawn Buttram, eighteen, and Mary Exzetta West, sixteen. Both of the latter girls were last seen in Seattle's Rainier Valley, Buttram in August of 1983 during the height of Nolan's crackdown on prostitution on The Strip, and West on February 6, 1984. West thus became the most recent known Green River victim. The missings now totaled fourteen.

Despite the progress on identifying the missings, the medical examiner's office had seven unidentified skeletons, the most in the history of the office. By this time, Adamson had decided that the two skeletons found near I-90 in February and March were in fact Green River cases, and had included them as well.

Late in April, Haglund and his dentists made positive identification of the jaw fragment found the day off Highway 410 before the Star Lake horror. When Debbie May Abernathy had been reported missing to Seattle Police on September 5, 1983, her age had been listed as twenty-six. Once investigators discovered that Abernathy was really only sixteen, it suddenly became a lot easier to find her dental records in Waco, Texas. Abernathy was also added to the list. So was Amina Agisheff, despite the lack of evidence of any prostitution background.

The skeleton found in Pierce County was included, too. After reading about the victim's braces in the newspaper, a father called the detectives to alert them to the missing persons report he had turned into Seattle city police on his braces-wearing, runaway teen-aged daughter in late December of 1982. The dental records of Colleen Rene Brockman, only fifteen, matched the teeth found with the Pierce County skeleton. Because it was now official that the killer had committed a crime in Pierce County, one of that agency's detectives was detached to join the task force. With Amina Agisheff, Debbie Abernathy, and Colleen Brockman, the list of identified dead reached nineteen. Counting the unknowns, the toll was at least twenty-six.

By this point, the lack of identifications of the seven unknowns was making it very difficult for detectives to foreclose suspects using the time-and-place matrix. As a result, Adamson gave permission for three detectives primarily responsible for the missing-persons effort to contact area dentists directly for help. With the cooperation of the state dentists' society, the charts of the teeth found with the unidentified skeletons were published in the area dentists' monthly magazine. Dentists were asked to check their records to see whether they recognized any of the charts. No one did, at least among the dentists who bothered to look.

Meanwhile, there was Melvyn Foster to deal with. By now Adamson had resolved to push Foster up or down on the list. He decided to give Foster yet another crack at the polygraph machine.

The way Foster told the story later, the police very politely asked him to come back to Seattle and resume their discussions. So Foster did.

After the first day of talks, Foster told reporters that the police were thinking of eliminating him. He had alibis, he said, for the Star Lake crimes, and the police were inclined to accept them. The next day, Foster again spoke to reporters, and said the police had given him a new polygraph on some of the Star Lake victims. This time, Foster claimed, he had passed. Police declined to comment.

Didn't that eliminate Foster? It did lessen some of the task force's interest in the man, Adamson admitted, although he still refused to rule him out on all the crimes.

But Adamson knew that if Foster was responsible for only some of the crimes, that meant the single-killer theory was discredited completely. While Adamson admitted that it was possible two different killers, each operating independently, were responsible for the murders, he still believed that it was only one man, or possibly two men acting together. It didn't make much sense any other way, he said, because of all the commonalities in the crimes, river and dry land alike. And if that were so, then Foster probably wasn't guilty of anything worse than being a buttinsky.

Meanwhile, all the publicity about the murders—augmented by the intensive work of the street team in making contact with the women—had virtually cleaned The Strip of prostitutes by the summer of 1984. The murderer, it seemed, had done what the police could not.

*　　*　　*

Then, in early August, two violent criminals lodged in the San Francisco County Jail confessed. *They* were the Green River murderers, they said, and Susan Sward, the reporter for the *San Francisco Chronicle*, bannered their claims across the top of the front page. The story created an enormous sensation, with the two men claiming that they had killed sixteen "and possibly more" women throughout the Pacific Northwest in the summer of 1983. One of the men told *The Chronicle* reporter, "Do I think I am the one they are looking for? I would have to say yes."

One thing was certain: Richard Carbone and Robert Matthias were not nice people. Carbone was facing sentencing after a recent conviction in San Francisco on rape, robbery, and sodomy charges. Matthias was waiting trial on armed robbery charges. Both men had served time in California prisons. They had called *The Chronicle*'s reporter from a telephone located within the jail.

But the claims of the two men had a history that was not unknown to Adamson. Beginning in mid-July, a man claiming to be an acquaintance of Matthias and Carbone made a series of telephone calls to Seattle area newspeople, telling reporters there that he knew of two men in the San Francisco jail who were claiming responsibility for the murders. Under questioning, it became clear that the two men probably did not have anything to do with the crimes; for one thing, the two men claimed to have put the bodies of victims in the Green River in the summer of 1983. That was a year off, of course. Told the men's claims didn't sound right, the "acquaintance" then said the two men weren't saying they were *the* Green River murderers, but only copycats. "They wanted to throw the police off the track. They thought it would be funny," said the "acquaintance."

After the calls, reporters checked with Adamson, who termed the claims, as usual, "interesting, very interesting." But then Adamson suggested that his detectives were aware of the two men's claims, and that no one gave them much credibility.

How had the police learned of the claims so far in advance of *The Chronicle*'s "scoop?" As the story later developed, an "acquaintance" of the two men had also called a Seattle writer who had been following the Green River murder case with avid interest. Ultimately, the writer was to admit she had talked with Matthias and Carbone themselves more than thirty times. The writer said she had been passing the claims onto the Green River Task Force "with the permission" of the two men.

But the communication between the men and the writer was apparently a two-way street. In questioning the men, Adamson learned, the writer inadvertently gave them enough information about the crimes to enable them to provide a convincing story to *The Chronicle* reporter two weeks later. The "acquaintance" who had started the whole thing was none other than one of the inmates himself. That simply illustrated the dangers of not keeping control over the investigation information, Adamson thought; journalists and writers untrained in such information control could easily be used by false confessors, and the investigation's resources needlessly diverted.

But now that the claims had been made public, the task force had to go through the exercise of determining their validity, for public relations purposes if nothing else. As it happened, a task force detective, Paul Smith, was vacationing in San Francisco when the story hit the newspapers. Adamson asked Smith to go interview Matthias and Carbone to see what they had to say.

Within a few hours, Smith had easily determined that Matthias and Carbone had nothing to do with the murders. Neither man could describe the Seattle Space Needle, for example. It was simply inconceivable that the two men could have been in Seattle as long as they claimed to have been and never noticed the city's most distinctive landmark. Even sillier, neither man could tell Smith whether Puget Sound was freshwater or saltwater!

Meanwhile, *The Times* obtained the two men's California prison records. The records clearly showed that both men were in California penitentiaries when most of the Green River crimes were committed. Even more telling, it appeared quite likely that neither man had even met the other until both were jailed in San Francisco only weeks before they made the claims.

By nightfall on August 7, the claims were completely discredited. The truth, Matthias told Paul Smith, was that he and Carbone had made up the story in an effort to induce Washington State authorities to bring the two men to Seattle. The idea, Matthias said, was that when the task force detectives took the two men out into the woods of the Great Northwest to find the bodies of their supposed victims, the pair would make a break for it. The entire hoax was nothing more than an elaborate escape plan.

43

REMAINS

August 1984/October 1984

As the summer waned, Jo Adamson was struck by how much her family's lives had been changed by this unknown man, this killer. Frank had never been close-mouthed with her about his work before, but this case was different. Jo noticed that each new discovery seemed to wear harder on her husband. Sometimes Frank would clam up, responding in monosyllables. Jo took responsibility during those times to force Frank out of it, to get him to talk. There's no purpose in bottling it up, she told Frank. And when Adamson retreated into his impassive, taciturn behavior, Jo would challenge him, argue with him, until Frank exploded at her. Jo began recording their conversations. Afterward she played the tape back to Frank, to let him know how he sounded. Gradually Adamson began to confide in her, using her as a sounding board.

At night around the dinner table, Adamson would discuss the day's events. Soon the conversation was all about femurs, mandibles, pelvises—bodies and bones—hookers, murder, prostitution; until finally Brian, then 15, would have to say, Enough. But then would come the telephone calls, usually at night from Haglund at the medical examiner's, and the talk about bones, bones, and more bones would begin anew.

As the weeks and months wore on, Jo found her own outlet to deal with the macabre subject that had taken over their lives. Sitting in her study overlooking the backyard's fruit trees, Jo began to write a play. She pinned photographs of the victims on the wall and stared at their faces; slowly, they began to talk to her, telling her about their lives, their hopes, their disappointments. She saw through them, their feigned hardness, their studied casual vulgarities, and knew them for what they were—very young girls with no place to run, victims of serial murder in three acts. It began with two fifteen-year-olds, waiting for a trick. And then came the killer, alternately sly, then cajoling, finally angry, burning with self-righteousness and hatred of women; followed by the timelessness of the river, which became a character itself as it told of how it had been used. Jo wrote and the play took form, giving her a place to put all the feelings, all the rage. Jo called it "Remains," and when it was done, she put it in her desk and shut the drawer. It would never see the light of day, she knew; *it was too close to the bone.*

As the summer progressed, Frank became an increasingly familiar face on television. Once a week he and Jo would have dinner at a different restaurant.

People approached him, recognizing but not quite remembering who he was or what he did. Some thought he was a politician. "I voted for you," some would say, and Frank, not wanting to explain, would just smile and say, "Thank you." Others who put his face together with the investigation wanted to discuss it with him. Are you ever going to catch the guy? "We're working on it," Frank would say in his cheerful, laconic way.

Many wanted to discuss their own ideas about the crimes, and Frank listened patiently. "Interesting," he said, "very interesting." Wild ideas poured forth, and tips about neighbors, ex-husbands, and coworkers were provided. Often Frank wrote these down, just to be polite. Occasionally, he put them into the task force's suspect hopper.

Soon Frank was receiving telephone calls at home from the public. Most callers were well meaning, wanting to help Adamson solve the case. Some were from self-professed psychics, and after Barbara's discovery of a skeleton, Adamson received calls from psychics who wanted to turn in *other* psychics. The calls ran the continuum of human sanity, and occasionally, very disturbed people found Adamson's number in the book and called him. But Adamson refused to change his number; there was just a chance, however small, that someone who knew the killer might call. Or even the killer himself.

Then, in late August, Jo answered the telephone while in her study. A man was on the line, claiming to be the killer. "I'm the Green River killer," the man said, "and now I'm going to go after the top dog." As Jo stared at the pictures of the victims on the wall, the phone went dead. Jo was shaken, not because she believed that it was really the killer who had called, but because she realized that she and her family had become targets for a universe of deranged minds.

Jo told Frank and Brian about the call. Both were upset. Jo was spending a lot of time out at night, helping to rehearse one of her plays. Was it possible that the killer, or someone else, would try to kill her because she was the wife of a public figure? Jo wasn't worried, too much; but Frank now knew just how Kraske had felt ten years earlier.

44

EYEWITNESS NEWS

November 1984/December 1984

The press problems that simmered through the summer and into the early fall finally boiled over in November. Throughout the previous months, news agencies peppered Adamson, Vern Thomas, and County Executive Revelle with complaints over the lack of access to the Green River detectives. One all-news radio station proposed that Adamson allow the station's reporters complete access to the investigation, promising to withhold all or most of the information until the killer was caught. Revelle's press aide pointed out that if one news outlet were granted that sort of access, all the others would want the same thing. If that happened, the detectives would soon only be giving interviews, the aide said, and then the work on the case would slip even further behind. The radio station's pitch was politely rejected. Similar approaches came from newspapers and television stations. Resolutely, Revelle and Thomas held them off.

Then in October, Seattle television station KIRO made an offer that made Adamson think twice: the station would offer a $100,000 reward for information leading to the arrest and conviction of the killer. In return, the task force would have to open its doors slightly to show the taxpaying public what they were up to. KIRO began conducting interviews with task force members and victims' families, and assembling file footage of the obligatory processions to the gray van. The programs would be aired during the quarterly "sweeps week," in which surveys of the Seattle-area television stations' ratings were conducted.

Without doubt, the programs were certain to substantially increase the station's ratings at one of the most critical periods of the year, thus increasing the revenues earned through advertising sales. KIRO's coup did not take long to leak out. Although Adamson and Brooks firmly denied that KIRO would get any inside information, the other news outlets doubted that. Just getting through the task force front door would give KIRO a chance to get to know the detectives and establish some back-channel relationships, other reporters believed. Relations between the press and police turned even more snappish. The reward, it was cynically pointed out, would only apply to information turned in to either the task force *or* the television station during the thirty days after the programs aired in November. Afterward, the reward would be withdrawn.

The complaints from the other news media outlets went up the line to Revelle, down to Thomas, over to Adamson, and finally, back to the KIRO management itself. Adamson understood about the complaints. But on the other hand, it seemed to Adamson that this was exactly the sort of proactive media strategy Douglas and the other FBI experts recommended. Using a television station to bang the drum so loudly might shake something loose, possibly even the killer himself, or even more likely, someone who knew him. As long as the information provided to KIRO could be managed, it would probably be worth the risk.

In early November, just after the election, the station began running a week-long special on the murders, complete with dramatic music and a handful of ominous mood shots, all heavily promoted with the slogan, "Somebody Knows Something!" coupled with pleas for calls. Thousands of telephone calls soon flooded the task force offices. The resulting tip sheets poured into the crime analysis section and sat there like a giant, indigestible lump while the analysts struggled to evaluate the information and assign investigative priorities to the tips. But there was nothing that seemed to provide the key.

Publicly, Adamson defended the KIRO program as a worthwhile investigative strategy. But within the ranks of the task force, doubts over the effectiveness of the effort took hold. Instead of giving the detectives the key to the crimes, the program had simply quadrupled the amount of chaff to be worked through.

Then, just as the KIRO gambit was ending, another news management problem blew up with *The Times*. Reporters there had begun poking into Kraske's original investigation of the river murders, and had learned that police had overlooked a number of leads in the aftermath of the discoveries in August of 1982, and that, for most of 1983—while many of the murders and disappearances were taking place—police had been seemingly oblivious to the crimes. The police, said *The Times*, had blown their best chance to catch the killer in 1982.

After all the effort to pump up the reputation of the task force through the KIRO week-long special, the newspaper stories were like popping a balloon. The bad relations between the police and the press grew even worse. More importantly, some detectives worried that *The Times's* publication of all the investigative gaffes would sour the mind of the public toward the task force. Would the negative news coverage affect calls to the police? Would it make the public feel that the police were incompetent, or worse? Adamson hoped not, but he just couldn't see how the newspaper had helped improve the chances of catching the murderer.

The paper put most of the blame on Winckoski and Kraske. The stories blamed the retired sheriff for not giving Kraske the help he needed (or even recognizing that help was required), and on Kraske for not asking. Kraske felt terrible. He had been so sure about Foster, but here were all these other skeletons. It *was* just like Ted, he thought, all over again.

By now, Kraske had left the Criminal Investigations Division, and was in charge of the county's north precinct. He found himself looking back again at what he had done, and couldn't find much he would have done differently. He watched as Adamson had come in, had gotten teams of detectives; a separate headquarters; travel money; interagency cooperation from the Port of Seattle, the city of Seattle, and Pierce County; priority assistance from the FBI; a separate headquarters; complete backing from his sheriff; even a $200,000 grant from the state to acquire a sophisticated computer system to keep track of all the tips. Revelle was also trying to get a federal grant to help pay for the investigation, after earlier deciding to hire thirty-four new officers to take up the slack left by the transfers to the Green River group. Indeed, it seemed to Kraske that Adamson had gotten a blank check from the county, a mandate to spare no expense, to leave no stone unturned in the search for the killer.

But Kraske knew he was no Adamson; he had never had the power or the politics to unlock the same doors of opportunity for himself. Cops weren't supposed to ask for help in his day. He should have, he thought, but it just wasn't in him. Just as it hadn't been in Winckoski to see that help had been needed.

Now, with the newspaper beating him up over what was promising to turn into the worst serial murder case in American history, Kraske realized how lame it sounded—in defense against such second-guessing—that no one had known when he was in charge just how how bad it would turn out to be, how many victims there really were. The newspaper hadn't cared about his excuses. Its stories kept suggesting that *he should have known*. Well, he wished he had.

A week after *The Times's* criticism, two weeks after

the KIRO reward was withdrawn, Kraske went to visit
his relatives in Montana, collapsed, and was hospital-
ized. Something inside, the doctors told him, was
making him bleed.

45

TED AGAIN

December 1984

In December, in his prison cell in Florida, Ted Bundy
read about the Green River Murders going on back
in his home state. He thought he might be able to
give the police some help. But that was vintage Ted;
while he had never confessed to any crimes, he still
believed that he had special insight into the minds of
murderers like him. Bundy wrote to Keppel. Keppel
went to Florida.

The main thing, Ted said, was that police should
keep the sites where victims' remains had been discovered under surveillance. Serial killers, he said, had a
strong affinity for the places where they left their victims. They were almost certain to return to those
places to relive the events that led them there. Bundy
willingly climbed into the brain of the Green River
murderer and explored with Keppel just how such a
killer might feel, what triggers might set him off. Keppel listened patiently while realizing that Bundy was
projecting his own fantasies onto the Green River
crimes. And, thought Keppel, Ted probably has
another motivation: *He wants us to catch the killer
before he passes Bundy's record.* Keppel was dis-

gusted. He also knew that Ted was bargaining with
him, trying to make himself valuable to the police in
the hope that Keppel or Adamson or someone would
ask the Florida governor to issue a stay of execution.
How like Ted to use anything and everyone around
him, to pose as the expert, Keppel thought. Well, this
time Bundy was out of luck, Keppel decided.

Bundy's ideas did not surprise Adamson. Really,
they were simply variations on what the FBI's John
Douglas and Keppel had already said. But the conversations jogged an image in Adamson's mind. He
remembered the times he had been fishing, how he
had taken the fish he had caught and put them under
water. Beneath the surface, the fish looked bigger,
Adamson recalled, magnified as they were by the
water. He saw the Green River killer carrying the
bodies of the dead women down the bank of the river,
first Wendy Coffield, then Dub Bonner, Marcia Chapman, and Cynthia Hinds. The killer put each in the
water and weighted them down with rocks. Afterward,
the killer sat in the grass on the river bank, enjoying
his catch, now larger than life beneath the slow, clear
currents.

Yes, the killer probably did return to the places
where he left his victims, thought Adamson. Or, at
least he had until the television had told the world
that it was too dangerous to continue when it revealed
the surveillance of the river back in August of 1982.
Now, no one knew where the killer was.

46

PATTERNS

September 1984/May 1985

Throughout the rest of the fall and into early 1985, as Adamson's task force continued to whittle away at the pile of information they were collecting, the pile of suspects grew steadily.

The street team continued to search the prostitution areas for witnesses and sick tricks, and the victim detectives dug deeper into the lives of the dead and missing. New names were generated for possible interviews, and the crime analysts continued searching for patterns. Was the killer a daytime worker, or on the night shift? Did he work at all? Was there any pattern to the days of the week that victims disappeared? Did the locations of the disappearances correlate with the days of the week? About the only pattern that could be discerned was that the killer seemed to go into a murderous frenzy in the spring of 1983, murdered steadily throughout that summer, and then embarkled on another frenzy in the fall of that year.

Meanwhile, quietly, special investigations were begun into a number of police officers, some in the county department, others in Seattle, and still others in the suburban departments. The idea that the killer was a cop had begun with the prostitutes themselves, but the apparent ease with which the murderer continued to evade detection caused some analysts to conclude that the killer was indeed someone with refined knowledge of evidence procedures and police techniques.

Publicly, Adamson steadfastly maintained that it was unlikely the killer was a bona fide policeman. The killer's behavior would have given him away to other police officers by now, Adamson said, especially as the psychological strain from the murders mounted.

It was far more likely, he said, that the killer was someone on the periphery of law enforcement, possibly a private security guard, perhaps even a corrections or parole officer. But leads about real cops continued to come in, and Adamson knew they had to be checked out. The fact that the task force was even looking at other police officers soon became known, inside the police brotherhood, and some of the officers investigated reacted bitterly.

Five times during the fall of 1984 the task force officers went to new dump sites, and twice Adamson decided to add new victims to the Green River list. Three of the other crimes seemed different to Adamson; and in at least one case, police had made an immediate arrest of a murderer, but not the man responsible for the Green River crimes.

Two of the new skeletons had been found on Highway 410, the road to scenic Mt. Rainier, within a few miles of the place where Abernathy's jawbone had been discovered just before the April 1 discoveries at Star Lake in the spring.

The first new skeleton was found off to the side of the scenic mountain highway on Columbus Day, in mid-October, when a mushroom hunter stumbled across the bones some fifty yards into the trees from the highway. The medical examiner's office was quickly able to identify the latest remains; Haglund and the dentists identified the skeleton as the remains of Mary Sue Bello, the woman reported missing to Seattle Police in October 1983. The effort to assemble the dental records of so many missing girls was beginning to pay grim dividends.

Bello had disappeared from someplace in Seattle

almost exactly a year earlier to the day her bones were found. Seattle Police had offered her name as a missing person to the county police in November of 1983. Within two weeks of placing her on the missing list, however, Nault had removed her when a policeman in Texas sent word to the detectives that he had seen Mary Sue Bello *after* her reported disappearance. The Texas cop had even sent fingerprints, and they had matched Mary Sue's. But here was her skeleton off to the side of Highway 410. Adamson concluded that Bello *had* been in Texas, but well before her grandparents had reported her missing in Seattle. The Texas cop, Adamson concluded, was confused about when he had last seen Bello. Or maybe he had seen someone who looked like her, and thought it *was* Bello again. In any event, the case only illustrated once again the difficult necessity of properly evaluating and investigating missing persons reports.

A month after Bello's remains were discovered, two hunters not far from the spot where Bello's remains were found went into the woods in pursuit of an elk. Thirty yards away from the road, they found a skeleton lodged behind a large fallen log. The following day, again using dental charts, Haglund and the dentists identified the remains as Martina Authorlee, who had last been seen in May of 1983. The Highway 410 victims followed a familiar pattern: First, the killer tested the site with Authorlee's body. When it wasn't immediately discovered, he returned with Abernathy in September of 1983, and a month later with Mary Sue Bello. The identified victim toll had reached twenty-eight.

The new discoveries rekindled a debate within the task force. Some detectives wanted to spend more time searching places where the killer logically might have dumped other victims. They argued that the families of the missing women deserved that much. And, they said, there was a chance that new sites could yield critical physical evidence.

But Adamson kept thinking about the twenty-two hundred square miles in the county. There were literally thousands of "logical" dumping spots. It seemed to him that finding remains was mostly a matter of luck, anyway. But a search *could* generate certain proactive opportunities, Adamson thought, the sort that the FBI's John Douglas might suggest.

Just before Thanksgiving of 1984, at Adamson's direction, Detective Fae Brooks announced to the news media that a search of the forested areas next to Highway 410 would be undertaken—but not until sometime after Thanksgiving. If there *were* other bodies off the highway, Adamson thought, the advance announcement might prompt the killer to go back, just in case, to see if he had inadvertently left anything incriminating behind. Naturally, the highway would be under covert surveillance in the days leading up to the actual search.

Meanwhile, the police and medical experts continued to plug away on the identification of the remaining unknown skeletons. Slowly the names were pried out of the teeth and bones as relatives and friends, realizing they had not seen the dead for too long, belatedly contacted the police or the medical examiner and directed investigators to old dental charts and x-rays.

One of the two skeletons found near I-90 in early 1984 was identified as Lisa Yates, a nineteen-year-old woman who had been missing since late December of 1983. Yates was the victim with the tiny pink glass particles. And the skeleton found near the half-buried remains of Connie Naon on South 192nd Street late in 1983 was identified as having been Kelly Ware, twenty-two, who had last been seen near a bus stop in Seattle's central district drug-peddling zone. The skeleton found March 31, 1984, whose skull had led to the Star Lake discoveries, was identified in December as Delores Williams, a seventeen-year-old who had last been seen on The Strip near the Red Lion, in March of 1983.

The September 18, 1983 victim, found when a resident was searching for a lost chicken, was identified by skeletal x-rays late in February of 1985. She turned out to be twenty-three-year-old Gail Lynn Mathews. Mathews had been in a boating accident some years before her death, and had broken her pelvis and collarbone. Relatives directed investigators to hospital records, which provided x-rays of broken bones that matched faint lines of healed bones in the skeleton. The relatives told police they had last seen Gail on The Strip in early April of 1983.

Still, four other skeletons or fragmented remains defied identification: the first skeleton found along I-90; the very young girl found by the caretaker's dog at the Highline Little League field early in 1984; the bones found wrapped in the plastic tarp by Barbara Kubik-Patten; and the fragment of lower jaw found in early 1984 by the other dog not far from Kimi Kai Pitsor's remains, near Mt. View Cemetery. That bone fragment was so small it was impossible to tell whether the victim had been a man or a woman.

Looking for solutions to the identification puzzles, however, generated new leads for detectives to follow up. Investigators worked hard to find people who had known the victims. Again and again, detectives found themselves dealing with information that was difficult, almost impossible, to refine. When did you last see Lisa, Kelly, Gail, or Audrey, as Delores Williams called herself? The answers were frustratingly vague in all too many cases. People rarely remember exactly where or when they saw someone when they were accustomed to seeing them come and go. Exact dates were almost impossible to pin down. The locations were a little easier, but investigators continued to be aware that the dates of disappearances that were so crucial to their work were all too fluid.

On the last day of January 1985, a detective assigned to the task force by the Seattle Police Department, Ed Striedinger and county detective Dave Walker, thought they had a possible breakthrough on a suspect. Another SPD man investigating a routine burglary obtained a file that had belonged to the suspect in the burglary, who could no longer be located. The burglary suspect had been the boss of a topless dancing club in downtown Seattle that had employed Lisa Yates. The day she disappeared was to have been her first day at work.

Inside the suspect's file folder, the burglary detective found a snapshot of two naked women, both lying in a field. He told Striedinger and Walker about the discovery.

"The photo shows two females, both nude," Striedinger reported to the task force. "The faces are not visible. There is grass and weeds grown to about two and one half to three feet. There is no horizon shown in the photo. Both girls are on their backs. Each of them has one leg extended and the other raised at the knee. Neither of them appear to have any obvious signs of trauma. The female on the left of the photo appears to be white and the other may be white or may be a racial mix. There are signs of swelling and bloating of the left leg of the girl on the right. The girl on the left has her right hand extended and the hand bent forward at the wrist. Both females shown in the photo appear to be dead."

Striedinger and Walker showed the photograph to other cops. All had the opinion that the women looked dead. That afternoon they took the picture and showed it to Dr. Reay. Reay examined the image, and agreed that the women appeared to be dead. The left leg of the girl on the right appeared to show some signs of postmortem lividity, Reay said. "He also pointed out the fingertips of the female on the right, and gave the opinion that it appears to show signs of decomposition," Striedinger reported.

Next the detectives took the photo to the University of Washington and showed it to two professors who worked in the university's earth sciences department. One professor examined the picture and suggested that from the vegetation it appeared to have been taken in July or August, and probably in a field in the northern half of western Washington.

The following day, a hunt for the burglary suspect

was launched. Detectives heard reports that the man and his girlfriend may have headed for California. Contacts were made with the welfare department in California, and three days later, a welfare official in that state told the investigators that the suspect's girlfriend had applied for welfare in that state, and had given an address in San Francisco. One hour later, Striedinger and Walker made arrangements to fly to San Francisco to locate the suspect.

By 5:00 P.M. on February 5, Striedinger and Walker had developed a line on the suspect's whereabouts. The trail led them from cheap hotel to cheap hotel. The detectives learned that the suspect's girlfriend was working in a nude dancing emporium in the tenderloin called "Fantasies in the Flesh." At one hotel, the detectives learned that the couple had been evicted because of their visitors, "specifically," wrote Striedinger, "a woman named 'Rita Erotica,' a young blonde girl who wore a lot of leather clothes and carried a whip." They had left no forwarding address.

Striedinger and Walker went to the tenderloin and started checking the adult bookstores and dancing establishments. The detectives met with the local San Francisco police and asked them to turn up the heat in the search for the suspect.

The following day, a trip was made to the hotel of "Rita Erotica's" boyfriend, who had also checked out. Then the detectives drove across the Bay Bridge and checked two addresses over there that had been associated with the suspect. The detectives found the address of the suspect's parents, and went there. No one was home.

That afternoon, the detectives went to "Fantasies in the Flesh," where the suspect's girlfriend was supposed to be working. She wasn't there. No one knew where to find her. The detectives went back out on the street, and shortly after two-thirty in the afternoon, spotted a car that looked the same as that reportedly driven by the suspect. They went into a nearby cheap hotel and found that the suspect was registered there. The two detectives and an inspector from the SFPD went to the room and knocked on the door, saying they had a warrant for the suspect's arrest. The man was taken into custody, along with his girlfriend, the topless dancer, and her baby.

About four o'clock, six days after it had all begun, Striedinger and Walker interviewed the girlfriend. They read the woman her Miranda rights.

"We then showed her a copy of the photograph in question and explained where we obtained them. We again asked if she was willing to discuss the photograph. She again agreed. I asked her to explain about the picture," said Striedinger. "She told us that the girls in the picture were not dead and she was, in fact, one of the girls in the picture." The suspect's girlfriend couldn't remember the other girl's name. "We asked her why the picture was taken and where. She said they had a friend take the picture along with several others, because they wanted to have some good nude pictures." The girlfriend said she planned to send some to *Hustler* magazine.

After the girlfriend was given a polygraph test and found to be telling the truth, Striedinger and Walker returned to Seattle. Now the detectives looked for the second girl to see if they could confirm the girlfriend's story. Another cop tracked the girlfriend down, and she came in for an interview. Yes, she said, she was in the picture. She and the suspect's girlfriend had worked together as topless dancers several years before, and had decided to have art photographs of themselves taken. A photographer named Pierre was hired to do the job. The woman had taken half of the thirty or so pictures, and the suspect's girlfriend had taken the rest. She had thrown her half away, she said. But the girl told the detectives that she had sent one of her photos to her sister. The sister lived in San Francisco.

Striedinger called the sister and confirmed the existence of the second photograph. He then asked the SFPD to pick it up and have it sent to Seattle. Five days later, the picture arrived. "I examined it," wrote Striedinger, "and saw that the location is the same.

The two females in the photo are [the two dancers]. In this photo, both girls are sitting up and smiling." So much for fantasies in the flesh.

In early February of 1985, Thomas met with the chief of the State Patrol, Chief George Tellevik, who promised support for the Green River investigation. But somehow the crime lab always seemed to have more pressing things to do. Tellevik explained the system to Thomas, who already knew it: The lab's first priority was to process evidence needed for trials, and there were a lot of those. And some things the lab simply wasn't equipped to do. As a result, in late February, Thomas and Adamson sent a large evidence package back to the FBI for the bureau's analysis.

Early in the month, Adamson and his detectives pulled off a coup of sorts when an undercover officer bought Melvyn Foster's aging sedan for $1,200 cash. Foster was led to believe he was selling the car to an ordinary person. Once detectives had the vehicle, the FBI was asked to send a three-agent team to consult in the processing of it for trace evidence. The car was dismantled. Thirty-four different pieces of the car, including the dashboard and interior mouldings, were sent east to the FBI laboratory for intensive analysis. Sophisticated equipment, including a laser, would be used to search for hard-to-find fingerprints not discernible by the traditional chemical methods. When the fingerprint analysis was completed, the FBI would send back another agent with any hairs, fibers, or bits of other trace evidence taken from the dismantled car for comparison with evidence taken from the death scenes. That way, Adamson and Thomas hoped to get some sort of definitive answer on the troublesome cab driver.

On March 10, 1985, yet another skeleton was found near Star Lake Road. A seventeen-year-old boy walking through the woods not far from where Sandy Gabbert's skeleton had been found discovered the new remains partially buried in thick mud. Once again the detectives cordoned the scene off and began the laborious process of reclaiming the bones from the earth. Within a day, the skeleton had been identified as that of Carrie Rois, the fifteen-year-old who had run away from the state receiving home in March of 1983. The newest victim, Adamson said, had probably been overlooked by the searchers when Gabbert, Williams, Milligan, and Smith had been found. Adamson ordered another massive search for the Star Lake area for the following day.

"If there's one thing we've learned during these homicides," he said, "it's that we've got to expand our search area." The Police Explorer Scouts were called once more, and the brush and forest was beaten for more than a mile down a muddy creek south of Star Lake Road. But no new skeletons were found.

A few days later, Adamson said publicly what had been apparent for more than six months: The murders seemed to have stopped, though not all of the victims had yet been found. An exhaustive review of all the city and county missing persons records and other information, Adamson said, seemed to indicate that the killer had stopped murdering early in 1984. That, of course, was also about the time that street prostitution in the Seattle area had taken its nosedive. While people had been reported missing throughout 1984 and into 1985, none of those who remained missing fit the victim type of the killer, Adamson said.

"In spite of our best efforts," said Adamson, "it is possible there are missing people we don't know about. It's conceivable other jurisdictions are not keeping as close a tab on the missing as we are."

Adamson said it was too soon to conclude that the killer had left town. Instead, Adamson said, the killer could be merely waiting for the heat to die down before starting up once again. The way to prevent further murders, if not in the Seattle area then somewhere else in the country, was for the police to identify the killer before he struck again.

*   *   *

Just four days later, however, the detectives added one more name to the missing list: Cindy Ann Smith, a seventeen-year-old topless dancer, had vanished just like so many others while hitchhiking on The Strip late in March of 1984. When police finally narrowed down the date she had disappeared to March 21, 1984, they were surprised to note that Cindy Smith, also known in the topless trade as "Vanilla," had thumbed her way to a likely death at the same time the task force was so carefully sorting through the remains of Cheryl Wims at the Highline Little League field not a mile away.

Reporters rushed to interview Cindy Smith's mother and stepfather, who lived in a deteriorating house on the edge of Tacoma's industrial section. Joan Mackie was a recovering alcoholic; her husband was suffering badly from emphysema. The pair told how they had tried but failed for more than two years to separate their daughter from a pimp who had peddled her outside topless joints from Anaheim to Anchorage. Cindy had finally returned home on March 20, 1984. She had gone out to hitchhike the following day to "My Place," the topless tavern on The Strip, they said, but she had never arrived.

Joan Mackie's eyes were red with weeping. In the background, a small portable television set broadcast the news of her daughter's addition to the missing list. "I hate that damn TV," she said. "Every time you turn it on, you hear another body's been found. That sets me right back. I have to start thinking about Cindy again, I start wondering if . . . I can sympathize with any parent who's going through this. I certainly wish they would hurry up and catch whoever or whatever it may be who's doing this . . .

"I don't know," Mackie said. "I've just turned everything over to God . . . I'm praying."

Late in March, Thomas and Revelle's aide Shelly Sutton conducted a complete, confidential review of the investigation. While Adamson, Thomas, and Revelle kept saying publicly, over and over, that things were going well, the reality was considerably starker.

The major problem, wrote Sutton in a secret memorandum to Revelle, was still in the crime laboratory.

"There are a number of problems related to processing physical evidence and fingerprints that impede the progress of the investigation," Sutton wrote. "First, the volume of physical evidence continues to overwhelm the Washington State Crime Laboratory. As of this writing [March 22, 1985], the task force has collected and catalogued 3,995 pieces of evidence, and each piece of evidence may contain hundreds of fibers, hairs, or other evidence that needs to be processed, analyzed for commonalities, and then compared. The backlog of lab requests stands at 123—80 with the State Crime Lab and 43 with the FBI Crime Lab. It is important to note that a single lab request may contain hundreds of items of evidence. For example, some of the lab requests are 12 pages long, with ten or more items listed on one page."

In short, the investigation was in danger of being strangled by its own evidence.

In addition to the backlog, the lab had completed processing on less than forty items submitted by the task force—just over 1 percent of all the evidence so far collected. Of course, those items were the richest in trace evidence, so the actual number of separate items examined by the lab experts was very much higher: Each time an article was submitted to the lab, the technicians with their magnifying glasses and microscopes found tens and sometimes hundreds of subitems to examine further. Thus, the evidence had a tendency to multiply geometrically.

At the rate of processing indicated by the current backlog, it would take more than *fifty years* to examine every bit of evidence so far collected. Adamson was haunted by the fear that the smoking pistol the detectives needed might be somewhere in the mass of evidence that would probably never make it to the lab.

Another important obstacle, Sutton wrote, was in

the processing of fingerprints, normally a police department function. Even though Revelle had added a new fingerprint technician to the county department four months earlier, Sutton wrote, processing the prints was taking far too long. Already the task force had developed nearly six hundred unknown partial finger- and palmprints from various pieces of evidence. The prints needed to be compared to the prints the department had on file—a tedious, time-consuming process.

To help speed up the fingerprint processing, a new device that used a computer to process the prints would be made available in both Anchorage, Alaska and San Francisco. The Alaska machine held the prints of eighty-five thousand people, and the San Francisco database was even larger. Plans were made to take the six hundred Green River partial prints and run them through both computers in the hope that some of the prints might be identified.

Finally, Sutton turned to an even more sensitive subject, the use of outside consultants. While other places had hired outside consultants in coping with their own serial murder cases—notably Atlanta with the child murders—Thomas and Adamson had come to believe that outsiders were often counterproductive. Big-name consultants, they felt, often used their consulting for self-promotion purposes; political leaders liked them because they gave the appearance of doing something and spreading the heat. But bringing consultants into the investigation often meant, at a minimum, delays while the consultants were brought up to date on the case. Worse, there was the risk that the consultants might leak confidential information, "to try to get some political mileage out of the situation," as Sutton put it.

Still, Sutton contended, consultants might be useful if their services were carefully defined. Already, she noted, the task force had obtained the services of Douglas from the FBI, two Seattle area psychologists, and the forensic dentists. A team of outside police analysts had been brought in during May of 1984, Sutton said, to review the task force's paper flow methods, and had made suggestions for improvements. The Border Patrol tracker had provided useful information, as had a forensic anthropologist, who had reviewed the medical examiner's methods for classifying skeletal remains. Even a professor who specialized in insects had proved useful.

But overall, said Sutton, the idea of bringing in a high-powered team of murder experts to assist in the investigation had more drawbacks than advantages. "These types of teams often serve more political than substantive needs," Sutton said. The county would be better off to go it alone, Sutton recommended.

In mid-April, again using old x-rays of previously broken bones, the medical examiner's office identified the other skeleton found early in 1984 near I-90. Delise Plager had been twenty-two when she had disappeared while waiting at a bus stop in south Seattle. Plager's story was a familiar refrain: She had been a runaway as a juvenile; had a lengthy record of juvenile arrests for petty crimes; had several arrests as an adult; and had generally lived a life of poverty and disappointment, punctuated by deep depressions and feelings of worthlessness. She was the mother of two small children.

Plager's identification brought the number of the unknowns down to just two, not counting the lower jawbone fragment.

Early in May, Adamson was asked to give a speech about the murders before the Seattle Rotary Club, one of the centers of business and political leadership of the city. Speaking before the Rotary Club was one way of maintaining crucial political support for the investigation, Adamson knew.

"It looks like the killings may have stopped in King County," he told the Rotarians. "But can we be sure?"

Serial murders, he said, were far more common in society than had previously been believed. Even if the Green River killer were no longer active, that did not mean that another person or even several other people might not commit the same kinds of crimes in the future.

"Some people have a desire to murder, and murder, and murder again. It's a chronic condition," he said. And no one should think that just because a killer makes street prostitutes his victims, he always will. "None of us is safe, or none of our wives, or none of our children," Adamson said.

One of the major challenges posed to modern society by serial murderers was the need to recognize such crimes far earlier, said Adamson. Police agencies all too often suffered from "linkage blindness"—the reluctance to look farther abroad, often out of their own jurisdiction, for similar crimes.

"I don't believe for a minute that these crimes started with the bodies found in the river in 1982," he continued, adding that task force detectives had reviewed homicide cases involving young women in King, Snohomish, and Pierce counties from 1973 to 1982, and had found thirty-eight unsolved murders over that decade that were similar if not identical to the Green River crimes. The task force was stunned to discover the extent of violence directed against women, he said. Even when the detectives limited their records search to only men convicted of actually murdering women, they were aghast at the number that resulted.

"This is indeed a regional crime," said Adamson, "and it may be a national crime. It may touch all of our lives."

47

GOING SOUTH

May 1985/June 1985

As May turned into June, the task force continued to struggle with the mountain of information it had acquired. Nearly twenty thousand tips had come in, many naming the same suspects over and over again. Each scrap of information had to be scrutinized, even when it involved someone previously discounted by the investigators. No one could be sure that the new information might not change a prior decision about a suspect's viability. The evidence backlog jumped to over forty-two hundred separate items collected by the investigators; as some of the items were passed to the lab for more intensive examination, technicians discovered hundreds more.

Meanwhile, the efforts to use the fingerprint computers in Alaska and California had brought no positive results.

Was it that the killer hadn't left any fingerprints at all? Was he wearing gloves? It was more complex than that, Adamson explained. While it was true the task force had about six hundred partial prints, some of them were so fragmentary that it was impossible to pluck out likely candidates from the two databases. There were simply too many possibilities. The fingerprints would come in handy only if a good suspect could be found.

Still, Adamson remained convinced that the name

of the killer was somewhere inside the task force records. But where? And how to recognize it when it came up? That was the trick, Adamson acknowledged.

Well, what about Melvyn Foster? Adamson refused to say so, but all the high-tech processing of the thirty-one parts of Foster's car had netted no matches to any of the known victims. Still, Adamson refused to completely rule Foster out as a suspect.

In early June, Foster went a little nuts. Foster's pedal-to-the-medal driving style resulted in a traffic dispute between the former cab driver and a twenty-one-year-old man near Olympia. Both drivers wheeled into a restaurant parking lot and got out of their cars to continue the confrontation. According to the younger man, Foster advanced on him with a knife while making threatening statements. Police were called and arrested Foster and clapped him in jail pending a mental evaluation.

The Green River Task Force was asked to comment on Foster's arrest. "He remains one of the numerous suspects we've got," said a spokesman for the task force, not mentioning the fact that Foster had been cleared of the Star Lake crimes, and probably all the others except for the river victims.

Meanwhile, the possibility that the killer had gone elsewhere was being given serious consideration. A review of other serial murder cases showed that when police came close to a suspect, it was not unusual for the suspect to move to a new part of the country and start all over again. The classic example was Bundy.

Were there other similar homicides involving prostitutes elsewhere in the country? There were indeed.

Portland, Oregon, was the Pacific Northwest's third largest city after Vancouver, B.C. and Seattle. Just three hours away from Seattle down the I-5 freeway, Portland likewise had a thriving sidewalk trade in prostitution. It also had seven homicides of prostitutes, at least four of them somewhat similar to the Seattle-area killings. Most, but not all of them, had taken place before March of 1984, the month Adamson and the others felt marked the end of the murders in King County. The most recent crime in the Portland area had taken place in October of 1984.

For months, the detectives had been watching the Portland cases to see whether any arrests were made. A solution to any one of the Portland cases would provide a prime suspect for the King County murders because of the proximity between the two cities.

Portland police were less than forthcoming with information about their crimes, however. They continued to insist that not only were their murders not connected to the Seattle crimes, they weren't even related to one another. Adamson and his detectives weren't so sure. Now that the crimes in King County appeared to have stopped, Adamson and the task force had to consider the clear possibility that the killer they sought had fled south after the task force had been formed.

In late April, the task force had circulated a bulletin to all local police officers that listed as many as sixty-one victims—including five of the Portland murder victims. The list was labeled "Green River Murder Victim–Missing Persons List," and had never been intended for public distribution. But somehow, after a month, it made it into *The Times*. The list was the most inclusive ever drafted by the police. In addition to the Portland victims, two other young girls in Spokane, Washington, were included, as were many of the women murdered in Seattle in early 1982—victims the police had previously refused to include. Did this mean that Adamson and the task force were finally admitting what the women's groups had been saying for more than a year? That the Green River murders were far larger than the police and politicians had been willing to admit? That even Portland and Spokane were within the killer's range?

Adamson was embarrassed by the publication of the list. So was Sheriff Vern Thomas, who apologized to County Executive Revelle.

"I would characterize it simply as a list of women who died and might be of interest to other law-enforcement agencies," explained Adamson. "There are names on that list that are not related to Green River."

But why was the document labeled "Green River Victim–Missing Person List"?

"The label is a little incorrect. There are people on that list that I'm almost positive are not related." Well, then, which cases *weren't* related?

"I'm not going to go into that," Adamson said.

The fact was, as Adamson had suggested at his Rotary Club speech, no one really knew for sure which cases were in and which were out. Some cases were more typical of the classic Green River murders, especially those cases involving clusters of victims. But no one could say with absolute assurance that the non-clustered victims in Seattle and Portland weren't the work of the same murderer. And the Spokane cases involved two hitchhiking, teenaged girls who had disappeared together, and whose nude bodies were found floating in the Spokane River—strangled—in the fall of 1983. These crimes were chillingly similar to the five victims found in the Green River only a few months earlier. The fact that Spokane could be reached by car from Seattle within a few hours by driving east on Interstate 90 increased the odds of possible connection.

Why was Adamson so cautious about these other crimes? After all, hadn't he already claimed that the Green River murders were "indeed a regional crime, maybe a national crime?" The answer was politics.

Starkly put, for Adamson to contend publicly that the Green River crimes had taken place under the noses of many other police jurisdictions throughout the Pacific Northwest was to bring the political heat on those jurisdictions as well, and to implicitly question the competence of those authorities. Bringing the heat was no way to get anyone's cooperation.

While one might think that it would be comparatively simple for police in one city to get the cooperation of their counterparts in another, in the real world of cops nothing is quite so straightforward. As in most other government activities, politics rules all. The politics of policing is, if anything, even more byzantine than ordinary electoral politics, conducted as it is behind the facade of poker-faced professionalism that Americans have come to expect from the forces of law and order.

But in the real world of diplomatic relations between police jurisdictions, there are matters of ego to be addressed, as well as sensitive questions of who gets credit or blame when things go right or wrong. Most important is the question of competence. Appointed police professionals are exceedingly touchy about suggestions that they have failed to do their jobs adequately. To have an outside agency—such as the task force, or even the FBI—come into a jurisdiction to conduct an investigation is tantamount to an accusation of incompetence, many ranking police officials feel. Barriers to information sharing are quickly erected behind the screen of retaining confidential information, and paranoia about possible leaks impedes cooperation. The failure of law enforcement nationally to come to grips with its parochialism is one of the major problems in dealing with crime in a free and highly mobile society.

Such was the situation when, on June 11, 1985, a partial skull found outside of Portland was identified as having belonged to Denise Darcel Bush, who had lost a coin flip with her pimp and had gone out for a pack of cigarettes, almost three long years before.

The bones were discovered by a bulldozer operator in Tigard, Oregon, a suburb southwest of Portland in suburban Washington County. The equipment operator was tearing up brush to prepare the ground for the planting of a tree farm when he noticed the partial skull. He called local police, who searched a small area around the initial discovery and located a few more remains, and the partial remains of a second skull as well. Was this another cluster, this time in Oregon?

Detectives with the Washington County, Oregon,

Sheriff's Department notified the task force of the discovery, but not before officers controlling the crime scene allowed the bulldozer operator to resume operations. That might have been an error, given the possibility that still more bones might have been present, but then destroyed by the equipment.

Meanwhile, dental charts and x-rays from both skeletons were sent to Chief Medical Investigator Haglund at the King County Medical Examiner's office. Within a day, the first skull was identified as having belonged to Bush.

How had Bush gotten to Portland? After all, she had last been seen on The Strip about noon on October 8, 1982, when she had left the motel after the coin toss to buy the cigarettes. She had left her belongings in the motel room. It simply wasn't very likely that Bush had decided to go to Portland on her own. It seemed obvious someone had kidnapped Bush and taken her to the Portland area. It couldn't have been Melvyn Foster, because that was when Foster was under surveillance.

But was it the Green River Killer, or someone else? And was Bush dead or alive when she crossed the state line? The latter question was significant, at least in political terms. For one thing, it might for the first time give the FBI a legal justification for entering the case. Bringing a kidnapping victim across a state line was a federal offense. Bringing a dead body was not.

And who was the second skeleton? Also the remains of a female, the proximity of the second skeleton to the first was very reminiscent of the clusters of victims found in the King County area. If the second skeleton was also a Green River missing person, the possibility that the killer had crossed state lines early in the series would become far more likely.

A week after Bush's remains were discovered, the FBI announced on June 21, 1985, that it intended to review her death to see whether it had jurisdiction.

"Information publicly reported in both newspapers and on television indicated that we should conduct this preliminary inquiry," said the FBI's Seattle special agent in charge, Allen Whitaker. "I contacted Sheriff Vern Thomas to discuss this case. We met yesterday and discussed it and here we are." The bureau would have up to ninety days to decide whether it had any jurisdiction, Whitaker said.

"We'll wait and see what the preliminary inquiry shows us," he said. "I wouldn't want to speculate on the structure but we certainly wouldn't compete or conflict with the locals." The ninety-day rule was a bureau regulation. But more important, it effectively allowed the agency to work without restrictions on the Green River case for three months. That meant that agents who had previously only fulfilled a consulting role on the case would now have the opportunity to go into the field.

Meanwhile, Adamson and four other members of the task force headed for Washington County, Oregon, to review the Bush case, and to discuss the other Portland area murders.

A few days after Adamson and the Green River group arrived in the Portland area to consult with the local police and the FBI, a renewed search of the place where Bush's skeleton had been found turned up a pelvic bone, and several smaller bones that were matched to the other remains found with Bush. While in Washington County, the task force members also reviewed two other cases of young female skeletons found, again together, several months earlier in Tualatin, Oregon, another Washington County suburb just south of Portland. Neither of those skeletons had been identified. Plans were made to compare all three of the unknown Oregon victims to the King County library of dental charts and x-rays.

Two days later, in the middle of June 1985, Haglund and the dentists made a positive identification of the woman found with Bush. Shirley Sherrill, the nineteen-year-old woman who had been arrested on The Strip the day Bonner's body had been found—the woman who had gone to Portland to get away from the murders—hadn't gone far enough.

48

LOTTIE

June 14, 1985

While Adamson and some of the task force members were driving down to the Portland area, a young woman named Lottie got into a nondescript silver van parked in the lot of a bowling alley in south Tacoma. It was early evening. The van's driver had removed the middle seat. He sat on the rear bench of the van, unzipped his pants, and gestured for the young woman to begin earning her money. The young woman reached for the man's unerect organ and looked up at his face. Something about it froze her. Suddenly, the man produced a long, sharp knife from somewhere on the seat and held it to her throat.

"Put your hands together," the man ordered the twenty-two-year-old Lottie. "Do what I say or I'll cut your throat." The man grabbed Lottie by the right wrist and tied a section of rope around it. The man had the rope in his pocket, already cut. Lottie started trying to talk to the man, to convince him to let her go. Just then a station wagon full of people went by, and Lottie started screaming for help. The car went on past. The man put the knife to Lottie's throat again and said, "If you don't put your hands together, I'm gonna kill you right here." So Lottie put her hands together and the man tied her up.

The man told Lottie to lie down on the floor of the van. Lottie did it. She watched as the man reached

311

under the seat and pulled out a plastic bag. The bag was stuffed full of rubberized cords with hooks in them, the kind used to tie things down while camping. While Lottie lay face down on the floor, the man tied her legs together with one of the rubber cords, then stretched it to hook one of the hooks around a post on the side of the van. He used another cord to tie Lottie's legs to the other side of the van, then did the same thing with two other cords he wrapped around her chest. The man retied Lottie's hands so she couldn't reach any of the cords, then reached behind the seat again and pulled out two pieces of duct tape, already cut, and put them over Lottie's eyes. Lottie started crying.

"What are you gonna to do to me?" she asked the man, over and over. "Just tell me, what are you gonna do to me? If you want to . . . just take me, I'll give it up . . . just tell me what you want."

The man said: "I won't tell you. We'll get there, then you'll find out."

The man put two blankets over Lottie, then an air mattress. Finally he tied another rope to Lottie, and pulled on the end of it to show that he had control.

"Don't move," said the man. "Don't make any sounds. If you move I'll know it and I'll come back there and kill you."

The man went back to the driver's seat and started the van. He began driving away. Lottie felt the van start and stop several times, then make some turns. Lottie could hear other cars on each side. After a few minutes the speed of the van increased, and Lottie knew they were on the freeway.

After a while the man pulled off the freeway. Lottie had managed to push back the blankets a little. She knew they were going someplace weird because in the twilight she could see branches rushing past the windows of the van. Lottie knew she was going to die.

As the evening grew darker and the van rushed on, Lottie worried at the ropes around her hands. The driver felt her move. "Stop that," he ordered. "It's for your own good."

Lottie stopped for a few minutes, then started trying to loosen the cords around her legs. By using one of her feet to push the cords down, she got her legs loose. Then she went back to the rope around her wrists.

"Don't move," the man said again.

"All right, I won't," said Lottie, and she stopped for a little while. But after a minute or two, Lottie started on the rope again, this time using her teeth to pick at the ends. Somehow, she wasn't sure how, she loosened them.

"Don't move, I'm telling you," said the man.

"I can't breathe," said Lottie.

"Don't move. If you don't want to get hurt, then leave the covers over your face."

Lottie lay quiet for a minute, then abruptly sat up, unhooked the rubber cords, then jumped to her feet. She ran straight for the knife that was lying on the floor next to the driver's seat. The van was traveling about thirty miles an hour.

The man shot a look over his shoulder as Lottie made her run for the knife. Lottie got the blade in her hands as the man continued trying to drive while fumbling his right hand for the haft of the weapon, trying to keep it away from her. Lottie raised the knife and started stabbing at the man. She gashed him above the eye. A car went past in the opposite direction. The man lost control of the van and it piled into a ditch, stalled, and threw both of them onto the floor. The man got the knife away from Lottie and cut her. They continued fighting for the knife, Lottie screaming, the man saying over and over that he had a pistol, that he would shoot her, and Lottie thinking, *I don't care, I don't care, if he's got a gun, why isn't he using it, he hasn't got one* . . .

Just then the sliding door of the van was shoved back and Lottie saw another man staring at them. She screamed again and called to the new man to help her. "Knock it off!" the samaritan shouted, then turned away and tried to flag down some other cars. Then the man Lottie had cut suddenly gave Lottie a shove and pushed her out of the van onto the ground. Lottie got up and ran into the nearby trees. The man who had tried to kidnap her was wandering around outside the van, acting dazed, the blood streaming down his face. Lottie turned and ran toward the cars that had stopped. Two other men were advancing on the driver of the van, who threw something into the bushes. A woman in one of the cars that had stopped gave Lottie a ride to a nearby gas station to call the police. Lottie still had the remnants of the ropes around her wrists. She had bitten them all the way through.

Within a matter of a few minutes after he first met Richard Terry Horton, Thurston County Sheriff's Department Detective Sergeant Mark Curtis wondered whether he was interviewing the Green River killer.

The Thurston County authorities had arrested the forty-one-year-old Horton outside a rented van that had crashed on Marvin Road, an isolated road that made the way to a rarely occupied days-only park at the edge of the southern part of Puget Sound, two counties south of King County. Witnesses who had stopped to help after the crash had noticed Horton wandering around outside the vehicle. A young woman was shrieking hysterically. The woman still had the remnants of ropes tied to her wrists. Both Horton and the young woman were bleeding. The witnesses had seen Horton throw something into the brush. A Thurston County deputy later recovered a brown duffel bag filled with a weird assortment of what looked like surgical instruments and syringes, and still later, a bone-handled knife with an eight-inch blade. The young woman had identified the knife as the weapon Horton had used to kidnap her.

Horton didn't seem to be the right type to be a kidnapper, Curtis thought. He was pudgy—about 210 pounds on a five-foot-eight-inch frame. He was married and the father of three children. He seemed pretty bright. He was a hospital corpsman for the U.S. Navy, a twenty-year veteran. He had done two tours as a Marine medic in Vietnam. Everything about the man screamed quiet, polite, slightly above average. Horton had been assigned to the *U.S.S. Ohio*, the first Trident submarine. Curtis asked if Horton minded if they searched the van. Horton said he didn't mind.

Curtis had already heard about the ropes and the rubber cords, and the deputy had shown him the brown duffel bag, which held another bag holding several large empty syringes, a few smaller ones, a recently purchased package of douche solution, a large forceps, and a wicked-looking trachea hook. Elsewhere in the van Curtis found a gas-operated pellet gun, a well-thumbed Bible, a copy of Joe McGinness's book, *Fatal Vision*, and a religious tract showing a minister being threatened by a huge maniac with a gleaming, foot-long silver knife.

Curtis opened the Bible to a place that had been marked by Horton. The mark was in the book of Ezekiel, Chapter 16:

> But you trusted in your beauty, and played the harlot because of your renown, and lavished your harlotries on any passer-by . . .
> And I will give you into the hand of your lovers, and they shall throw down your vaulted chamber and break down your lofty places; they shall strip you of your clothes and take your fair jewels, and leave you naked and bare . . .
> They shall bring up a host against you, and they shall stone you and cut you to pieces with their swords . . .
> And they shall burn your houses and execute judgements upon you in the sight of many women; I will make you stop playing the harlot, and you shall also give hire no more . . .
> So will I satisfy my fury on you, and my jealousy shall depart from you; I will be calm, and will no more be angry. . . .

At that point Curtis called the Green River Task Force in Seattle. Here was this well-thumbed Bible, marked to a verse about killing prostitutes, stripping them, taking their jewelry, and stoning them, and a motive: ". . . and will no more be angry." Curtis had seen the stuff in the duffel bag, and he had heard the gist of the young woman's story. It was clear to Curtis that Lottie was a prostitute: Lottie herself admitted it. And Curtis also believed that if Lottie hadn't chewed through the ropes on her hands, she would probably have been murdered.

The Green River Task Force had long since put out the word to police departments in western Washington to be alert to violence directed against prostitutes. This little caper seemed to fit the bill perfectly.

The task force, naturally, was extremely appreciative of Curtis's tip. They would send someone down the freeway to Thurston County the first thing in the morning, they said. In the meantime, Curtis thought he would take a statement from Horton—if he cared to give one. The problem was, Curtis didn't know exactly what to ask Horton, at least as far as the Green River crimes were concerned. And while Horton might be in his most psychologically vulnerable state—having just been arrested—not having a Green River detective on hand to ask questions meant that the best course would be to wait until morning to ask Horton about those crimes.

In the meantime, however, Curtis resolved to do his own job: Find out about the assault and kidnapping of Lottie.

Shortly after 3:00 A.M., Curtis and another detective with the Thurston County Sheriff's Department asked Horton if he would discuss the incident with them. Horton agreed to talk.

After reading Horton his rights, the two detectives told Horton they were investigating an assault. They asked his permission to record the interview. Horton agreed.

Horton worked hard to sound sincere. His halting voice seemed calculated to portray himself as some sort of victim of a bizarre lapse in judgement. He had decided to hire Lottie for oral sex, Horton said, but then changed his mind. He decided to get his money back, and the only way he could think of to do it was kidnap the woman! Horton told the detectives that he had panicked, and the whole incident had escalated out of control.

Later, Horton would try to portray the incident as self-defense. It was Lottie who had attacked *him*, Horton said. That seemed even more farfetched. Horton told Curtis that he had never had a date with a prostitute before. Curtis doubted that very much. Horton's description of the events made it sound like Horton had merely bumbled his way into the situation. Curtis kept thinking about the precut duct tape and ropes, the conveniently placed knife and rubber cords, and most all, Horton's *failure to reclaim the thirty dollars he said he wanted to retrieve!* The bills had still been in Lottie's possession, blood soaked though they were. Curtis took the money as evidence.

The following day, Mike Hatch, a King County detective assigned to the Green River Task Force, drove south to Thurston County. Search warrants were obtained for both the van and the U.S. government vehicle Horton had left parked in Tacoma. It appeared that Horton had been assigned temporary duty at the naval nuclear reactor facility in Idaho, and had decided to leave his government-issue car in Tacoma. He had rented the van to go camping, he said. The rental place removed the middle seat. Curtis was ready to charge Horton with first-degree kidnapping and assault.

But by morning Horton had thought over his situation. He had contacted an attorney. Detective Hatch asked to be allowed to interview Horton about the Green River murders. No way, said Horton's lawyer. Would Horton agree to take a polygraph test? Horton said he would. His attorney said, You're joking. The offer of the test was rejected.

Hatch drove back to Seattle. It was clear that Horton would be an "A" suspect. But the question was, could the task force prove that he was the right man, in the right place, at the right time? Hatch started assembling a timeline on Horton's whereabouts over the past few years. He obtained an inquiry subpoena for Horton's credit car records and his telephone bills. The credit car billings did not begin until after the Green River murders were over. They were no help. The telephone billings showed only one interesting thing: Someone using Horton's home telephone number had made a call from the Mariott Hotel on The Strip on May 28—the day after Marie Malvar's driver's license had been found in the airport. Yet the hotel had no record of Horton having been registered as a guest.

The answers about Horton, the detective realized, would have to be found by the Navy. The Naval Investigative Service began an investigation into Horton's whereabouts in 1982, 1983, and 1984. After several weeks, while Horton was held for trial in the kidnapping and assault of Lottie, the investigation was completed. It showed that Horton had been serving aboard the nuclear submarine *U.S.S. Ohio* when it docked at its base at Bangor, Washington on August 12, 1982—the same day that Opal Mills supposedly disappeared at Angle Lake on The Strip, and the same day that Dub Bonner's body was found at the PD&J slaughterhouse by Frank Linard. If Horton was aboard, he probably couldn't have been the river murderer, because all of the river victims except possibly Opal Mills were murdered while the submarine was making its way from Groton, Connecticut, through the Panama Canal to Bangor. That assumed, Hatch realized that Horton was really aboard the submarine, as the Navy's records suggested.

The N.I.S. obtained more records. These showed that Horton was probably at sea again in early 1983 when two of the Star Lake Road victims were murdered. Finally, the records indicated that Horton was serving shore duties at the base medical dispensary at Bangor during at least three other disappearance dates, and had been on vacation with his wife in Ore-

gon in early June when Constance Naon vanished.
That seemed to definitely eliminate Horton. Hatch
recommended that the investigation of Horton be
closed, due to his alibis for dates associated with the
Green River, Star Lake, and south airport clusters.
But for those who believed that there was only one
man doing the sort of things the Green River Killer
was doing, Horton was an eye-opener.

Several months later, Horton pleaded guilty to one
count of second-degree kidnapping and was sentenced
to two years in prison. The Navy gave him the boot,
and his wife divorced him. Curtis kept the duffel bag.
He couldn't let it go. Lottie went to Texas.

49

PORTLAND

June 1985/September 1985

As the summer unfolded, Adamson and the task force
detectives found themselves increasingly interested in
the Portland area. The more interested Adamson and
his detectives became in Portland, the more prickly
relations between the task force and local police got.
The task force had been balked in late May when they
asked for information relating to two men Portland
Police suspected in the strangulation homicide of a
young Portland-area prostitute. Portland Police at first
declined to disclose the names of their two suspects,
saying the two men could not have committed the
Green River murders.

Fine, said the task force members, but why don't

you let us check for ourselves? What? said Portland
Police. Don't you trust us? And the battle was joined.
Portland Police insisted that the Green River murders
were a Seattle-area problem, not something they had
to be concerned with. Don't try to push *your* problem
off onto us, they told the Seattle cops. Matters were
made rather worse when a Portland homicide lieutenant offhandedly remarked that getting murdered just
happened to be an occupational hazard for street prostitutes, giving the King County contingent the idea
that prostitute homicides weren't much a priority in
the city of Portland.

After the complaints by Adamson and Thomas to
newly appointed Portland Police Chief Penny Harrington, more detailed information on the two men was
turned over to the task force detectives. Neither of
the Portlanders could be linked to the Green River
crimes. We told you so, said Portland Police; keep the
Green River problem where it belongs.

But in the wake of the discovery of Bush's skull,
and then Sherrill's, as well as the two still-unidentified
Tualatin remains, the Green River detectives came to
believe more and more that their killer had either
gone to Portland, or at least had spent considerable
time there. The task force asked Oregon authorities
for more information on the various Portland-area
prostitute murders, which by now were nearing an
even dozen, counting the four in suburban Washington County. Washington County's detectives were
completely cooperative. They visited the task force in
Seattle to see what they could learn, and brought their
own files on their four homicides, the two in Tigard
and the other two in Tualatin, to Seattle with them.

But the city of Portland's Police Bureau steadfastly
refused to open any of its case files to the Seattle
detectives, who felt that, on the surface, at least four
Portland cases were possibly quite similar to the Seattle murders: Trina Hunter, seventeen; Tonya Harry,
nineteen; Essie Jackson, twenty-four; and Kimberly
Ramsey, also nineteen. All had some history of street
prostitution in Portland's prostitution area on North-

east Union and Interstate Avenues, and all had been strangled. Northeast Union and Interstate Avenues formed the extension of U.S. Highway 99 into Oregon from Washington State across the Columbia River.

Trina Hunter's death was intriguing. She had been found half naked, dumped head first into a watery bog northeast of Vancouver, Washington, in December of 1982, after having worked for several years as a prostitute in Portland's prostitution area. Portland police had initially declined to investigate her disappearance after her family reported her missing. After an outcry from the city's black community, however, a more aggressive investigation was undertaken, one that centered on Hunter's husband. In the course of that investigation, Portland Police concluded that she had disappeared from Vancouver, Washington, on the night of December 6, 1982, when she had entered a red Cadillac while working. The car was similar to the vehicle described in Cynthia Hinds's disappearance only four months before, in August of 1982. Portland Police had washed their hands of Hunter's murder after learning that she had last been seen across the river in Vancouver.

But Hunter's disappearance date put her murder *after* those of Denise Bush and Shirley Sherrill. The discovery of Hunter's body late in the first year of the Green River murders, a few miles off the freeway running between Portland and Seattle, was an argument that she too was a victim of the Green River killer, who could have been headed back to Seattle after his October–November stay in the Portland area. That the Green River killer had been in the Portland area now seemed obvious from the discoveries of Bush and Sherrill.

Task force officials looking into Sherrill's disappearance developed shaky information that she had come back to Seattle sometime in late October or early November. Some sources told the task force investigators that they had seen her in downtown Seattle as late as the second week of November in 1982. That probably meant, as in Bush's case, that the killer had taken Sherrill to Oregon.

Three other city of Portland homicides were also somewhat promising. Tonya Harry was murdered around July 8, 1983, during what appeared to be a brief gap in the Green River series. She was found the following day in a pond in a park in north Portland. Essie Jackson was last seen in February of 1983 during another, similar gap in the Green River series. She was found dead on a wooded hillside in a park in northeast Portland.

And Kimberly Ramsey had last been seen on Northeast Union Avenue October 26, 1984. She was found only a few hours later along the bank of the Columbia River a few miles east of Portland. The dumping ground was very similar to many of the Green River sites, with household trash, junked cars, and the like strewn nearby. Investigating detectives from the Multnomah County Sheriff's Department found the faint imprint of a newspaper page on her buttocks. The page was from the southwestern Washington edition of a free advertiser circulated in Vancouver and Longview, Washington. Detectives theorized that the paper had been in the killer's vehicle while he transported her body.

Despite her initial cooperation, Harrington, the first woman police chief in a major American city, ultimately backed her own detectives in their refusal to share all their information with the Green River Task Force.

"I don't believe a serial killer is here," she said. "We're not going to close our eyes if we see a pattern, but we don't see anything." As a result, she said, Portland would not form a task force to investigate its murders, and indeed, would not even investigate them on a daily basis unless new information were developed. Task force detectives concluded that the Portland reluctance was less a desire to withhold confidential information as it was to conceal the embarrassing lack of work on the crimes from their Seattle-area counterparts.

In late July, medical investigator Bill Haglund and several members of the task force went back to Washington County for an extended search of the area where the two unidentified Tualatin skeletons had been found. A few small bones and a reconstructed tooth were all that could be located, neither enough to identify the dead without more specific information. But it did seem likely that the Green River killer was leading them farther afield.

50

VOTES

August 1985/September 1985

For some time, County Executive Randy Revelle had been counting his positives and negatives, the sort of thing politicians are wont to do as they get ready to face the voters, as Revelle would do in November. The executive knew he had a mixed balance sheet. One of the negatives was the new jail, built at a cost of $67 million to replace the old, decrepit lockup located on the top floor of the county courthouse. The damn building had gone millions over budget in cost overruns, and its opening had been delayed for more than a year. Finally, the end appeared in sight. But then a computerized lock system had malfunctioned, and some of the builders had been accidentally locked inside their own creation. Other workers had to tear some of the cells apart to rescue them. The whole county was laughing at the situation, but it wasn't funny to Revelle or his reelection campaign. The jail had become a campaign issue, and Revelle was charged with being an inept manager.

Even worse, from a political point of view, Revelle was being hammered on a daily basis by the owner of the Seattle Mariners baseball team over the team's lease with the county-owned Kingdome. George Argyros, the team's owner, was threatening to declare bankruptcy and move the baseball team to another city if Revelle refused to renegotiate the lease. Revelle didn't want to run for reelection as the man who helped kill major league baseball in Seattle. That would definitely be fatal.

Those were two of the negatives. The positives were far more abstract. Revelle had tried to modernize the patronage-ridden county government's bureaucracy, and had helped focus the county on the problems of managing its rapid growth. He had brought numerous improvements to the police department. But the murder investigation, which ironically had helped make those improvements possible, remained a political push-you-pull-me.

On one hand, Revelle could justifiably say that he had recognized the murder problem and had moved to deal with it. After all, his ally Vern Thomas, the sheriff, had formed the task force, and at the very least, it appeared that the killings had stopped. And he had replenished the police department's personnel, so no one could claim that they weren't getting service from the police. He had also lined up a federal grant to help pay for the investigation.

But on the other hand, he and his police department could be faulted for having spent—so far—nearly $4 million on the investigation with no results. While no political candidate would dare ask the question publicly, there was likely to be a bottom line with the voters: *Was it worth it?* Had Revelle shortchanged regular police operations, diminishing police response time, to support a quixotic attempt to find the murderer of people who many did not really care about, anyway? Would Revelle be vulnerable to his opponents' attacks on vaguely worded charges that he had mismanaged the police department, just as he had supposedly mismanaged the jail?

Already there had been a few signs that Revelle's opponents sensed his vulnerability on the Green River matters. His most important rival had already intimated that Revelle had mismanaged the Green River case by not bringing the FBI in sooner.

Republican Tim Hill, the elected comptroller of the city of Seattle, was, like Revelle, a familiar name politically in the county. He had served on the Seattle City Council with Revelle. In his late forties, Hill's long, angular frame was topped with a shock of blond hair that made him look boyish despite his age and experience. He liked to ride his bicycle to work, which made him seem, somehow, younger and environmentally aware, just the sort of politician younger voters favored.

While blessed with photogenic looks and a progressive public image, Hill was handicapped as a politician by his discomfort in the sort of social schmoozing that most elected officials revel in. One-on-one, Hill often had a hard time maintaining eye contact. In solo interviews with the news media, Hill often seemed to fumble for his words, as if picking his way across a minefield of potential explosions. When pressed for answers or commitments, Hill would take a deep breath, pause, and slowly let the air out of his lungs, audibly blowing the air past his lips in a sigh that seemed to express an enormous reservoir of unarticulated anxiety. The habit sometimes made Hill seem like an old mare, blowing heavily after an arduous walk back to the barn. Others in Seattle government circles thought him a cold fish, or worse, indecisive.

But behind these personality traits, Hill was a first-rate thinker. One of Hill's abiding philosophies was the belief that government activism—Revelle's stock in trade—often carried hidden costs, and that government decision making needed to take those costs into account. For the previous decade as the main budget watchdog, Hill had carved out a reputation as a cautious man with a dollar. Now, in the keep-taxes-down consciousness of the Reagan era, Hill's minimalist philosophy of government was gaining momentum. At several campaign stops, Hill had made glancing references to the Green River investigation, saying that while he supported the effort to find the murderer, the investigation would have to be carefully monitored to make sure that real progress was being made. If the effort stalled, Hill said, the county would have to decide whether to reallocate the resources to other areas. And Hill suggested that if *he* had been county executive, he would have called in the FBI to assist in the investigation long before.

Hill's comments about the murders and the FBI made their way to the Revelle campaign. Revelle's first instinct, he said later, was to clobber Hill for his ignorance over the bureau's true role in the investigation. But Vern Thomas and Adamson dissuaded him. Making the investigation into a political issue—even one that would benefit Revelle—was likely to undermine the broader political support necessary to keep the effort going. If the Republicans thought Revelle intended to use the task force in any sort of "look what I did!" political manner, they wouldn't be quite so willing to support the effort later when it came time to pay the bills, they said.

Other serial murder investigations, chiefly the one in Atlanta, Thomas and Adamson pointed out, had run into trouble over similar political frictions. At all costs, the Green River murder investigation should be protected from politics if it were to have any hope of a successful resolution, the two men told Revelle.

Revelle took the advice of Adamson and Thomas. Instead of blasting Hill, Revelle sent him a private message: Back off on the Green River Task Force. If Hill continued his criticism, Revelle promised, he would accuse Hill of attempting to use the murders of scores of young women for his own selfish political gain. Hill muted his criticism about the FBI's role, but continued to say the investigation would have to be monitored to make sure the resources were not being misdirected.

THE GREEN RIVER KILLER 327

In the meantime, Revelle felt a need to have someone from the outside review the Green River investigation and at least pronounce it on course. Thomas and Adamson were less than enthusiastic. What good would it do? They had already told Revelle there *were* no experts in serial murder. The experts hired in Atlanta, they said, had only complicated the politics involved.

But Revelle thought an outside review would be good for the investigation, good for the detectives' morale, and also helpful in reassuring him that the investigation was getting somewhere. It also might prove useful in protecting Revelle against any charges that he was presiding over a multimillion-dollar wild goose chase, some of Revelle's political advisers thought.

Early in August, the county contracted with retired former Los Angeles Police Department Detective Pierce Brooks to review the Green River investigation. In signing Brooks, the county would be asking one of the nation's most famous experts on serial murder to look Thomas and Adamson's task force over. Brooks would get $3,000 for his work.

But even before Pierce Brooks could begin, a young Portland prostitute—a girl from Seattle, no less— climbed into an old blue taxicab on Portland's Northeast Union Avenue about 3:00 A.M. on a night in early September. Four or five hours later, about thirty-five miles east of Portland, a passing driver found her near death by the side of the road, her throat severely slashed.

But the young woman lived, and within a few days was able to provide the Oregon State Police with a vivid description of her attacker. Adamson's detectives and the FBI rushed to Portland. The FBI's Douglas, finally back in harness after a convalescence of nearly a year, dropped everything and went to Portland too. Here, at last, was a possible survivor of the Green River killer. This time, everyone resolved, they would not let him get away.

51

THE BLUE TAXI

September 1985/October 1985

By the second week in September, Adamson had a
full street team in place in Portland. It wasn't easy to
get them there, either.

The turf boundaries so jealously defended by the
Oregon cops were daunting. There were, first of all,
the Washington County cops and the Multnomah
County cops; next there were the Portland Police, and
the police of the surrounding suburbs; across the
Columbia River, there were the Vancouver, Washing-
ton cops, and the Clark County Sheriff's Department.
There were the Oregon State Police, the Multnomah
County District Attorney's Office, the Washington
County District Attorney, and finally the FBI and the
U.S. Attorney for Oregon. All of these agencies had
carefully defined relations; now the Green River Task
Force, which wasn't even an agency but instead was
sort of an ad hoc group formed and administered 180
miles away, wanted to jump into the middle of the
pond. Naturally, there were waves.

Adamson didn't much care about the interjurisdic-
tional niceties, but he knew that it would be fatal to
lose his temper. The most important thing was to get
some proactive strategies going in the Portland area.
The odds were that the killer was still active. That
meant, with luck, the killer could be caught before he
moved somewhere else. Detective Larry Gross and

the other members of the Green River street team tried to show the Oregon people what they had learned: how to follow prostitutes, how to establish some rapport with the frequently suspicious girls and their pimps, how to organize tip sheets. There were resentments: *If the Green River types were so good, why hadn't they caught anybody yet?* Gross and the others tried to swallow their retorts and get on with the job at hand. Other frictions between the jurisdictions flared up from time to time; once Gross chased a man who had snatched the purse of a prostitute. It seemed to Gross that the man had pulled a gun, so Gross had fired his own weapon.

"I didn't hit him, thank God," Gross said later. But the firearms question only exacerbated the relationships. Finally the Oregon State Police gave the Green River people temporary authority as state police officers, in case one day Gross or one of the others shot and *didn't* miss. Other flaps over the treatment of prostitutes also boiled up, but were smoothed over.

Meanwhile, an all-out effort to find the blue taxi that had picked up the surviving prostitute was launched. FBI agents, Oregon State Police investigators, and the street team visited every taxi company in Portland, western Washington, and the Columbia River gorge in search of the cab and the driver described by the victim.

The victim was a fifteen-year-old Seattle girl with a history that almost perfectly matched those of the Green River victims: runaway reports, occasional arrests for petty crimes and prostitution. She had come to Portland with friends. Sometime between 2:00 and 4:00 A.M. on September 6, she had accepted a ride from a round-faced, blonde-haired man with a mustache. The man was twenty-five to thirty years old, somewhere between five-feet-nine and six-feet-one, with a ruddy complexion, probably from old acne scars. His hair hung down over his collar. The cab was an American-made station wagon, maybe a Dodge, dark in color, probably blue, with blue vinyl bench seats. The girl remembered that the car had the name of a taxi company on the door, but couldn't remember what it was. The car also had a lighted taxi sign on the top. Inside, the cab also had an old-style mechanical meter, the type with the manual flag, mounted on the dash.

Almost as soon as she settled into the taxi's front seat, the girl said, the driver produced a knife and made her lie on the floor. Pulling over to the side, the man tied her up with ropes he had in the back seat. Then the man put the taxi onto the freeway leading east from Portland. After about half an hour, they pulled off the freeway and drove into the woods near a state park named Horsetail Falls. The man jerked her out of the car, the girl said, and began punching her in the head. The man threw her down on the hood of the car and raped her, then beat her again. He ripped her remaining clothes off. Then the man stabbed her several times with his knife.

Bleeding profusely from the wounds and in shock, the girl lost consciousness. She came to as the man dragged her through the woods to an embankment. There the man shoved her over the side of the embankment and watched as she rolled down the hill. The man came down after her, gathering brush and leaves, and threw them on top of her. The girl played dead. The man watched her for awhile, then climbed back up the embankment. Under the branches, in the light of the moon through the clouds, the girl saw the man light a cigarette and calmly smoke it. Then the girl lost consciousness again.

When she awoke once more, it was nearing daylight. She managed to crawl up the embankment and out toward the road, where she passed out, naked in the rain. A bit later a man and a woman driving by found her. They took her to a hospital. A day or so later, the girl told the Oregon State Police the entire story.

The attack in many ways matched the style of the Green River killings, particularly the bit about the branches, Adamson thought. Clearly, the man was a calm, methodical killer. And a composite drawing of the suspect's face, prepared by the Oregon State Police with the girl's recollections, could be interpreted as resembling the earlier composites of men sought in the Green River case.

Finally, the detail of the mechanical meter, with the metal flag that had to be flipped down, was very helpful. Most taxis had long since given up the mechanical meter for the electronic kind. Adamson and others in the task force believed that the survivor had given them a particularly strong lead. Now it would be up to them to make the most of it.

Meanwhile, detectives in Seattle were sent downtown to pick up copies of taxi licenses issued by the city and county. Each photograph was scrutinized for resemblance to the composite. Records from the weights and measures bureaucracies were checked for references to old mechanical meters. Taxi drivers were interviewed in both cities. A man who made a living repairing meters was questioned. Literally every old station wagon taxi ever operated in the states of Oregon or Washington was tracked down. Junkyards in both states were checked. A man who was a Portland taxi driver who had an uncanny resemblance to the composite drawing was questioned several times, and finally was given a polygraph test. He passed.

After more than a month of effort, the task force decided to involve the public. The composite drawing was released to the news media, as was the description of the car. More tips were phoned in by the public in both states, but none of them bore fruit. It was as if the cab and its driver had utterly vanished.

Douglas arrived in Portland in mid-September. The only hangover from his near brush with death was a faint tingling in his left arm. All of his mental faculties had returned completely, which had been a relief to Douglas and his wife, to say nothing of the insurance company.

The Horsetail Falls attack gave him the opportunity to draft a profile of the Portland attacker. The Port-

land man was similar to what he now believed about
the man being sought in Seattle. Both men were calm,
methodical criminals. They both had clever ways of
contacting their victims. Both men had tried to conceal their crimes. Both drove a lot, smoked, probably
drank. Both men were nocturnal, probably from
unstable intimate relationships.

And Douglas's trip to Portland brought with it some
hidden advantages for the task force. For months, the
Portland Police Bureau had kept back their files on
their own prostitute murders: Hunter, Jackson, Ramsey, Harry, and several others. Now Douglas was able
to break through the wall and review the Portland
documents. Portland may not have wanted to talk to
Seattle, but Douglas faced no such inhibitions.

There *were* differences between the Portland homicides, Douglas saw, but they were slight. It was
entirely possible that the Green River person might
have committed the Portland crimes, if one allowed
for a change in modus operandi. Sometimes killers
under pressure *did* change their m.o., Douglas knew.
Ranking the victims in order of possible connection,
Douglas went first with Ramsey, then Hunter. The
others were less likely.

After a few days in Portland, Douglas flew to Seattle to meet with Adamson and the other members of
the task force. He indicated that on balance the Portland murders seemed the work of a different man than
the Green River killings. But there was another thing
he wanted to discuss with Adamson.

Over the past year, an idea had taken shape in
Douglas's mind. In thinking about the murders, Douglas had begun to see that maybe, just maybe, there
were two different killers involved in the Green River
crimes. Not tandem killers—that was always a possibility—but two completely different murderers entirely, acting independently of each other.

The idea had come from the differences between the
victims found in the Green River, and those found
in the woods. It seemed to Douglas that the river
victims had some aspects of staging to them that the

wooded-area victims did not have. At some level, Douglas guessed, the killer of the river victims *wanted* his deeds discovered. That wasn't at all true about the wooded-area killer, who had gone to such great lengths, like walking down a step hillside, to conceal them.

It was possible that all along there had been two different killers, Douglas suggested, one for the river, and the other for the wooded areas. Douglas had decided that this was the most logical explanation for the differences: fresh bodies versus skeletons, risk-taking by dumping even after the site was discovered versus extreme caution—to the point of killing a dog. It really doesn't make much difference, Douglas assured Adamson. Both killers, if there really are two, are much the same sort of personality. Techniques that will work to catch one will work just as well for two. When you get someone, Douglas said, that's when we'll know for sure.

52

PIERCE BROOKS

September 27, 1985

While the task force detectives, Oregon State Police, and FBI agents took the Portland prostitution areas apart in their search for leads on the latest attack, Pierce Brooks began his review of the investigation.

Brooks was sixty-three years old, and a legend in the world of homicide detectives. For more than twenty years, Brooks had been a Los Angeles policeman, much of the time an investigator of murder. Brooks helped solve numerous killings, including the killing of two Los Angeles cops that Joseph Wambaugh later wrote about in *The Onion Field*. Years later, as a consultant, Brooks had worked on the effort to identify the person who had contaminated bottles of Tylenol in Chicago, and still later, on the Atlanta child killings. In contrast to John Douglas's essentially vicarious psychological perspective, Brooks's approach to homicide investigation grew out of his own experience. At this point in 1985, Brooks was retired, but he had some definite ideas about what the country needed to do about serial murders.

In July of 1983, Brooks was one of several witnesses who testified before a U.S. Senate subcommittee about the growing threat of serial murders. The nation, Brooks testified, was at growing risk from serial murderers who moved from police jurisdiction to jurisdiction. The problem had become so severe, Brooks testified, that no one knew how large it really was. Somewhere between five thousand and twelve thousand people were being murdered *every year* in the United States, Brooks said, by people who didn't even know their victims. Police, he said, were at a loss to solve the crimes.

What was needed, Brooks testified, was an information clearinghouse. He had been working with the FBI to plan such a clearinghouse, one that would work directly with the bureau's Behavioral Sciences Laboratory. The clearinghouse would be a program of a proposed National Center for the Analysis of Violent Crime, which would be headquartered at Quantico. The major component of the program, as Brooks envisioned it, would be a computerized data bank called the Violent Criminal Apprehension Program, or VICAP.

The way Brooks visualized VICAP, each and every police jurisdiction would be asked to complete computerized questionnaires on their unsolved homicides, and send the questionnaires to Quantico to be entered into a computer. Once enough cases and their methodologies were entered, analysts would be available to consult with local agencies on the likely travel patterns of serial predators. The bureau would find similar cases in the databank, and act as sort of a marriage broker between the two or three different local agencies. Brooks's testimony was instrumental in convincing the Senate to fund the murder data bank.

But as Brooks prepared to review the Green River investigation for Revelle, Thomas, and Adamson, the VICAP program was still struggling to get off the ground. The problem wasn't money, or even federal will, as much as it was reluctance of the local agencies across the country to take the time to fill out the forty-four page VICAP forms designed by Brooks. Letting the feds look over their shoulders, many locals decided, might be more trouble than it was worth.

Now Brooks was being asked to give his benediction to the Green River investigation. Overtly, Revelle wanted to know whether things were being done appropriately. But on a more primal level, Brooks's endorsement of the investigation so far might be worthwhile insurance to have *if* Tim Hill decided, after all, to attack Revelle on the conduct of the hunt for the killer.

After two weeks of leafing through the investigation's enormous volume of paperwork, and having discussions with the task force's detectives and supervising sergeants, Brooks was ready to make his report. Brooks wanted to give it orally. Revelle wanted it in writing. A compromise was reached: Brooks's oral discussion of the investigation would be taped, and later transcribed. The county would then boil the report down into a press release for distribution to the news media. The transcript itself would be withheld.

The briefing was held in Thomas's office behind closed doors. Thomas, Adamson, Bob Keppel, and Shelly Sutton, representing Revelle, were the only ones present.

Brooks went right to the heart of the issue: "It is

most important," he said, "that there be no reduction
in force, or decrease in the present personnel strength
of the task force. If anything, it should be increased."
From here on in, Brooks said, the task force needed
to focus on the commonalities of each of the crimes,
to look for ways of seeing the same factors in each
case. Cutting the task force would be absolutely
wrong, he said. "Keeping sufficient personnel aboard
in the task force to collect, collate, analyze, evaluate
and follow up many thousands of leads received these
past several years is the only way this case is going to
be solved, other than a lucky traffic stop by a patrol
officer of the killer transporting his latest deceased
victim, and that may not happen."

The most striking thing about the Green River
crimes, said Brooks, was the killer's selection of the
dump sites. What drew the killer to those places? Now
Brooks tried to go inside the mind of the killer:

"I don't believe this killer selected the body disposal
sites at random," Brooks said. "If he did, he is the
luckiest serial murderer of all time. He knows pretty
well, or even exactly, where he will dispose of his
victims before the murder occurs.

"Just for a moment, let's focus on four of the most
prominent cluster sites. The four that I am most familiar with I call airport north, airport south, Star Lake,
and the Green River. They are heavily wooded, somewhat concealed, and you think at first that this is an
ideal location where someone would take anything to
hide it—a body in this particular case, but anything
valuable, and in this case it was a body that was
valuable."

The thing that was valuable to the killer, said
Brooks, was his relationship to the victims. If the victims weren't valuable, Brooks suggested, then the
killer wouldn't have bothered to hide them. The killer
was excited about his relationship to the victim and
the remains; the secret of the murders represented by
the bodies somehow defined him. To safeguard the
secret and its power, the killer liked places where he
felt safe being secretive. To Brooks, these were proba-

bly places the killer had been to many times before
for other secret activities.

"It is a very high risk situation to go into an
unknown area that is heavily wooded like that without
knowing something about that location," Brooks said.
"I just do not believe . . . that the killer went there
with his victim the first time he had ever been there.

"I try to put myself in the position," said Brooks,
"where, here I am a stranger to the area; and if I
want to dispose of a body, and I'm just driving down
the road and here comes this nice little winding hill
and I have this body I want to get rid of, that would
probably be the *last* place I would stop. I noticed
maybe perhaps there are [trash] dump sites in the
area, but I would be very nervous about stopping
there.

"First of all, it is somewhat difficult to stop without
partially being in the road. It would seem to me that
the person that disposed of the bodies at those sites
had perhaps used the dumps before, maybe lived in
the area or had worked in the vicinity.

"I think the Green River location is perhaps one of
the greatest examples of what I am trying to talk
about. To just, at random, drive down a road and then
stop at what is obviously a river, and then, despite tall
grass, to carry a body down there and dispose of it
when there could be people fishing down there or people watching, makes me believe that this killer had
some intimate familiarity with that site."

Brooks paused to gather his thoughts. He was trying
to draw a picture of the murders, trying to lead his
listeners to understand what he meant by case commonalities. He began again:

"So why, or how, did the killer select the sites? By
random, chancy selection, I think not. By reconnoiter-
ing beforehand, possible but not probable. The best
bet is the killer was familiar with the site because of
a prior relationship with the area.

"There are a number of ways this relationship could
have occurred. The suspect could have lived in the
area, that's the most obvious." The task force should

check out the names of people who live near each of the clusters, Brooks said. "Property tax roles, public utilities, and school records are a good resource for resident names," he said. "Names of renters would be much more difficult to obtain, but it could be done. Perhaps the use of volunteers could be considered for making these routine and tedious name searches."

Or, said Brooks, "The suspect could have worked in the vicinity. He could have worked at the airport site, could have worked on the ballpark, could have worked at the airport himself as one of the airport employees. I realize the airport sites are very close to the pickup points on Pacific Highway where some of the girls were picked up and that's how the killer might have become familiar with that area, but it is still difficult for me to believe that a person would walk back into those woods with a body and feel comfortable about it.

"I would look for a list of anyone employed on any project in the area, including the airport employees. There are other jobs and occupations the suspect may have had that would make him familiar with the body disposal sites, such as a home builder. Perhaps the killer was involved in building a home, or in bridge construction. You all know that a bridge was being constructed at the time the bodies were disposed in the Green River and very, very close to that location."

Now Brooks discussed the killer himself. "You have to look at the times the victims disappeared and you will see they are quite scattered. They cover quite a period of time. It does not appear that this person has steady employment, eight to five every day or whatever; it might be a delivery person, someone in private security, maybe a salesperson.

"I would also check the unions. The unions sometimes keep files of people that get involved in working labor-related jobs. Cab companies should be checked and I am aware of the situation with the cabs who were cited under suspicious circumstances and I know they're being checked out.

"Now, as far as the military is concerned, you have

a heavy military population in the area. We have both Army and the Air Force and the Navy. I have always felt this person might either be in the military or could have been in the military.

"Now that the FBI is fully involved in the case, they might have the best resources for follow-up on a possible military suspect, because I think that you can't just go locally. But I definitely think a military person could be a suspect.

"In my personal profile of the killer—based on the killer's behavior—we have a person who has killed a number of times. And I realize it could be more than one person, but if I was a betting person, I'd bet maybe a dollar that I think it is one.

"So, my thinking that it is probably one person, it is next, possibly two persons working together, occasionally together, occasionally separate. In other words, similar to the situation of the Hillside Stranglers, the two cousins in Los Angeles.

"As far as the profile is concerned, my, again my personal profile . . . I certainly see the male. I think the odds are that it would be a Caucasian. I think that there's a good chance that this person is military, or had a military connection, is an outdoors type, is somewhat of a loner but is certainly not a total introvert. I can't believe that a person that picks up prostitutes on the street as this person has done is the kind of person who walks into some kind of singles bar and tries to make it with some of the girls. I think this fella's a little bit backward that way, introverted in other words, does not come on strong with women and that's why he goes for prostitutes, which in my thinking are the easiest victims. Of all the high-risk victims, they are the highest.

"It is possible that he could be a trained killer. In other words, we do have in the military, we have special forces who are trained to kill in that manner. They know how to, they have done it, during the war, particularly in Viet Nam, and it could very well be that person has had some familiarity with training such as

that. It would also go with his success up to this point
as to avoiding capture.

"In other words," said Brooks, "he could be a
trained survivalist, knows how to kill and kill quickly.
He is not a mutilator, has no interest in that. His
sexual gratification is just with the kill. For whatever
it's worth, that's my profile of this person."

Thomas, Adamson, Sutton, and Keppel remained
silent for a few minutes while they considered what
Brooks was saying. Boiled down, it seemed that the
homicide expert was suggesting that the best way to
solve the case was to actually *increase* the information
the task force was collecting. Not evidence so much,
or tips, but rather, indexes to possible commonalities.
Property owners, workers, soldiers, sailors, cops, cab
drivers—anyone with a discernible tie to the cluster
sites.

Brooks's ideas made sense in the abstract. Rather
than waiting for a tip to be phoned in that might lead
investigators to the killer, Brooks was essentially recommending that the investigation go out and generate
more of its own tips. Collecting lists of names of people familiar with each of the dumping sites, then comparing the names to see who had the sites in common
was one way to focus the investigation further. But
the work!

Adamson knew he already had a problem loading
the task force computer with the tips and other case
documents. After receiving the computer, relatives
and friends of task force members had volunteered to
input the thousands of pages of documents into the
data base. But after six months, it was clear the volunteer system was not the answer. It was taking too long,
and Thomas and Adamson were pressing Revelle to
find the money to hire professional data-entry people.

Now here was Brooks, proposing that the task force
increase the data-entry task enormously. And where
did it end? Property tax records were one thing, but
the equal necessity of obtaining the names of renters,
workers, students, even the unemployed. The dimensions of Brooks's proposal seemed staggering. To do

it right, the task force would have to obtain many lists *for each* cluster site. The names would run into the tens of thousands. It would take months, probably years, and the accuracy of the lists would be dubious. One could imagine all the investigators spending all of their time doing nothing more than assembling lists, day after day, month after month, sort of modern-day monks scribbling endlessly in a vain effort to write their way to salvation. If that happened, who would follow up on the tips that kept coming in? Brooks's idea seemed both logical and impractical.

One lead, Brooks said, that was particularly good was Marie Malvar's driver's license, the one that had been found in the airport a month after her disappearance.

"I think that is an outstanding lead and this goes back to my investigative blood," said Brooks. "I still think that following it would be productive because, how did that girl's driver's license get there? Either she dropped it or—but she's missing. She's totally vanished. So if you run that down, looking at airplane manifests, aircraft manifests, maybe you are going to find her and you can eliminate her forevermore as a problem child. It's strange that a person like that is getting aboard a flight that costs a lot of money. So who else could have dropped, accidentally dropped it there? This is where you board the planes. Wouldn't it be interesting if a name came up that was a cab driver or someone like that, somebody that's really a top suspect? That's my point on a lead like that."

After more discussion about the computer and the need for more index lists, Thomas turned to a new subject.

"The next thing is," Thomas continued, "I noticed you never said at any time, mentioned the law enforcement officer."

"Frank [Adamson] and I already discussed law enforcement officers," Brooks said, "and that came up early on when Frank and I were talking, and of course it is one of the persons I think of because they have the obvious excuse of being there and also, who

best could park the car alongside a road and be halfway out in the road and not be stopped? For somebody who has a blue light and siren on top of his car
... I think you always have to include, as much as
we don't like it, the possibility of a police officer or
former police officer or one who wanted to be a police
officer."

After more discussion about the task force morale
and the imminent arrival of the FBI, Adamson asked
Brooks to go over the tandem killer hypothesis—the
idea that the murders were the work of two people
acting together, like the Hillside Stranglers. As far as
Adamson could see, the location of Gabbert's body
so far down the hillside at Star Lake was a powerful
argument that at least two people would have to be
involved. Carrying a dead weight down the slippery
hill would be difficult for just one person in the daylight, let alone at night.

"I would not be surprised if two people were
involved," Brooks said, "but if they are, I think they
know each other and they have worked together on
occasions and that kind of bothers me. Because I
know that you eliminate people on the basis of time.
If a prostitute is missing on a certain date and then
that suspect is out of town, that suspect could be eliminated but maybe his partner did it and they're just
separated for the time being.

"The first time it really struck me was Green River
and then I went up on Star Lake and I saw the sites
where particularly [Sandy Gabbert and Carrie Rois]
were placed, that's somebody who is pretty sure of
himself and the place. To walk down that hillside carrying a body, for just one person to do that, it's certainly possible, but he's no lightweight."

"What about the dog in the Gabbert site?" Adamson asked. "What's your feeling about that?"

The dog, Brooks said, was one of the more interesting aspects of the Star Lake dump site. Had the dog
been present while the killer was dumping Gabbert's
body? Had the killer killed the dog because he did
not want the dog finding the body before it had a

chance to decompose and trace elements to wash away? Brooks's feeling was that the dog was part of the Star Lake neighborhood. Because an examination had showed the dog had not died naturally, it was logical to assume that the killer had killed it. That meant that someone needed to canvas the nearby houses to see whether anyone owned a dog that had disappeared in April of 1983. Another possibility was that the killer simply hated dogs, and thought it would be amusing to kill a dog and leave it with the victim. Psychological experts, Brooks pointed out, often contended that serial murderers had childhood histories involving cruelty to animals. Overall, said Brooks, the dog was "just one more thing. But it's nothing by itself that's going to lead us to the killer."

After a few more minutes, the meeting broke up. Brooks had given the task force a qualified endorsement, if one steered away from index files question. Now, how to use it?

Or should it be used? While some of his advisers suggested that a press release recounting Brooks's endorsement might be very helpful in the last days of the campaign against Tim Hill, it seemed to Revelle that making a public announcement of how great everything was going for the task force could be construed as an attempt on his part to take political credit for the effort. Revelle could see the editorialists taking swipes at him for trying to take political advantage from the deaths of all the young women.

No way, Revelle said. Brooks's endorsement was kept back. Instead Revelle would rise or fall on the rest of his record.

53

ABSENTEES

November 1985

On November 5, 1985, Revelle lost his bid for reelection as county executive by fourteen hundred votes, a small fraction of those cast. In losing Revelle, the task force lost its most potent political card. After all, Revelle was the man who had staked the reputation of the county police on the successful outcome of the Green River investigation, the man who had supported them through all the difficult start-up years, the man who had used his political power to get them a state-funded computer system, the man who put the department in line for a $1 million federal grant.

Most of all, Revelle had been the man who had protected the investigation from becoming a political football from the very beginning. Now Revelle would be replaced by a cost-conscious Tim Hill. And hadn't Hill already said that the task force would have to be reviewed to see whether it was doing any good? Sure, Revelle had said the same thing, but to task force members, it seemed like Hill really meant it.

Hill's margin of victory was contained in the county's absentee vote. Hill's political strategist had bombarded those voters with mailings, anticipating that the majority of the absentees were Republicans. Revelle's people had let the absentees go by—largely because they *were* Republicans. Revelle's campaign didn't want to waste any resources among a group that wasn't likely to vote for them anyway.

In the aftermath of the election, some of Revelle's aides reviewed the decision not to use Brooks's endorsement of the task force and the Green River investigation as a political issue. The campaign had turned on other issues. But would a few kudos to Revelle for having had the courage to try to solve the murder case have helped or hurt? Now it didn't make any difference.

Now the cost-conscious Hill was about to take office. Hill insisted that he supported Revelle's commitment to finding the killer. But in almost the same breath he noted that there were a lot of competing needs, and the county was limited in just how much it could afford.

And what of Vern Thomas? Just as Revelle had brought Thomas in to take over from Winckoski, Hill might find *his* own man to run the county police. With Revelle gone, followed by Thomas, was there any future for the investigation, no matter what Pierce Brooks had said? Still, as he prepared to occupy the courthouse suite being vacated by Revelle, Hill was getting the message from numerous law enforcement figures through the state: Hill should seriously consider keeping Thomas in place, and the murder investigation under way. Now was not the time to fold, Hill was told, not now, just when the task force was reaching the point of being able to sift through all the leads and get something done.

And there was a second factor. By the fall of 1985, the murder investigation had become a matter of intense publicity. Each of the news agencies had spent time learning about the crimes, and had covered them closely. It was almost as if the news media had a vested interest in the investigation continuing, Hill realized; certainly, reporting on the task force sold newspapers and filled their airwaves. It was a topic that the news media had taken a proprietary interest in. Hill didn't think it was likely that the press would just allow him to dismantle the effort, even if he was inclined to do it. There would be all kinds of questions; editorial boards would criticize him for being insensitive to the plight of the victims and their families. So would women's groups.

No, now was not the time to think about cutting the investigation. Politics made that imprudent. Perhaps when the politics changed, something might be done. Hill met with Vern Thomas, and asked him if he was willing to remain as sheriff. Thomas agreed. But Hill advanced the same bargain extracted earlier by Revelle. If the murder investigation seemed to be going nowhere, or if other crime problems got out of hand, Thomas had to be willing to cut the effort back. Thomas agreed.

54

OPTIMISTICALLY SPEAKING

January 1986/February 1986

Two days before the end of 1985, a couple walking along a road near Mountain View Cemetery, not far from the spot where Kimi Kai Pitsor's skull had been found two years earlier, noticed a newly wrecked car in a ravine just off the road. The couple called Auburn police to report their find. The police came and looked at the white Lincoln Continental, and by running the license plates through the computer, discovered that the car had been stolen from a tavern near The Strip several days before. No one noticed the human bones nearby that the wreck of the car had disturbed.

Later the same day, two workers from the cemetery hiked down the ravine to look the car over. They found a human skull. Auburn police returned to the scene, and this time, the Green River Task Force was called in.

The following day, the Police Explorers were again pressed into service. The terrain was remarkably similar to that at Star Lake, which was, after all, only two miles to the north. The ravine off the road was one of four or five similar, steep gullies that were choked with blackberry bushes, ferns, and other low-lying brush, all mixed together with alder and fir trees. Within a few hours, about four fifths of a complete skeleton was recovered. Eight officers wielding machetes and rakes cleared the site near the car for the detail work. It was bitterly cold.

After taking New Year's Day off, the Scouts and the police went back to the ravine on the second day of the new year. Working not far away from the site of the first discovery, the searchers discovered another skull. This one matched the lower jawbone that had been found in the area in early 1984.

This time, Adamson himself was present at the scene. The new discoveries were almost certainly victims of the Green River killer, Adamson said.

"My thoughts are that the remains are probably Green River," said Adamson. "When these people are identified, we'll have two more victims. It's obvious this is a group scene."

The two newest skeletons made three found not far from the cemetery, counting Pitsor's skull, which had been found about four hundred yards away on the side of the road. No other bones had ever been found with Pitsor, and although police in 1983 had searched both sides of the roadway, it was only the latest discoveries that attracted their attention to the ravine itself. As he stood along the road, Adamson suddenly saw that it was going to be necessary to go into all the ravines with the usual, arduous, hands-and-knees search. Who knew how many other bodies might be found? And where was the rest of Pitsor?

Several things about the Mountain View cluster—clearly, that was what it was—intrigued Adamson. One was the proximity to the cemetery itself. The cemetery was reached by several key roads in the investigation: Military Road South provided access to the area from the west, and where the ravines all bottomed out in a single canyon below the road, there was the infamous Highway 18. Second, situated up on the hill the way it was, the cemetery's rolling expanse of green lawn provided a sweeping view of the Kent Valley, including the Green River and Mt. Rainier. Was the cemetery meaningful in some way to the killer? Did the killer, for example, have relatives buried there? Adamson kept remembering what Pierce Brooks had said about the killer's prior familiarity with the dump sites. Here indeed was an example of how an index list could be effective, but how to whittle the information down? Getting a list of all the survivors of those buried in the cemetery would be an enormous task. What about the cemetery's employees? Or those who had built it? Good Lord, the possibilities seemed endless.

Third, the discovery of Pitsor's skull offered certain possible insights into the character of the killer. Normally, Adamson knew, heavier parts of a disarticulated skeleton were carried *downhill* by smaller animals. Yet Pitsor's skull had been found along the roadway—about fifteen or twenty feet away from a sign marking the Auburn city limits. Pitsor had disappeared in April of 1983. Had the killer returned to the site, found Pitsor's skull, and placed it on the side of the road so obviously in King County territory in order to taunt the police? The skull had shown no signs of animal gnawing. But it was impossible to say with any certainty; there was no way of truly predicting what an animal might do with a bone.

The next day, the searchers expanded their efforts, searching a number of ravines. The usual media pack was there, waiting. A reporter for *The Times* and one for KIRO stood together on the road not far from the police command post, a van parked along the roadside. Reichert, Nolan, and several other task force members were talking to one another. Suddenly Reichert lashed out at the two news media people.

"Get away from there!" he snapped, glaring at the two reporters. Nolan quickly came over and told Reichert to be cool. He led him away by the elbow. What was *this* all about? Reichert had long ago become sick of the news media's pushy behavior. He thought Nolan and others on the task force had become just a little too cozy with some of the reporters. Some of the television people had set their cameras up on the edge of the ravine and, Reichert thought, were using their telephoto lenses to pick up what the investigators were doing down below. Sometimes it seemed to Reichert that the news media thought the whole thing was being done for *their* benefit. He climbed down into the ravine and erected a cardboard screen to shield the scene from the prying cameras.

The reporters were surprised at Reichert's outburst. *Something's going on*, one of them thought. *They're acting pretty cocky*. Later, *The Times* reporter approached Adamson. Adamson seemed a little bit different than usual, the reporter thought. Something about his attitude triggered the reporter's antennae. The reporter tried to put his finger on it. Got it! Adamson seemed a little more hyped up than usual, just a shade more confident and ebullient. He was actually smiling. What did Adamson make of these new developments, the reporter asked, and did he foresee another year of discoveries like the one just past?

"By this time next year I'm fairly optimistic we will have him in jail," Adamson said. "I'm being optimistic about 1986. I feel good about this year."

They're on to something, the reporter thought. Adamson was practically predicting the capture of the killer *this year!*

Adamson saw the wheels turning in the reporter's brain and knew he had just made a mistake. *They're going to say I said we'd catch the guy this year*, he thought. Sensing that he had gone a little too far, Adamson tried to backtrack a bit and put his remark in perspective, explaining that the investigators were making progress in the case because relatively few bodies had been discovered during 1985. Unlike the first year of the task force, he said, when the remains of fourteen victims had been found, the discovery of only five in 1985 had given the detectives more time to "do a lot of work toward identifying the killer."

But Adamson's explanation only confirmed the suspicion growing in the reporter's mind. "Identifying the killer" was after all the name of the game, and "a lot of work toward" that end meant the cops thought they were closing in.

The following day, *The Times* bannered Adamson's remark across the front page: "Serial Killer Hunter Predicts Capture in 1986." Seeing the newspaper's headline confirmed Adamson's fears, especially when the story in the newspaper pointed out that Adamson was normally a very cautious person. Inadvertently Adamson had raised the expectations of the news media, and by extension, the public, who would now expect the task force to do what Adamson had predicted.

After reading Adamson's prediction in the newspaper, the newly sworn-in Tim Hill called Vern Thomas to ask what was going on. Thomas told Hill that while the investigation was progressing well, it was too soon to say for certain whether an arrest could be made *this year*. Frank had just made a mistake, said Thomas. Hill said he understood. But Hill's chief aide, Rollin Fatland, was unhappy. Fatland was Hill's closest political adviser, and the man Hill relied upon most to do the dirty work that the nonconfrontational Hill sometimes needed to have done. It was a role Fatland relished.

From Fatland's perspective, the commitment made by Revelle to solving the murders was something of a political albatross. In private conversations, Fatland—often described by political reporters as Hill's closest friend and alter ego—doubted the wisdom of putting so many resources into such a seemingly unsolvable puzzle.

Hill had come into office on the strength of his contentions that the "liberal" Revelle had badly managed the county. Hill, the former Seattle city comptroller, had pointed to his own credentials as a fiscal manager and had said the county needed to do more with less. The police budget was a case in point. Tying up so many officers and their support in the investigation of the murders meant fewer resources for other police activities, Fatland contended. That in turn created political pressures to hire more police officers. Hill was worried that more police officers meant other, hidden costs: more jail space; more prosecutors; more defense lawyers; more courtrooms, judges, and clerks; more janitors to clean up after them; more electricity for the light bulbs; more copy machines; more heating bills; more of everything. Where would it end? Somebody needed to stop reacting to crime and start planning, Hill believed. And if the Green River investigation was going nowhere, then maybe some or all of those Green River resources should be put back on the street. That way, Hill and Fatland reasoned, the county could improve its police services at no extra cost.

Hill's reservations about hiring more police officers fell on the police department as if he were recommending that the police let the bad guys go. The cops couldn't believe it, and privately ridiculed Hill for his naiveté about crime and criminals. Hill pointed out that he was a former prosecuting attorney, and that as the man who had to approve the bills, he had a different perspective on crime than the cop on the beat.

But meanwhile, the task force had begun to assume a political life of its own. Women's groups and the news media had raised the profile of the crimes and the need for their solution to the status of a political icon. Hill couldn't very well simply announce that the hunt was over: *Sorry folks, we couldn't do it.* He certainly couldn't end it now, not with Adamson publicly predicting the imminent capture of the killer. In his own mind, Fatland believed that Adamson had made no mistake, that he had instead made a political preemptive strike to make sure Hill did the right thing.

Over the next few days, Haglund and the dentists pored over their collection of dental records. None of the charts matched the teeth recovered from the two newest skeletons. Both girls appeared to have been killed some time in 1983. One victim appeared to be white, somewhere between fourteen and seventeen years old, and about five-feet-four to five-feet-eight. The other girl was black, twenty to twenty-five years old, and somewhere between five-feet-one to five-feet-four. Getting an exact height on skeletons that had been so badly weathered was nearly impossible. Detectives began searching their assembled collection of missing persons reports and prostitution citations looking for missing women that fit the criteria. But no matches materialized.

Meanwhile, more searching at the Mountain View cluster area produced the bones of a third person. Those bones were matched with Pitsor's skull. *That* mystery, at least, had been solved, though the question remained of whether the killer had deliberately placed her skull where it might be found.

Meanwhile, Adamson's remark had galvanized the news media even as it had confused Hill and irritated Fatland.

By now reporters covering the murders had become used to looking for nuances in the investigation. Even Adamson's frequent "interesting, very interesting" coda could be infused with different meanings, depending on Adamson's facial expressions, and by careful phrasings of the questions. They knew Adamson had a very difficult time dissembling; it simply wasn't in his nature. And in part because of the information blackout imposed by the police, the news media had also become more skilled at relating disparate facts to the whole, and deciphering hidden meanings in events. It was often like reading tea leaves, but at least it helped refine the questions reporters used in their frequent give-and-take with Adamson and other police officials.

Thus, when it was announced in early January that another ten FBI agents had hit town in order to help on the Green River investigation, the news media put that event together with Adamson's prediction and concluded that matters were nearing a head. The new FBI arrivals brought the total task force complement to fifty-six people, not including the county officers brought into the case from time to time for special assignment.

Reporters put out their lines. A few nibbles came back. *Something would happen soon*, reporters learned on deep background. *Watch. Be ready.* At both newspapers, editors met behind closed doors with reporters and made plans to cover the big event, if and when an arrest was made. Artists were brought in to draw maps of where all the skeletons had been found. Emergency staffing arrangements were drafted. Photographers were briefed. Telephone numbers were assembled. Assignments were handed out. A push was made to learn even more information.

The television stations heard the same rumors and came to the same conclusions as the newspapers. KIRO's Hilda Bryant redoubled her efforts to cultivate sources inside the task force. Something was cooking. The tension began to build.

And at a Seattle all-news radio station, a reporter named Roger Nelson was sure he had the inside track to the story. Several months previously, a federal source had told Nelson that the task force was narrowing the hunt. A suspect was in the cross hairs. With persistence, Nelson learned the man's name, and some things about his background, and how the man had come to the attention of the task force. The case was very sensitive, Nelson was told. The man was under covert surveillance. Broadcasting the facts as he knew them wouldn't do anyone any good. He certainly

didn't want to go down in history as the man who had
blown the task force's opportunity to put the nation's
worst serial killer away, did he? Of course not.

Nelson kept his own counsel through the fall and
into the winter. But to prepare for the story when it
broke, Nelson obtained the man's prison file under a
freedom of information request. Reviewing the file,
Nelson noted that the man under suspicion had twice
been convicted of burglaries several decades in the
past, *and that he had told police some of the things he
had stolen had been thrown into the Duwamish River.*
The Duwamish River, of course, was the downstream
extension of the Green River.

Nelson also learned that the man was now one of
the state's most productive fur trappers. Pulling the
man's state fish and game licenses and the accompany-
ing report of his catches showed that the man had
trapped in many areas where Green River victims had
been found. Finally, Nelson learned from a confidential source, the man under suspicion had once told
other trappers that he had killed and skinned a dog
caught in one of his traps. That was *very* significant,
Nelson was told. Nelson confronted Adamson with
what he had learned.

On February 6, 1986, Adamson invited Nelson out
for coffee at a spot in Seattle's north end, miles away
from the precinct, to talk about Nelson's discoveries.
Nelson believed that Adamson was doing him a favor.
He had no way of knowing that the straight-shooting
Adamson had just suckered him away from what was
to turn out to be the biggest story of the year. Nelson
and Adamson, in fact, were still talking when three
cars of FBI agents swooped down on two men driving
a truck in rural King County, and arrested one of
them in connection with the Green River murders.

"What took you so long?" asked the man the agents
had arrested.

55

THE CIRCUS

February 6, 1986

About four-thirty in the afternoon of February 6, neighbors in a residential area just off The Strip known as Riverton Heights were amazed to see a number of police vehicles pull up and park in front of a rather ordinary wood-frame, split-level house on South 139th Street. The neighbors saw police wearing the distinctive green jackets marked GRTF go up to the house and knock on the door, then begin stringing up the remaining crime scene tape. As the last of the remaining daylight faded, the neighbors called the television stations. The cops, they said, were in Riverton Heights and had arrested the Green River killer.

After weeks of tension and waiting, the telephone calls broke the dam of media restraint. Within minutes, camera crews were setting up in the street outside the house. News bulletins were quickly flashed over the radio and television stations, triggering a rush of even more reporters. Soon the entire street was jammed with newspeople, the neighbors, and curious rubberneckers who had driven to the scene after hearing of the reports. Inside, shadowy figures could be seen swinging a lighted video camera back and forth. Police officers streamed to and from the house, carting out sack after paper sack of what was obviously evidence. Several cameramen got fuzzy shots of someone being bundled into a marked police car. The figure wore a garment over the head to conceal the identity. The marked patrol car roared off, while inside the car, officers held a large book over the person to conceal the shape. Police said little, other than that they expected to be searching the house for some hours to come.

Back at the precinct headquarters of the task force in Burien, just west of the airport, another regiment of reporters, photographers, camera operators, and soundmen gathered in the gloom. After some time, task force spokeswoman Fae Brooks emerged from the building. The task force, she said, had served a search warrant that day. But Brooks refused to characterize the subject of the search warrant as a "suspect." Instead, the man was only a "person of interest" to the investigators, Brooks said.

Was this a major break in the case at last? Brooks was asked. She shrugged noncommittally. Only time would tell, she said.

But inside the building, Ernest W. "Bill" McLean saw things much differently. From his point of view, it looked pretty grim. Here were all these cops around, many of them glowering at him, and there, on the wall, was a huge blow-up picture of himself, and running between his picture and all these other pictures of women, which McLean understood quite rapidly to be the photographs of the Green River murder victims, were all these strands of red string. Along the walls were rows of file cabinets, each of them labeled with *his name!* On the table in front of him were two small rocks encased in plastic. "I sure hope you guys have been known to make mistakes," McLean told the police. That remark, matched with McLean's earlier quip about things taking so long, sent the investigators' hopes soaring. This had to be the guy. McLean told them he had known for weeks that he had been under surveillance.

We know you're the killer, the cops kept telling McLean. Look at all this evidence we have on you. The best thing you can do right now is tell us all about it. Nobody's gonna get mad at you, it's just that you're sick. We want to get some help for you.

I didn't do it, McLean said again and again. He found himself with the insane urge to laugh. It would be funny if it weren't so serious, he thought. *These guys want to stretch my neck!* He had to convince them somehow that they had made a mistake. "It looks like you've been pretty busy," he said, sending detectives hopes soaring again. "But I'm not the guy."

In another office at the precinct, Douglas sat drinking coffee, waiting to see what would happen. He had flown out to Seattle just before the arrest to consult in the handling of the suspect. His profile had helped establish the legal justification for the search. In addition, Douglas had recommended all the stressors—the rocks, the photograph, the red lines, the files, the shock arrest, followed by the sympathetic invitation to confess. The question was: Would it work?

Detective Jim Doyon and an FBI agent conducted the interrogation. An hour after it started, Doyon emerged. "He's not the guy," he announced. Jaws hit the floor. "I felt like I'd just left a turd in the punchbowl," Doyon later recounted. Douglas couldn't believe it.

What's he doing? Douglas asked. The detective described McLean's behavior. "He's not the guy," Douglas agreed.

Inducing serial murderers to confess required a different approach than playing on the murderer's guilt. Douglas had long ago observed that most serial killers *had* no guilt. Often, he knew, they felt *justified* in their murders. That was particularly true in a case involving a murderer who had killed prostitutes and had dumped their bodies near trash. This Green River killer, Douglas believed, saw his victims as trash. He would have no guilt whatever in murdering them. Guilt was out as a means of detection.

But fear was in. If such a killer saw or believed that police had hard evidence—really specific evidence, like the rocks—against him, his fears would be triggered. He would react in some discernible way. He would lie; or might break down; or display some clearly distinctive reaction related to his awareness of the significance of the evidence. McLean showed nothing more than the normal apprehension anyone might feel if placed under similar circumstances. The rocks, it was clear, meant nothing to him. And his nervous bemusement at all their efforts seemed to speak of someone who knew he was innocent.

The detectives went back in to continue discussions with McLean. As the conversations progressed, McLean told them he was perfectly willing to answer any questions they asked, as long as they weren't about game violations or about burglaries. The detectives agreed. They asked him about statements that acquaintances had attributed to him. Wasn't it true that he had once said it might be fun to pick up a prostitute and do whatever one wanted to her, and then kill her? No, said McLean, he had never said that, somebody had told them some bullshit. Had McLean ever picked up a prostitute? No, he said. And in fact, the police had no record—or even any tips—that showed McLean had had any contact with prostitutes. It just didn't seem to be in his lifestyle.

Well, how could McLean account for the fact that while under surveillance, he had been followed driving to many of the areas where victims had been found, particularly up on Highway 410? That was where he happened to trap, McLean said; that was where fur-bearing animals could be found.

Okay, said detectives. Would you be willing to take a polygraph examination?

McLean felt as if he had just been given a choice between mortal disease or eternal poverty. He could refuse the lie detector, which might rekindle the detectives' suspicions. Or he could take it, and what if, for some reason, he failed? *It's just a computer,* McLean thought. *Computers screw up; they make mistakes. Do I want to trust my life to a machine?*

"Okay," said McLean.

About 8:00 P.M. detectives escorted McLean out a rear exit and drove him to the federal building in downtown Seattle. None of the reporters saw them leave. Downtown, an expert polygraph operator from the FBI was waiting. This would be no twenty-minute examination like those used for Foster and Tindal. Each test would take up to an hour, and by 2:00 A.M., McLean would take five of them. He passed every one.

All of this remained unknown, however, to the packs of reporters still gathered outside the precinct headquarters and McLean's house in Riverton Heights. They milled about aimlessly at both locations, sharing rumors and keeping a sharp eye on the doors for new developments. They believed the "person of interest" was still inside the precinct.

The crowd at McLean's house had by ten or eleven o'clock grown so large that a store owner for The Strip had arrived to sell soft-drinks, coffee, and popcorn to the crowd. Meanwhile, television reporters interviewed any neighbor who would agree to go on camera. Almost all of them said they were shocked by the search. Their neighbor was a nice man, a good neighbor, friendly, they said; it was almost impossible to imagine Bill McLean as a serial killer.

But reporters by this time were in full frenzy. Hadn't the cops kept saying over and over again that when the killer was caught, all the neighbors would say he was a nice man, a good neighbor, friendly, and that it was impossible that he could be a serial killer? Things were going according to script.

By late evening, the television stations had gone into extended coverage of the event. Over and over, each of the stations showed the fuzzy picture of the unknown person being bundled into the patrol car. Over and over, the stations showed indistinct figures moving about inside the house, and others carrying sacks of something out of the house. As the hours wore on, the reports grew more shrill, until seemed as though all caution had been cast aside.

A reporter for KIRO dramatically recounted how a "source" had told him that the house held a "shrine" to the occupant's hunting, making the racks of antlers and deer heads hung on the wall sound sinister and cultish. Others talked of how the man had been stopped by the FBI—"Stop! It's the FBI! Hands up!"—and how no one except the police knew what secrets were then being revealed. And in final paroxysm of breathlessness, KIRO's Hilda Bryant confided firmly that "the task force has told me that they believe they have got their man, that this IS the Green River killer," when of course, the task force was just discovering the opposite.

Back at *The Times*, the editor in charge of the paper's coverage watched the television coverage and slowly went mad. It seemed to him that everyone in town knew exactly what was happening except his reporters. As the night wore on, Rick Rafael got angrier and angrier. Hadn't the paper made all these great plans to cover the event, if and when? And now it was when, and the damn reporters didn't have any information to report! Fuming, Rafael walked out on an outdoor catwalk used as a bridge between different parts of *The Times*' building. That was the only place at *The Times* that employees were allowed to smoke, and Rafael was smoking now, in more ways than one.

"Shit," he said, stubbing his cigarette out angrily in the littered ashtray on the catwalk. "We're getting our asses kicked." He glared at one of his reporters and went back inside to watch more television.

Over at the *Post-Intelligencer*, things were even worse, however. Like *The Times*, *The P-I* had prepared a big package to be published if and when an arrest was made. Unlike *The Times*, however, *The P-I's* deadline was that night—in fact, the first deadline was not long after 9:00 P.M. What to do? Use the package, with all the maps and photographs, the faces of the sad staring victims, the pictures of the grim-visaged cops as they carted away skeleton after skeleton over the years? But what if the cops were wrong? What if the guy they had searched wasn't the killer? Then what? Wouldn't the use of the package with all the maps and pictures make it seem like the paper was saying the guy was guilty? Probably. But what if he *was* the guy? Didn't the paper owe it to its readers to tell them everything it could about the momentous events? And there was no time to decide.

At 9:00 P.M., when the deadline closed, McLean was still being interviewed, and as far as *The P-I* could tell, was a bona fide suspect in the worst serial murder case in American history. The paper decided to use its package. They also decided to print Bill McLean's name.

By 2:00 P.M., as *The Times*'s reporters scrambled to catch up to the television people, the events seemed to enter a period of dead calm, much like the center of a hurricane. More was to come, but at that point, none of the television or radio stations was reporting anything new that *The Times* by that point had not either confirmed or discounted. Now the moment was drawing nearer to *The Times*'s own point of decision: Use the photos and the maps and charts and chronologies so carefully prepared, or not? *The P-I* had used theirs. Wouldn't readers expect the same from *The Times?* The same debate as at the other paper now unfolded at *The Times*. Rafael had to make the decision. His only source of guidance, apart from his instincts, were the same reporters he had been berating so vehemently only hours before for their ignorance. Rafael liked to think that glaring at and criticizing his subordinates motivated them; and usually it did. Afterward Rafael would repair the damage by clapping them on the back and telling them what a fine job they had all done. Usually that worked too.

Let's lay back in the weeds a little bit, one reporter advised. Let's be very careful here. If the guy was The Guy, we would probably have seen some activity to indicate it by now. We don't want to use our package if we aren't sure. It could imply the guy is guilty. And for God's sake, let's keep his name out of the newspaper.

But on the other hand, said Rafael, what if he *is* The Guy? What good is all this preparation if we can't use it when we need it most? Let's write it down the middle, Rafael was told, and after another smoke, he agreed. He decided to hold back all the maps, charts, and photographs until the last possible moment, which would come shortly before 8:00 A.M.

But at 3:30 A.M., Fae Brooks emerged from the precinct building once again. "The person of interest has been released," she said. "He is free to go. He was never arrested. We have taken him to a destination of his choice."

56

TILT

February 1986

The following day, Adamson was ashen faced. He had been up all night. He had counted on McLean's viability as a suspect, far more than even he had realized. Now he was suffering from the aftereffects of the return to earth. The man who was searched, Adamson told the television cameras while standing in front of the headquarters, was only one of ten thousand people the task force was interested in, no more, no less. All the stuff that had been taken in the search would soon go to the state crime lab for analysis. Adamson refused to say whether the man who had been searched had been cleared. But downtown, another official quite familiar with the night's events, put it quite simply: "If he was The Guy, do you think we would have let him *go?*"

And later that day, Fatland was nearly beside himself. He was angry at Thomas, angry at Adamson, angry at the news media for going too far, and worried, very clearly, that the county had just let itself in for a major lawsuit on the part of the man who had been searched.

Adamson had led them all down the garden path, Fatland said bitterly; now look what happened. The wheels had come off. I can promise you one thing, Fatland told a *Times* reporter; We're going to get that task force *under control*. Frank Adamson is out, as far as we're concerned. We're gonna review the whole thing, from the top down. You can count on it.

57

TURNABOUT

February 1986/June 1986

In the aftermath of the McLean fiasco, the news media found itself scrambling to disclaim any responsibility for what had happened. Each of the television stations extolled its own virtues of restraint, noting over and over again how *they*, unlike some of the others, had responsibly withheld the name of the person searched; most also replayed their tapes showing the friends and neighbors of the man expressing incredulity about his culpability.

Inevitably the scramble to get away from the disaster focused criticism on the task force. Television commentators expressed concern for the man who was searched, noting that his privacy had been horribly invaded by the police and "some" irresponsible news media. Just how had the task force settled on the man, anyway? Had they made a mistake? Why had the police made such a big deal about the search? They should have known their actions would touch off a media event, or so the comments went.

The Times's editorial cartoonist, Brian Basset, published a cartoon in two panels, the first showing a radio-wielding cop in tall grass and wearing a SWAT team cap, peering through a pair of binoculars and saying, "He's white . . . he's male . . . harbors a deep resentment toward the opposite sex . . . and he knows these woods inside out." The second panel showed the heavily armed police surrounding a small bewildered boy dressed in a tee shirt. One of the cops holding a submachine gun was shouting, "Freeze, dog-breath! Green River Task-Farce!" In the background was a kids' treehouse with a sign reading "No girls allowed!," with the "r" in girls reversed. An inner tube swing hung by a rope from a tree limb.

The media criticism ignited Vern Thomas. The whole thing was *your* fault, Thomas angrily told reporters; *all* the newspeople had overreacted. The Basset cartoon particularly enraged the sheriff. He railed at a *Times* reporter about the newspaper's irre-sponsibility. The reporter, who hadn't yet seen the cartoon, couldn't understand what Thomas was talking about. Hadn't *The Times* withheld the man's name, the pictures, the maps, the whole nine yards? Later the reporter saw the Basset gibe and was appalled at the damage the drawing promised to do to his already ticklish relations with the police.

Meanwhile, McLean decided to go public with his side of the event. He chose *The Times* to tell his story, since that paper had done the most to minimize the privacy invasion. As he sat in his house with his still-furious wife, surrounded by all the game trophies, McLean told how the police had handcuffed him, how he had been give the "silent treatment" by the FBI agents on the way to the Burien precinct offices, about the specially set up "McLean room," with the photo-graphs and the red lines and file boxes and the rocks. Sure, he was scared, McLean said. But he knew he was innocent, and finally he had been able to convince the police of that fact.

Now, said McLean, he was just mad. The cops had torn his house apart, cutting up swatches of carpeting, emptying drawers, burrowing into closets, and scattering work records. The whole house was a mess. They had embarrassed him in front of the nation. Even angrier was McLean's wife. She had been the one filmed by the television people getting into the patrol car. The police had taken her to FBI headquarters in Seattle and had demanded that she give hair and blood samples, as if the agents had considered *her* a suspect in the murders!

They had been in touch with lawyers, the McLeans said, and the police and news media would be hearing from them soon.

At the task force headquarters, Adamson wrestled with the dilemma. McLean had seemed to fit the FBI's psychological profile quite well; the FBI had seemed so certain that McLean was the murderer. Hadn't the man been followed to places where bodies had been dumped? And there was the supposed dog episode. The trouble was, in the absence of eyewitnesses or a valid confession, the only way the crimes could be solved was through the use of trace evidence like hairs, blood, and fibers. The only legal way to get that evidence was to perform a legal search. If Adamson wanted to solve the case, he had to make the search. If he had it to do over again, Adamson thought, he would have handled the news media differently, but he still would have had the search performed. Okay, it didn't net them anything, *this time*. One down and maybe three hundred others to go. There would be more searches in the future, he told a reporter. Maybe not quite so public, though.

The FBI's crack surveillance team of fourteen agents, brought in especially for McLean, packed up and left town. So did Douglas. Too bad, said Douglas. Maybe next time.

As the week neared an end, some politicians also scrambled for daylight between the task force and the criticism. One county councilman—the politician who represented McLean's district—said he was unhappy with the way the police had conducted the search. "I don't know what kind of character this person is, but he doesn't deserve that kind of notoriety if he is innocent," the councilman said. And several others criticized the police and the news media for the way the whole thing had been handled.

But would the mistake cost the task force—and Thomas—their credibility with the politicians? More importantly, would the money dry up? For Hill, the McLean episode had provided an opening, the opportunity to suggest publicly for the first time that cuts *were* possible, without running into a buzzsaw of criticism from the news media and victim's advocacy groups.

"I have full confidence in Vern Thomas and I think that he's doing a professional job," Hill said. "He and his staff are intent on catching the Green River killer and intend to do a professional job." But, said Hill, "If there are very few good leads, if the possibility of coming up with good leads is not strong, then we would consider a reduction in resources appropriate. If the assessment is that the killer is still active and in the area, then that's a different matter. We've got to recognize there are a wide variety of county priorities . . . we have to simply look at demands for county services." Hill said Thomas now intended to review the manpower allocated to the task force, and to consider some reductions.

In the midst of all the media criticism—fueled in part by the reporters' own guilt for the excesses—the politicians' lingering doubts about the whole program now resurfaced. Many politicians concluded that Thomas *had* oversold them in 1983, and that the murders probably can't be solved, no matter how much was spent.

In political terms, the investigation was now a loser, some politicians said privately. The time was right to cut their losses, go on to other things, more popular causes, like the war on drugs. The investigation was no longer the media darling, and therefore it was safe to cut. Green River had become "bad PR," said one politician. The unsuccessful search had tipped the precarious balance that Thomas and Revelle had so painstaking assembled two years before. Pierce Brooks's advice to stay the course was completely forgotten.

After McLean, jokes and taunts about the task force also swept through the police department. Adamson again became the target of whispered attacks by his rival commanders. The McLean disaster was Adamson's fault, some said privately. He was just a politician, they sneered; he was no investigator, that was for sure. "Frank Adamson," sniffed one commander, "couldn't find an elephant with a bloody nose in the snow."

Adamson pulled his head in a bit. There's no use giving everybody an easy target, he thought. At home he discussed the fiasco with Jo. There wasn't any good in second-guessing himself, he told her, and she agreed. He had done the right thing in searching the fur trapper, he said, and he would do it again. He wouldn't be able to live with himself if he hadn't conducted the search, knowing what he knew before the event, no matter what anyone else thought *now*. All those pictures on the wall told him he was right, too.

58

BLAKE'S MAN

April 1986

Even before Pierce Brook's had suggested assembling index files to help narrow the search for the killer, one task force detective had been working along the same direction. Crime analyst John Blake had become fascinated with the possibilities held by a criminal lawyer from Kent who had been arrested by police for soliciting a police decoy prostitute on The Strip just five days after Wendy Coffield's body was discovered, back at the very beginning of the murders.

Investigating suspects was not Blake's job. The way Adamson had set up the task force, the three crime analysts were supposed to be rating the tips that came in, making sure that the tips were followed up, and maintaining the task force's data base. Additionally, the crime analysts were charged with looking for any hidden patterns and trends in the crimes, such as days of the week, times, locations, and the like.

But as a part of that work, Blake had become interested in real estate owned by a lawyer who had been arrested. The lawyer seemed to own or have connections to many parcels near where victims had been found, or that had road access provided by the critical transportation routes. Those connections might give the lawyer, Blake speculated, intimate familiarity with the places where victims had been dumped, as Brooks had suggested.

Blake began culling other information about the lawyer from various records. Soon he had obtained information from various prostitutes about their contacts with the man. Blake also developed an informant who knew something of the man's personality, who told him the lawyer refused to discuss the Green River murders even when it was a widespread topic of conversation. Finally, Blake learned that the lawyer was well known to some of the oldtimers inside the King County Police Department. The man had a law office in Kent not far from where the first five bodies had been found, had access to several vehicles, including a van, and practiced law in the area where most of the victims had last been seen. Who better than a lawyer, thought Blake, would be so conversant with evidence? Had that been why the victims had been found near so much trash, as an effort to confuse them? Blake came to believe that was imminently plausible. Slowly, bit by bit, Blake worked to build a case against his man.

In the weeks following the McLean affair, Blake succeeded in convincing a prosecutor and the inquiry judge to issue subpoenas for the lawyer's near-daily credit card billings. Painstakingly, Blake charted the billing dates against the known disappearance dates. Over and over he checked the victim dates against the charges, and the locations where the lawyer had incurred the charges.

In comparing the billing dates to the disappearance dates, Blake made what he thought was a startling discovery: on *none* of the dates in which victims had disappeared had the lawyer incurred any credit card charges. The absence of use of the credit cards on days when the victims had disappeared was the reverse of what investigators had found with Bundy a decade before, when gasoline credit card slips were used to place Ted near some of his victims. But to Blake, the *absence* seemed a powerful suggestion that the man had been somehow involved in the Green River murders—especially since purchases could be tracked on almost every other date during the period of the murders. Was the absence of charges the result of the lawyer's familiarity with how Bundy had been tripped up? To Blake, it seemed likely.

Blake grew more excited about his idea: Here was a lawyer, someone educated in the rules of evidence, who had represented prostitutes, who had frequented them as a customer, who had an office not far from the dump sites, who could not seem to account—at least on paper—for his whereabouts on the assumed dates of the crimes. I think this is The Guy, Blake told anyone who would listen.

The other detectives were mildly interested in Blake's hypothesis. But they pointed out that many other candidates seemed equally good prospects. Don't lose your objectivity, they told Blake; don't get tunnel vision. And in the meantime, how are you coming on rating today's tips? Inwardly, Blake gnashed his teeth. How could everyone be so *blind?* Reichert particularly bugged him. As one of the "Chosen Few," Reichert had reviewed his findings and had dismissed them, suggesting that Blake didn't know all of the things that he, Reichert, knew. While he boiled inside, Blake knew he had to maintain the image of the impartial cop, the calm, fact-oriented analyst. But it was becoming harder and harder.

Blake pushed for a search of the lawyer's home, cars, and office. But after McLean, the idea of going after a lawyer seemed truly dangerous. Blake's findings were "interesting, very interesting," he was told, but he didn't have enough to justify a search warrant. If you could somehow show that the man's time during the *hours* of the disappearance was unaccounted for, you might have something, Blake was told.

Blake returned to the prosecutor and explained his problem. He wanted to see the lawyer's appointment books. They would show the hours the lawyer was in his office. Whoa! said the prosecutor. You're crossing the line with that. You are probably going to violate confidential attorney–client privileges. Can't you find some other way?

Blake tried some other things. But it kept coming back to the appointment books. Somehow, he had to get them, Blake kept thinking. The answer was probably in there someplace. Already he had heard unconfirmed reports that the lawyer had represented at least one of the victims, and further that the victim had called the lawyer *on the day she had disappeared!* That seemed powerfully persuasive to Blake.

Finally Blake returned to the prosecutor and said it couldn't be done without the appointment books. He had to have them. By now Blake was secretly beginning to wonder whether the lawyer had some sort of political pull with the police department and the prosecutor's office. The prosecutor offered a compromise. He would go with Blake to the lawyer, explain the situation, and ask the lawyer to turn the books over to the judge; then the judge would copy the books, omitting the clients' names. The times of the appointments, and the destination of the trips that the lawyer made to court and elsewhere, would then be turned over to Blake for his analysis.

Blake didn't like it, but it was the best that could be done, the prosecutor said.

The lawyer didn't like the arrangement either. The idea of his being a Green River suspect was ludicrous. If only he hadn't been arrested that night by the policewoman! The prosecutor was patient, sympathetic. It's the best way to end this, he said. Finally the lawyer agreed to the proposal. An appointment was made to review the books; then the lawyer had to postpone the appointment. Blake's suspicions were further aroused. It looked to him that the lawyer had something to hide. The lawyer still had misgivings about the propriety of the arrangement. Blake called the prosecutor and pressed hard: *When* would he get the expurgated books? Finally the appointment was set, and after several days, copies of the censored books were turned over to Blake.

Blake sat down once more to fit the new information into the matrix. He spent hours tracking the lawyer's movements, growing more and more convinced of the man's viability as a suspect. The dates and times in the books seemed to indicate that the lawyer had been in the area on the days that disappearances occurred. Even when entries in the appointment books showed the lawyer was in court, Blake concluded that the lawyer *could* have left court early. Again, there was nothing to positively eliminate the man as a suspect.

Once again, Blake tried to induce the task force brass to serve a search warrant. Again they refused. By now Blake was nearly convinced that the lawyer was the killer, and that higher-ups in the police were covering up for him.

By now, however, the task force commanders had become increasingly worried about Blake. He seemed to be on a crusade. He wouldn't listen when others tried to dissuade him from his beliefs; somehow, Blake always found a new explanation for a seeming inconsistency in his theory. Blake's bitterness had grown to the point where he had suggested quietly to others in the task force that *someone, somewhere* was covering up. Worst of all, Blake's performance of his assigned duties began to suffer. Tips that looked

promising were unconsciously being set aside as Blake
focused on his man.

Finally, to put the matter to rest, Adamson offered
Blake an alternative: Blake and someone from the
FBI would go to see the lawyer personally and interview him. If the man did something, or acted in some
way that indicated guilty knowledge, them Adamson
would consider asking for a warrant. Blake and the
FBI man made an appointment with the lawyer. The
man was angry at Blake, and denied any involvement
in the murders. The FBI man looked over the clothes
the lawyer was wearing, including a pair of expensive
leather shoes. The man's office was neat and clean.
The man himself was well groomed. Afterward, Blake
and the FBI man left. He's not the guy, the FBI man
told Blake. That man wouldn't feel comfortable getting his shoes and clothes muddy. He's out. The task
force commanders agreed with the FBI, and put the
lawyer in the inactive file. Blake refused to accept it.

59

RETREAT

April 1986/May 1986

In the week that followed the McLean search, the task
force morale plummeted. Cops around the task force
water cooler made snide remarks about the FBI. Several said they had always doubted McLean's viability.
Some of those who had been assigned to the surveillance team said it had always bothered them that
McLean had never made contact with prostitutes.

Reichert had had his own doubts, partly conditioned

by his bias toward Foster. Inside their own minds, others were laughing. McLean had always been a longshot, Blake thought, but the brass had been blinded by the hotshit FBI. Inside, Blake's hopes for his lawyer suspect went up.

After two years of operation, the fact was that the task force had begun to splinter into cliques. In the inner circle—"The Chosen Few," as some detectives referred to them—were those who had been with the case almost from the beginning, such as Reichert, Fae Brooks, Larry Gross, and several others. To some, the inner circle seemed privy to secrets not extended to the rest of the task force. Outside that ring were those detectives working on the suspects, which had become something of a drudge, since there were so many of them. Further out still were those officers rotated into the task force on a temporary basis as part of light duties assigned after illness; many of those officers had no idea of what was going on, and felt shut out.

And outside the task force itself, the bitterness of exclusion continued to eat away at the remainder of the county's police force, particularly those assigned to the Burien precinct. For two years they had given the precinct over to the elites, and they were sick of it. The arrival of the FBI had further overcrowded the limited office space, and the overcrowding was only marginally improved when the bureau's surveillance team left town.

To improve morale, Hill reluctantly agreed to allow the task force to move from the Burien precinct to an unused junior high school facility nearby. The move cost $16,000. Hill's budget office demanded that Thomas pay for the move by cannibalizing one of the task force positions. But Hill made it clear to members of the county council and to Thomas himself: The task force had to be substantially reduced. There was no way the county could afford the task force at its current level without a tax increase, and there was no way that Hill was going to propose a tax increase in his first year in office.

* * *

Meanwhile, Hill wanted to be sure that any cuts in the task force would be Thomas's doing, not his. The politics of the murders and their investigation required that reductions be for valid police reasons, not because of any other causes, and especially not because Thomas had been his opponent's appointee. Both men knew other police priorities were demanding attention. Stopping drugs was the current program, not chasing after a murderer who had obviously left town. Thomas was the top cop—what was he going to do about *drugs*?

To help Thomas get the picture, Hill's office had passed around a questionnaire to residents of the county, a slick political brochure that asked what people thought should be priorities for county spending. Hill showed Thomas the results: The Green River Task Force wasn't even rated. What people wanted was new park and recreation facilities, Hill said. Thomas noticed that the Green River investigation wasn't even listed as a choice. Thomas cut three positions off the task force, and agreed to convene a panel of his top commanders to review the entire task force operation.

But as the spring warmed up, Thomas felt he had to find a way to protect his creation, the task force. All the experts kept telling him that it might take years to solve the crimes. The worst thing he could do, the experts said, was to give up too soon. Hadn't Pierce Brooks actually suggested that the task force be *increased*? But under the current political climate, the question was: Could he maintain the task force at a high enough level of staffing to yield results? If not, he might as well throw in the towel and save them all a lot of trouble. But Thomas wanted the case to be *solved,* dammit. He had to walk a narrow line between maintaining the investigation and responding to the political demands for doing more with less. If only McLean had been the killer.

In early April, Thomas wrote a memorandum to Hill. "Since I reduced the task force by one person in January," Thomas wrote, "and by two more in March . . . to finance the cost for moving the task force to the Glendale Junior High School, I recommend the task force be maintained at the present level. I do recommend, however, that we reassess manpower requirements for the task force on a quarterly basis to insure that resources not needed by the GRTF by reassigned to regular department duties as soon as they become available.

"With the narcotics workload increasing so rapidly, I do intend to release two more force members to work in the narcotics area as soon as possible."

There it was—Thomas's counterproposal in the bargain he had made with Hill the previous winter. He had already cut three jobs from the thirty-four originally assigned to the murders. He did not want to make any further reductions: "Not recommended," said the memo. However, Thomas would be willing to review everything once again in three months, giving Hill a tighter leash. And he held out the hope of cutting two more detectives soon for assignment to the drug wars.

But even the limited cuts by Thomas had begun to stir opposition from women's groups and victim groups. Cookie Hunt's Coalition to Stop the Green River Murders was particularly vocal. The police, said Hunt, were backing away from their commitment to catch the murderer, and it was all because of politics.

Beginning in June, Thomas's top commanders began the reassessment of the task force requirements promised to Hill by the sheriff. Included on the review team were Kraske, chief Jim Nickle, and Major Terry Allman, Kraske's successor as the commander of the department's criminal investigations division. After two years of watching the task force get nearly anything it wanted in terms of police resources, all three men had their eyes on the goodies Thomas had provided to Adamson. Was there any reason to believe that Adamson could get the job done without so many people? That was what Thomas wanted to know. One alternative was yes, the other no. With a mandate from his command staff to keep the investigation at its current level, Thomas would have something to bargain with when he met with Hill. Without a mandate, Thomas would be forced to cut the investigation back. Politics, thought Thomas, more politics.

Adamson didn't like it. What sort of outcome could Thomas anticipate when the fate of the task force was being turned over to some of those who had opposed it in the first place? Thomas tried to convince him.

"Hey, Frank," Thomas said. "Come on, we've got to do it. *You've* got to do it. I can't sit here and allow it to run on without having somebody take a look at it. And I don't have time to do it myself.

"I picked three people who I think will give you a fair shot. They'll give you a shot, but they'll give you a fair shot." They'd give me a shot, all right, thought Adamson. A *coup de grace*. But Adamson was an experienced administrator, and knew the time and the climate were ripe for the first substantial reduction in the attempt to find the killer. To pretend otherwise was to ignore the realities, and whatever else he was, Adamson prided himself on being a realist.

60

CUT TO THE BONE

May 1986/November 1986

By the time the management review began in mid-June, three new skeletons had been discovered, bringing the list of known dead to thirty-six. Ten others remained on the missing list.

The last three skeletons had been discovered in familiar locations—two east of Seattle, near I-90, and one along the banks of the Green River. The Green

River skeleton was only partially recovered. All that could be found was a part of the spine, some of the ribs, and a collarbone and a shoulder blade. It was impossible to tell how long it had been there. The rest of the remains had been lost to the river's flow over the years. Without a skull, it was impossible to tell who the victim might have been; and without the pelvis, not even the sex could be determined. The only thing for sure was that whoever the dead person had been, he or she was very small. Lacking the sex, age, or race of the victim, investigators decided not to add the bones to the Green River victim list.

The other two victims were quickly identified. The first turned out to be Maureen Feeney. Her name had been among those given by Seattle Police to the county in December of 1983 as possible Green River victims. The task force had declined to list her as a victim because they could find no links between Maureen Feeney and the world of prostitution. But the discovery of her skeletal remains near I-90, in almost the same circumstances as Delise Plager and Lisa Yates earlier, caused the investigators to look again. While Maureen's family protested that she had never been involved in prostitution, investigators found a pimp who had known her as Kris Ponds.

The pimp said her family hadn't known about Maureen's other life. A few days later investigators talked to a Seattle patrol officer who had given "Ponds" two jaywalking tickets within five minutes in Seattle's International District on September 26, 1983—just two days before the pimp had last seen her. The officer said he was sure the woman had been working as a prostitute. "Ponds" had given the same address as Feeney.

The identification of the second victim, found in mid-June, provided the solution to two mysteries. The first was the fate of "Tina Tomson," the friend Paige Miley had left on the bus bench on November 1, 1983. By this time the investigators had learned that Tina Tomson was a false name, and that "Tomson's" real name was Kim Nelson, and that she had come from

Ann Arbor, Michigan, as had her friend Denise Bush. Nelson, it turned out, was the tall, blonde woman who had told Larry Gross that she intended to get "that prick" who had killed her friend. Instead, it appeared that the killer had gotten Nelson.

But poking further into "Tomson's" identity pried loose yet another identification, this time one of the unidentified remains remaining from 1984. Checking all the files for all variants of Tina Tomson, investigators found that a woman they had assumed had been Nelson was in fact an entirely different person—real name, Tina Thompson. Dental records obtained for the real Tina Thompson were matched with the skeleton Barbara Kubik-Patten had discovered wrapped in the plastic tarp. Tina had last been seen on The Strip July 25, 1983—a year to the day after Dub Bonner's disappearance. So now the unidentified list was back down to five—the two found in Tualatin, Oregon in 1985; the two found near Mountain View Cemetery in early 1986; and the small white girl found near the Little League Field in early 1984, near Cheryl Wims. That victim was particularly frustrating because of her age. Someone had to know of a missing person that young, Haglund kept thinking.

On July 15, the fourth anniversary of the day Wendy Coffield's body had been found in the Green River, Cookie Hunt and the Women's Coalition to Stop the Green River Murders paid a surprise visit to the task force headquarters at the junior high school and started a sit-in.

The sit-in, said Hunt, would last for forty-six hours—one hour for each of the Green River victims. "I don't think we would be here if we thought the police were any closer than before to solving the murders," she said. When it began to rain, Adamson invited the group into the task force headquarters for shelter, and Reichert brought in donuts for the protestors.

The food and shelter didn't change the protestors' mood much, however. The public was apathetic about the murders, Hunt insisted, because the police and news media continued to portray the victims as prostitutes. And now, she said, the police were thinking of cutting the task force even further. They were, indeed.

By September, Kraske, Allman, and Nickle had finished their review. The trio presented their findings to Thomas in a confidential report. The recommended a 40 percent cut in the investigation's staffing. More importantly, they recommended that Adamson be moved back under Allman's command; that would act as a control on Adamson's spending, because now Adamson would have to justify his decisions to someone other than Thomas. The reasons advanced by the three commanders made sense, at least on paper. The most important reason for the reductions, they said, was that it appeared that the murders had stopped.

"The reasonable assumption at this point is that the killer is *not* presently operating within King County," the panel reported. "The fact that [Adamson] has elected to transfer street unit people to investigation and actually assign caseloads, missing persons, etc., is a strong indicator that the need for a street unit has been greatly reduced."

Adamson *had* transferred four detectives out of the proactives to help with the follow-up work, in part because the number of prostitutes remaining in the Seattle area—after the murders had received so much publicity—was steadily dwindling. But at the same time, the amount of follow-up investigation kept increasing, which was why Adamson used the four street cops for the follow-up work. Now the panel was pointing to Adamson's own management efficiency as the reason he should lose personnel.

But what if the murders started up again?

"In the event that a need for a street-unit style of operations should arise," the panel reported, "it would present no problem to temporarily assign street-unit–experienced Green River Task Force detectives to such duties." In other words, if the murders began again, Adamson could simply assign his follow-up people to work the street on the new murders.

But what about all the follow-up that still had to be accomplished? The raw numbers were staggering. In addition to the thirty-seven known homicides, there were the ten missings; more to the point, the task force had zeroed in on the more than 4,100 individuals named in nearly 18,000 tip sheets and had come up with a list of 978 different "A" suspects—those thought by investigators to be most capable of having committed the crimes.

So far, only 268 of the 978 had been conclusively eliminated; another 452 people had been placed in the inactive files by the "investigator's opinion," pending receipt of more information.

Then there were all the other categories of "A" suspects, any or all of whom could still be viable, but who had also been placed in the inactive files: fifty-three people detectives had been unable to either locate or even identify; eighty-four who had passed polygraph tests; eleven who had refused to take the test; three who had utterly refused to cooperate; two who had inconclusive polygraphs; and thirty-six who were inactive because they had died, moved elsewhere, or because of some other reason.

That still left sixty-nine people who remained under active investigation, an even dozen of whom detectives were not even able to identify. That made for an average caseload of ten current "A" suspects for each detective, all of them originally trained to consider only one suspect at a time.

And, of course, the numbers were constantly fluctuating as new names came in, and as information moved names from inactive to active status.

The review panel, however, concluded that the task force computer—by now loaded with tens of thousands of tip sheets and other documents, including a master list of the evidence—would make it less necessary for Adamson to have as many detectives. The computer, said the panel, could do much of the work detectives traditionally did with shoe leather.

Of course, the panel said, it would help if Adamson could be a little more careful in defining what constituted a Green River suspect. The tipsheet criteria tended to be so elastic that it could be giving a false impression of detective workload. And what was Adamson doing with *two* lieutenants? One was supposed to be supervising the street-unit people and the crime analysis team; but those units were so self-starting, often taking assignments from the follow-up units, that that lieutenant was doing Adamson's administrative work instead. One lieutenant could be cut, the panel contended.

A fingerprint identification position could be cut. A sergeant should be eliminated. Then, because the computer was clicking along so well, the four street cops Adamson had transferred to follow-up were also put on the cutting board.

Finally, the panel said the public information officer job filled by Detective Fae Brooks should also be eliminated; publicity was not the task force's need, not now, after McLean.

All these liberated resources, said Allman, Nickle, and Kraske, should go back into the pot for reassignment to other commanders, mainly to narcotics enforcement and to boost the proactive patrols in the precincts.

Thomas now had his review. What should he do? Clearly, Hill and the council would be watching. Thomas had proposed hiring twenty-nine *new* officers just to keep up with the routine workload the department already had. He needed Hill's support to hire as many of those twenty-nine as he could get. It certainly wouldn't help that cause to get into a squabble with his boss over the task force. He had promised both Hill and the council that if other crimes increased, he would reassign the resources. Well, other crimes *had* increased. Thomas sent the panel's recommendations on to Hill with a letter saying that he had decided to make the reassignments as they had been proposed. Now he just had to hope that the murders wouldn't

start up again, and that Hill would hire the new personnel he was requesting.

It did not take long for the cuts to surface in the
news media. The county council divided over the
issue. One councilman was upset over the proposed
reductions. As chairman of the county's police operations committee, Ron Sims considered holding hear-
ings to ask the police whether the cuts would reduce
the chances of catching the murderer. Sims sat
through a series of meetings with Thomas, Adamson,
and Hill's budget director, in which the budget director made it quite clear that the Hill administration
considered the Green River investigation a luxury the
county could no longer afford. Arguments flew back
and forth. The question Sims faced was whether to
surface the debate in a public forum. But Sims knew
the budget numbers weren't lying, and that the only
way the investigation could be maintained without the
cuts was to go for a tax increase. Sims could count
votes with anyone, and he knew the votes for an
increase just weren't there. What good would a hearing do, in that case, except make Hill mad at him,
maybe open himself to the charge of grandstanding?
After awhile, Sims thought better of the idea, and the
cuts were allowed to happen "administratively," as
Sims put it later.

Others on the council thought the cuts were probably a good idea. "They've been at it for two or three
years now," said a Republican councilwoman, Lois
North. "Maybe it's time to use those resources for
those who are still here."

And another councilman, Paul Barden, a former
county policeman, said the cuts were "terrible."

"We shouldn't have to make this choice," he said.
Barden had been pressing Hill to increase the personnel in the entire police department by three dozen
new officers. Things were so bad in some areas of the
county, Barden said, that twelve of the county's regular patrol districts were going unstaffed by police. The
county had less than half of the manpower per thou-

sand population than the city, he said. But Hill had been unmoved by his arguments, instead contending that the county didn't need to hire new officers, only that is should use those it had more efficiently. Barden could count votes too, and knew that Hill had won.

In the end, Hill asked for the hiring of six new officers. That's all the county can afford, he said. The new six, coupled with the reduction of a dozen positions from the task force, would effectively give the department eighteen new positions to work with. But Hill didn't want it to be said he didn't care whether the murders were solved. "The Green River investigation," he said, "is a high priority of my administration."

Now it was Cookie Hunt who blew up. "Of course it's political," an angry Hunt charged after Hill and Thomas announced the cuts at a joint news conference. "If the county had come under the same pressure to catch the killer as it has about the drug problem, I think things might have been different.

"The task force was cut back once before, when most of the murders where taking place," she pointed out. The county, said Hunt, was making another bad decision.

Tom Estes, the father of Debbie Estes, was also bitter about the reductions. "This is an election time of the year," Estes said, "and naturally, political people have to cut budgets. They have to put money to other things to improve their image to the voters, and meet other voters' needs. But after those needs are met, unfortunately, the killings may go on. They're borrowing from Peter to pay Paul, and it's going to come back and haunt Peter."

And Judy DeLeon, the mother of Carrie Rois, was also angry. "It makes me and some of the other parents feel like the deaths of our daughters aren't important to anybody," she said. "It's bad enough that this has happened. But now it's like the King County executive is saying, 'Well, that's too bad, but now we're going to do something else.'

"If someone came in and shot us all dead, there would be continual outcry, but what they're telling us is, 'Who cares?' That's how I'm taking it, that my daughter's life meant nothing. He [Hill] should spend a couple of hours walking in my shoes."

After first objecting to the cuts, Adamson swung into line behind Thomas and Hill. Publicly, he tried to put a good spin on the reductions. One could argue, he said, that the street-unit component of the task force *was* a luxury, even if it had been the critical eyes and ears of the investigators in the prostitution areas. The murders *had* stopped, and other crimes had gone up. Adamson also agreed that the increased efficiency of the task force and the availability of the computer offset some of the effects of the cuts. And, he said, the uniformed patrol officers could pick up part of the burden of keeping the prostitution areas under surveillance.

Adamson did not add, however, that the patrol officers had had that responsibility when all the murders were going on.

Now Adamson had the duty of deciding who would go and who would stay. It's like making cuts on a football team, the thought. Just because someone had to go didn't mean they weren't good enough, it was just that there were only so many spots on the roster. Several members of the street unit were sent back to the department, as well as several detectives. So was John Blake.

Later, Blake confessed that something in him just snapped when he learned that he was being dropped from the task force. Adamson tried to tell him that it was nothing personal, it was just that cuts had to be made. But Blake had a hard time hearing Adamson. "I blew up," he admitted later. What transpired between the two men remained secret. But in the end, Adamson suggested that Blake take a few days off to think things over. Instead, Blake took a temporary disability leave for reasons of psychological stress. Ultimately, the leave became a permanent retirement for a psychological disability. The Green River murder case had driven John Blake to mental illness.

*   *   *

In November, events from the cuts took a new turn. Mike Nault, who had been commanding the department's newest precinct in suburban Maple Valley, became caught up in a controversy over sex harassment among the officers in his command. Nault had apparently ignored the complaints, or at least had not taken them seriously enough to suit Thomas. Thomas's press spokesman said simply but devastatingly: "The sheriff has lost confidence in Mike Nault." Thomas wanted to reassign Nault. He asked Adamson to take Nault's place.

Adamson thought briefly about what Thomas was offering: a promotion, and a chance to step out of the line of fire, for a while at least. He was tired, Adamson knew. He had tried to assemble a task force to solve a terrible series of crimes. He had been a zealot for maintaining the task force at the higher level, but had been attacked by his fellow commanders, the public, the news media, and the politicians. Maybe, he reasoned, it *was* time for someone else.

"Frank, I'm not kicking you out," Thomas told Adamson. "I'm giving you an opportunity to get a promotion if you want it, and a chance to leave the task force. You make up your mind, it's your decision. But you've got to take a look at it. You've been there a long time. You're getting tired. I've been watching your eyes. You've been getting particularly sensitive with the press. You're getting overly sensitive, and I'm a great one to talk about it, because I've been sensitive too. But . . . when you sit back and see somebody else do it, you can see it better. I recommend you take it. That's not an order, but . . ."

That night, Adamson went home and talked it over with Jo. It's over, he told her. He had taken his best shot at the job, he said, and felt good about what he had created; he knew in his heart that his men had stopped the murders. But now it was time to go on. He knew what was needed for the task, and what was left in the task force after the cuts just wasn't enough.

The following day, Adamson told Thomas he would accept the promotion to major and the chance to run the new precinct. The smaller task force would be turned over to a new commander.

Cookie Hunt greeted the announcement of Adamson's departure with more criticism.

"They keep saying everything's okay, but everything's *not* okay," Hunt said. "There would be a big public outcry if they flatly got rid of the task force, but instead they're chipping away and putting out propaganda that everything's cool.

"There've been a lot of changes in the last several months," she said, "and it seems they're trying to integrate the task force into the department and phase it out."

Adamson denied it. "The task force is not fading into the sunset," he said. "Patience is very important. It may appear the task force is disappearing, but it's not.

"I believe fully the task force will solve the case. In terms of the task force, I'm just one person. I think my loss will be minimal."

In Adamson's place, Thomas named Captain James Pompey, who had been head of the department's technical services division, which included the SWAT team and the marine patrol.

Pompey was the department's highest-ranking black officer. "It was nothing I volunteered for, " Pompey said of the assignment to the task force. But Pompey said, "I feel I can meet the challenge. I think I could have said no."

BOOK THREE

POMPEY
1986–87

61

POMPEY'S RUN

November 1986/April 1987

After the summer of cuts, personnel shifts, and political maneuverings, the trimmed-down task force under Pompey settled back into its routines. Work proceeded on attempts to assemble the various index lists suggested by Pierce Brooks, among them a computer listing of military personnel assigned to the region. Another project had been launched to identify pickup trucks by make and color in the hope that somehow the right pickup could be located. Those lists were coordinated with other lists, including traffic citations and Port of Seattle field interview reports.

The seeming halt in the murders continued to suggest several possibilities: The killer was dead; the killer was in jail for some other crime; or the killer had left the area and had gone somewhere else to begin anew. Some detectives assembled lists of dead men, and still others began a project to identify every male in the state who had been incarcerated near the time the murders had stopped.

Meanwhile, the crime analysis unit continued to pay close attention to similar homicides in other parts of the country in the hope that other murder cases might give detectives some new leads to work with.

The detectives had already consulted with their counterparts in Honolulu, where a serial murderer had strangled and dumped the bodies of seven women over a period of months. Three of the victims had been discovered near water next to an airport runway. Most of them had last been seen at bus stops. But Hawaiian detectives discounted the possibility of a link to the Green River crimes, mostly because the women killed there appeared to have no background in prostitution. The task force detectives were inclined to agree.

Other homicides in Spokane and Oakland were reviewed, as was a series of prostitute murders in Los Angeles. In each case, there were enough differences to discount any links. All that could be done was to hope that the other police agencies were successful in resolving their cases. If arrests could be made, it would be possible to see whether the out-of-state suspects had ever been in the Seattle area.

Then, in mid-December, a man searching for a Christmas tree to cut in a forested area north of Vancouver, British Columbia, discovered the nude, decomposing body of a young woman lying partially exposed in a shallow grave. The following day, a search by police uncovered a bone that did not belong to the first body. An expanded search was undertaken, and twenty yards away, a second victim was discovered lying behind a large log. The two murders had eerie similarities to the Green River crimes: the clustering of two victims close together, the log, and the shallow burial. No identification and very little clothing had been left with the victims.

Further review of the Vancouver records showed that four prostitutes had been murdered in the city over the previous twenty months. The Vancouver area had been a magnet for prostitutes since the opening of Expo 86, the world's fair. Over the year of the fair, the city's prostitution population nearly doubled to fourteen hundred people, most of them women, according to police estimates.

Had the killer gone north? Just as Portland was three hours to the south, Vancouver was a mere three-hour drive to the north. With all that publicity about the murders and the investigation in Seattle, a move by the killer to a place where there was an abundance of prostitutes and an absence of proactive tactics designed to catch him was certainly plausible.

Prostitutes in Vancouver certainly believed it. Marie Arrington, a spokeswoman for a prostitute's organization, said she thought the Vancouver murders could be connected. "Some of the tricks in town have said they are the Green River killer," Arrington said. "The girls feel he's been here. Whether he's here or not, the girls are really afraid."

Efforts over the next month to identify the two latest Vancouver victims proved successful. One was Karen Ann Baker, twenty; the other was Darlinda Ritchie, twenty-seven. As Canadian investigators looked deeper into the lives of the two women, they discovered that not only had the two women known each other, they were close friends. Both had worked at the same Vancouver nightclub as topless dancers. But what was startling about their deaths is that they appeared to have taken place more than a month apart. That focused investigators' attention on the nightclub where both women danced, and suggested that their killer was someone who knew both women. That in turn tended to discount the murders' connection to the Green River case, where the victims appeared to have been selected at random.

On the heels of the Vancouver cases came a news report about an obvious serial murder case, this one in many ways similar to the Green River crimes. The bodies of five young black women had been found dumped in woods just outside of Washington, D.C. Detectives there said that two of the women had been stabbed, and that all four had been sexually assaulted. But detectives were at a loss, at least initially, to identify the victims. All five of the victims had been dumped within three hundred yards of one another. Task force detectives contacted investigators in Prince Georges County, Maryland, to compare notes. But it was impossible to demonstrate any links between the eastern case and the Green River problem.

*　　*　　*

By January, almost all of the tip sheet information, along with all the supporting investigative documents, had been loaded into the task force computer. Organization of the material and its automated analysis and retrieval was beginning to pay dividends, particularly when the information was cross-matched against some of the index lists that were being accumulated. Earlier in the previous summer, a task force investigator had begun to notice some peculiar coincidences about a thirty-eight-year-old man who had previously been investigated, but placed on the inactive list after passing a polygraph test.

The man had been arrested for soliciting a police decoy on The Strip in April of 1982. As detective Matt Haney looked deeper into the man's background, he discovered that the man himself had contacted the task force to offer information in May of 1984. The man told police then that he had met one of the victims in the fall of 1983. Who was that? The man didn't know the woman's name. But he had seen her and her friend along The Strip and had talked with them. The man was shown photographs of the victims, and identified Kim Nelson, whom investigators then knew as Tina Tomson. The fact that the man had contacted *them* rather than the other way around was open to two interpretations. One was that the man was simply trying to help. But another possibility was that the man really wanted to find out what police knew about him.

Investigators in 1984 had conducted a preliminary investigation of the man, which ended after the man voluntarily agreed to take a polygraph test. The examiner reviewing the test results concluded that the man had passed the test, and the investigation of the man was put on inactive status. But there was more to the man's background than investigators had known at the time, and the computer helped Haney find it.

Burrowing through Port of Seattle police records, Haney uncovered information in which a prostitute had accused the same man of choking her, in 1980, while they were parked on a dark road in the area of condemned houses south of the airport. The woman had run to a nearby occupied house for help. Police were called and stopped the man. He claimed that the woman had bitten him, and that he had retaliated by choking her. Port police let him go.

Then Haney found another Port of Seattle report, this one a field interview conducted by patrol officers, which showed that police had encountered the man while he was parked in a truck near the Little League field in 1982. The place where the man was interviewed was only a few yards from where Cheryl Wims's skeleton was recovered two years later. The Port's paperwork showed that a woman with the man was identified as Jennifer Kaufmann. Haney checked the computer for hits on Jennifer Kaufmann, and was surprised to learn that Kaufmann was a false name used by Green River victim Keli McGinness.

And the computer wasn't finished. The same man, Haney found, had been named as a possible suspect in the abduction of Marie Malvar on the last day of April 1983. The computer had turned up the report filed by Des Moines Police detectives when Joe Malvar and Bobby Woods tracked down the truck with the primer spot after Marie disappeared, four long years before. The man linked to McGinness owned the truck with the primer spot, and it was his house that the Des Moines officers had visited when called by Malvar. That was *three* victims linked to the same man, thought Haney. This was getting interesting.

Haney showed the man's 1984 polygraph to the FBI lie-detector experts. The experts looked over the test and its interpretation and decided that the test had been flawed. the questioning, they said, was incomplete because no questions had been asked about Marie Malvar or Keli McGinness. Consequently, the test could not be used to clear the man.

Bolstered by these discoveries and the FBI's opinion, Haney and other investigators then began assembling as much information as they could about the man. Paige Miley, Nelson's friend, was tracked down in Las Vegas. She immediately identified a photograph of the man as the same person she had seen in the Seven-Eleven a few nights after Nelson's disappearance, the man who had asked her about her "blonde friend."

Other detectives assembled a complete list of all the vehicles the man might have used during the years of the murders. The list totaled nine different cars or pickup trucks, several with campers. Another effort was made to track down the man's former wife. She provided a wealth of background information on the man, including the fact that he liked to search out places where people had dumped things to scavenge for old auto parts. She took detectives on a tour of some of the places. Some of them turned out to be not too far from the places where victims' bodies had been dumped.

A number of prostitutes and former prostitutes were contacted about the man. Several identified his photograph as a man they had frequent contact with as he had cruised The Strip in 1982 and 1983.

The statements of eyewitnesses who had seen pickup trucks associated with some of the disappearances—including Denise Bush, Kimi Kai Pitsor, Gail Mathews, and Alma Smith—were compared to the vehicles owned or operated by the man. Allowing for the bad lighting conditions, the trucks reported by the witnesses could have been the same as those operated by the man, the detectives concluded.

The man was a U.S. Navy veteran, a lifelong resident of south King County, and worked the graveyard shift as a painter in a Seattle-area truck manufacturing plant. The man's shift records were obtained from his employer under an inquiry subpoena. Analysis of the man's work records showed there was *not one* occasion when a victim disappeared when the man was at work, and that on several occasions when victims had last been seen—including the date of Nelson's disappearance—the man had called in sick.

Finally, the location of the man's residence and place of employment were plotted against the dump sites. To get to and from work, the man often drove along The Strip. And the man lived on a small cul-de-sac just off Military Road South, just north of the road that led down to the Green River. The closest turn off The Strip that led to his house was at 216th Street—the same intersection where Dub Bonner, Keli McGinness, Gail Mathews, and Marie Malvar had last been seen, and where Bobby Woods had jammed on his brakes to avoid running the red light.

For years, the FBI had been telling task force members that the day they encountered the man they were seeking, they would know it in their gut. All the signs would point to the man, if he were the right one. Now Haney had that gut feeling.

Late in the afternoon of April 8, 1987, teams of task force detectives fanned out across south King County. One team met the man as he emerged from work, and served him with a search warrant which allowed them to take hair samples. The man's truck was towed away for a thorough vacuum-cleaner search. The detectives asked the man if he was willing to take a second polygraph test. The man declined. Detectives gave him a ride to his parents' house, located some six blocks east of The Strip near Military Road.

Meanwhile other detectives had seized other vehicles owned or operated by the man for similar searches. Still another team went to the man's house and took carpet samples and other trace evidence from an outbuilding. Within a few hours, the entire search was over. It had almost been completed before most of the news media had even learned it was going on.

The single exception was *The P-I*. Tipped to the search by someone in the know, two teams of *P-I* reporters and photographers had staked out the man's house and workplace. Detectives serving the warrant at the truck plant saw them and mistook them for FBI agents. When the detectives learned the journalists' true identity, they asked that the paper keep it quiet until it was all over. *The P-I*, sitting on an exclusive story, happily agreed. They certainly weren't going to broadcast the news.

Other detectives in the man's neighborhood went door to door and asked neighbors to refrain from calling the news media. Most agreed. But just before the search at the house ended, a television station stumbled onto the story and sent its traffic helicopter on a fly-over. The station, still leery after the McLean disaster of the previous year, decided not to air any pictures.

Late in the afternoon, just as detectives were preparing to cart the evidence away, the police issued a short, terse statement confirming that a search warrant had been served, and emphasizing that the man searched had *not* been arrested. In contrast to the McLean affair, the latest search warrant was as clean as a surgical incision.

Two days later, Pompey surveyed the results of the task force's second major search and said he was very happy with the way things had come out.

"The press did its job," said Pompey. "This is a case of widespread interest. They aren't the enemy. This was going to come out, anyway. The game plan was to get in and out with a minimum of disruption, no more than we have on any other search warrant.

"People have a right to their privacy," he said. "We've got to remember it's a matter of intense interest when we serve a search warrant in this case. We've got to look at all the tips, we have an obligation to do that. But we've also got to protect the people.

"Last time they really thought they had their man. Everyone got real excited. Everyone got pumped up, until it came out full blown—'This is the guy.'

"Well, that hurts you. It hurts you with the public, it hurts you with the prosecutor's office and it hurts you with the court when you want to get another warrant.

"This one, we took slowly. We went along, checking each thing, saying, 'Yeah, he looks good, but we've got to take it one step at a time.' You can't get in the frame of mind that says 'This is the guy,' which is what we did the last time and what they did in Atlanta.''

Now, said Pompey, the case would go to the crime laboratory.

Despite their low-key approach, Pompey and the detectives were nevertheless excited about the search. The man's reluctance to be interviewed and take a second polygraph test—later confirmed by the man's lawyer—looked like it might be an evasion.

But Pompey cautioned everyone: Let's take it one step at a time. Let's let the lab look at the evidence and see if any of it matches.

62

BREATHING ROOM

May 1987

A few weeks after the search, a pair of reporters approached the truck painter's father. The father was a retired bus driver who had once been assigned to the run that covered The Strip. The father was still reeling from the shock of the search, which had included some of the vehicles owned by the father himself. When the reporters suggested that the task force had been known to make mistakes, the father could only shake his head. The police, he said, had told him they were sure this time. A lump appeared in the father's throat, and he appeared on the verge of tears. "They mean to pin it on him," he said.

But a month after the search, it seemed likely that

the task force had missed again. The collection of
hairs and fibers obtained from the search of the truck
painter's house, workplace, and the vehicles could not
be matched to any of the similar evidence found at
several of the Green River sites, and most specifically,
with the Opal Mills case, which remained the investigator's best evidence. But that did not necessarily
eliminate the man from *all* the crimes. The possibility
remained that the person who had killed Opal Mills
and the other victims in the Green River was someone
different than the person who killed the women found
on dry land. More tests would have to be conducted,
said the supervisor of the State Crime Lab, Kay
Sweeney.

Pompey was philosophical about the findings. He
wasn't ready to completely give up on the truck
painter. If the lab couldn't find an immediate link, he
said, the investigators would just have to look harder.
More seized materials would be sent to the lab, Pompey said.

Two days after the lab announced that it could not
find any connecting evidence, Pompey decided to go
fishing. An athletic man drawn to physical challenges,
Pompey wasn't interested in simply throwing a line
over the side of the boat. It was more fun to go to
where the fish were: underwater.

Ever since he had commanded the department's
marine patrol with its diving unit, Pompey had had an
interest in scuba diving. He had taken lessons, and
had a moderate amount of diving experience.
Recently he had purchased a top-of-the-line, air-pow-
ered speargun. He wanted to demonstrate it for
county detective Bob Stockham, also a former member of the diving unit.

Stockham, an ex-Marine, had learned to scuba dive
in the service. He was an accomplished diver. Pompey
had been asking Stockham for weeks to take him
along an a spearfishing trip. The two men had gone
diving together twice before. On this Sunday, Stockham and his brother met with Pompey and Roger

Dunn, a former county detective who had become a private investigator in Seattle. The four men put their diving gear in Stockham's fourteen-foot inflatable boat and set a course for a buoy several hundred yards off Richmond Beach in north King County. The water in the area was about ninety feet deep, and the floor of the sound at that location was covered with huge chunks of demolition concrete, which provided something of a habitat for bottom-dwelling fish.

Because the inflatable boat wasn't large enough for all four men to get into their tanks at once, Stockham and Pompey suited up first. Then the two men went over the side. Dunn and Stockham's brother followed.

Stockham and Pompey worked their way down the heavy chain securing the buoy and began to search for fish in the gloom near the bottom. The plan was for both men to make a circle around the chain while hunting for fish. Stockham and Pompey saw one fish, and Stockham let Pompey have first crack. Pompey missed. He reloaded his speargun, and the two men continued working their way around the chain. Stockham looked at his bottom timer and saw that the two men had been down about fifteen minutes of the planned thirty-minute dive. Dunn and Stockham's brother could not be seen.

Suddenly, Pompey approached Stockham, and pointed to the air pressure gauge on his tanks. Stockham checked the gauge and couldn't believe what he saw. Pompey had less than four hundred cubic feet of air pressure. Stockham had fifteen hundred. "You're supposed to come out of the water with a five hundred pound reserve," Stockham said later.

Stockham decided that the two men should forget trying to find the chain again, and instead signaled to surface immediately.

"So we did," Stockham later recalled. "We went straight up. Facing each other. We got about thirty feet from the surface, where visibility wasn't too bad . . . we got to about thirty feet and we were home free in my mind. All of a sudden, he stopped and started to sink. And I had to turn around and go back after him.

"Well, when I got back down to him he was sinking. And I reached down to try to pull off his weight belt and he had this carbon dioxide cartridge on his vest . . . I tried to grab that [to inflate it]. About that time, I couldn't see. It was a little bit dark. I was trying to see his eyes . . . to see if he was conscious. He had spit his regulator out of his mouth. And he wasn't kicking. He was just sinking.

"So, while I'm doing this all of a sudden he jerks my regulator out of my mouth and drags me down and we both land on the bottom. Then I'm trying to get . . . by this time I'm thinking: I've got to get my regulator back. So . . . I'm facing him and I'm kind of grabbing his arm and I'm thinking, I either have to get my regulator back or I have to strip all my gear off and go to the surface. He's holding me by my regulator. And he's not looking at me. I can't catch his eyes, which is something you try to do. I can't make eye contact with him. Or he won't look at me . . ."

Stockham was beginning to think they were both going to drown.

"Finally he gave my regulator back to me, and stripped all his gear off and shot up to the surface. I tried to stop him. I followed him and I tried to grab his fins. I couldn't. He just went too fast . . . then he ended up, when I got up to the surface, he was on the surface. He was obviously suffering a trauma . . . from coming up too fast. He was floating. His tank was still attached to his suit.

"What happened was, he didn't expel any breath when he went up, like he's supposed to. Or not enough. Probably he would have been O.K. if he had done that." In short, Pompey was suffering from the bends.

Stockham swam over to where Pompey was floating on the surface of the water. He seemed to be unconscious. Foam was issuing from his mouth. Stockham saw a small boat in the vicinity. "Call the Coast

Guard!" he shouted. He maneuvered Pompey over to the inflatable boat and pulled him in. Now Pompey seemed to be conscious. Stockham talked to him. Pompey kept saying he was sorry. Stockham told him not to worry about it. Stockham ran the inflatable over to the nearby boat. Other divers on the boat helped Stockham pull Pompey aboard.

Ten minutes later, a Coast Guard vessel arrived, and Pompey was transferred to that boat. Stockham stripped Pompey's wet suit and tanks off. A few minutes later a helicopter arrived. Pompey was placed in a litter and winched up to the chopper. Stockham wanted to go too, but the Coast Guard wouldn't let him. He had the idea the doctors would want to know how deep they had been diving and for how long. Then the helicopter clattered away. Dunn and Stockham's brother were still diving. The entire incident had taken less than twenty minutes.

Pompey was taken to Virginia Mason Hospital in Seattle, where there was a decompression chamber. By the time the helicopter arrived, to outward appearances Pompey seemed in pretty good shape. Pompey was still conscious and talking, even joking a bit. The hospital people put Pompey in the chamber and increased the pressure to balance the air in his lungs and blood vessels. They put a tube down Pompey's throat to try to remove the fluid congesting in Pompey's ruptured lungs.

About two hours later, Stockham, Dunn, and Stockham's brother arrived at the hospital. "I get there and he's fine," Stockman recalled. "He appears to be fine. They were talking about how they wanted to put me in the chamber too, how they had to make sure I hadn't surfaced too fast myself. They were saying how he had some fluid in his lungs that they wanted to try to aspirate."

But before Stockham could be put in the chamber, Pompey went into cardiac arrest. Stockham watched as the emergency doctors tried to revive Pompey. It was hopeless. Everyone suddenly stopped moving. Pompey was dead.

Stockman was devastated. He left. "It was about all I could handle," he said.

"I just knew that there was nothing they could do for him. I knew he had suffered a bad injury. He was obviously hurt, although he was conscious and everything, at the hospital it was obvious . . . I just know from prior experience that you can't surface that fast and hold your breath. If you panic, you hold your breath, and if you hold your breath you're going to die. There's just no two ways about it. That's essentially what happened."

The death of Pompey cast a pall over the department, and more particularly, the investigation. Stockham blamed himself for Pompey's death. Looking back, he said, he should have realized that Pompey was not an experienced diver. One of the biggest challenges inexperienced divers face is learning to regulate their breathing, to make the supply of air last longer. Pompey had consumed too much air too fast while hunting for a fish.

Or had he? Was there something wrong with Pompey's tank or air regulator? Stockham wanted to find out. He visited the local diving shop where Pompey had filled his tanks, and obtained a sample of the air Pompey had used. Stockham sent it to a laboratory at the University of Washington for tests. Stockham wanted to know whether carbon monoxide had inadvertently been mixed with the air. There was a trace of the gas, but not enough to make a difference.

Dr. Reay conducted an autopsy, and Pompey's death was attributed to a pulmonary embolism following a diving accident. It was amazing, Reay said later, that Pompey had lived as long as he had after surfacing so quickly. It was as if he had been dead from the time he had surfaced, but his body just hadn't known it.

The department undertook an investigation into the death. Stockham wrote a statement about what had happened. He felt terrible. He couldn't help thinking that somehow the whole thing had been his fault, that he should have known that Pompey was not experienced enough to dive in the place Stockham had selected. Later, Stockham talked to Pompey's instructor, another department detective. The detective told Stockham that Pompey had always consumed his air too rapidly, that he had been warned before about the need to breathe more slowly. It was just one of those things, thought Stockham, a combination of factors. He shouldn't blame himself. But he did.

63

SCAPEGOATS

May 1987/November 1987

There was an aftermath of Pompey's death, one that illustrated all too clearly how the years of frustration over the murders had begun to seep into the ordinary lives of the police, the public, and the news media. It was difficult for some to accept the fact that Pompey's death *had* been an accident. To some, the fact that the commander in charge of the investigation had died under such mundane, preventable circumstances seemed to argue for darker theories.

Paranoias about the police and the failure to apprehend the murderer had long led those only peripherally conversant with the case to speculate that somehow the police had been covering up for the killer. Hadn't the police admitted that they believed someone posing as a law enforcement officer might be responsible for the crimes? What steps had been taken to make sure that a *real* cop wasn't the killer? Pimps and prostitutes continued to suggest that a real policeman was the murderer. The very secrecy that surrounded the investigation made suggestions of cover-up seem more plausible. And when the police declined to release the details of the investigation into Pompey's death, the speculation only increased. Some refused to believe it when police said they wanted to protect the feelings of Pompey's family and those involved in the accident. These subterranean rumblings were still going on when, beginning in the late spring of 1987, *The Times* resolved to try to uncover the reasons for the Green River investigation's apparent lack of progress.

A large part of the newspaper's inquiry would be focused on the operations of the vice unit during the months when the murders were taking place. At the very least, *The Times* hoped to be able to answer the question of whether anyone involved in the vice unit had anything to do with the crimes.

Letters were sent to Thomas requesting the public disclosure of every vice arrest undertaken in 1982, 1983, and 1984; the vice officers' expense records and mileage logs; and the names, serial numbers, and work schedules of the officers assigned to the vice unit during the years of the murders.

It took very little time for the police, particularly the members of the vice squad, to learn what the newspaper was up to. There were several confrontations over requested information. Lawyers were called in. A police legal adviser scrutinized every release, and refused to provide the names of those arrested under a state privacy law. Most of the names had already been obtained by the newspaper from the court records, but not every person arrested was charged in court. Who were *those* people? What if those arrested but never charged were the victims? It didn't seem very likely, but the state of confrontation between the newspaper and the police by that point had convinced the newspaper that it should leave no stone unturned.

That was the situation when Stockham began hearing police department scuttlebutt that *The Times* considered a former vice officer still with the department, Detective Rick Gies, to be a suspect in the crimes; that Pompey had learned incriminating information about Gies; and that Stockham, a close friend of Gies, had somehow murdered Pompey to cover up for his friend.

In actuality, the newspaper had no such beliefs beyond a momentary consideration of that scenario as an unlikely possibility. For one thing, the newspaper's reporters knew that Gies had long since been investigated and cleared as a suspect, not only by the department, but also by the FBI. Scores of pimps and prostitutes had named Gies as a suspect to detectives, in part because of Gies's tremendous success as an undercover officer. Gies's whereabouts during the crimes had been thoroughly checked by detectives, and he was placed in locations far away from the crime scenes. And while Gies had a reputation for sometimes treating prostitutes with hostility, he simply had the wrong personality to be the killer, detectives had reasoned. Still, members of the department, familiar with Gies's reputation as a master of disguises and his long experience policing prostitution on The Strip, liked to kid Gies about his supposed role in the crimes, sometimes asking him whether he had taken the victims home before killing them or afterwards, and similar police locker-room teasing. Gies would sheepishly and occasionally indignantly deny that he was the Green River killer.

But Gies did not know that the newspaper knew that he had been eliminated; all he heard was that reporters had obtained his complete work schedule for three years, and that they were trying to prove that he was the killer. Gies was furious with the newspaper, and particularly with the reporter who had made the request for his work schedule. One day Gies encountered Stockham in the police department hallway.

"Goddamn Carlton Smith," Gies told Stockham.

"Bob, you don't think I'm the Green River killer, do you?"

"Gee, Rick," said Stockham, still teasing Gies, "I really don't know." But then Stockham saw that Gies was genuinely upset. Then Stockham realized a new fear: Was the newspaper investigating the rumor that *he had killed* Pompey to cover up for Gies? Suddenly, the idea of Gies being a suspect in the crimes didn't seem so funny at all to Stockham. It was ridiculous. The goddamn media!

"Don't let it bother you," Stockham told Gies. "The reason they're looking at you is because you went out there and kicked ass when you were a vice cop."

Stockham thought that was the end of the matter. But it wasn't. Someone within the department—Stockham never found out who—also began thinking about Pompey's death, and referred Stockham's name to the task force as a possible suspect in the death of Pompey. Some officers just had a hard time understanding how Pompey could have made such a fundamental mistake. There had to be something more, they thought. So an investigation was undertaken of Stockham as well, focused on whether he had for some reason murdered Pompey. The whole thing seemed stupid, to Stockham. But he understood why it had to be done: What if the newspaper discovered that no investigation had been undertaken? What would the fucking reporters think about *that?* He didn't have to like it, though.

The two *Times* reporters had already been turned in as possible suspects. Several people thought that since they seemed to have such an interest in the case, perhaps they knew more about it than they were saying. And certainly, some thought, they would have a motive to keep the story going. But they had already been considered as suspects years earlier, Adamson had admitted, and cleared. Still, the paranoia and anger about *The Times*'s project had spread throughout the department, allowing people to believe what they wanted to believe.

* * *

Late in June, another skeleton was found near Green River Community College, far down the Kent Valley and about three hundred yards off Highway 18. Three boys searching for aluminum cans discovered the skeleton, covered with leaves and brush, in a heavily wooded ravine near the school. Nearby were four or five large boxes filled with over two hundred bones of animals—including dogs and dear. The task force collected *all* the bones and sent them to the medical examiner's office on the chance that other human bones might be mixed in. None were.

Within three days, however, Haglund and the dentists identified the skeleton of Cindy Ann Smith, the topless dancer who called herself Vanilla, and who had last been seen hitchhiking on The Strip in early 1984. Cindy had vanished the same day, in fact, that police were finding the remains at the Highline Little League Field. The discovery of Cindy Smith's remains brought the known victim toll in the Green River murders to thirty-seven known dead. Nine others were still missing.

As the summer of 1987 unfolded, Vern Thomas and his department waited for *The Times* to complete its work. Some, like Allman, hoped that the newspaper would turn up some sort of key that the investigation had missed, by accident if nothing else. Meanwhile, Pompey was replaced by Captain Greg Boyle, who also headed the department's major crimes unit. In reality, however, most of the day-to-day decisions in running the task force were left up to Lieutenant Dan Nolan, the only commander left from the original task force created by Adamson.

As the summer progressed and more demands were made by the newspaper on the police, relations grew increasingly bitter. Every time it wanted something from the police—a record or a memo—it sent a copy of the demand letter to County Executive Tim Hill. That was just another problem for Thomas, whose relationship with Hill was beginning to deteriorate.

Now, having the newspaper burrowing into the department's files, giving copies of the disclosure demands to Hill's office, and complaining about perceived obstructions, only made things worse between the executive and the sheriff.

The two men had been at odds throughout much of the year, primarily over budget matters. Hill still wanted Thomas to hold the line on police spending. But the county was growing so rapidly that calls for police services were escalating sharply. Thomas knew he would have to go back to the county council to request a supplemental budget authorization to cover the department's overtime pay. Hill told Thomas he would not support him in that, and that he would just have to find the money someplace else. What did that mean? Thomas told Hill it couldn't be done. The only way, he said, was to lay off several dozen officers. Did Hill want him to do *that?* No, said Hill; you're the sheriff, you're the department head, you figure it out.

A major disagreement blew up over Thomas's role in a county decision to buy one of the fingerprint computers. The review panel that recommended the task force cuts the year before had also recommended that the county buy one of the high-tech computers, the Automated Fingerprint Information System, or AFIS. The cost was $7.8 million to acquire and operate over five years. Hill's budget office red-inked the request. Then Ron Sims and Paul Barden on the county council said it would buy one anyway, using a property tax levy of about $2.50 a year for the average homeowner.

Thomas asked Hill whether he should cooperate with the council in providing information about the system. Hill said go ahead. Thomas provided the information, the council passed a law putting the issue on the ballot for the voters to approve, and then Hill vetoed the legislation. The council rewrote the law, and Hill vetoed it again. Then the council overrode Hill's veto, and the issue was placed on the ballot anyway. Hill blamed Thomas when the issue was approved by the voters. "We have Vern to thank for that," Hill complained to the other county department heads at their weekly meeting.

And as the year went on, other disagreements occurred. Hill began pointing out Thomas's deficiencies to other county department heads in the group's closed-door meetings. Thomas gritted his teeth. He had survived years of abuse for his principles at the Seattle Police Department, and this is what his career was coming down to? Was his job so important to him now that he was willing to take this from a *politician?* But he wanted to solve the Green River case, and Thomas feared that once he was gone, Hill would dismantle the task force entirely. So the cold war between the two men continued.

Sometimes Thomas would meet with Hill, and to Thomas, it seemed as though Hill couldn't be bothered to listen to him. The way Thomas saw it, Hill's eyes would sort of glaze over, and later, Hill would complain that Thomas hadn't told him something, when he actually had.

Thomas began confronting Hill directly in meetings when Hill got the faraway look in his eyes. Leaning forward, Thomas would tap Hill on the knee, saying, Listen up, here, I'm telling you something that I don't want you to say later that I didn't tell you.

Naturally, Thomas's actions irritated Hill. "I don't know why we had the friction we had," Hill mused later. "I didn't really ever understand Vern Thomas." Asked if he thought that Thomas was a bit sensitive to criticism, Hill seized on the word. Thomas *was* sensitive, Hill said.

An open rupture nearly took place near the end of the summer over the budget question. Hill criticized Thomas at one of the weekly meetings of the executive's cabinet. Thomas lost his temper. He started to get up. He opened his mouth to tell Hill, "Stuff it!" But then he caught himself and started laughing when he remembered one of his own top commanders—a man well known throughout the department to have a volatile temperament—had counseled *him* to keep calm in such situations. The irony of taking advice on deportment from the excitable commander secretly amused Thomas. Instead, chuckling, he sat back down, and the others in the room stared at him curiously.

A few weeks later, Hill threatened to have Thomas arrested for overspending his budget allocation for the overtime. Council supporters of Thomas rushed in and made an emergency appropriation, getting Thomas off the hook. But Hill was angry; bit by bit, Hill began to see Thomas as the Democrat-controlled county council's man inside his own administration.

"He felt that I had more influence with the council than he did," recalled Thomas. "We had discussions about that. I tried to tell him that the council would do this, or do that." But in Thomas's eyes, Hill wouldn't listen to him; Hill's eyes would glaze over.

From Hill's point of view, Thomas needed to work on running the department and leaving the politics to him. Sometimes, though, Hill got into disputes with the council that Thomas thought he could have avoided, if he had only listened to Thomas. "And therefore he got eaten alive a number of times because he did not know the politics of the council," said Thomas later.

As a result, by the fall of 1987, Thomas knew that Hill doubted his loyalty to Hill's administration. But by now, Thomas was doubting it too.

In early September, another body was found. This one was fresh. The body of Rose Marie Kurran, sixteen, was found wrapped in a plastic tarp. It had been thrown over an embankment between Military Road South and I-5, just south of South 188th Street.

The new victim was just over five feet tall and weighed only ninety pounds. She had been known to hitchhike on The Strip. Detectives soon learned that she had an all-too-familiar background, including trouble with alcohol and probable prostitution. She had last been seen in the prostitution zone around South 144th Street. Reporters went to see Rose Marie's grandmother, who talked about the girl.

"She never seemed to want to do anything she *had* to do," her grandmother, Ruth Matelski, said. "The minute you'd say 'You gotta do this or that,' off she'd go."

Just three weeks before, Matelski recalled, "Rose Marie came to visit, and I had just been reading in the paper about some man who was convicted in Tacoma for doing terrible things to a girl. So I told her that you don't know how many kooks are running around.

"And do you know what she said? She said, in effect, 'I'm too smart for that; I know my way around.'

"She was such a beautiful child when she was young," Matelski continued. "I keep asking myself what we could have done, if we could have tried harder. I sometimes blame the juvenile system. There's no such thing today as the old woodshed to make children mind. If you get strict, it's child abuse."

Matelski thought that over, and then said, "Maybe that isn't fair, criticizing the system for everything. She was a girl who wanted a father image. That was why she kept trying to go back to see her real father. She didn't find any of the things she wanted. She fell in with street kids. A girl does that, and what do you expect?"

A week after Rose Marie's body was found and while task force investigators were still trying to decide if she should be included on the Green River victim list, *The Times* published the results of its look at the department, the investigation, and the vice subculture. The newspaper had discovered that the county department under Winckoski had failed to take seriously many of the missing persons reports involving the victims. Perhaps even worse, the newspaper said, police had failed to appreciate the fact that many of the murders were going on right under their noses throughout much of 1983.

And the newspaper reported a rather curious fact: Of the forty-six disappearance dates then known, for some reason, the vice squad had made no arrests on forty-one. Since it was rare for the unit to go more than two days without a prostitution arrest, that correlation seemed significant. How had the killer known the police would not be in the area on the days he chose to victimize the women?

The police said they were not surprised at the latter finding. They had come to believe that the killer was someone with a highly refined sense of the street, particularly when it came to knowledge of police operations. Somehow, the police said, the killer had known or realized when the vice squad was operating. But how? The killer was just very clever, the police replied.

A further fact brought to light was that once the police, under Adamson, had begun keeping The Strip under surveillance, the murders seemed to have stopped. The two exceptions were Mary West, who had been seen in the city of Seattle's Rainier Valley, which was *not* under surveillance, and Cindy Smith. She had disappeared on the same day the task force was processing the scene at the Highline Little League Field where Cheryl Wims and the second, still-unidentified victim had been found. Had the killer known the police were otherwise engaged? It was suggestive, but impossible to say with any certainty.

The series of *Times* stories put Thomas in a somewhat difficult position. One the one hand, he wanted to defend the work of the task force. On the other, he didn't want to publicly criticize Winckoski. He refused to critique the early stages of the investigation. He said what had happened no longer mattered. "All I know," he said, "is that *I've* got a problem, and my problem is the worst serial murder case in American history. Don't ask me about what happened before I got here.

"You can criticize me if you want," he said, "for not acting soon enough, but don't ask me to criticize what somebody else has done." It was simple, said Thomas, for someone to years later second-guess the police. But no one had known that it would ever become as bad as it had.

As for the vice squad, *The Times*'s stories concluded that it was almost impossible that the crimes had been committed by any of the unit's members. None of those assigned to the squad met the test of being unaccounted for each time someone disappeared. The only other possibility was that several of the vice unit members had acted together, and that was seen as highly unlikely. Someone would have told on the others by now, *The Times* reasoned.

But the Kurran case had posed that troubling question: Was the killer back? And was it time to redeem the promises to return all the investigators to the job? Investigators themselves were divided over whether Kurran was in or out. There were differences between the Green River victims and Kurran's murder—most notably, the ease of her discovery.

But the differences were no guarantee that Kurran was not killed by the same man who had killed the others. The troubling fact was, it was impossible to say for sure one way or the other. The only thing that seemed obvious after working on the Kurran case for a week was that she had been killed by a serial murderer, if not the Green River man, then another one.

On almost the same day, detectives in Oregon were called to a wooded hillside outside of Portland, where the remains of seven murder victims were found in a cluster.

But the Molalla case, as it soon came to be known, seemed to be quite different from the Green River cases. For one thing, the crime scene area where the bodies were found seemed much more disorganized. And with each victim, investigators found a small cache of used vodka bottles, the kind sold on airplanes, as if the killer had sat down next to each corpse and had gotten drunk. *That* was totally different. The task force sent Detective Haney to the scene to look it over; he reported back that the cluster site

seemed substantially different from the Green River
case.

Haney's view was soon borne out when Oregon officials arrested a man already in jail for the murder
of a prostitute. Eagerly, the Green River task force
detectives ran the man's name through their computer, and checked the man's alibis for the time of
the Green River murders. They quickly discovered
that the man had been incarcerated during most of
the Green River crimes. That eliminated him as a suspect in the Green River case, it was decided.

Late in September, yet another body was found in
King County. Partially skeletonized, the newest victim
was discovered by someone riding a dirt bike in the
brush off Auburn-Black Diamond Road—the same
rural highway where the body of Yvonne Antosh had
been found in late 1983, and not far from where Cindy
Smith had so recently been discovered. The place
where the body was found was known to be a spot
where teenagers often gathered for "keggers," or
drinking parties. The latest victim appeared to be
somewhere between fourteen and twenty years old.
She had been strangled. The only clothing left on her
body was a single pink sock.

Reichert and about ten other task force detectives
came to the scene. So did Barbara Kubik-Patten, the
would-be psychic. But no one, not even the psychic/
detective, was now prepared to say whether the new
victim had been killed by the Green River murderer
or—perhaps even worse—a new serial murderer entirely
different than the last. A week later, the body was
identified as the remains of runaway Debbie Ann
Gonzales. She was just fourteen years old.

By mid-October, when relationships between Hill
and Thomas had degenerated to their nadir, someone
in the county department used a piece of letterhead
stationery from the police department's Criminal
Investigations Division to put a political bomb under
Thomas. An anonymous letter written on the official
paper suggested that Thomas and others in the depart-

ment had conspired to obstruct the Green River murder investigation. Exhibit A was former crime analyst John Blake. The letter was mailed to Hill and every news media outlet.

"As concerned civilian employees and police officers, we feel that this open letter is necessary since it appears that the person or person(s) responsible for the 'Green River' killings may have become active again," the letter said.

After mentioning *The Times*'s investigation of the investigation, the letter went on: "Up to this point, we have felt we were associated with a professional police agency. We are fully aware of the complex and frustrating nature of this investigation; however, we have to wonder exactly what course our department is on."

The recent murder of Rose Marie Kurran suggested that the department's course was all wrong, the letter writer went on to say. "We trust that recent statements by the task force and the Sheriff are not a downplay of the probability that the Green River killer has started again. We don't need *another* black eye."

Then the letter mentioned Blake, the crime analyst who had retired after becoming obsessed by the lawyer suspect, and suggested that Blake's investigation of the lawyer was sabotaged by the police department. "The disturbing rumor is that a former task force detective, John Blake, investigated a suspect who is an attorney practicing in Pierce and/or King County, who seems to have connections to our department. If what else we have heard about the investigation is true, we find it incredible and reprehensible that if that particular investigation was deliberately suppressed . . . in the meantime, more disappearances and bodies!

"If that suspect is indeed responsible and someone is covering for him, we see this as a cruel hoax on the families of the victims and the public who are expecting results.

"Given the magnitude of the 'Green River' cases,"

the letter concluded, "we have to be critical of this department's actions. We hope that the state's $200,000, the federal government's $1 million, and the countless hours spent by detectives, FBI agents, and police officers have not been in vain. King County obviously blew it on the Ted Bundy case. We don't need more of the same.

"Sorry, Mr. Hill. No names. We would like to finish our careers."

The letter was signed, simply, "Us."

Hill immediately called a press conference to respond to the letter. Hill told reporters that he had no idea whether the letter was legitimate, but that he intended to discuss the allegations with Thomas. That made it seem as if Hill were taking the allegations in the letter seriously.

"I don't know who it's from," Hill said. "The general policy of the King County Police is not to respond to anonymous letters, but I think that the issues raised, and the fact that it was made a public letter before I even received it, have to be answered." Hill didn't add that the fact that the letter was on Thomas's department's own letterhead gave it additional credibility.

Could the police really be covering up for the murderer? Hill said he didn't know. "It would have to be an unusual conspiracy for a number of these charges to be borne out," he said. Still, "There are some allegations here I want to talk to Sheriff Thomas about." That indeed made it sound as though Hill were going to call Thomas in on the carpet.

So, who was "Us"? How did they know about Blake, whose suspicion of the lawyer had remained one of the task force's secrets, and whose "blow-up" had never been publicized? The letter was off on several important facts, but the use of the letterhead coupled with Blake's name seemed to indicate that the writers *were* a part of the police department. Clearly, someone seemed out to get Thomas.

Thomas declined public comment on the letter. So did the task force. But inwardly, Thomas seethed.

Several days later, he met with Hill to talk about the letter. Thomas explained that there was no substance to the allegations, and Hill seemed satisfied. Two years later, in fact, both men could barely recall the discussion. But the fact that Hill hadn't immediately dismissed the letter as the work of a provocateur said volumes about how far the two men's relationship had sunk.

Six days later, Thomas resigned.

As he later recalled the event, Thomas simply decided not to put up with it anymore. The letter, he said, had nothing to do with his decision. He had looked at himself in the mirror and wasn't happy with the way Vern Thomas felt about Tim Hill.

"The kind of guy I am, and anyone will tell you, when it comes to the man who appoints you, if you can't be loyal to that man, you shouldn't work for him," Thomas said afterward. He'd felt like quitting several times before, and had come close to doing so with the "stuff it" temptation. But each time someone on his staff had talked him out of it, saying the department needed Thomas.

But Thomas still found himself torn by irrepressible feelings of anger and disloyalty to Hill, and that was hard to accept.

"That's my philosophy," he said later. "You should never stick around just because you want the money or the position. A lot of people don't agree with me. But that's always been my philosophy and it's cost me some good jobs, and promotions at certain times. That's my philosophy and I would do that [not stick around].

"My feeling with Tim was, if we got to the point that I felt we could not work together, that I could not be loyal to that man and I was bad-mouthing him all the time . . . which I was, finally, well, that was terrible. And it was clear that it was time for me to leave. And I also took into consideration, that I should also give him enough time to chose his new sheriff before the next election comes along. I owe him that.

"I've been here two years. I have cut the task force for him, I've opened the door for him. That's there. He won't have to feel like *he* stepped up front."

On Tuesday, October 27, Thomas came into his office, called Hill's office and told Hill's aide Rollin Fatland that he was quitting. Hill was out of the office at the time, but called Thomas back immediately on his car telephone, and asked if he would attend a joint press conference to announce Thomas's "retirement." Thomas agreed to that as well. According to Thomas, Hill asked him not to talk about their difficulties in their relationship at the press conference. Thomas smiled and said, Of course.

The following day, Thomas and Hill faced the microphones. Thomas insisted that he had no ill will toward Tim Hill, and that he had been planning his retirement for some months. Hill lauded Thomas as a consummate professional. What would happen to the Green River investigation? Thomas said he believed the investigation would go on. "I wanted to catch this person before I left, " Thomas said, "but it hasn't happened. I still have faith that there will be a solution." Hill said that as far as he was concerned, catching the Green River murderer "is still a high priority of my administration."

Later, when Thomas and Hill left the area of the press conference and approached the courthouse elevators, Hill looked at Thomas and said simply, "Thanks, Vern." Thomas could have publicly skewered Hill in announcing his retirement, but had desisted. Hill was grateful. Thomas only nodded. It was the first time in their two years together, Thomas later recalled, that Hill had ever told him thanks.

BOOK FOUR

EVANS
1988–90

64

FATHER BOB

December 1987/January 1988

With Thomas gone, the department once again came under the acting direction of the chief who had run things after Winckoski had similarly "retired" in late 1982, Jim Nickle. Nickle had been one of the three top commanders under Thomas who had recommended the reductions in the task force in 1986.

This time, said Nickle, he wanted to be a candidate for sheriff. Nickle had the backing of Thomas and most members of the department. But Hill said he intended to conduct a nationwide search for the new man, using a personnel recruitment company. Hill said he wanted to take his time in finding a new sheriff.

While the search was under way, however, Nickle would run the organization much as it had been in the past.

One of Nickle's first moves was to bring Bob Evans back as commander of the task force.

Four years before, Evans had been the sergeant running the task force's original street unit under Adamson. He had received a long-awaited promotion to lieutenant late in 1984, and was assigned to run the uniformed patrol in the suburban Federal Way substation, located far south of the airport. For two years he had been on the investigation's sidelines, watching the investigators ride the roller coaster of

Foster, the San Francisco snapshot fiasco, McLean, the truck painter, and scores of other suspects. Like others, when McLean was cleared, Evans had felt a tremendous letdown, so sure had he been that the case had been solved.

Later, when Adamson had been promoted and sent to the Maple Valley precinct to replace Nault, Evans had been transferred there as well. Adamson and Evans shared an intense desire to catch the killer, but with Evans the motive was, if anything, even more personal.

Evans was a compact man in his late forties, bespectacled, and often, when excited, intensely profane. Once he had donned a clerical collar to pose as a priest, hoping to gain access to a bookmaker's office to serve a search warrant. The disguise hadn't been necessary, but later other detectives liked to tease him about the ploy by calling him Father Bob. And despite his salty tongue, there *was* something ecclesiastical about Evans's demeanor.

Years before the Green River murders, as a sergeant in charge of the department's vice detail, Evans had taken the unheard-of step of developing prostitutes as informants in the war against the massage parlors. In getting to know the women, Evans came to appreciate a fundamental fact about prostitution and prostitutes that police often ignored as part of their psychological armoring process: that the women who sold themselves were *people*, that they had families who loved them and children who depended on them; that they cried and laughed and felt terror, happiness, and hopelessness just like anyone else; and that, in many cases, they were driven to prostitution by a desperation few others in society could really understand.

The creativity in disguises and the empathy for prostitutes had been reasons why Adamson had selected Evans to run the task force's street unit in the first place. Back in 1984, as the weeks wore on and the street team developed productive contacts within the prostitution community, Evans also developed an abiding conviction: The investigation of the murders deserved an all-out effort.

When outsiders sometimes commented that the reason the police had been unable so far to catch the Green River murderer was because the police didn't really care about the victims, Evans became angry. "Bullshit! That's bullshit," he said.

"I believe in my heart that it wouldn't have made one iota of difference if these victims had been the daughters of politicians or a carload full of nuns," Evans said later. "This sort of investigation would have continued and an effort would have been made to solve it. The community *did* care. The community at large has been very supportive of this. The community jumped in many times and offered a lot of help.

"The problem that existed at times was that when the few vocal people that got up and said, 'The Seattle community doesn't care because they're prostitutes or the police don't care,' some dickhead media person who had too little to do that day would capitalize on that aspect of it, and I think unfairly. Unfairly to the families of the victims, to the victims and to the cops who were working hours and hours and hours to resolve this. The community cared and supported this investigation from the beginning. And I think that the cops who have worked on it did too."

As he moved into his new job, Evans couldn't help but reflect on how things had changed from 1984. For one thing, Evans had been a sergeant in 1984, and Dan Nolan had been a lieutenant. Now Evans was a captain and Nolan was working for *him*. The reversal in roles didn't particularly bother Nolan, who, with Reichert, was one of the few who had remained with the investigation since Adamson's new beginning. Nolan liked Evans personally, and while Evans retained the final authority, little was done without agreement between the two men.

Evans remembered when Adamson had first approached him about being on the task force. "No one expected it to last more than six months," he later recalled. "I know I didn't. I thought it would be over in three months and we'd be looking for something else to do." He remembered looking at a collection of suspect files on Reichert's desk in late 1983.

"Well, this looks like the guy. Look at this and this and this," Evans told Reichert at the time. "Hell this is exciting. Maybe we can put this thing to bed pretty quick. We need to go arrest this son of a bitch right now and start putting the evidence together." Reichert had started laughing.

"When you get done reading that," Reichert told Evans, "I have ten more just like it." And Reichert did. Six months later, as Evans was preparing to leave the task force to become a patrol lieutenant, the victim count had soared to twenty-six. But throughout each of his ten months on the task force, Evans never lost the feeling that the investigators were right on the edge of breaking the case. Now, it seemed like a long shot to Evans. But he would give it his best effort, he decided.

Just as Evans took over, the task force moved again. The school district decided to reopen the school that had been used by the task force since early 1986. The detectives, their telephones, all the files, and the computer were moved back to the county courthouse. The old jail on the twelfth floor was remodeled to accommodate the group's two dozen remaining detectives. The rest of the major crimes people were moved in with them, and also placed under Evans's command.

Meanwhile, Chief Nickle began to rotate detectives out of the unit in preparation for the inevitable end. Nickle, a representative of Hill's budget office, a deputy prosecutor, Adamson, and Nolan began another review of the investigation's staffing and the work that remained to be done. A decision was made to lop five more detectives off the task force. Events were beginning to come full circle, back around to the way things had been at the beginning of 1983.

THE GREEN RIVER KILLER   457

65

MONTGOMERY

January 1988/May 1988

Shortly after the first of the year, there was a great
deal of excitement in the crime lab. After months of
picking through the material vacuumed from the truck
painter's pickup truck, criminalist George Johnson
thought he had finally found something: a single tiny
shard of what appeared to be pink glass. Pink glass!

To the detectives, the particle looked quite similar
to those particles found or associated with Connie
Naon, Lisa Yates, the still-unidentified girl at the Little League field, Colleen Brockman, and the body discovered by Barbara Kubik-Patten, Tina Thompson.
The fragment also looked similar to particles found
with two other murdered women not previously connected to the Green River case, one of them involving
a prostitute last seen in Tacoma. Was the particle
found with the man the same stuff found with these
victims? If it was, the detectives might finally have a
case to take to court.

Evans and his detectives were ecstatic. It looked
like it was finally all over. They had done what had
seemed to be impossible: They had finally recovered
a piece of physical evidence that promised to bring the
killer to justice. Pink glass. How did it get to places
where the victims were found and in the man's truck?

A likely scenario was advanced: Some thought it
possible that the man's truck had once contained a

pink glass structure, perhaps a bottle, that had shattered, casting tiny fragments of the glass all over a portion of the vehicle. Later, as the man killed the victims, tiny fragments of the glass might have been transferred to the victim's bodies as the man transported them to the dumping grounds. Evans told others, "I feel like I'm on third base and heading for home." But more tests of the glass would be required to make sure the glass was the same material as that found with the victims. The testing process was begun.

Meanwhile, early in March, Haglund and the dentists made a breakthrough in identifying one of the two girls found near Tualatin, Oregon, in 1985. The identification was made possible when a sister of the victim notified Evans's detectives that her family hadn't seen sixteen-year-old Tammy Liles in years. Detectives following up the tip obtained Liles's dental charts, which were matched to the records from the Tualatin victim. Detectives later learned that Liles had last been seen in downtown Seattle on June 8, 1983—one day after Connie Naon had disappeared from The Strip. Here was another case that seemed to indicate the Green River killer had traveled with victims between Washington State and Oregon.

"The Tualatin cases indicate to us that the killer was more mobile than we thought in the past," said Lieutenant Dan Nolan of the latest identification. "This now begs the question of, What is the killer doing in Oregon? What is he doing there? He could be a tourist. He could be working there. He could have a dozen reasons to be there. What draws the killer there?" No one knew, although the speculation was limitless.

The identification of Liles led to the decision to add both Tualatin victims to the Green River list. That put the total of known dead at thirty-nine. Nine other woman remained missing.

As March turned into April, Hill was narrowing his search for a new sheriff. The search had been conducted by a Bellevue, Washington, personnel recruitment firm. One of the five names submitted to Hill by the firm was the police chief of Boise, Idaho, James V. Montgomery.

Montgomery had been in Boise nearly five years. Before that he had worked for the Jefferson County, Kentucky, sheriff's department, which encompassed the urbanizing area around Cincinnati, Ohio. He was regarded by police officials in both Boise and Jefferson County as being bright, well-educated, and politically astute. That last was a quality that helped endear him to Hill after all the fractious years with Thomas.

The way Montgomery later recalled his recruitment, he initially expressed little interest in the King County job. People in Boise warned him about King County. Some thought that the sheriff in King County still had responsibility for running the jail, Montgomery recalled, but that hadn't been true for years. The other downside of the job was the Green River investigation.

"I remember some friend of mine over there in Boise said that's a problem: You're going to be stuck with the notoriety of the Green River Task Force," Montgomery later recalled. "Obviously, it's a window of opportunity if you solve this thing, during the time you're there.

"But absent that . . . and I was aware of the fact that it had been four or five years, and I knew the statistics of the chances of solving it weren't real good. I knew that this was one of those hanger-oners that we weren't going to be able to get rid of very easily."

But the Bellevue recruiters were persistent, and after some weeks, Montgomery agreed to join four other candidates on a tour of King County that would include a stop at the offices of Tim Hill.

"Well, they flew us all in here," said Montgomery, "and I came in with the understanding there were no strings attached. They flew us in, put us up in a hotel, and gave us a little tour for a day or so. I remember meeting one-on-one with Tim. The meeting lasted, perhaps, thirty minutes or so. It was pleasant, upbeat.

Not terribly in depth." Hill discussed the Green River investigation only very generally, recalled Montgomery. He certainly did not come away with the impression that if he wanted the job, he would have to agree to cut the task force down to size, Montgomery recalled. Or that it was a "high priority of my administration," as Hill kept insisting publicly.

"I was concerned about the overall management of the organization, trying to get some feel for what kind of a job this was," Montgomery recalled. "And who is Tim Hill, all that sort of thing. [The conversation] didn't rivet my attention only on the task force.

"We parted company. I went back to Boise. Later, he or as I recall, maybe Rollin [Fatland], anyway, somebody called and said: Well, we're interested in you, and so forth . . . and we're going to be going to the east coast. On the way back we'd like to stop by and visit you in Boise a little bit . . . just to see how things go over there. See what kind of a place you're working in . . . and maybe talk to your boss."

In late April, Hill and Fatland stopped in Boise and resumed discussions with Montgomery. Again the Green River investigation was not a major topic of conversation, according to Montgomery. By that time, the negotiations between Montgomery and Hill had advanced far enough so that Nickle had sent a thick binder of various issues confronting the police department to Montgomery for his perusal. One entire section dealt with the Green River investigation. Despite Nickle's briefing, if Hill or Fatland had discussed any of the investigation's controversial staffing issues, Montgomery two years later did not recall it. At no time, said Montgomery, did Hill or Fatland tell him they wanted to see the task force ended. Any decision to do *that*, it was clear to Montgomery, would have to be made by him, not them.

And it was likewise clear that Montgomery was willing to do that. That neither Hill nor Fatland nor the personnel recruiters had completely briefed Montgomery on the political consequences of cutting the investigation became clear almost immediately, however.

On May 10, after Hill had offered the job and Montgomery had accepted it, Hill introduced Montgomery at a press conference. Naturally, one of the first questions was about the Green River investigation. By now the news media had grown suspicious of Hill's commitment to the investigation. Montgomery was quickly asked what he would do with the murder investigation. Montgomery said he didn't know enough about it to comment intelligently. The news media accepted that, but the idea took root that somehow, Montgomery would be Hill's hatchet man on the investigation.

Two days after Montgomery was named sheriff, Evans laid the groundwork for further shrinkage of the task force. The killer, said Evans, was almost certainly one of the between fifty and seventy remaining "A" suspects still being investigated by the police.

"I think he's in there. He's got to be in there," Evans said. The focus of the task force from now on, he said, would be to work each of these fifty to seventy names until each but the killer was eliminated.

"There have been no recent outside distractions," said Evans. "There have been no recent body finds or other events that take away from investigative time, so we've been able to concentrate on looking at suspects." That sounded suspiciously like Adamson's pronouncement in early 1986, the one that had surprised Hill and infuriated Fatland. But Evans turned the assessment into a rationale for further reductions in the investigation. Already, the FBI, the city of Seattle, and the Port of Seattle had withdrawn officers assigned to the investigation, Evans noted. That left just nineteen people on the task force, including Evans.

"It's no big deal," Evans said. "The [other] agencies are in the same situation as everyone in the country. They need manpower. I think we can get through the rest of this case with the current manpower. If something else happens, everyone has promised to jump back in a heartbeat."

Just what that "something else" might be, however, was never made clear. Over the past year, the area had new murders, as the incidents with Kurran, Gonzales, and several others had shown. But no one was willing to link the new crimes to the Green River case. For one thing, detectives were reluctant to stigmatize the new victims by including them on the Green River list, even though several of the victims had been known to commit prostitution, use drugs, or hitchhike.

But the reality was that no one could say for sure that the new victims did not represent new murders in the series. The only surety seemed to be that the new victims were not disappearing *only* from The Strip, and not nearly at the rate they vanished in 1982 and 1983.

On the other hand, the police admitted when pressed that they had not been monitoring the prostitution population and the runaway teenager problems as thoroughly as they had in 1984 and 1985. It was always possible, Evans admitted, that the number of dead was far higher than presently known. Maybe the killer was simply better at hiding the victims. Hadn't he buried several? Sure, it was possible, Evans said. But he didn't think it very likely.

Then, on the last day of May, a Sunday, a construction crew digging postholes for a new fence at an apartment complex in Federal Way dug up a human bone.

Just what that "something else" might be, however, was never made clear. Just in case, the area

66

MUFFIN

May 1988

Evans got the call just after attending church with his wife. He told her that he wanted to run over to the discovery site, located not far from The Strip near South 348th Street, about six miles south of the airport, for a few hours. Evans thought it would be good for the task force morale if he at least put in an appearance.

Still dressed in his church clothes, Evans arrived at the scene. Bill Haglund was already there. Whether the skeleton had actually been buried, or whether it had inadvertently been covered by workers who had graded the site several years before when building the apartment complex, remained unclear. Haglund was busy digging a trench alongside the remains. He had found that the best way to remove buried victims was to use archaeological techniques. Once the trench had been dug, Haglund and his assistants would attempt to slip the metal sheet under the bones so that any hairs, fibers, fingernails or other minute evidence would not be accidently lost. Soon Evans was down on his knees in the mud next to Haglund.

"Uh oh," said Haglund as he pried out a piece of the jawbone. "We're in deep shit." After so many years of studying the dental charts of the missing, Haglund knew most of them by heart. The newest jaw had a steel crown, and Haglund immediately recognized it as a Green River chart. But whose?

Hours later, after the remains had been taken to the medical examiner's office and as the task force packed away its digging tools, Evans looked around at all the apartment units that had been built on the site. If there had been other victims dumped at this location, he knew, the chances of finding them now were almost nil. The county couldn't very well tear down all the apartments at this point. Evans considered the likelihood of other victims having been dumped at the location and decided it wasn't very likely. "Most of our victims have been on the surface, covered with brush," he said. And because the area had been well traversed by people and wildlife over the years, said Evans, he was convinced that the chances that others had been placed at the location were slim.

If there *had* been others, he said, "I'm inclined to think we would have known it by now."

That night, Haglund knew he had been right when he recognized the tooth with the crown. The dead girl, he discovered, had been Debra Lorraine Estes— "Betty Jones" on the street, but little "Muffin" to her parents, the long-suffering Tom and Carol Estes. Debbie had been found at last, not fifteen blocks away from where she had last been seen so long before in September of 1982, when the Green River killer had only just begun.

67

SAN DIEGO

June 1988/July 1988

Two weeks later, just after Montgomery was sworn in, Evans received a report from the crime lab that infuriated him.

On June 15, Evans was notified that the lab had *lost* the particle of pink glass taken from the truck painter in the search. The key evidence in the case had disappeared. The comparisons could not be made. How had it happened?

Evans immediately called Kay Sweeney, the administrator of the lab. What the hell was *this*, Evans wanted to know. The county had spent millions of dollars and years of effort to find a single piece of trace evidence tying a suspect to the crimes, and then the lab can't keep track of it? What did Sweeney expect them to do? Go back and serve another search warrant? It was ridiculous.

Sweeney downplayed the incident: Accidents will happen, Sweeney said, pointing out that the lab had thousands of cases to process every year. Besides, said Sweeney, there had been no way to tell whether the glass particles were *truly* significant. It might turn out, he said, that the glass was so common that it could be found anywhere. Evans wasn't mollified. He wrote a bitter letter of complaint to State Patrol Captain Paul Schultz, who had administrative responsibility for the lab. Schultz did not respond.

But several weeks later, Evans was notified that the lab had "found" two more glass particles from the search of the truck painter, and was about to begin the comparisons. Stop! said Evans. Instead, he sent a detective over to the lab to collect *all* the particles, including those found with the victims. Then he called the FBI and asked if their lab could conduct the comparisons. The FBI agreed to do the work, but its resident glass man would not be available for two months.

Fine, said Evans, we'll wait. The particle samples were placed in the task force property room under lock and key for safekeeping in the interim. Now Evans had to worry about the viability of his best evidence. Once a defense attorney—assuming there was even a trial—learned that the lab had "lost" the first bit of glass only to "find" more, the reliability of the evidence could be laughed out of court. Evans couldn't believe that the laboratory hadn't taken more care.

In fairness to the long-suffering criminalists, the shard of glass was so tiny that it was almost impossible to control in any event. A criminalist had been attempting to examine the minute particle to see whether it was made of the same material found with one of the victims. In moving the particle from one location to another, it had fallen off a tiny probe. The particle was so small, that once it was gone, it was gone forever, despite all the efforts to find it.

Meanwhile, the task force returned to the vexing problem of trying to determine why the murders had stopped. All the experts had insisted from the beginning that once a serial killer began murdering there would be no end to the killings until the murderer was either captured or dead. "You just don't go down to the Treatment Center for Serial Killers and get your treatment and stop killing," was the way one detective put it.

Task force members continued to cull the lists of those men arrested in the spring of 1984, or those men who had died in the same time frame. But more and more, the investigators were swinging around to the point of view that the killer had simply moved elsewhere and had started a new, so far undetected string of murders. By the spring and early summer of 1988, the top candidate on the "moved to" list was the city and county of San Diego, California.

Beginning in early 1984, the San Diego area had experienced a large upsurge in unsolved murders of women involved in prostitution. The murders had coincided with a campaign by city and county officials to crack down on the street prostitution problem. By June of 1988, it appeared that there were at least two serial murderers operating in the San Diego area. One killer seemed to operate only within the city limits of San Diego, capturing his victims in city-policed prostitution areas and dumping them in urban locations. Three victims, for example, were placed in dumpsters behind stores or businesses just outside the downtown core.

But another twenty-five women had been murdered and dumped along rural roads in the largely undeveloped San Diego County countryside. Those murders resembled the Green River killings in many ways.

Beginning in the late fall of 1987 and continuing through the spring of 1988, Reichert had been in contact with a San Diego detective named Tom Streed. Streed believed that the twenty-five San Diego county murders were the work of a serial killer. He also believed it was possible that the Green River killer had moved to San Diego.

Considering the facts of the San Diego murders, that was a distinct possibility. And in addition, both communities had several obvious commonalities. San Diego and Seattle were both important employment centers for aerospace workers, for example. Both communities had sizeable fishing and shipping fleets. Both communities had a number of large military installations. And coincidentally or not, both were quite close to international borders.

While Reichert and Streed compared notes over the telephone, there was no substitute for actually visiting the place where a crime victim was last seen and where they were subsequently found. Small, subtle details of terrain, vehicular access, and inferred site behavior had to be seen to be appreciated. Reichert wanted to go to San Diego to see for himself. But there was no money to pay for the trip. What to do?

A possible solution was found with the creative use of another project Nolan and Evans had been working on for some time.

Beginning in early March, Evans and Nolan had begun discussions with a newly formed police support group, the nonprofit Seattle–King County Crime Stoppers. Like other, similar groups across the country, Crime Stoppers was formed to help get more citizen involvement in solving crimes. This was done by videotaping reenactments of unsolved crimes, then airing them in public service slots. Viewers who knew something about the crimes thus displayed on television were urged to telephone Crime Stoppers confidentially in return for a modest reward. The organization had been formed with assistance of the Seattle Police Department, which donated the services of one Seattle Police Department detective, Myrle Carner, as well as office space and telephones.

In early March, Carner had been invited to make a presentation about the Crime Stoppers program to the King County police command staff. Afterward, Carner was invited by Evans and Nolan to continue discussions in the task force headquarters.

We have a problem, said the two Green River commanders: We want to get some intensive media exposure, but our relations with the local news media outlets are very strained. We're interested in what Crime Stoppers might be able to do for us, but there is a condition. We must have total control over what is broadcast. We have to approve everything. Can you help?

Carner said he thought he could. Evans and Nolan said they needed to think it over for a while longer. Two weeks later, Nolan called Carner back. "Go for it," Nolan said.

Carner went to PEMCO, an insurance company with offices in Seattle. The PEMCO board had long been known for its support of such public projects. PEMCO officials heard Carner's pitch. He needed money for a very confidential project, Carner said, a plan to air a major Crime Stopper's broadcast about the Green River murders. Carner thought he required a minimum of $25,000. He asked the PEMCO officials for $150,000. Might as well aim high, Carner thought. "You got it," the PEMCO officials told the startled Carner.

Carner then began working with his own taping director, a Canadian named Grant Fredericks. Fredericks thought the Green River murder case was of such national interest that the task force might obtain the best results by having the program broadcast nationally. In that case, other people would have to become involved. Fredericks put Carner in touch with a producer he knew in southern California. Arrangements were made for Carner, Reichert, and Fredericks to fly to California to discuss the possible project with the producer, at Crime Stopper's expense. While there, Reichert would have an opportunity to make the three-hour drive down to San Diego to meet with Streed and his superiors.

On March 29, Reichert and Streed met and discussed their cases again. That afternoon a San Diego County Sheriff's Department helicopter gave Reichert a tour of the San Diego dump sites, and that night he and Streed went out to look over San Diego's version of The Strip, El Cajon Boulevard.

As Reichert talked to Streed and looked over the situation, it seemed more and more a case of *déjà vu*. Here was Streed, who kept saying that his agency was facing a serial killer, only to be discounted by his superiors. Here was the San Diego County Sheriff's Department, trying to figure out how to come to grips with a string of murders that appeared to involve multiple police jurisdictions, including the San Diego city police. Here was the city department, yawning disinterestedly at Streed's theories, and privately knocking him as an egomaniac. Linkage blindness was not confined to Seattle, it seemed clear.

The San Diego cases, Reichert saw at once, were very close to the Green River murders: Most victims worked as streetwalkers on a long stretch of El Cajon Boulevard connecting the suburbs to the city proper; most had last been seen on the sidewalks of the boulevard, soliciting passing cars; few had been reported missing at the time of their disappearance; and many were found dead miles away in terrain that seemed remarkably similar to the Green River cases, usually off isolated roads with quick access to an interstate freeway, I-80 or U.S. 395. Often there was trash or debris not far away. The distances between the places of disappearance and the locations of the bodies seemed to indicate that the San Diego murderer had somehow immobilized his victims before dumping them; perhaps like the Green River killer, the San Diego killer was murdering his victims in a vehicle and transporting the corpses to the dumping grounds.

Had the Green River killer gone to San Diego? Reichert didn't know. He also realized that the proposition probably couldn't be proved one way or the other, unless someone was arrested and positively linked to the crimes. But that seemed even more remote a prospect in San Diego than it was in Seattle. The reality in San Diego was that no one—not the police brass, not the politicians, not even the news media—seemed to care about the murders. The news media in San Diego had consistently underplayed the crimes, and three years after the murders had begun, no one except Streed seemed to be willing to even say the crimes were related to one another, let alone to the Green River case. The news media had reported each of the murders as an isolated incident, usually in two to three paragraphs. The crimes only rarely made the television news. No one except Streed had tried to link them together or to see any commonalities.

But Streed himself was in an increasingly untenable position. Holder of a graduate degree in psychology, fluent in Russian, Streed fancied himself an expert on psychopathology and serial murders. He often lectured to his fellow detectives from a posture of intellectual superiority. Naturally, the other detectives resented him, and complained that Streed thought he was better than they were. Streed was seen as bombastic, acerbic, opinionated; his attempts to induce the city police to cooperate with him were regularly rebuffed.

Reichert returned to Seattle more than half convinced that the killer he sought had moved to San Diego. If there were only some way to get the authorities in San Diego to work together to catch someone in their cases; then Reichert and the rest of the Green River task force could see if the San Diego man had been in the Seattle area during 1982 through 1984. But police officials in San Diego did not seem very interested in the prospect that the Green River murderer might be in their backyard. In ways reminiscent of Portland, police officials there seemed loath to acknowledge any problem at all. Task force officials were told by San Diego officials in fairly clear terms to keep their problem to themselves.

Still, after six years of learning to deal with the politics of murder, task force officials knew of ways to get things started, no matter the reluctance of those who did not wish to cooperate. Shortly after Reichert returned from San Diego, a task force official met secretly with reporters for *The Times*. What's the latest with the evidence from the truck painter? the reporters asked. Forget about that, the task force official said. The real hot item now is in San Diego. And then the task force official proceeded to explain about all the politics of San Diego's thirty-two unsolved prostitute murders, and how task force officials had been largely stymied in getting any cooperation from San Diego law enforcement.

The reporters had been following matters in San Diego for some time, but the tip from the task force official put the events there in a new light. The similarity of the San Diego crimes to the Green River murders *was* startling. So was the task force official's assertion that cooperation had been far too limited. Most interesting of all was the news that most of the murders had been downplayed in San Diego. The parallels to the early years of the Green River case were obvious. And what if the San Diego killer *was* the same person as the Green River killer? If there were any chance at all that the two killers were one and the same, it would be irresponsible of the newspaper to ignore it.

In late June, the two reporters also went to San Diego. Armed with autopsy reports showing the circumstances of death of most of the San Diego victims, and after obtaining background information on those who had died, they visited many of the sites where victims had been last seen, and those places where they were later found. The similarities to the two cases did not seem exaggerated. Local political officials were asked about the friction between the two San Diego police units, and acquainted with the facts about serial murder; interviews were conducted with local news media on why the case had not received any substantial publicity.

The resulting story in *The Times* was the first spark in a political explosion in San Diego. Within two weeks, the story had been picked up by the national television news networks, followed by local news media organizations in Los Angeles and San Diego. Soon the politicians jumped in, and by the end of August 1988, San Diego police authorities formed a joint city–county task force to search for their killers. Increased information then began to flow directly between the Green River Task Force and the San Diego unit.

Meanwhile, the planning continued on Carner and Frederick's idea for a national television broadcast about the Green River murders. By July, the pieces were falling into place. A New York scriptwriter was hired, and plans were made to syndicate the program nationally. The task force supplied the information to be used in the program, and retained, as agreed, final control over what was to be aired. Like the local Crime Stoppers programs, the Green River project would be designed to elicit toll-free telephone calls about the crimes from the national public. The hope was that someone, somewhere would call in and provide the key to solving the murders. Maybe, it was hoped, the killer himself would call.

68

PINK GLASS

October 1988

In October, the FBI's glass man was finally ready. Evans sent Detective Brent Beden, the task force's evidence control supervisor, back to Washington to the FBI lab, carrying the precious pink cargo locked in a briefcase.

Once in Washington, D.C., Beden made arrangements to stay at a hotel until the analysis was done. Some thought it might take as long as a week.

At 8:30 AM. on the day after he arrived, Beden reported to the FBI's lab with the briefcase. Carefully he handed the materials to the FBI's glass expert, who signed a formal receipt. The expert took the materials into the lab. Beden found a nearby chair and sat down to wait.

At 9:00 A.M., Evans took a call from Beden.

"Bob, this is Brent."

"Hi Brent, what's going on?"

"Bob, are you sitting down?"

"Should I be?" Evans asked.

"You should."

"Ok, I'm sitting down. What is it?"

"You know your pink glass particles?"

"Yeah?"

"They aren't pink, they aren't glass, and they aren't particles."

"*What?*"

Beden repeated himself. He explained. The FBI glass man had looked at this stuff under his microscope for less than thirty minutes before emerging to tell Beden that what the state lab had been identifying for years as potentially vital evidence, "pink glass particles," weren't really particles at all, or glass, or even pink, but instead were a natural element, a type of garnet stone that is often associated with sandpaper, roofing, and volcanic eruptions. The material is so common in the volcanic Pacific Northwest, especially after the 1980 eruption of Mt. St. Helens, that it was virtually useless as an item of incriminating trace evidence.

Evans didn't know whether to laugh or go crazy.

69

THE MOVIE

November 1988/December 1988

As the nights shortened in October and November, the television production went into full swing. The actor Patrick Duffy of the primetime soap opera *Dallas* was signed as an anchor for the program; he would be paid $75,000 for his time and name. Crime Stoppers' Myrle Carner obtained the assistance of The Boeing Company for studios to house the live portions of the program. Arrangements were made to install a bank of telephones in the studio for police to take the phone calls, and computer terminals were set up to allow the police to tap into the task force data bank immediately.

Meanwhile, the New York writers met daily with Reichert, Evans, Nolan, and other members of the task force. Ideas were pitched back and forth. Some were rejected by the police because they were considered too sensational. Others were rejected by the producers for the same reason. The script seemed to be a fluid commodity. Reenactments of several scenes were put on videotape. Interviews were conducted with several participants, including one harrowing conversation with the survivor of the Portland knife attack near Horsetail Falls.

In late October, several dozen teenage girls were brought in, put up in a motel along The Strip, and costumed as prostitutes so that scenes depicting the sidewalk soliciting could be videotaped. On another night, a camera crew followed Larry Gross around as he surveilled The Strip. The camera recorded the action as Gross rousted a john who had just picked up a real prostitute. The john's face was electronically altered, but the conversation between Gross and the man was real.

But the police, writers, and producers soon came to appreciate another problem: How should they bill their hybrid to the public? What *was* it, really? Was it a documentary? No, said the police and producers, because it would have reenactments. Was it news? Not that, because the police admitted they would have total control over what was aired. Maybe it was a docudrama. Nope, said the writers, because it was more than just a dramatization of what had previously taken place. "Current reality," they said, would be the primary focus, and to that end, plans had been made to have detectives standing by in San Diego, Nashville, and several other cities, all to be interviewed live by Duffy on the big night, sort of like the network news.

Then it *would* be news, right? No, no, no, said the producers, because news meant *objectivity*, and that was the last thing producers wanted. They wanted to help the investigation by stimulating the viewing public to call in with tips. That meant people needed to be riled up. In effect, the program would be a national public goosing on serial murders, particularly the Green River crimes. We call it reality TV, said the producers.

Reality TV! Sudden images of Geraldo Rivera stormed through the minds of the Seattle news media, along with a darker fear. All these years they had pestered the King County police for details about the Green River crimes, only to be shut out time and time again. And now that the *Geraldoites* were on the scene, who knew what secrets the cops were sharing? Reporters for several television stations launched lobbying campaigns against the police department's decision to cooperate with the Crime Stoppers program, to no avail.

Evans and Nolan kept saying they had considered the pros and cons of participating, and had decided they had little to lose by going national in a two-hour, in-depth program. That was a lot better, they said, then twenty seconds on the local channels, and hey, who knew? Maybe something would happen.

The biggest problem faced by the uneasy alliance between the task force and the program producers was striking the right balance. Enough information had to be released to make the program interesting. Yet it couldn't be too gory or no one would buy the advertising time. No advertising money, no program. At the same time, the task force's most important secrets had to be protected.

As November turned into December, the program began to shape up more and more as sort of a telethon on serial murders, with Duffy acting as the master of ceremonies, introducing videotapes and interviews with selected subjects, including John Douglas of the FBI on the killer's supposed personality. Meanwhile, task force members and other detectives from Nashville, Tennessee; Mobile, Alabama; Lexington, Kentucky; Rockford, Illinois; Las Vegas, Nevada; Phoenix, Arizona; Honolulu, Hawaii; Portland, Oregon; Palm Springs, California; Vancouver, British Columbia; and Thurston County, Washington, would be flown into Seattle at Crime Stoppers' expense to take the telephone calls that were expected to pour in. The detectives would be seated in front of computer terminals, which would allow them to immediately enter the tips into the task force's computer system. A toll-free telephone number would be flashed continuously across the lower portion of the television screen so the viewing audience would know where to call if they had information. Periodically, fragments of the recovered tips would be funneled to Duffy, who would tell the audience about them in sort of an evangelical hustle to induce even more calls. The program would be titled *Manhunt Live: A Chance to End the Nightmare*. A press release on the program was sent out nationally to hype interest.

"The goal of this important special," the release read, "is straightforward and direct: to mobilize the country in an effort to track down the most prolific killer of all time, the Green River Killer. More vicious than Jack the Ripper, Ted Bundy, The Boston Strangler and Son of Sam combined, this killer has terrorized the West Coast for the last six years."

On the day before the broadcast, December 6, 1988, the county police helped promote the program further by announcing that new information would be revealed on the program for the first time. A press release was distributed by the county police to discuss the new information. One victim, said the release, had been pregnant when she was murdered. And the other item was—a Green River victim had escaped death, *and had been able to describe her attacker*!

Now the local television reporters went nuts. This was exactly what they had feared. Worse, now the police department was shamelessly using *them* to promote a program that would be aired on another channel.

At a press conference held the day of the release, reporters hammered Montgomery, Nolan, and Evans hard on the pregnancy issue. Why hadn't the police released this information previously? Why were they releasing it now? Wasn't this a case of the task force thumbing their noses at the local reporters and using a sensational fact for manipulative ends?

Nolan tried to field the question. "Given what the [FBI's] Behavioral Science Unit tells us, the one key stressor we may have in this investigation is the fact that, if the Green River killer has a girlfriend—and we make an assumption here that it's a male, all right?—and he's got a live-in girlfriend or he's associated with a female, or there's a 'significant other' in his life, *she* may well have been able to . . . understand or dismiss the fact that he can go out and kill prostitutes.

"But now [she would learn] he's killed an eight-

month pregnant woman. And she's never known that.
Or, whoever is with him has never known that before.
Perhaps as a result of that sort of psychological stress,
that person who knows, if there is a person who
knows, who the Green River killer is, may say 'I can't
deal with this. I've got to come forward now and make
it known: John Doe is the Green River killer.' " Simply put, the idea was that the announcement of the
murder of an unborn baby might trigger someone to
turn in the killer.

After a few more questions, Nolan expanded on his
answer. "We were looking for ways [to get the killer
to come forward]. It was apparent through our investigative efforts we weren't budging the Green River
killer. And he may well be killing in San Diego, or he
may well be killing anywhere in the country. Routine
investigative techniques, traditional ways of solving
the case that we've used, have not worked. Here was
a way to get this particular psychological stressor to
the whole country in prime time, in one shot, in a
two-hour segment that is not a twenty-second bite
with a talking head." Take *that*, nattering nabobs of
negativity!

A KIRO reporter, Brian Wood, tried a different
tack. Did the use of this national whatever-you-call-it
signify the future in media–police relations? Was the
message to law enforcement across the country going
to be, from now on, just withhold information from
the local news media and save it for the time when
you can go national? Was the message, it's OK to
bypass the local media?

Nolan lost his cool.

"We're not bypassing you, jack," he shot back at
Wood. "This [the press conference] is obviously an
effort not to bypass you. And you guys are all bent
out of shape 'cause you've got a local interest in it.
That's great. We all understand that. This has become
your forum, for you to take a shot at the police
department. And we knew that you were going to do
that. That's great, if that's where you want to go. I

hope to God it solves a lot of cases because we'll stick it right up your—O.K.!"

Montgomery was leaning behind Nolan and tapping him on the shoulder to get him to stop.

Wood and Nolan exchanged more barbs for a few minutes before Montgomery got control of the situation.

"I don't think, well, this may be productive for you but I feel we're being badgered at this particular point," said Montgomery. "If there are any other questions that relate to the show rather than, uh, well, we understand you disagree with us professionally, fine. We agree to disagree."

The other issue was the so-called surviving victim of the killer. Why hadn't the police told anyone about *that*? They had, said the police. They were referring to the Horsetail Falls slashing victim in Portland. Since when was *she* a Green River victim? reporters then demanded. Why wasn't she on the list? She wasn't a Green River victim, said Nolan; it was just that some detectives thought the attack was quite close in methodology to the Green River attacks. Then why was it being included? To show viewers what might have happened to the Green River victims, Nolan said. Then the Horsetail Falls slasher *was* like the Green River killer? How do you know it wasn't really *him*? And so it went on, two sides locked in permanent combat over the meaning of words, and what they portended in the vacuum of clear information.

The next night, as the broadcast began, Patrick Duffy drove up to the Boeing Company's studios in south Seattle in a King County Police Department patrol car. The vehicle screeched to a halt at the curb, its red lights flashing. The door was flung open, and to the accompaniment of drums and dramatic music, Duffy strode into the building, looking as if he meant business. *Manhunt Live: A Chance to End the Nightmare*, was on.

Almost immediately the switchboard lit up with calls. Two hours later, after the program had shown the grisly police videotapes of the pregnant Mary

Bridget Meehan's exhumation, after a professional actress portrayed the Horsetail Falls victim staring up at her would-be killer from beneath the leaves, after Streed reported in from San Diego, and other cops from the other localities, and after Larry Gross had rousted the john, the calls were still pouring in. The lines were so busy, in fact, that most callers couldn't get through. The final push to find the killer was under way.

70

THE LAW STUDENT

December 1988/January 1989

The following morning, police were still taking calls. Arrangements were made to keep the lines open for several more weeks to give everyone a chance to get through. The studio floor was littered with papers and used coffee cups. Most of the cops were exhausted from fielding hundreds of telephone calls, many of them from people who obviously knew nothing. At one point during the night Reichert had received a telephone call from a man who said he wanted to confess; the tension in the room rose dramatically. Douglas had stood at Reichert's elbow and consulted with Reichert on the man's responses to Reichert's questions. Finally the man admitted, as Reichert had suspected, that he was not the killer.

But several of the calls did pan out. One, in fact, *was* for a Green River murder, but not one of those the task force was seeking to solve. A few weeks before the program, police had found the strangled body of a young woman dumped along the banks of the river. It was clear, however, that the victim had not been murdered by the Green River killer. Detectives had been pursuing a suspect with great diligence when someone called in after the program and provided information about two totally different suspects. The tipped suspects turned out to be responsible for the crime, and the original suspect was exonerated. Already the program had paid dividends, Evans thought.

Another dividend came when a woman who had previously claimed to have been home with a Portland-area suspect in the Horsetail falls attack called to say that she had lied. The suspect had told her about the incident, but had left out the brutal details, and blamed the whole thing on the fifteen-year-old girl. But after watching the reenactment on television, the woman decided that the man was a monster. The Green River police quickly checked out the man's whereabouts during the dates of the Green River crimes, and discovered that the man had ironclad alibis for the Green River murders. While that part of the program had done what it was intended to do—help solve the Horsetail Falls attack—it did not advance the Green River case at all. Worse, because three years had gone by, the statute of limitations made it impossible to prosecute the Portland man for his vicious attack.

The main problem, however, was sorting through all the tips. That had been one reason the answering police had been seated in front of the computer terminals; the information from the caller—including a number where follow-up detectives could reach them later—was put directly into the task force computer. Over the next month, the information would be sorted and related to existing information. Much of it would be passed on to other agencies. If nothing else, the task force had become a sort of national clearinghouse of sexual predators, particularly the murdering variety.

By the end of the week, the phone company reported, more than *100,000* people had attempted to call. Less than ten thousand actually got through. Carner was ecstatic and depressed at the same time. No one had foreseen the effect of the program on the viewing public. It was, he said later, like a national cleansing. People who had kept things to themselves for years, even decades, had called in to report their suspicions. What haunted Carner was the fear that the person with the key piece of the Green River information had been unable to get through. After three weeks, the phones were simply unplugged. The Crime Stoppers people just couldn't get enough volunteers to man the telephones any longer.

By the middle of January 1989, almost all of the information had been fed to the computer and digested. The computer had enabled the police to process the tips faster than ever before. But because it had, now there was no longer any need to have so many detectives tied up, Montgomery reasoned. By early February—five years after Adamson's initial promise to get the killer no matter what it took—the task force was down to six detectives, six months ahead of schedule. The hunt was almost over, whether anyone was willing to admit it or not.

But there would be one last gasp to come.

Among the thousands who called the police as result of the television show were two people, one in Seattle, the other in Portland, Oregon. As they watched the show, both began to think of someone they knew: a person who was quite intelligent, who often acted mysteriously, and who liked to pretend he was a police officer. The tips from both telephone calls were routinely logged into the computer along with the thousands of others about other people.

Then a coincidence occurred. The day after the program, an investigator for the Veterans Administration fraud detection unit happened to call a King County detective assigned to the Green River Task Force about an old case. The VA man had no professional interest in the Green River matter; instead, he was only interested in what county detective Tom Jensen might be able to tell him about a man named William J. Stevens II. Jensen had investigated Stevens on a burglary case in 1979. The VA man told Jensen that a former accomplice of Stevens in the burglary was now working at a VA office at the University of Washington processing veterans benefit claims. The former accomplice had apparently opened a claim for a William J. Stevens II. Meanwhile, the VA investigator had determined that Stevens himself had opened his *own* claim while a student at Gonzaga University in Spokane. It seemed to the VA man that Stevens's former accomplice might be involved in some sort of fraud. What did Jensen know about this man Stevens, anyway?

Jensen couldn't help but be amused. Ever since 1981, when Stevens had walked away from the King County jail's work release program—while taking out the trash, no less—Jensen had wondered whatever had become of him. Now he was learning that Stevens was alive and well in Spokane. Because Stevens had been convicted of burglarizing a police uniform store then located on Pacific Highway South in 1979, Jensen had always considered Stevens a possible suspect in the Green River murders, albeit one of low probability. In 1986, in fact, Jensen had turned in a tip on Stevens to the task force. The nagging question was, where had Stevens been all those years after he had walked out with the garbage? Was it possible Stevens had gone not far at all, but was simply using another name?

Stevens had been a student in pharmacology at the University of Washington at the time of the burglary. He also held a degree in psychology, and had a background as an officer of the U.S. Army's military police. Jensen considered Stevens bright enough to be capable of committing the Green River crimes, if in fact it could be shown that he had been in the Seattle area during the time of the murders. For a motive, it was possible that Stevens might have murdered the women just in part to taunt the police. Stevens had told Jensen in 1980 that he had applied for an appointment to the Seattle Police Department after he had left the army, but had been turned down because of his bad driving record. And of course, there was the garbage angle to consider, possibly significant because of the trash found near the Green River victims.

To Jensen, the fact that Stevens had not been recaptured after his escape meant either that he had left town permanently, or that he had been very successful in changing his personal history. It had been as if Stevens had simply dropped out of sight after walking out with the trash. But now, thanks to Stevens's accomplice's inadvertence, Jensen knew right where to find the burglar.

Jensen ran Stevens's name through the task force computer, and struck immediate paydirt with the two tips that had just been telephoned in as a result of their program, both of which shed a glimmer of light on where Stevens had been for the previous eight years.

Jensen then called Spokane County police officials, told them there was a warrant out for Stevens's arrest, and that Stevens was a possible suspect in the Green River murders. With the assistance of the Spokane authorities, Jensen began working to fill in the background on Stevens's whereabouts from 1981 to 1988. One very good lead was provided by the person who had called from Portland, a woman who had lived in the basement of a house Stevens had owned in Tigard. Tigard! Where the skulls of Denise Bush and Shirley Sherrill had been found. Even better.

Follow-up interviews were then conducted of the people who had reported Stevens to the task force as a result of the television program. Small fragments of Stevens's past began to fall into place. Those who knew Stevens reported that Stevens owned police uniforms, was a police paraphernalia buff, had taken photographs of prostitutes, and had talked of murdering prostitutes. Some acquaintances told police that Stevens had a fascination with the Green River murders. Further follow-up by the task force showed that Stevens had used at least two different aliases in the Portland area after his escape.

Meanwhile, the Spokane authorities learned that Stevens had applied for a government-authorized exempt license plate for an old city of Everett police car that he owned, a car that Stevens had outfitted with police radios, a radar unit, and blue emergency grill lights. The car actually *looked* like a real cop car, the Spokane police discovered. Running the government-exempt license plate on the car, the Spokane detectives discovered that Stevens had been billing himself as the emergency services director for the city of Spangle, Washington. There was no such city.

On January 9, 1989, Spokane city and county police swooped down on Stevens at his elderly parents' home in Spokane and arrested him on the escape charge, and also served a search warrant permitting them to look for evidence related to the false application for the exempt license plates, and for any other records that might show Stevens had used false names to get licenses for other vehicles. A Spokane County detective serving the warrant found numerous documents in Stevens's bedroom, including several driver's licenses issued to Stevens under different names, credit cards in those names, and other records showing Stevens had spent much of the past eight years obtaining various items of surplus police equipment. The detectives also found thirty-three different firearms, a possible violation of the federal gun laws. In one part of the room, a Spokane detective found a small box filled with about fifty Polaroid photographs of nude women, some in sexually explicit poses. Other photographs found in the bedroom seemed to indicate that Stevens himself had taken the nude photos. Detectives recognized several of the photographed women as Spokane-area prostitutes.

The following day, Stevens was shipped back to the King County Jail to serve the remainder of his sentence for the burglary, plus a dividend for the escape. An investigation would continue in an effort to further pin down Stevens's whereabouts during 1982 through

1984. The years from 1985 through the end of 1988 were a bit easier to figure out: Stevens had been in law school.

In 1985 Stevens had left Portland to move back to Spokane. Perhaps believing that no one was looking for him any longer on the escape matter, Stevens applied for admission to the Gonzaga University Law School and was accepted in 1985. When he was arrested, Stevens was in his last semester. He had twice been elected president of the Student Bar Association.

By all accounts, Stevens was a popular student, helpful to other students and friendly with the faculty. A former professor at the law school, Craig Beles, was to become his lawyer as the investigation proceeded. The law school was embarrassed over the revelation—publicized soon after Stevens's arrest—that they had been educating a felon on the lam. It wasn't their fault, said Gonzaga officials; Stevens, they said, had lied on his application for admission. "If we knew that he lied, we would have barred him," said Associate Dean Vern Davidson. "I liked him," Davidson said. "I found him charming . . . and I still like him. I find him very friendly and helpful."

71

TED IS DEAD

January 23, 1989

Exactly two weeks after Stevens's arrest, Major Dick
Kraske sat at home as another former law student
many people had described as friendly and helpful
made the last walk of his life.

To the end, Ted Bundy had tried to be of assistance. Kraske found a curious roiling of emotions
inside him. His mind flashed back to the dark days of
1974, when he had been seized by the anxiety that
somehow the "Ted" killer would seek out and kill his
daughters. Kraske remembered the sleepless nights,
the tension, the pressure, his deteriorating relationship
with his family, all the pain and frustration Bundy had
caused. Kraske could still see the hillside where Bob
Keppel had scoured the ground on his hands and
knees looking for bone fragments; he remembered the
agony of the grief-stricken families, the screaming in
the news media; he could still imagine the terror that
Bundy's victims must have felt.

Yet Kraske felt sickened by the celebrations of Bundy's imminent departure from the living: the picketers'
signs that read "Buckle up, Bundy, It's The Law," the
jokes about frying and sizzling and similar sublimated
expiations of the collective guilt of indifference that
the Crime Stoppers' Myrle Carner had so recently
touched. Kraske's mind went back to his own boyhood
in Montana, where murderers had been hanged,

quickly and soberly. It was *justice* then, Kraske thought, not this carnival. Bundy's interminable appeals throughout the 1980s had turned the system into a joke, Kraske thought, and had pent up all of this public rage. Now Bundy would finally die for what he had done, but Kraske knew a part of him was dying, too.

Three thousand miles away, only hours earlier, Keppel had conducted his final interview with the man he had known only as the "Ted" killer. Bundy was still trying to help. The words had poured forth from the former Boy Scout, telling of abductions, assaults, mutilations, perversities that shocked even Keppel. Keppel had taped the final statements, somehow managing to keep his face a mask as Bundy had described his acts. The Book was closing on the murders that he and Kraske had failed to solve. Was it a final unburdening before death? Keppel did not think so. To the last, Keppel believed, Bundy was trying to manipulate the system for yet another stay of execution. Bundy was only trying to use him, Keppel, as his last card. How ironic, Keppel thought, that Bundy was seeking help from the very people who had wanted to catch him so badly for so long. But when Bundy told Keppel about one particularly atrocious act—the severing of the head of one of his victims—Keppel turned off his tape recorder. "At that point," said Keppel later, "I was done with him."

At 7:06 A.M. in Florida State Prison's death chamber, a woman—a fitting choice—stepped forward and pressed a button and sent two thousand volts of current into a copper-plated skullcap fitted over Bundy's head. Bundy's fists clenched spasmodically. Three minutes later, Ted Bundy had officially ceased to exist. But he had actually been dead for years.

Others, and the description that Stevens gave the
. . .

72

THE LAST DANCE

February 1989/July 1989

As the winter turned into spring, more information
about William Stevens continued to come in.

Ever since Stevens's arrest, Evans had been peppered with questions about the law student's viability
as a suspect. It did not appear to him, Evans said over
and over again, that Stevens was a *likely* suspect in
the Green River murders. Evans said investigators had
searched diligently for any evidence that Stevens had
been in the Seattle area during the time of the murders, and had found none. As it turned out, however,
that assertion would ultimately be replaced by more
ominous facts. Meanwhile, police continued to develop
other disturbing information about the former law
student.

Several of Stevens's acquaintances, including his
former accomplice, told police that Stevens seemed to
know an inordinate amount of detail about the Green
River murders. Stevens supposedly told one man that
the Green River women had been killed in so-called
"snuff films." Others talked of how Stevens had spo-
ken of desires to mutilate prostitutes, and how he
hated them and blamed them for the spread of AIDS.
Several acquaintances told police that Stevens gave
them the impression that he was an undercover agent
for various police agencies, including the Green River
Task Force.

Others had the impression that Stevens worked for the Central Intelligence Agency. The Portland woman recalled how Stevens had once shown her a secret room behind a bookcase in the basement of the Tigard house. Stevens told her, the woman said, that he could now show her the room because it had been "declassified." Periodically, Stevens's acquaintances said, Stevens told them he was going on a "mission," and that he would then be absent for a period of days or weeks. When he returned from these "missions," they said, he would be hyperactive, nervous, keyed up; he would watch television for hours until he calmed down. To investigators, the supposed periods of hyperactivity matched the model they might expect from a man who committed serial murder.

Where did Stevens get his money? That also became a focus of task force attention. As the investigators probed deeper, they learned that Stevens had charged many of his expenses to the credit cards issued under the false names; but then investigators learned that the names and duplicates of the cards also belonged to *real* people. Where did Stevens's charges end and those of the real credit card holders begin? It seemed that Stevens had become a master of disguises, weaving a paper trail deliberately intended to sow confusion. Detectives were also told by Stevens's former burglary accomplice that Stevens had shared in the proceeds of money orders taken during a post office burglary at Fort Shafter in Hawaii, and that Stevens had used some of these proceeds to buy the house in Tigard.

The house itself turned out to be less than a mile from where the skeletons of Bush and Sherrill had been found in 1985, and less than five miles from where Liles and the other Tualatin victim were found earlier the same year. That seemed significant. Detectives found that Stevens had acquired a collection of old police equipment from the demolition of the old Portland Police Bureau building in 1984. Finally, an inquiry subpoena issued for all the credit cards used by Stevens seemed to show that Stevens had traveled frequently between Tigard, Portland, Seattle, Spokane, and Vancouver, B.C., during the years of the murders. The credit card receipts indicated that Stevens had purchased fuel, auto parts, stereo equipment, and meals in all of the locations during the time of the murders in each of the cities. Suddenly, Stevens was looking better and better, thought Evans.

As Stevens settled into his cell at the King County Jail, he found himself merging into the jail culture quite easily. His wit, intelligence, and charm made the other prisoners easy prey for attempts to learn things about them he might be able to use to bargain for better treatment, or perhaps, even an early release. That was one way Stevens hoped to be "friendly and helpful" to the authorities.

As far as he knew, police did not consider him a suspect in the Green River murders; after all, following his arrest, hadn't Evans and other task force officials said publicly they knew of no connection between Stevens and the crimes? Stevens resolved to hunker down and finish his sentence as quickly as he could, then get out and disappear again.

Then, sometime during the spring, Stevens struck up a relationship with another inmate, a man awaiting trial on charges that he had raped and murdered a Seattle woman. Stevens told others he found the psychology of the man awaiting trial fascinating, and that he intended to write a psychological paper about him. As Stevens described his fascination with the murder to a third inmate, he supposedly spoke in animated terms about the murderer's bloody predilections. The third inmate then contacted jail officials and related the conversations that he had with Stevens. There is indeed no honor among thieves, particularly when they are incarcerated.

The information about Stevens's supposed fascination with bloody murder eventually worked its way back to the task force, and became yet another piece of the puzzle to Stevens.

In the meantime, Spokane detectives tracing the weapons they had found in Stevens's bedroom tracked one pistol back to a former law school classmate of Stevens, a man named Dale Wells. Wells, it turned out, was a deputy public defender in Spokane. Task force investigators interviewing Wells reported that Wells told them Stevens had talked about prostitutes a lot. Wells claimed Stevens said that prostitutes were diseased, and that they were responsible for the rapid spread of AIDS. Stevens used to frequent Seattle's prostitution areas, Wells said Stevens told him; and Wells said Stevens was prejudiced against blacks, and often spoke of using violence against those who thwarted him. Once, said Wells, Stevens had told him that a Gonzaga professor who had flunked him should be stalked and killed. Wells also said that Stevens conversed occasionally about Ted Bundy. Wells told the investigators that Stevens commented on Bundy's mistakes, and referred to Bundy as stupid.

Evans still couldn't quite convince himself, however, that Stevens was the killer. True, there were many disturbing aspects of Stevens's behavior, but the task force was a long way from being able to implicate Stevens in any of the crimes. Being weird wasn't the same as being guilty, Evans thought. The best way to proceed, Evans believed, would be to talk to Stevens directly. Literally hundreds of suspects had been eliminated simply as a result of interviews over the years. Most of those interviewed were only too glad to cooperate with the investigators. Detectives went to see Stevens in the jail.

Stevens was guardedly cooperative. But when it came to certain questions about his whereabouts and activities from 1982 through 1984, Stevens simply clammed up. Several efforts were made to convince Stevens to cooperate, Evans said later, but Stevens adamantly refused to answer certain questions. He suggested that the detectives submit written questions to him through his attorney, former law professor Beles. That was hardly the way to conduct an interrogation of a potential murder suspect. What to do?

Evans ran the problem through his mind. While he

still wasn't sure that Stevens was culpable in the murders, how could he be sure? Evans could not in clear conscience exculpate Stevens unless he was convinced that Stevens was not the killer. Well, if Stevens wouldn't cooperate, there was only one thing to do, Evans thought: Look for evidence that would decide the issue with or without cooperation.

On July 12, seven years to the day after Wendy Coffield was killed, Evans and a team of task force investigators obtained a King County search warrant and went to Spokane to paw through Stevens's belongings at two different locations. One was the house of Stevens's father, who was dying of cancer; the other was a storage facility where Stevens kept voluminous records. Police found over a thousand videotapes, and nearly fifty cardboard boxes filled with years of receipts, tax records, and other similar paperwork. All of this would have to be analyzed and put into some sort of order in the effort to figure out where Stevens had been during the time of the murders. It took a truck to cart all the material back to Seattle.

The news of the search was soon broadcast in Spokane, and then Seattle. Still Evans refused to say that Stevens was a suspect in the murders. "We need time now to review the documents and determine if we need to look further to see if this man can be linked to any unsolved crimes in King County," he said.

---

73

NEWS

July 1989/October 1989

But the following day, Evans was a bit more explicit. "If his attorney would have let him talk to us," Evans said, "we wouldn't have had to serve search warrants. I knew this would create a firestorm, but we had no other option. We were forced to move, it was the only thing left to do. There was a ton of bizarre circumstances that needed further investigation."

And the task force released every line of its affidavit in support of the search. "Records obtained thus far," Evans wrote in seeking court permission for the search, "Have failed to provide him with an alibi for any of the forty-nine [Evans was apparently counting Meehan's unborn baby as a victim] suspected Green River homicides, or any of those [seventeen others] in the cities of Portland or Spokane.

"Instead, interviews and records have produced . . . facts that tend to establish that Stevens is a viable suspect in the Green River homicides, and possibly others in the Pacific Northwest."

Viable suspect. That choice of words in Evans's affidavit created another media sensation, particularly in those areas of the country not well schooled in the nuances of task force talk. In other places around the country, "suspect" was often used synonymously with culprit, and carried an implication of guilt. Why else would police have called someone a suspect if they weren't guilty? A "viable" suspect was even more guilty.

A photograph of Stevens taken during his arrest in January, showing him handcuffed in the courthouse hallway, head hung down in apparent contrition, went coast-to-coast. The next day the story made the front page of *The New York Times* and countless other newspapers. Oregon's largest newspaper, *The Oregonian*, all but convicted Stevens in their coverage. And Ann Rule, the noted crime writer, chimed in with an interview contending that in her opinion, Stevens "was the best suspect yet," claiming that she had been "watching him since January." *Time* magazine published a story that suggested strongly that the murders were at last solved.

Through Beles, Stevens immediately issued denials that he was the Green River killer. "He is shocked and terrified," Beles said of Stevens. "He is a bona fide character, but not a cold-blooded killer." Six days later, Stevens had to be moved to an isolation cell in the jail. Other inmates had begun to threaten him.

By mid-August, Stevens had mounted a counterattack against Evans and the task force. While detectives were still poring over all Stevens's records in an attempt to determine where he had been during the murders, Stevens's brother, Bob, was doing the same thing. On August 16, Bob Stevens blasted the task force.

"Throughout these past few months, my family and the public have been told by the Green River Task Force that the ordeal that my family has undergone could have been avoided," Bob Stevens said. "That they were only interested in determining his locations from 1981 to 1985, and they assured my family that the task force had hoped to determine my brother's innocence.

"I don't believe any of these statements," Bob Stevens continues, "but I do believe that the task force has been reckless in their investigation and have done nothing but harass my brother, family, and friends."

Then Bob Stevens attempted to end the task force's

investigation of his brother once and for all. He produced photographs and more credit card records that seemed to show that William J. Stevens was on a car trip across the country in July, August, and early September of 1982—the very time when the murders had begun.

Evans was undeterred, however. Just because Stevens might have alibis for *some* of the murders didn't mean that he could be excluded from *all* of them, Evans said. The old debate about whether there was more than one murderer was back.

"Unfortunately," said Evans, "we don't deal in emotion but in facts. I understand he loves his brother but we still have a job to do. We have offered Bill, through his attorney, more than a dozen opportunities to clear this up quickly and quietly and he has declined." Then Evans got a little mad.

"It is not my fault he was a fugitive," he said, "that he told his friends he wanted to do things to prostitutes and that he collected police badges and equipment. If I would have walked away from that without checking it out, I should have been fired."

The investigation would continue, Evans said. And in late September, as Bill Stevens was nearing the end of his jail term, federal authorities in Spokane slapped him with a new charge: federal weapons violations. The gun Stevens had accepted from Wells, a forty-five caliber Colt, was the evidence in accusing Stevens of being a felon in possession of a firearm.

It was all a witchhunt, Bob Stevens said. "They're just looking for whatever they can to keep him in jail. They can't find anything on him in connection with the murders, so they do this."

In late September, Evans made another attempt to get Stevens to help them out. Stevens agreed to be interviewed, according to Beles, to help out a friend he thought the task force was trying to implicate with him in the murders. But he never named the friend, and the talks went nowhere.

"We had hoped we could get the information we needed and bring this to a conclusion," Evans said.

"Unfortunately, what we wanted to talk about and what he wanted to discuss were largely two different things. We are back where we started. I remain as concerned about him as I was when the search warrant was issued."

Two days after these conversations with Stevens stalled, Dale Wells killed himself. Wells had been the friend that Stevens had hoped to help, police were sure. Somewhere during the summer, Wells had come to feel that he himself was under suspicion with Stevens. Wells left no note. He simply shot himself in the head with a shotgun on a Saturday morning.

What was this about? The previous week Wells had been served with a federal subpoena in the Stevens gun case. There seemed to be no reason to believe that Wells did not wish to cooperate with Stevens's prosecution. But as investigators looked closer at Wells's death, new questions emerged.

For one thing, Wells and Stevens had remained in communication while Stevens was in jail. Letters and telephone calls had been exchanged. Then it turned out that in their search in January, Spokane police had seized a wallet from Stevens's bedroom that held a driver's license issued in Wells's name; the license had a Spangle address. Spokane police said they didn't think that Wells had ever had possession of the phony license, but its existence was now rather more troubling, with Wells dead.

Was Wells worried that he would somehow become caught up in Stevens's legal troubles? That the license might connect him to something? No one knew. The whole matter was puzzling. Why had Wells provided the information about the gun if he wanted to avoid involvement? Why had he talked to the task force and why had he provided information about Stevens and prostitutes? A search of Wells's apartment after the suicide turned up a two-page, unfinished letter to crime writer Rule. In the letter Wells compared someone he did not name to Bundy. Investigators said they believed that Wells was referring to Stevens.

As it happened, Rule had been in Spokane the night before Well killed himself, giving a talk about serial murderers. Detectives speculated that Wells may have attended the Friday night talk. Rule said she did not recall meeting Wells. "I'm as baffled as everybody," she said. "I feel bad. This is really getting to me. I don't know if he was in the audience or not."

A month later the Spokane newspapers reported that there had been an investigation of Wells, after all. Police detectives there learned that in the days before the body of a strangled prostitute was found in a field near Spokane's race track in January of 1986, Wells had been trying to find the woman. The manager of a Spokane motel where the woman, Ruby Jean Doss, had been staying, told the newspapers that Wells had come to the motel to ask about Doss. Wells had identified himself as a lawyer, and told the motel manager he wanted to find the woman because she had stolen a wallet from a friend of his who was a Spokane police officer. Was this the wallet with Wells's Spangle identification in it? With Wells dead, no one could now say for sure. But Spokane police acknowledged that they were investigating the dead man to see if they could clear up the mystery.

Meanwhile, Stevens began making his own arrangements for a book. Beles and Stevens opened negotiations with a California writer to tell Stevens's side of the story. "The task force has thrust Bill in the public eye, and opportunity has come knocking," said Beles. "It is partly an attempt by Bill to obtain funds to pay for attorney fees he owes and any he may owe in the future. Maybe it'll give Bill a chance to clear his name."

Evans suggested that Stevens's desire to gain the proceeds from a book may have contributed to Stevens's reluctance to cooperate with investigators. "I will *not* contribute to selling books," Evans said. "Maybe that's why he hasn't cooperated. All I want is to determine whether he has committed any crimes in this jurisdiction."

But two weeks later, Evans announced that he had cleared Stevens of involvement in the Green River murders. "We have come to the conclusion that we can no longer call him a viable suspect," Evans said. "We never had the opportunity to go to the source of this case, but reviewing what we had we've decided to eliminate him."

The last of the "chance to end the nightmare" was over.

74

CHILDERS

October 1989

Bob Evans stood motionless in the gathering chill of the October afternoon, protecting his hands against the cold by jamming them deeper into the side pockets of his heavy topcoat. Five hundred feet overhead, the deafening thunder of the outbound jets obliterated most of the conversation, and set the air atremble. It was O.K. Evans didn't feel much like talking anyway.

Almost two years had gone by since Evans had been promoted and had taken command of the King County Police Department's Green River Task Force. Now, like the killer it sought, the task force itself was fading away. Soon it would be just a memory, an old picture in a yellowed newspaper.

Well, it had always been a long shot, Evans thought as he stared down at the shallow grave of the latest

Green River victim, another one in the vacant lot on South 192nd Street, near the dark road by the golf course where so many tricks were turned. He wondered who this one had been. It was October 11, 1989, and the hunt was nearing an end.

This would be number forty-nine; and while no one except the killer himself—whoever the bastard was—could say with any certainty just how many had died, Evans knew one thing: Whatever the number, it had been a slaughter unmatched and unknown anywhere else in the western world.

Evans watched quietly as Haglund, Reichert, and the others carefully excavated the new remains. This one had been found less than fifty feet from the rock-bordered place where Connie Naon's skeleton was discovered in late October of 1983, and even closer to the tin-can–covered spot where the bones of poor Kelly Ware were found the following day.

Bill Haglund examined the new skull as it came out of the earth. This victim had been buried, much the same way Mary Meehan had been, just across the street. They cautiously packed up the remains while the detectives sifted through the dirt around the area. This was an old skeleton, Haglund said as he examined it; not a new one, but someone from the years of all the murders.

Not far away the television cameras and newspaper photographers did what they always did; one of them brought a tall step ladder, so that they might shoot down on the crime scene while the processing continued. Reichert erected a cardboard barrier to shield the things recovered at the scene from the prying eye of the camera. By now these movements had taken on the aspects of ritual for both the news media and the police; everyone knew their role without asking.

Later in the afternoon, Haglund checked his now-vast library of dental records, all stored on a computer, and instantly identified the newest victim; nineteen-year-old Andrea Childers. She had never been on the official missing list, even though police had been told of her disappearance in April of 1983. Nine months later, in January of 1984, as the detectives winnowed through the list of possibles, they had picked Childers as a potential missing, and had obtained her dental charts to compare to the unidentifieds.

Then word had come from U.S. Customs officials that a woman with Childers's identification had crossed the border at Blaine, Washington, in early April of 1984. Childers was removed from the list, but Haglund had kept the charts just in case.

Now it appeared that another woman might have used Childers's identification, and a search would have to be undertaken for *that* woman. Where would it end? How many others like Childers were still out there, lying undiscovered, reduced to disarticulated bones under some forgotten patch of blackberry bushes, or shallowly buried, as Childers had been? The horrifying fact was that searchers had combed this lot many times and had probably walked over Childers's shallow grave without even knowing it.

And the known missing had to be somewhere. Kase Lee was still out there, someplace; so were Becky Marrero, Marie Malvar, Keli McGinness, April Buttram, Tracy Winston, Patricia Osborne, and Pamela Avent. Someone knew where those bones were, but wasn't saying.

HEAD GAMES

February 1990

In early February of 1990, a city councilman in the Seattle suburb of Tukwila—just down the hill from the ridge—discovered some human remains on a wooded hillside next to a city park.

The councilman called his own police department, which in turn called the King County police. A search the following day turned up a few more bones. Then one of the searchers discovered something strange.

Along with the bones was a piece of medical equipment, of a type often used by patients suffering from epilepsy.

Because the location was only a few blocks from The Strip, the possibility that the remains were the remnants of yet another Green River murder victim was considered very high. The location of the discovery was in the brush off the side of a lonely road winding down the hill through the trees, just exactly the sort of place that the long-sought Green River Killer favored for disposing of his victims. But because no skull was found, it appeared that identification of the remains would be impossible.

As he sat staring at the bones on his workbench over the next few days, Chief Medical Investigator Bill Haglund kept thinking about the medical equipment. Something about its discovery was wrong, Haglund realized. Checking his records, he discovered that such a device had been used by Denise Darcel Bush—the young woman who had lost the coin flip with her pimp and had gone out to buy cigarettes in early October of 1982, never to return.

But Bush's skull had been found near Tigard, in Oregon. How could these bones be hers, too? Was the killer dismembering his victims, scattering their parts over two different states?

No, Haglund realized almost instantly. The hillside near Tukwila was where the body of Bush was originally left after her murder in 1982. It was even possible that the killer had actually killed her nearby. Later—probably much later—the killer had returned to the location, gathered up whatever bones he could find—Bush's skull, and perhaps Shirley Sherrill's as well—*and had taken them to the Portland area.*

Why? To throw confusion into the investigation, it seemed clear. Haglund thought over so many of the other discovered remains: Kimi Kai Pitsor's skull at the edge of the road near Mountain View Cemetary in December of 1983 stared back at him in his mind's eye; so did Debbie May Abernathy's jaw, found March 31, 1984 along Highway 410. Or Mary West, whose skull was found in Seward Park. Or the partial skeleton found near the Green River itself in the spring of 1986. Here seemed the answer to another mystery: The killer had been moving the bones around to sow confusion. That meant, as Ted and Douglas had predicted, the killer had returned again and again to the secret places where he had left his victims. And it meant that the killer was a man, as Ted and Douglas had predicted, who derived great enjoyment from taunting the police who had so far failed to catch him.

Another, larger search was conducted for still more remains. Bloodhounds were called in, and the Explorer Scouts came with their machetes and workboots once more. The entire hillside was completely overgrown with thorny blackberry bushes. Two days were spent laboriously hacking searchers' paths across the hillside, and when it was over, nothing more had been found. The killer had won again.

EPILOGUE
1990

OUTCOMES

June 1990

Four months later, the search for the Green River Killer was at an end. The passage of the man no one knew had altered almost everything, in ways both obvious and subtle. The King County Police Department had been radically changed by his existence. The murders proved to be a crucible of transformation, refining the baser metals of the oldtime Sheriff's Department into a modern police agency. In the most cynical sense, it could even be argued that the murders had been good for the department.

And why not? The number of police officers in the department had increased dramatically during the period of the murders; all the old complaints over lack of service were now a mere faint echo of the past. As for skill levels, the crimes had provided a grim training that years in the classrooms could never have equaled. The department had become a national resource on sexual predators; thousands of items of criminal intelligence about potential offenders were stored permanently in a sophisticated computer data bank; the department now owned a computerized fingerprint processor, laser-based fingerprint and fiber detection analyzers, and tens of thousands of dollars in high-technology surveillance equipment. And the county's police were widely considered to be the finest outdoor crime processors in the country.

But the serial murders had changed the King County Police in other ways as well.

Dick Kraske was forced to retire, for one thing; Frank Adamson was made a chief instead; Jim Pompey was dead; and Bob Evans was also promoted. He got Kraske's old job. Reichert and Fae Brooks were made sergeants, and assigned to the patrol force under Evans. Reichert's black hair had gone completely gray, and in seven years he had aged at least twenty, some thought. John Blake was still suffering from his psychological disability.

The Green River murder case had changed the lives of others as well. Barbara Kubik-Patten was divorced; her discovery of the skeleton under the tarp had changed her life irrevocably. Judy DeLeon, the mother of Carrie Rois who had bitterly suggested that County Executive Hill walk in her shoes, broke her leg while walking a year later and died the following month from a blood embolism. Herb and Ginny Coffield sued the state for negligence in failing to keep their daughter Wendy Coffield safe, but lost. Connie Naon's boyfriend collected the proceeds of a $10,000 life insurance policy on her life provided by her employer, after being sued by Connie's mother over the money. FBI profiler John Douglas was joined by ten more agents in profiling violent criminals, the agency began a program to train local police to do the same thing, and still it seemed impossible to keep up with the workload.

Randy Revelle was out of politics, having been defeated in an attempt to become county executive again in 1989; Vern Thomas had become the security director for the Goodwill Games. Tim Hill was reelected in 1989, once more drawing on absentee voters for his victory margin. The police officers' union campaigned actively against him.

Tindal was still driving a taxi; Foster was still unemployed and still threatening to sue; Horton was out of prison; McLean was still trapping and had collected $30,000 from several of the news media, and was suing the county for false arrest. The truck painter was still painting trucks, and still unpublicized.

The Strip itself was changed. Gone, demolished,

was the topless dancing tavern, "My Place," which had been such a prostitution magnet near the Red Lion Hotel, where eighteen-year-old Cindy Smith had intended to ask for a job in March of 1984. Gone were the short-time rates and the X-rated movies at the motels farther up the highway, at the nexus of so many disappearances; now the owners offered clean family rates. Gone were the crowds of drug dealers and the pimps who hung out at the drive-ins and at the convenience stores and in the parking lots; most of all, gone were legions of "hoes." It was as if The Strip were haunted by ghosts, and all who tarried there felt somehow their presence, and avoided it as much as possible.

A drive down the highway and a turn toward the valley below the ridge presented still other changes. The trash and garbage of the isolated death zone near Star Lake was still there, but now there was something new: real estate signs. The woods where so many bones were found in April of 1984 were for sale. At the gravel turnout where the Scouts had rested after finding so many dead, there was a suburban driveway, and at the end of the pavement, a wonderful custom house. It was hard for those who knew what had happened to drive past it without thinking of Sandy Gabbert and the dog, Delores Williams, Terri Milligan, Alma Smith, and Carrie Rois. It was hard not to wonder whether the happy homeowners knew the history that surrounded them.

The slaughterhouse was gone, burned to the ground after it had been closed in 1986. Now the charred remnants were the only sentinel to the death that had been discovered there so long ago. The Little League Field was improved, and near the place where the still-unidentified skeleton—still labeled Bones Number Ten after all these years—had been found by the caretaker's dog in March of 1984, there were now a row of self-storage units.

But the lessons of the worst serial murder case in American history remained bound up in the nearly five hundred volumes of reports, locked away in what had been the old jail on top of the King County Courthouse. Page after page of reports, interviews, evidence, photographs, maps, charts, drawings, analyses—all waiting for a day that may never come.

It was impossible to think of all those reports, all those pages of transcribed interviews, the tip sheets, the detailed inventories of evidence, the storage room with all the thousands of pieces of possible evidence, without thinking of the man and the questions.

In the end, it was possible to visualize only the dimmest of outlines of the nation's worst serial killer. There were tantalizing clues, but no one could say how accurate they were. He was a man, probably white, experts thought, and possibly between the ages of thirty and fifty. He appeared to wear shoes that were somewhere between sizes ten and eleven, and once owned a pair of shoes with a composite sole, no heel. He drove a pickup truck with a camper, which probably carried cutting and digging tools in the back, and occasionally, plastic tarps. He was a man familiar with hidden areas often found near golf courses, cemeteries, plant nurseries, parks, and places where household garbage and yard waste were illegally dumped. He may have worked occasionally with fiberglass, perhaps as an auto body repairman. He may have had experience in the military or as a security guard. He was familiar with police procedures. He probably was in the Seattle-Tacoma International Aiport in late May of 1983, either flying somewhere or meeting someone on a flight. He read the newspapers and followed the coverage of the murders on television. He kept things that belonged to his victims.

But the questions far outnumbered the answers.

Who was he? What happened to him? Had they successfully identified him, only to be balked in getting the proof, as some detectives still fervently believed? Was his name somewhere in the computer, merely unrecognized? Or, did they miss him completely?

Was he in prison for some unrelated crime, keeping quiet and waiting for the day of his eventual release?

Or was he dead? Some wondered if the man had been killed in a common, ordinary accident, a crash on the freeway perhaps, bringing an unnoticed end to a man who no one had ever really known.

Others visualized a more poetic conclusion. They saw the man picking up a young woman, driving to a lonely, dark secret place, then going for the kill. But this time the young woman was faster with her knife or gun or sharpened knitting needle. They saw the young woman and her "boyfriend" rolling the dead man's body into the woods, where it would be covered with brush and leaves, or better yet, into the waters of the Green River. The unknown man would die an undistinguished death, and no one would ever know how the horror had stopped.

But fanciful outcomes are for television or the movies. In the real world things are not so neat, and in this case, there is no ending, no resolution. In the real world, the unknown man is, more than likely not, very much alive, driving somewhere in America, looking for someone special to take to a very special place.